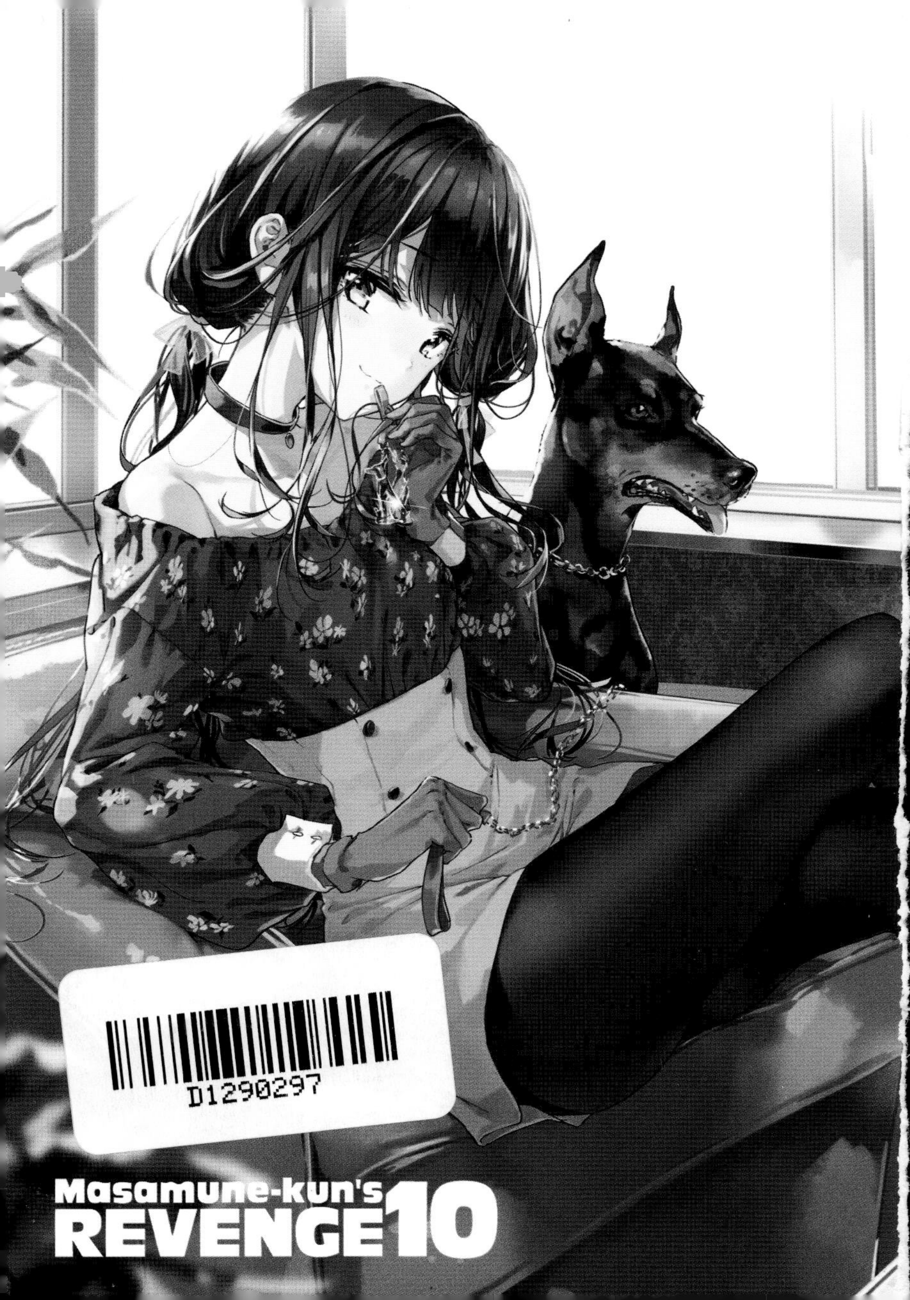
Masamune-kun's
REVENGE 10

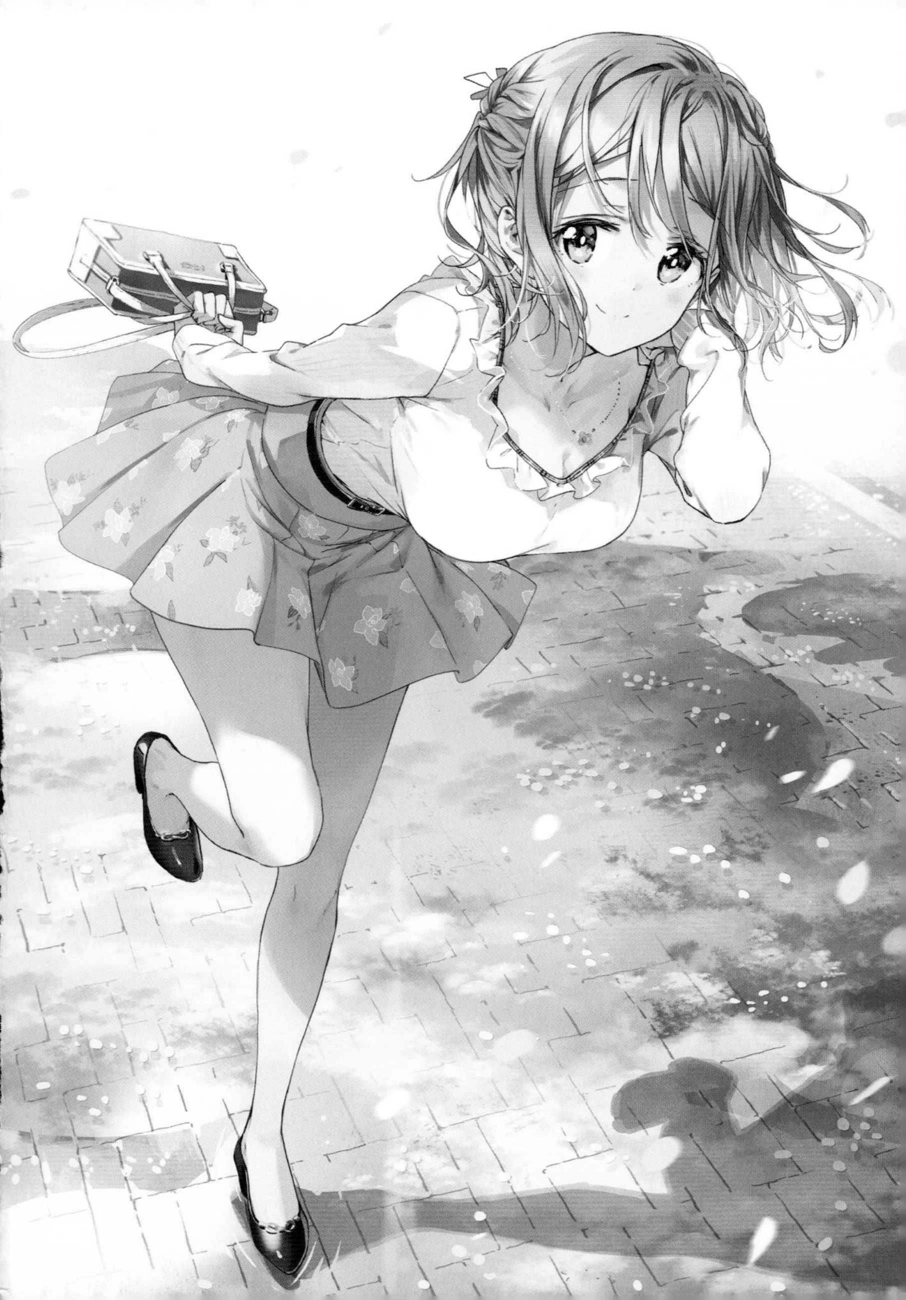

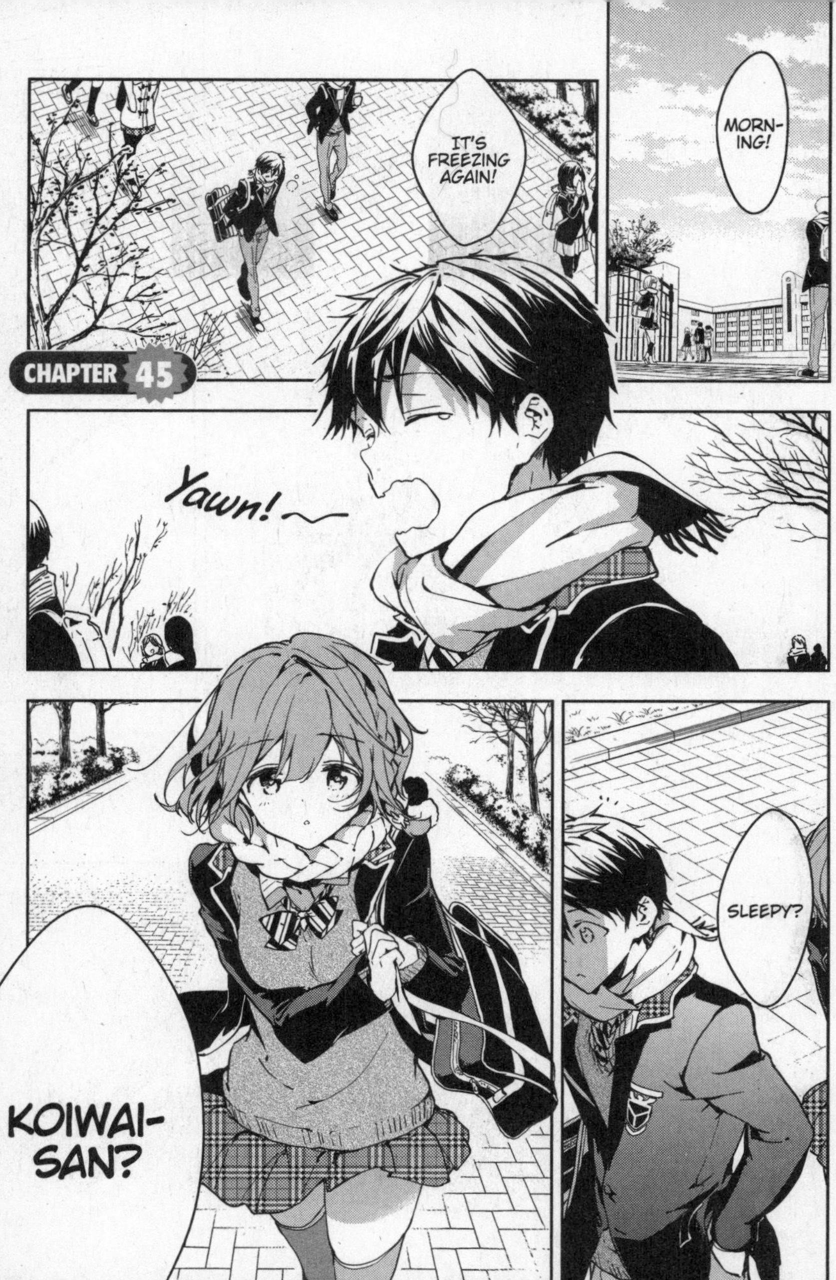
MORNING-ING!
IT'S FREEZING AGAIN!
CHAPTER 45
Yawn!~
SLEEPY?
KOIWAI-SAN?

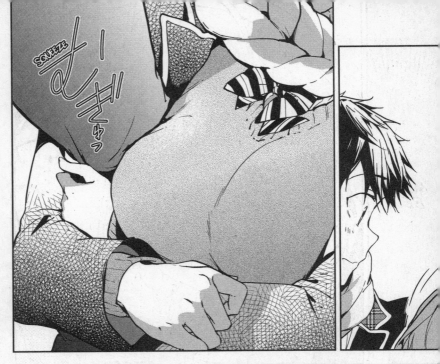

SQUEEZE

YOU'RE NOT SUPPOS- ED...

TO CALL ME THAT.

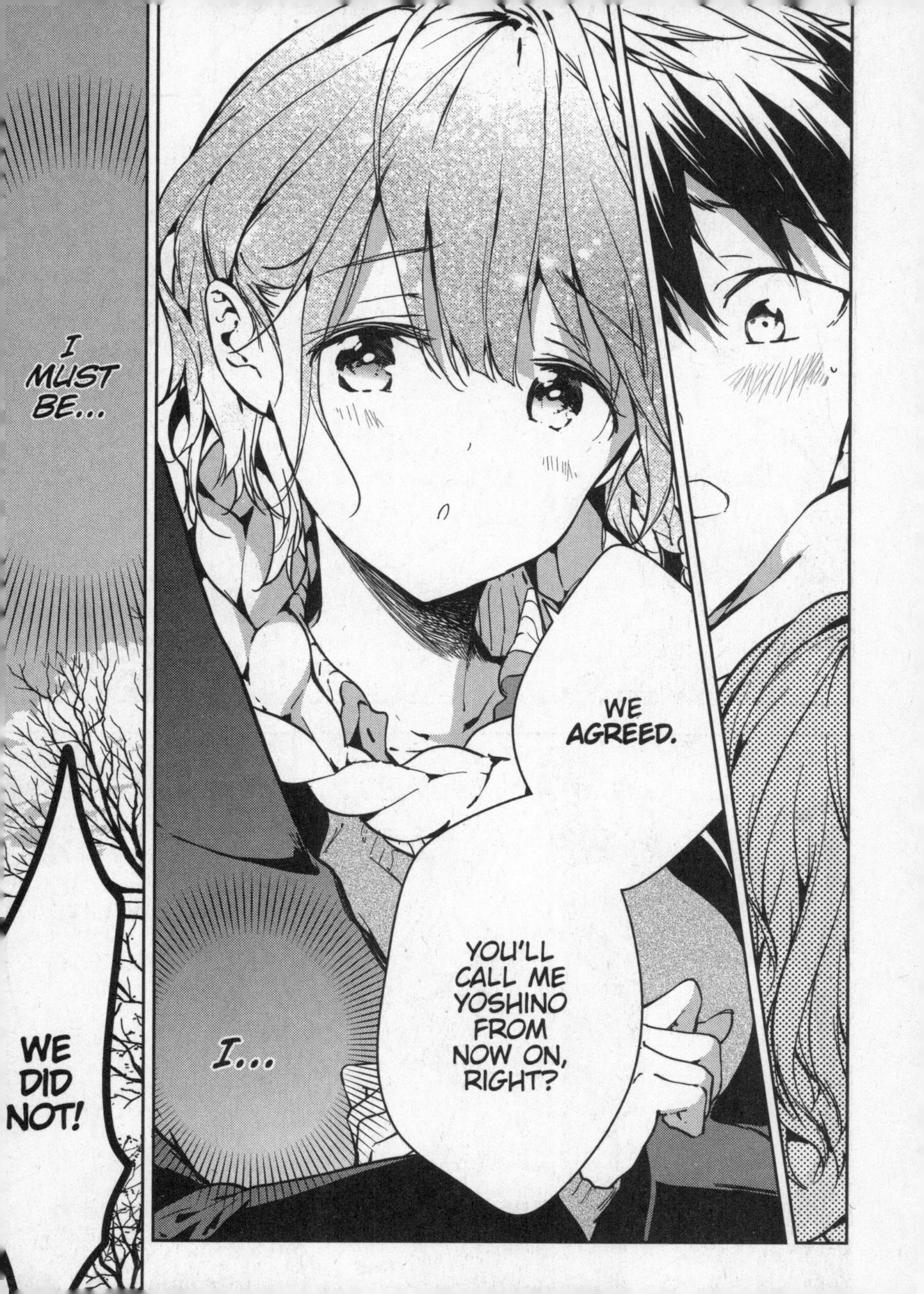
WE AGREED.
YOU'LL CALL ME YOSHINO FROM NOW ON, RIGHT?
I MUST BE...
I...
WE DID NOT!

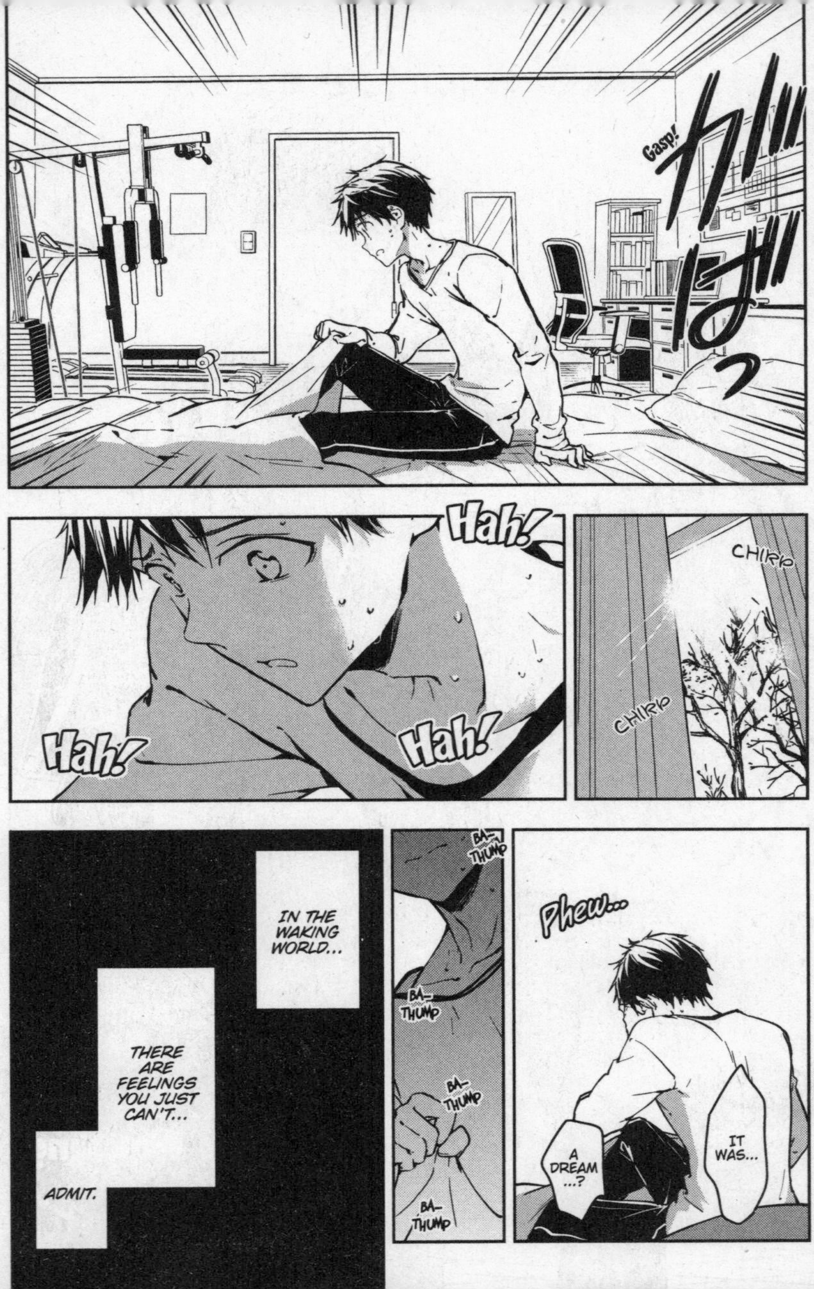
Gasp!
CHIRP
CHIRP
Hah!
Hah!
Hah!
Phew...
IT WAS...
A DREAM ...?
BA-THUMP
BA-THUMP
BA-THUMP
BA-THUMP
IN THE WAKING WORLD...
THERE ARE FEELINGS YOU JUST CAN'T...
ADMIT.

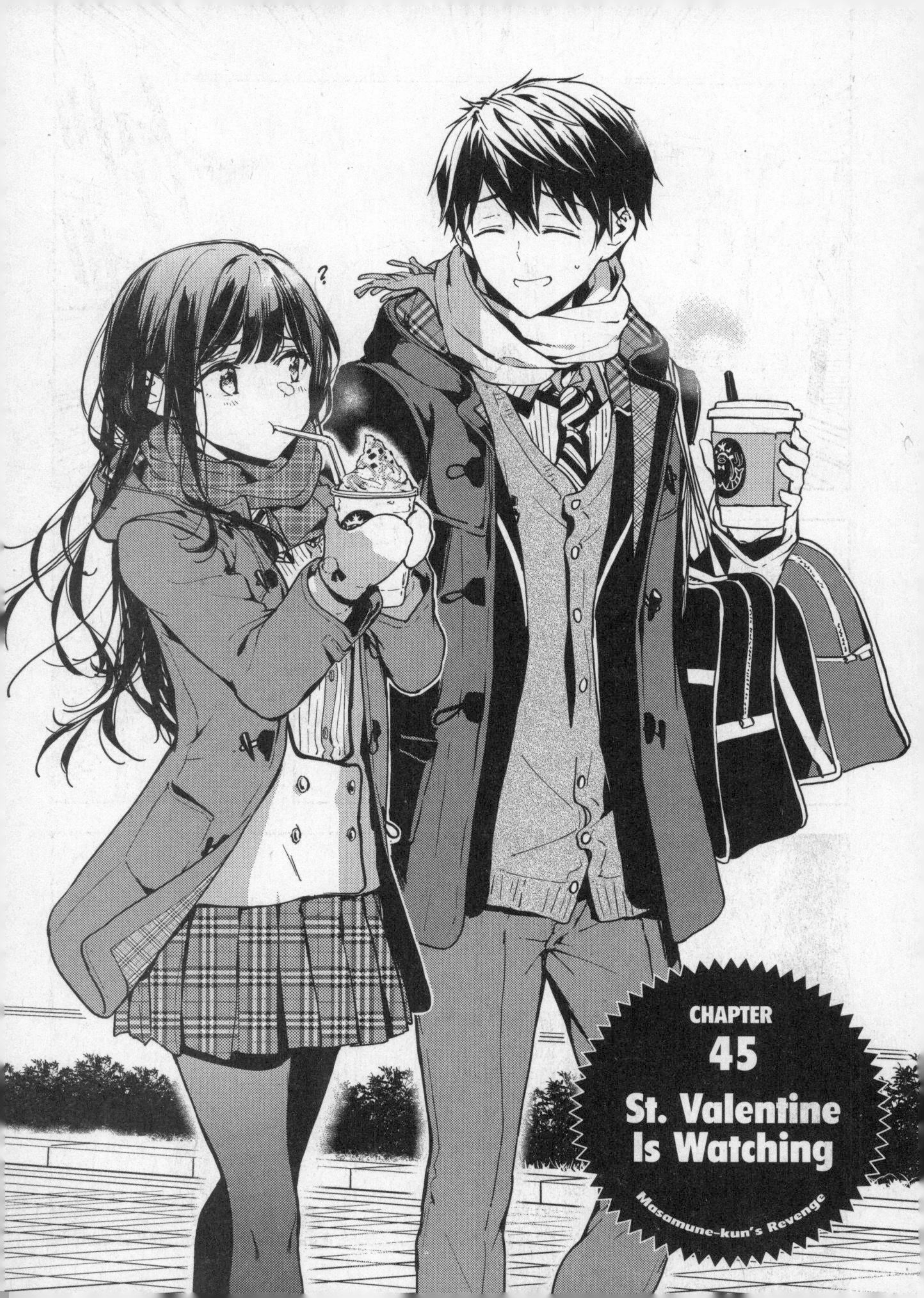
?
CHAPTER
45
St. Valentine
Is Watching
Masamune-kun's Revenge

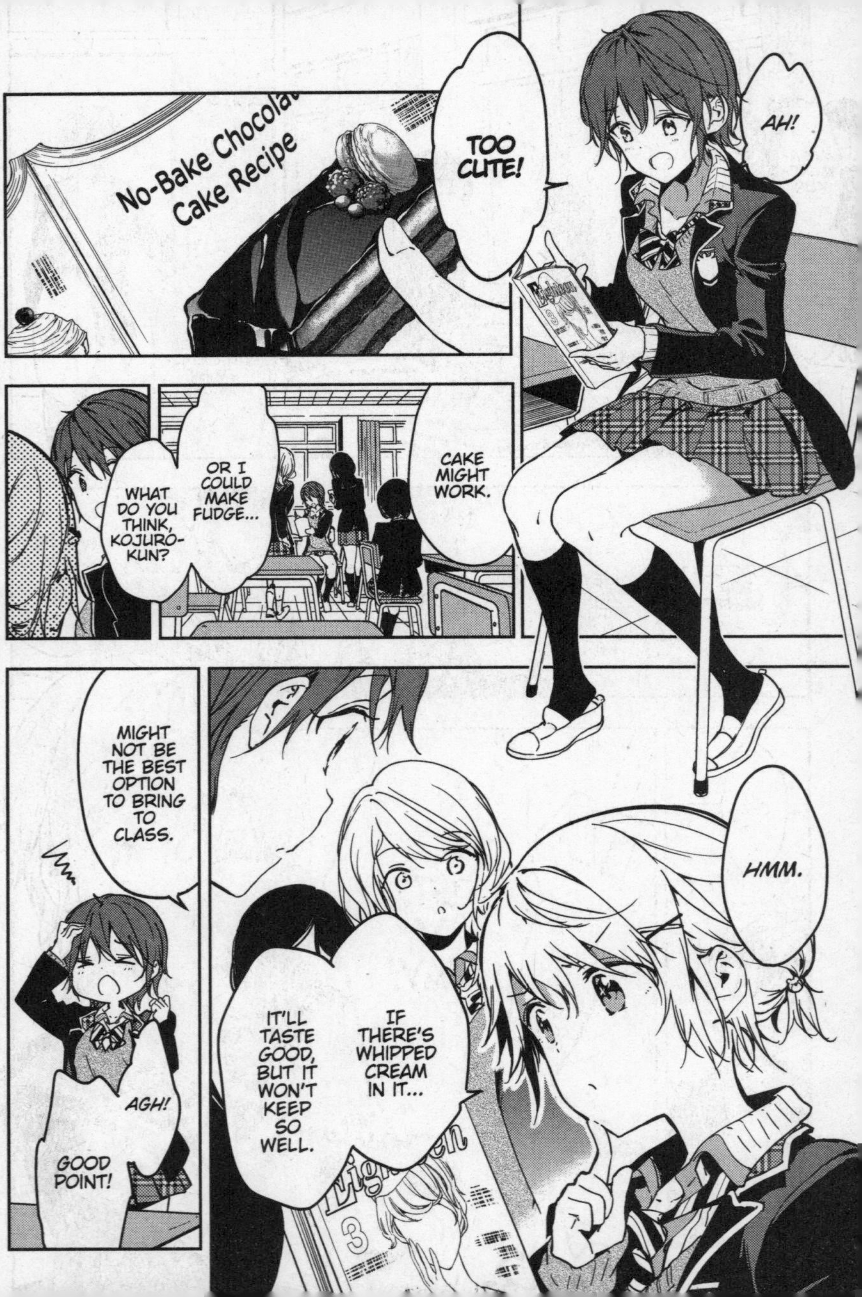
AH!
TOO CUTE!
No-Bake Chocolat Cake Recipe
CAKE MIGHT WORK.
OR I COULD MAKE FUDGE...
WHAT DO YOU THINK, KOJURO-KUN?
HMM.
IF THERE'S WHIPPED CREAM IN IT...
IT'LL TASTE GOOD, BUT IT WON'T KEEP SO WELL.
MIGHT NOT BE THE BEST OPTION TO BRING TO CLASS.
AGH!
GOOD POINT!

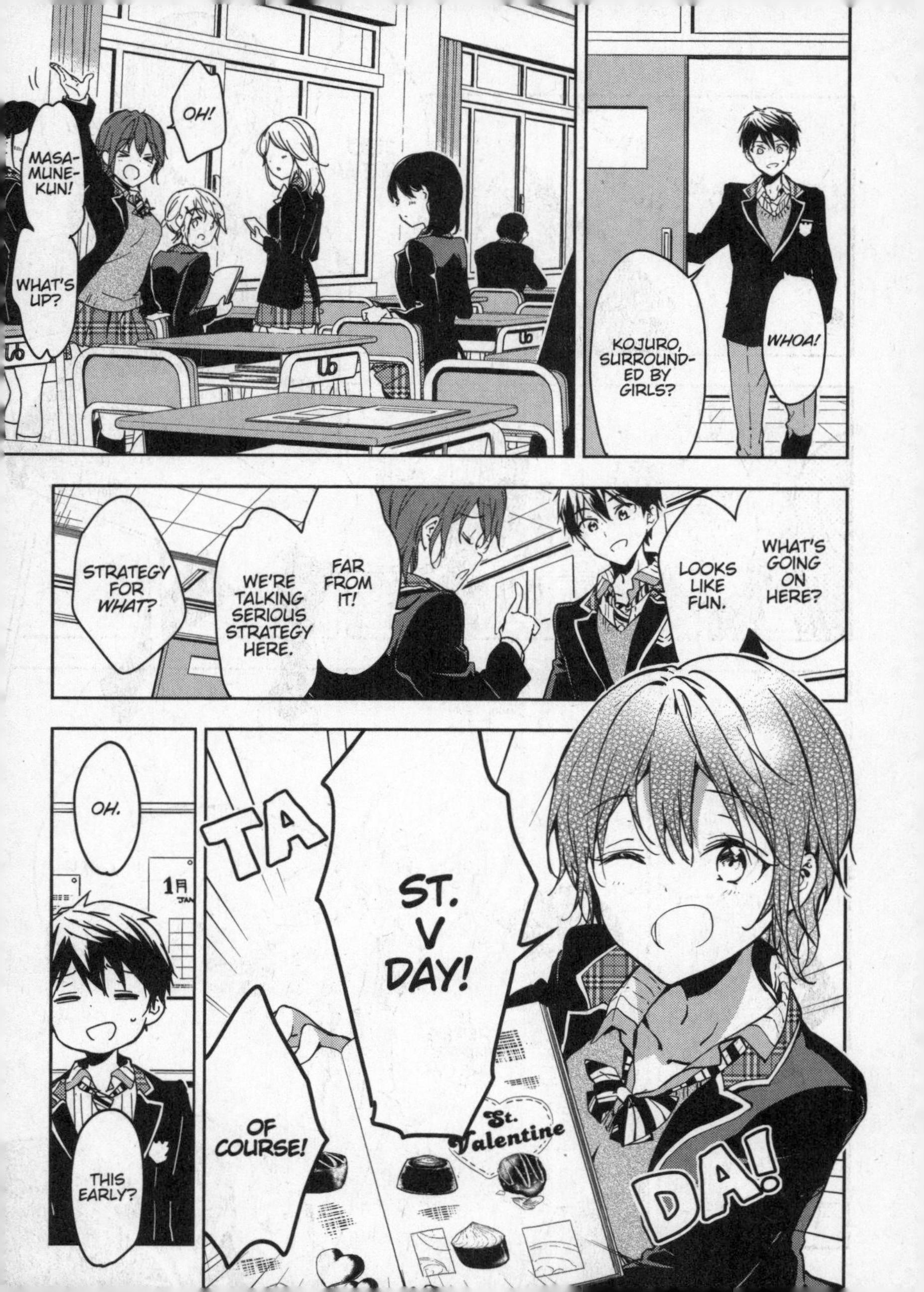
WHOA!
KOJURO, SURROUNDED BY GIRLS?
OH!
MASAMUNE-KUN!
WHAT'S UP?
WHAT'S GOING ON HERE?
LOOKS LIKE FUN.
FAR FROM IT!
WE'RE TALKING SERIOUS STRATEGY HERE.
STRATEGY FOR WHAT?
TA
DA!
ST. V DAY!
St. Valentine
OH.
THIS EARLY?
OF COURSE!

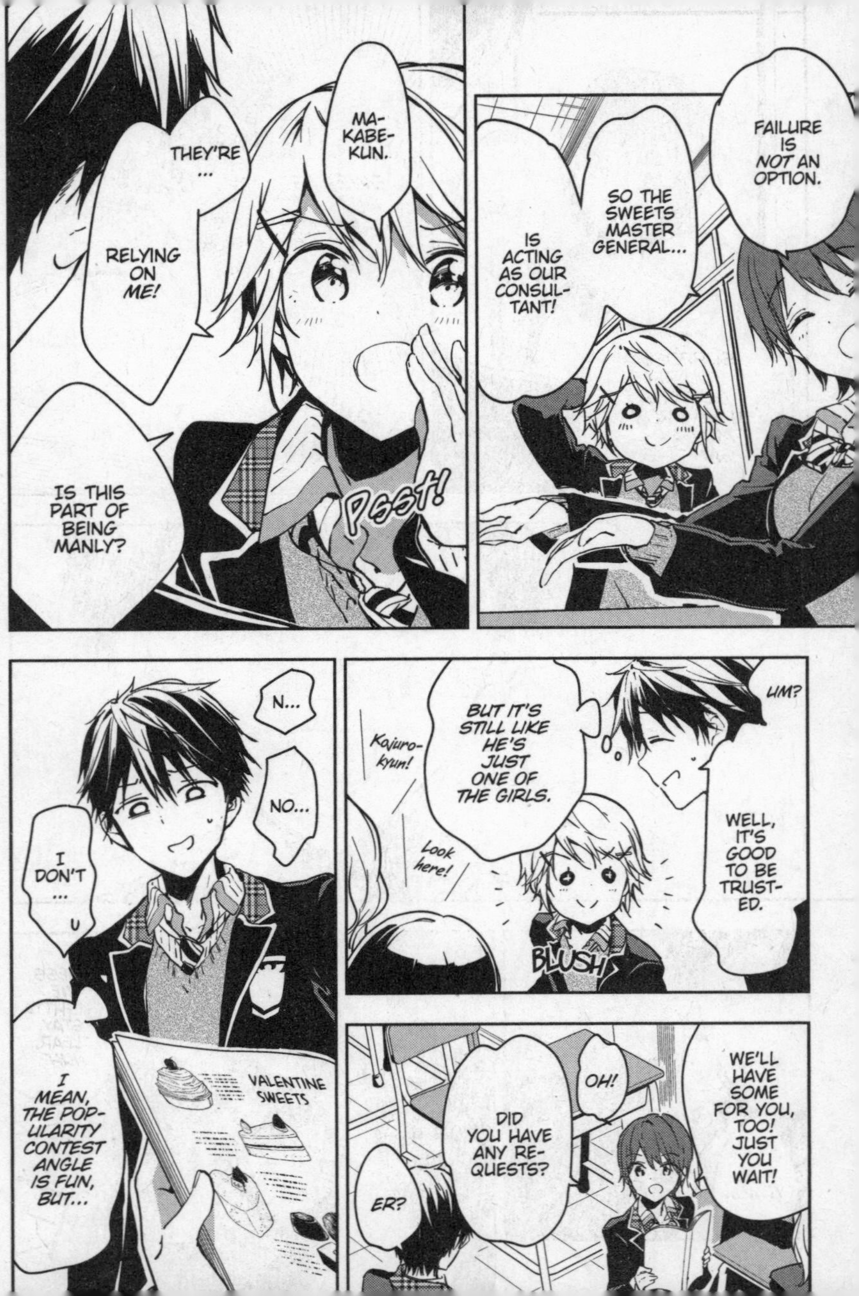
FAILURE IS *NOT* AN OPTION.
SO THE SWEETS MASTER GENERAL...
IS ACTING AS OUR CONSUL-TANT!
MA-KABE-KUN.
THEY'RE ...
RELYING ON ME!
Psst!
IS THIS PART OF BEING MANLY?
UM?
WELL, IT'S GOOD TO BE TRUST-ED.
BUT IT'S STILL LIKE HE'S JUST ONE OF THE GIRLS.
Kajuro-kyun!
Look here!
BLUSH
WE'LL HAVE SOME FOR YOU, TOO! JUST YOU WAIT!
OH!
DID YOU HAVE ANY RE-QUESTS?
ER?
N...
NO...
I DON'T ...
U
VALENTINE SWEETS
I MEAN, THE POP-ULARITY CONTEST ANGLE IS FUN, BUT...

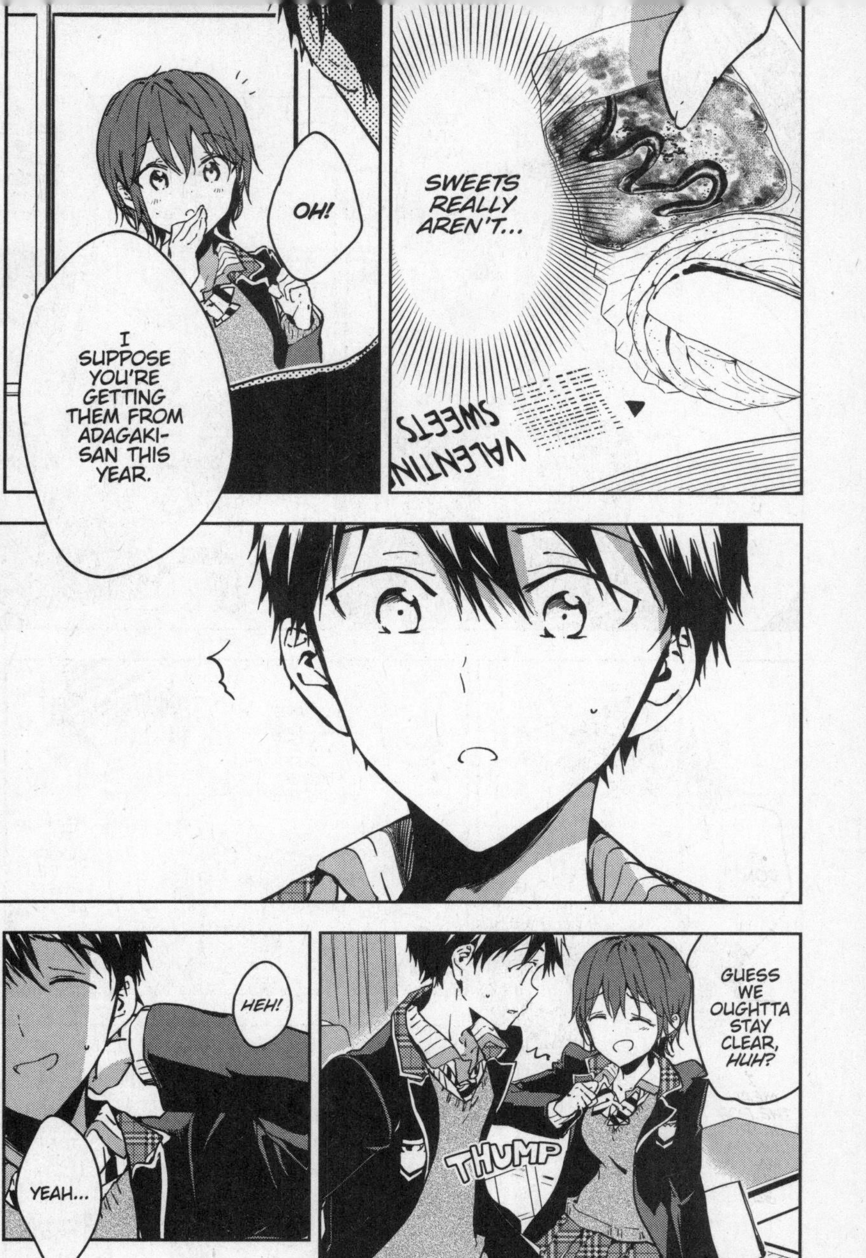
SWEETS REALLY AREN'T...
VALENTIN SWEETS
OH!
I SUPPOSE YOU'RE GETTING THEM FROM ADAGAKI-SAN THIS YEAR.
GUESS WE OUGHTTA STAY CLEAR, HUH?
THUMP
HEH!
YEAH...

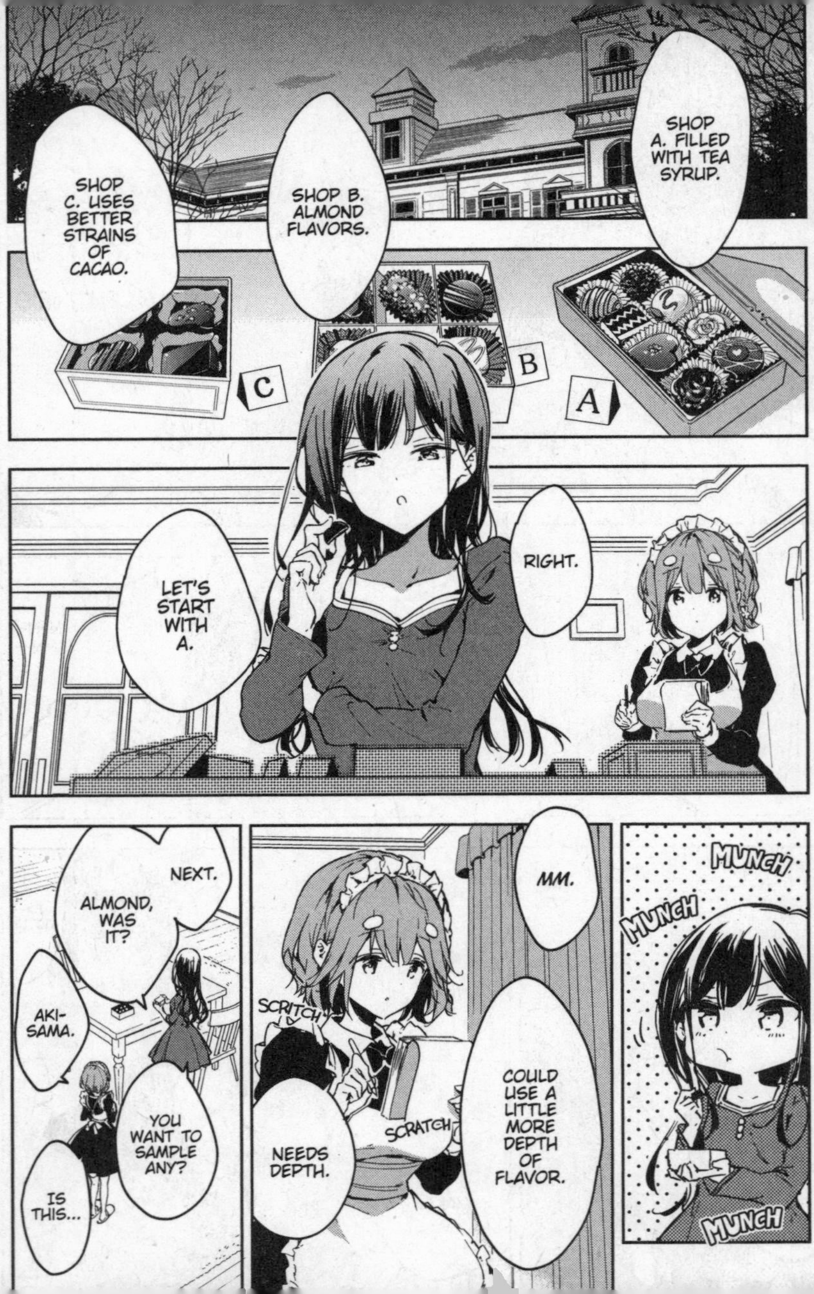
SHOP A. FILLED WITH TEA SYRUP.
SHOP B. ALMOND FLAVORS.
SHOP C. USES BETTER STRAINS OF CACAO.
A
B
C
RIGHT.
LET'S START WITH A.
MUNCH
MUNCH
MUNCH
MM.
COULD USE A LITTLE MORE DEPTH OF FLAVOR.
SCRITCH
SCRATCH
NEEDS DEPTH.
NEXT.
ALMOND, WAS IT?
AKI-SAMA.
YOU WANT TO SAMPLE ANY?
IS THIS...

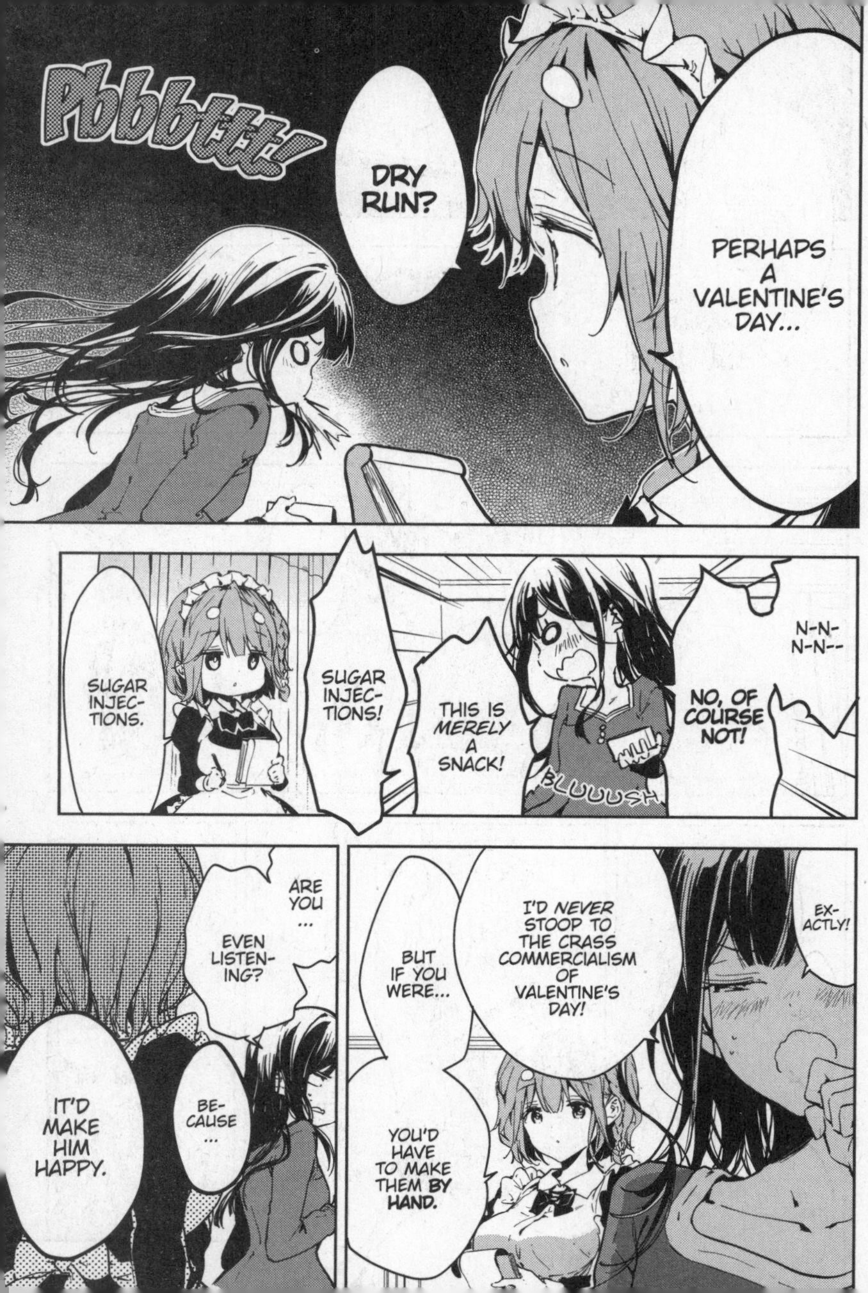
PERHAPS A VALENTINE'S DAY...
DRY RUN?
Pbbbttt!
N-N-N-N--
NO, OF COURSE NOT!
THIS IS MERELY A SNACK!
BLUUUSH
SUGAR INJECTIONS!
SUGAR INJECTIONS.
EX-ACTLY!
I'D NEVER STOOP TO THE CRASS COMMERCIALISM OF VALENTINE'S DAY!
BUT IF YOU WERE...
YOU'D HAVE TO MAKE THEM BY HAND.
ARE YOU ...
EVEN LISTENING?
BE-CAUSE ...
IT'D MAKE HIM HAPPY.

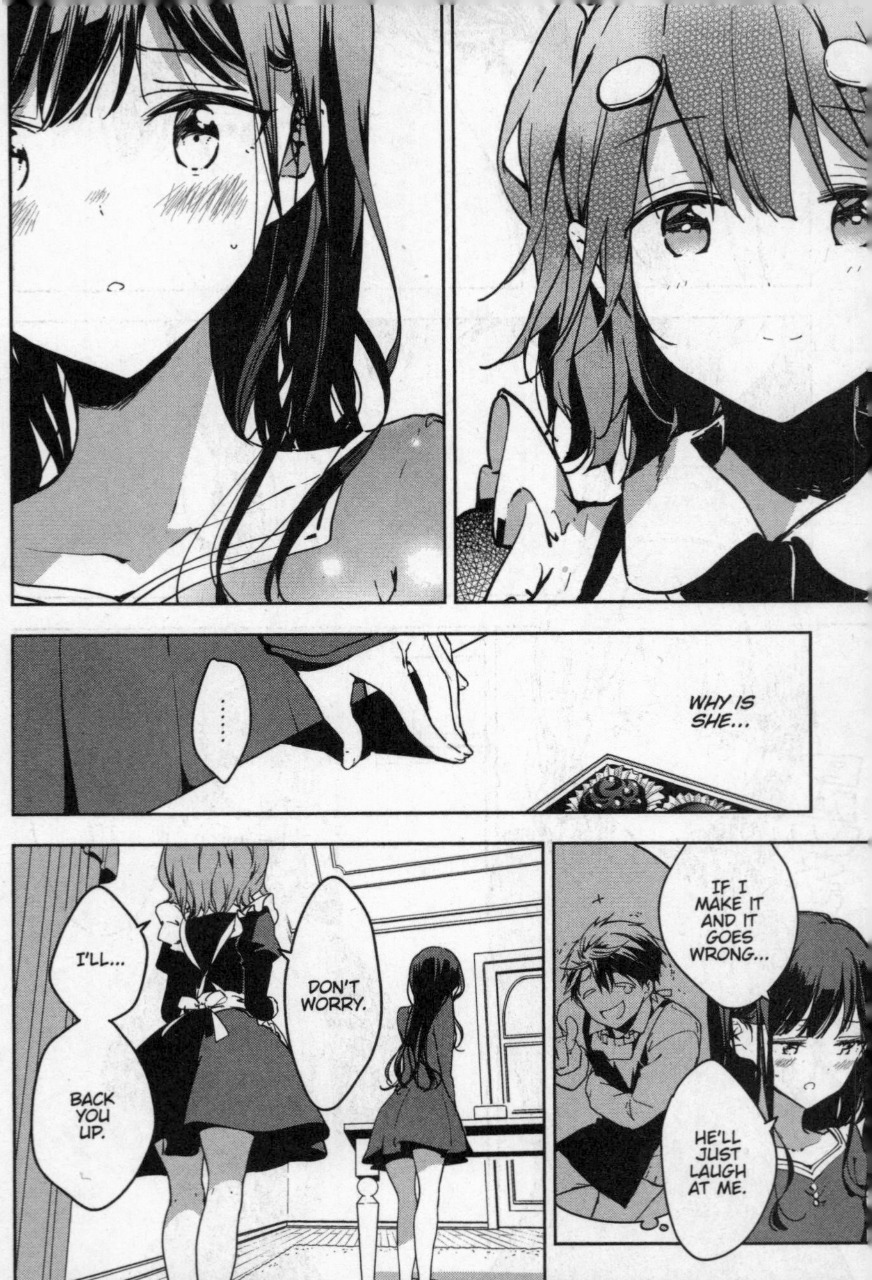
WHY IS SHE...
......
IF I MAKE IT AND IT GOES WRONG...
HE'LL JUST LAUGH AT ME.
DON'T WORRY.
I'LL...
BACK YOU UP.

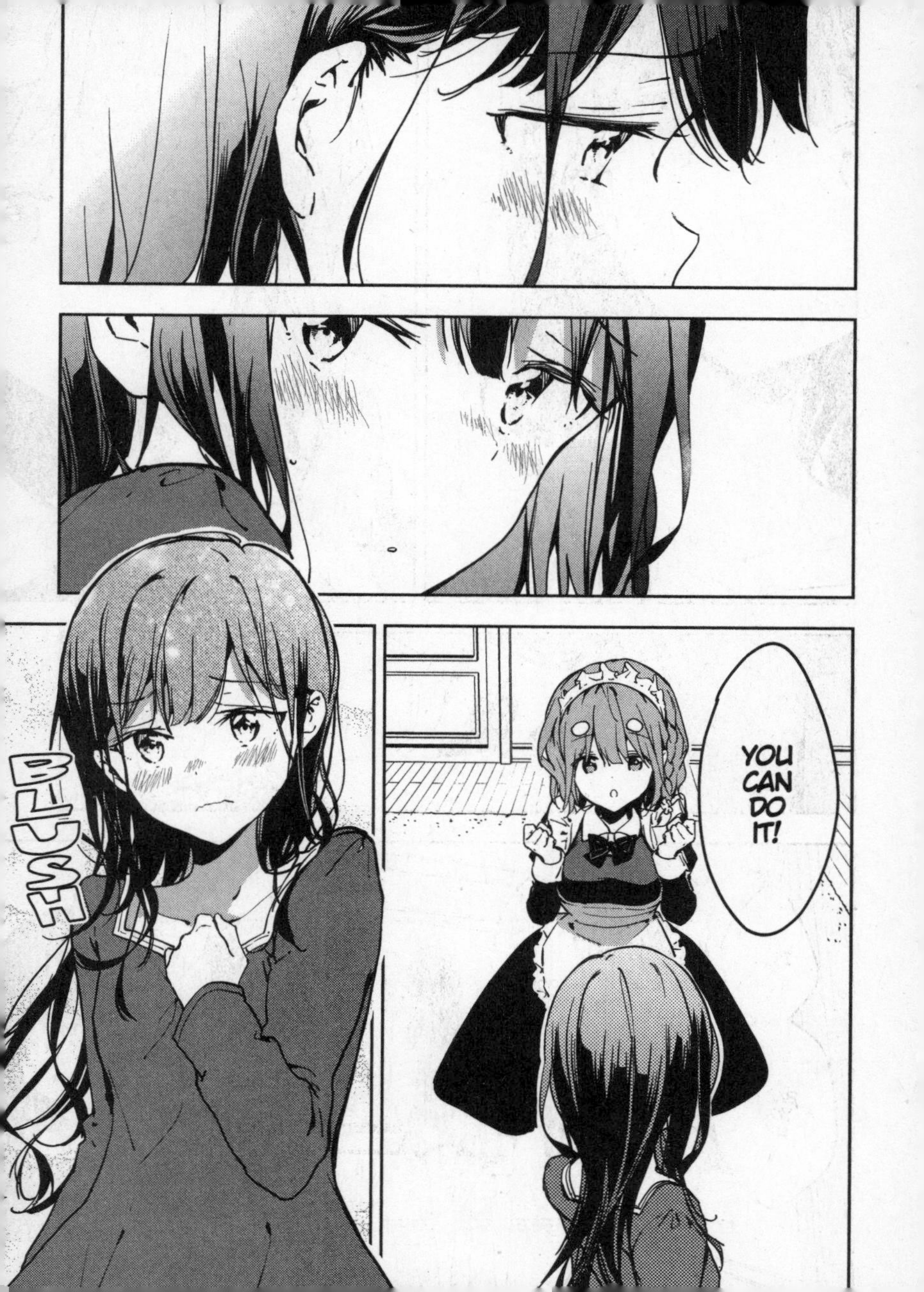
YOU CAN DO IT!
BLUSH

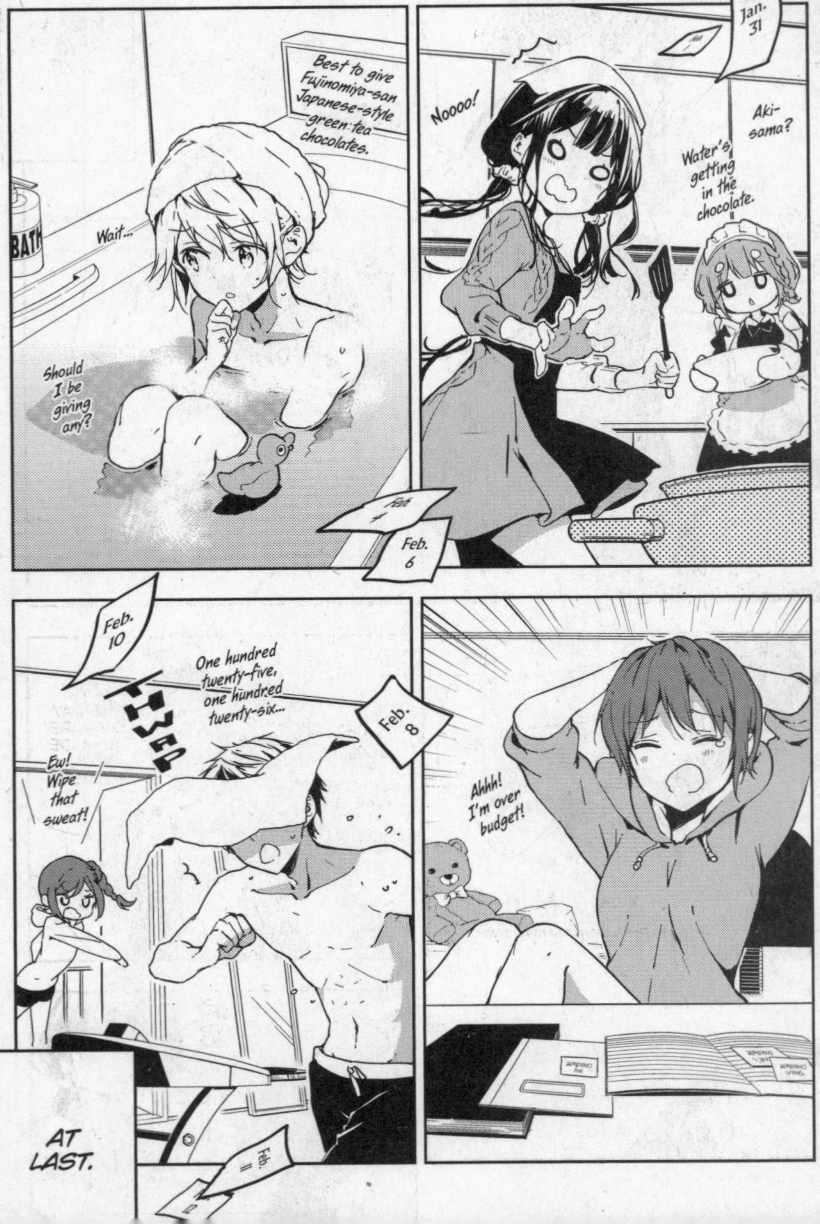
Jan. 31
Aki-sama?
Water's getting in the chocolate.
Noooo!
Feb. 4
Feb. 6
Best to give Fujinomiya-san Japanese-style green-tea chocolates.
BATH
Wait...
Should I be giving any?
Ahhh! I'm over budget!
Feb. 8
One hundred twenty-five, one hundred twenty-six...
Feb. 10
THWAP
Ew! Wipe that sweat!
Feb. 11
12
AT LAST.

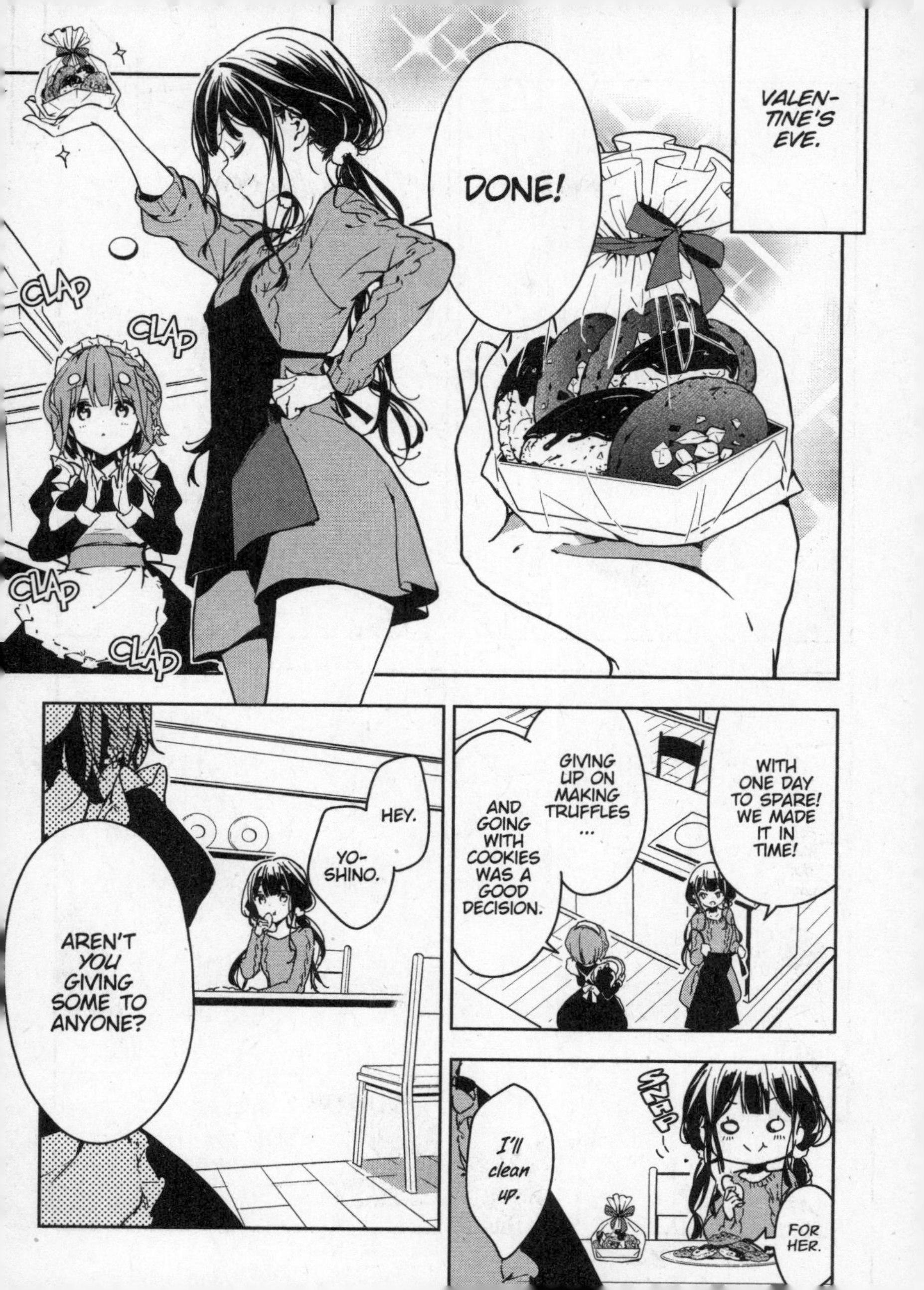
VALEN-TINE'S EVE.
DONE!
CLAP
CLAP
CLAP
CLAP
WITH ONE DAY TO SPARE! WE MADE IT IN TIME!
GIVING UP ON MAKING TRUFFLES ...
AND GOING WITH COOKIES WAS A GOOD DECISION.
HEY.
YO-SHINO.
AREN'T *YOU* GIVING SOME TO ANYONE?
*I'll clean up.*
FOR HER.

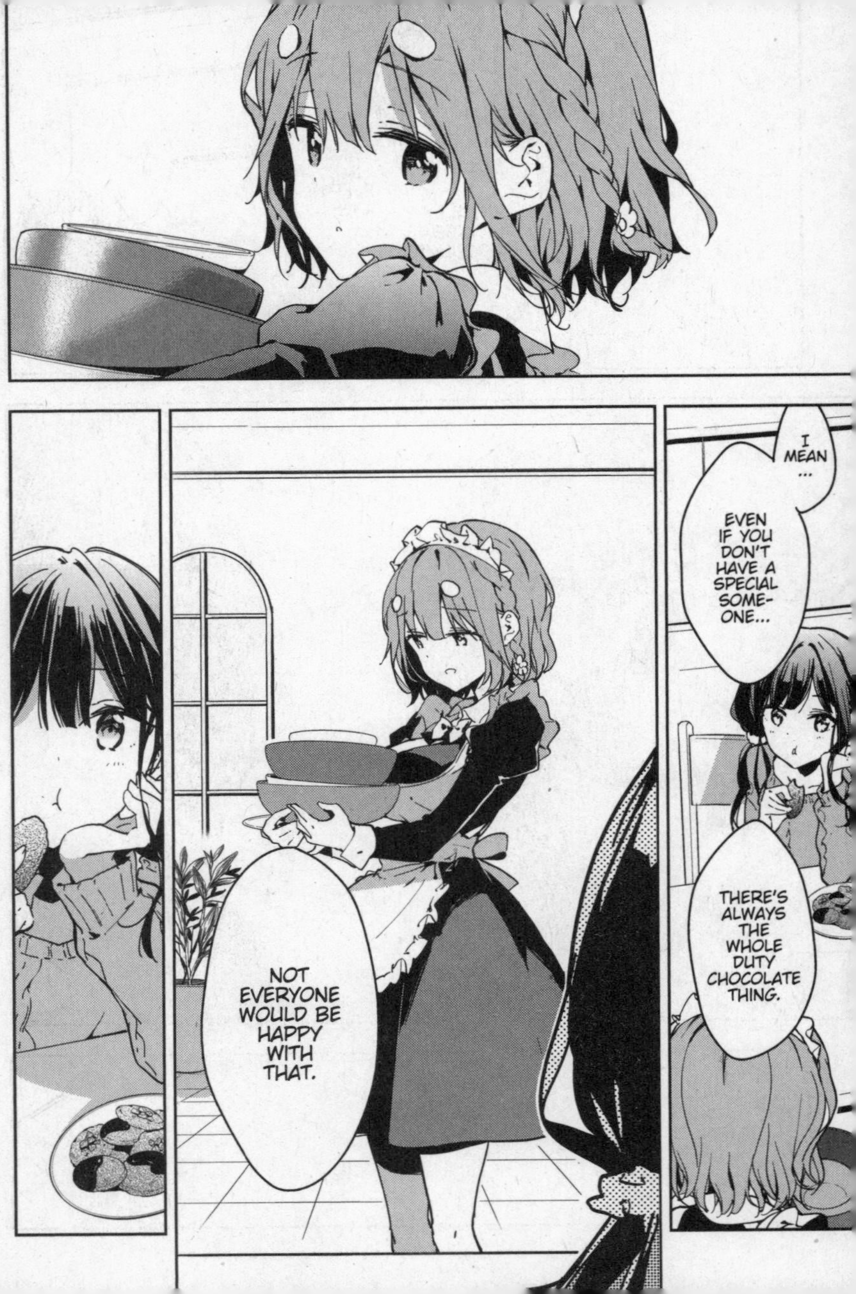
I MEAN...
EVEN IF YOU DON'T HAVE A SPECIAL SOME-ONE...
THERE'S ALWAYS THE WHOLE DUTY CHOCOLATE THING.
NOT EVERYONE WOULD BE HAPPY WITH THAT.

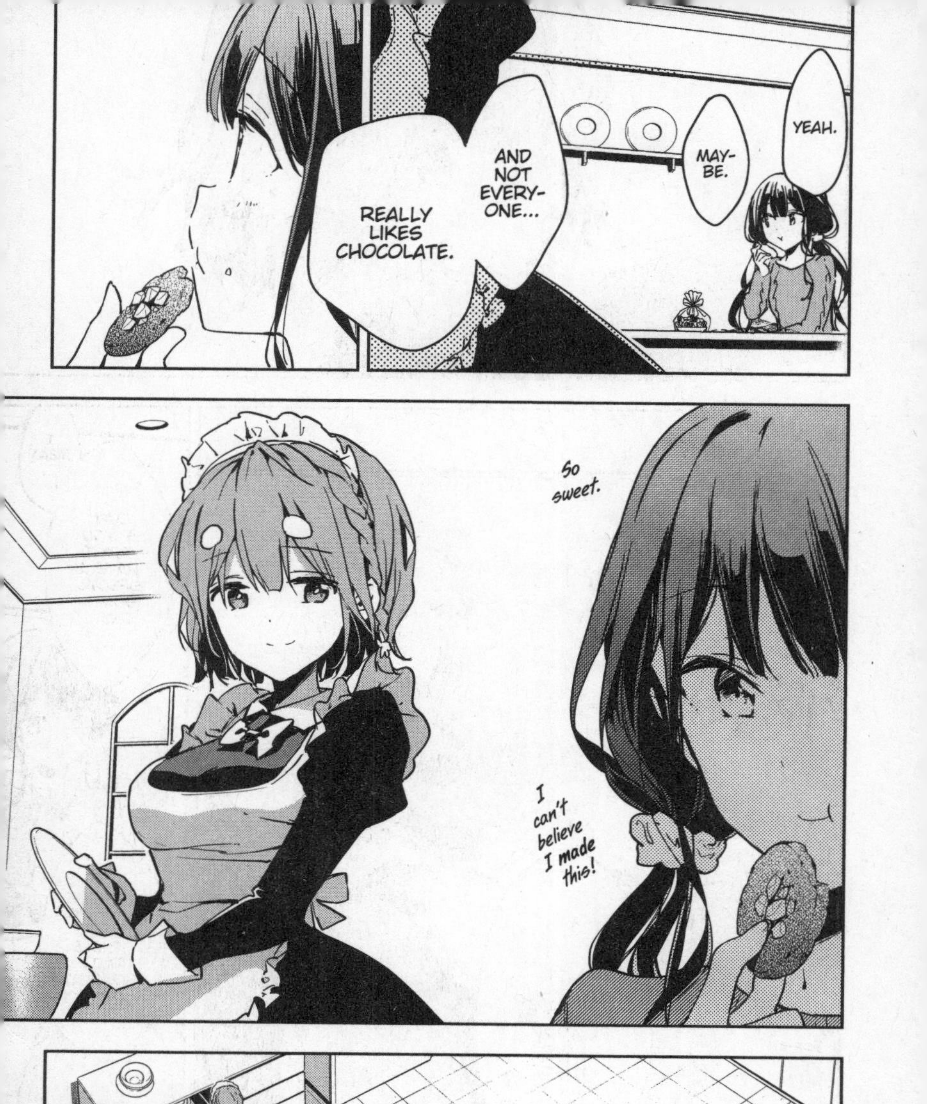
YEAH.
MAY-BE.
AND NOT EVERY-ONE...
REALLY LIKES CHOCOLATE.
So sweet.
I can't believe I made this!

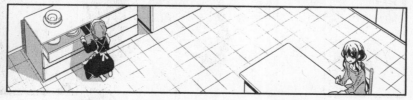

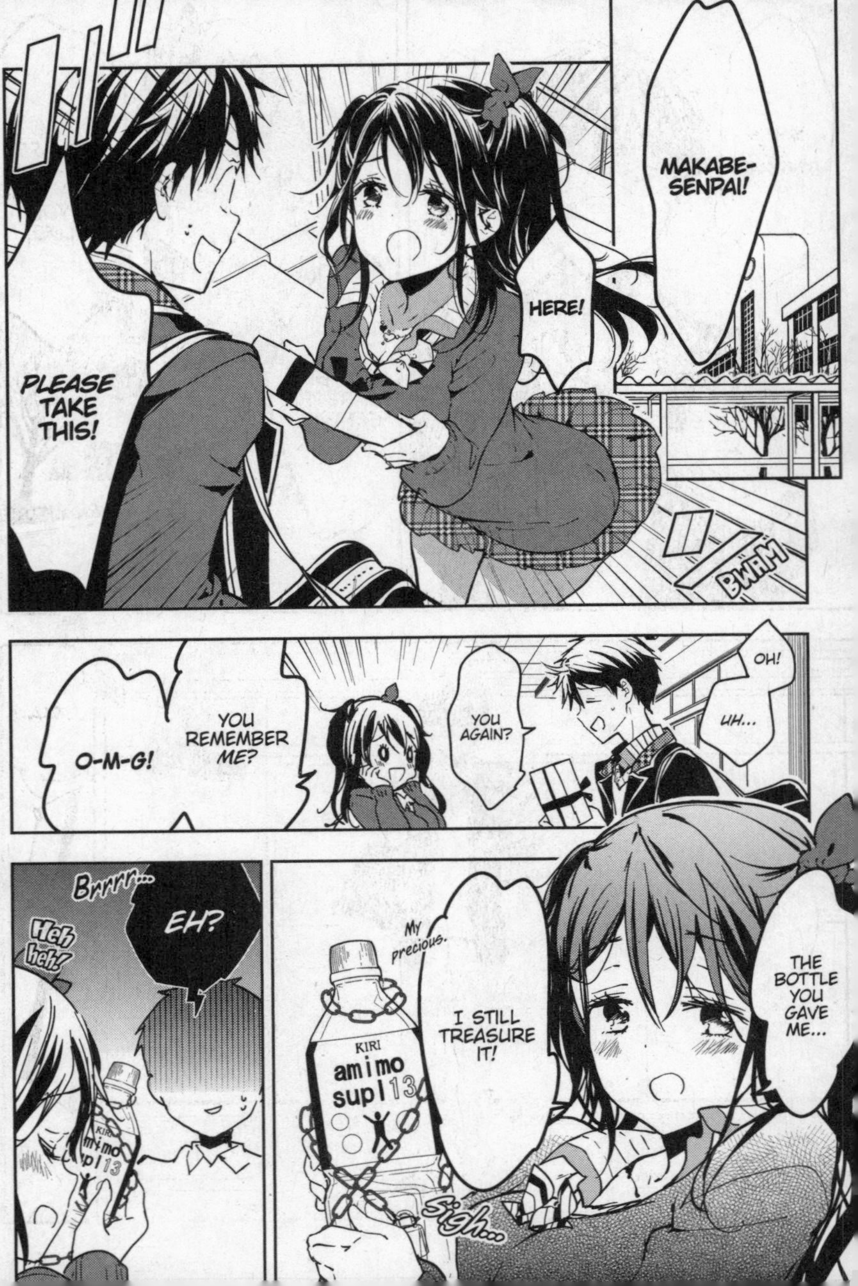
MAKABE-SENPAI!
HERE!
PLEASE TAKE THIS!
BWAM
OH!
UH...
YOU AGAIN?
YOU REMEMBER ME?
O-M-G!
THE BOTTLE YOU GAVE ME...
I STILL TREASURE IT!
My precious.
KIRI
am i mo
sup l 13
Sigh...
EH?
Brrrr...
Heh heh!

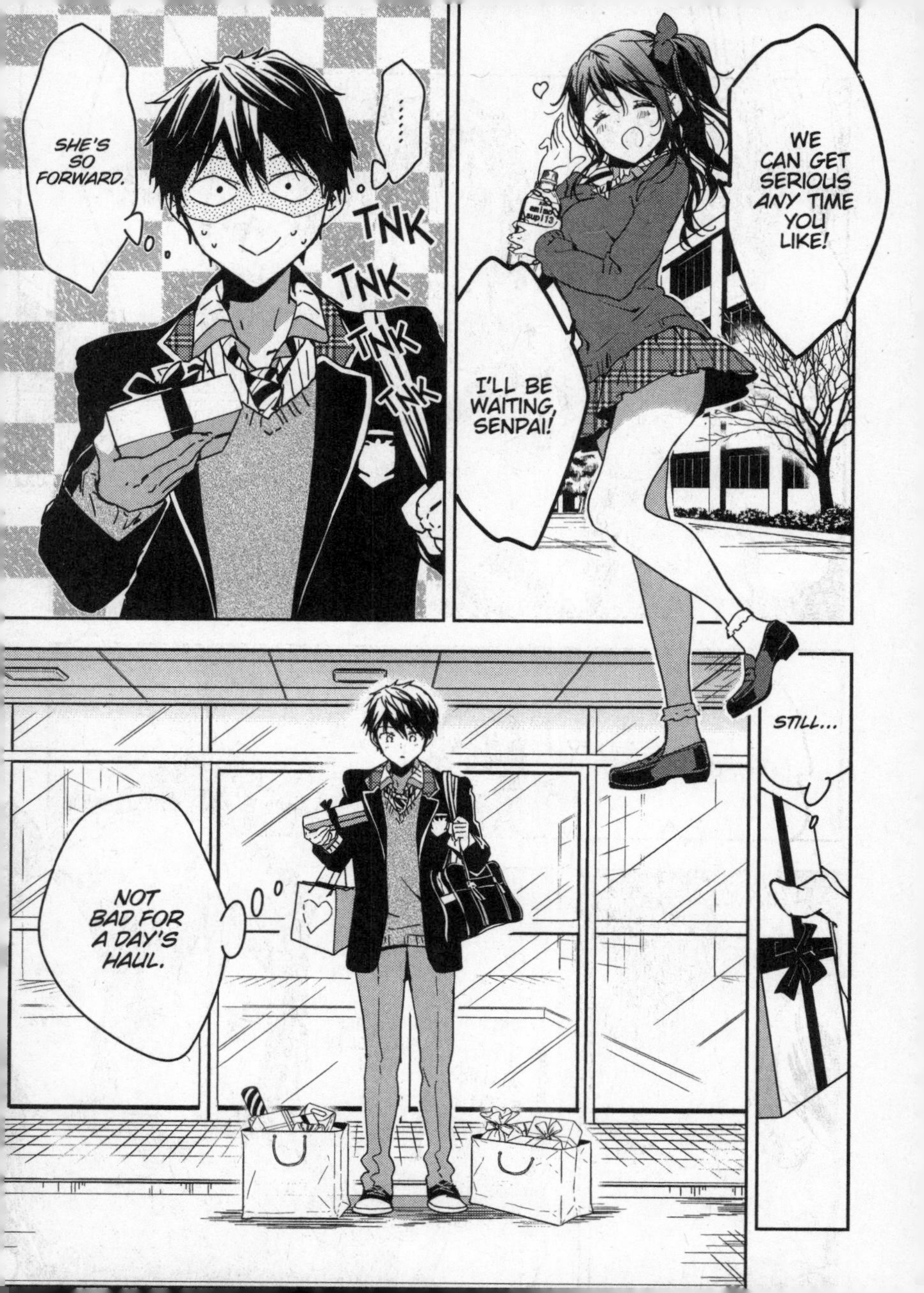
WE CAN GET SERIOUS ANY TIME YOU LIKE!
I'LL BE WAITING, SENPAI!
......
SHE'S SO FORWARD.
TNK
TNK
TNK
TNK
STILL...
NOT BAD FOR A DAY'S HAUL.

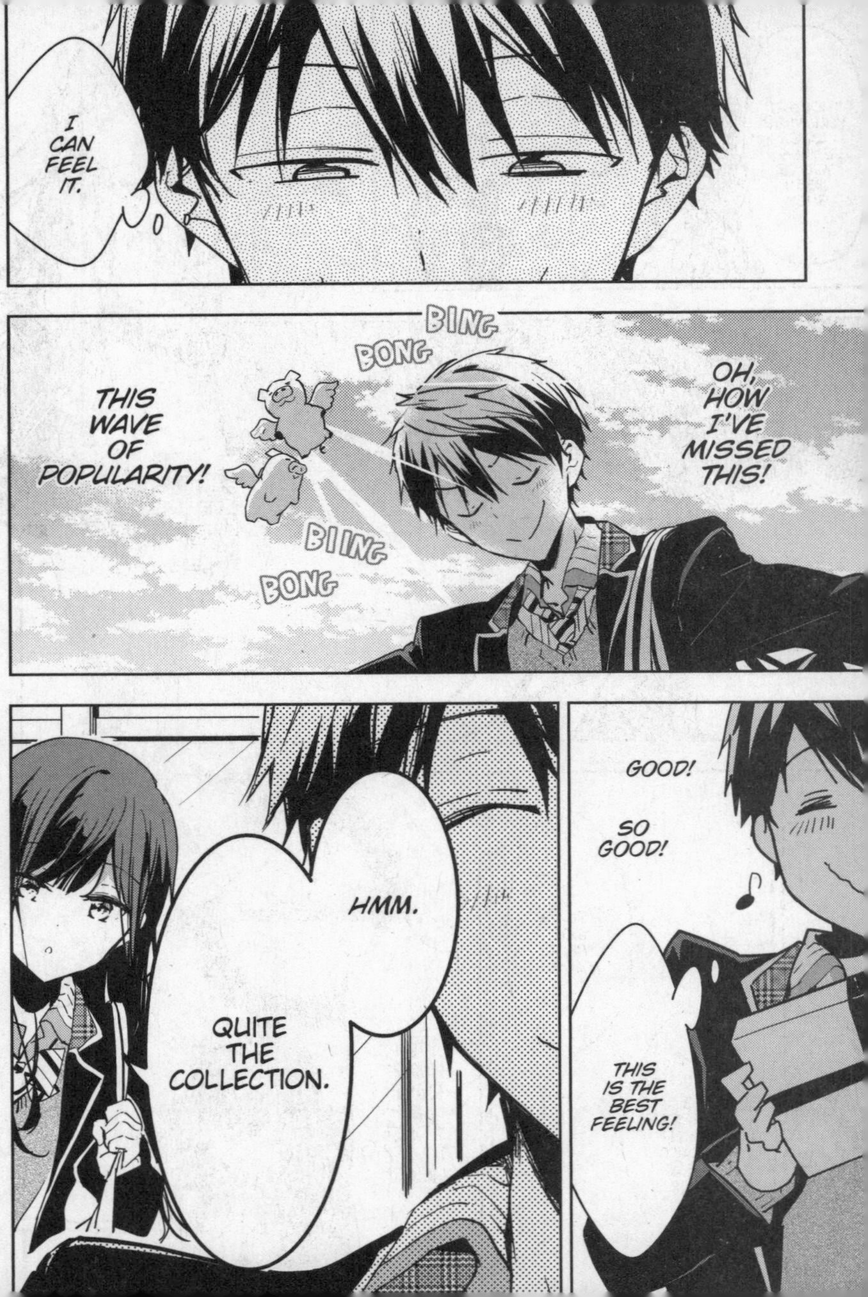
I CAN FEEL IT.
BING
BONG
OH, HOW I'VE MISSED THIS!
THIS WAVE OF POPULARITY!
BIING
BONG
GOOD!
SO GOOD!
THIS IS THE BEST FEELING!
HMM.
QUITE THE COLLECTION.

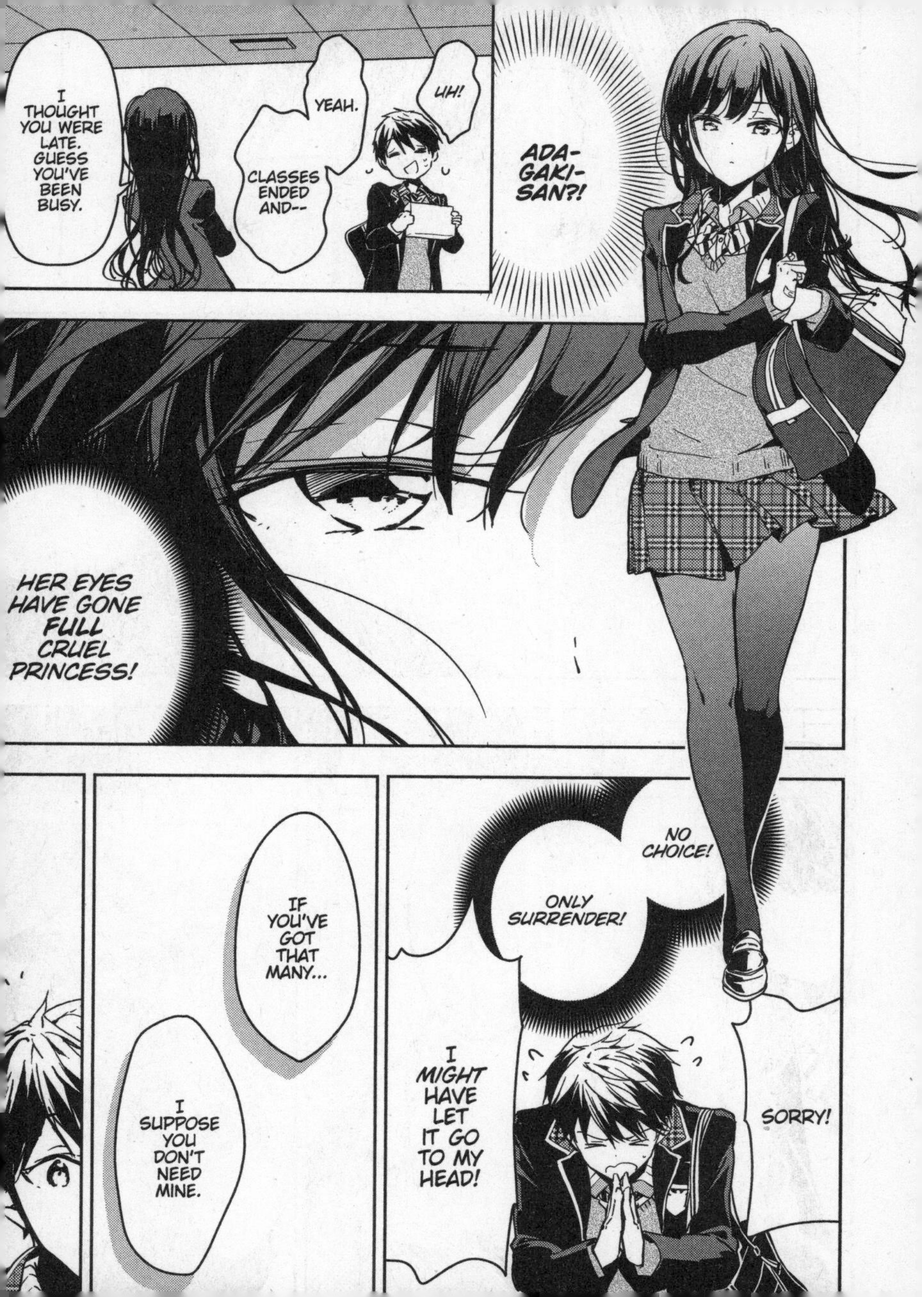
ADA-GAKI-SAN?!
UH!
YEAH.
CLASSES ENDED AND--
I THOUGHT YOU WERE LATE. GUESS YOU'VE BEEN BUSY.
HER EYES HAVE GONE FULL CRUEL PRINCESS!
NO CHOICE!
ONLY SURRENDER!
SORRY!
I MIGHT HAVE LET IT GO TO MY HEAD!
IF YOU'VE GOT THAT MANY...
I SUPPOSE YOU DON'T NEED MINE.

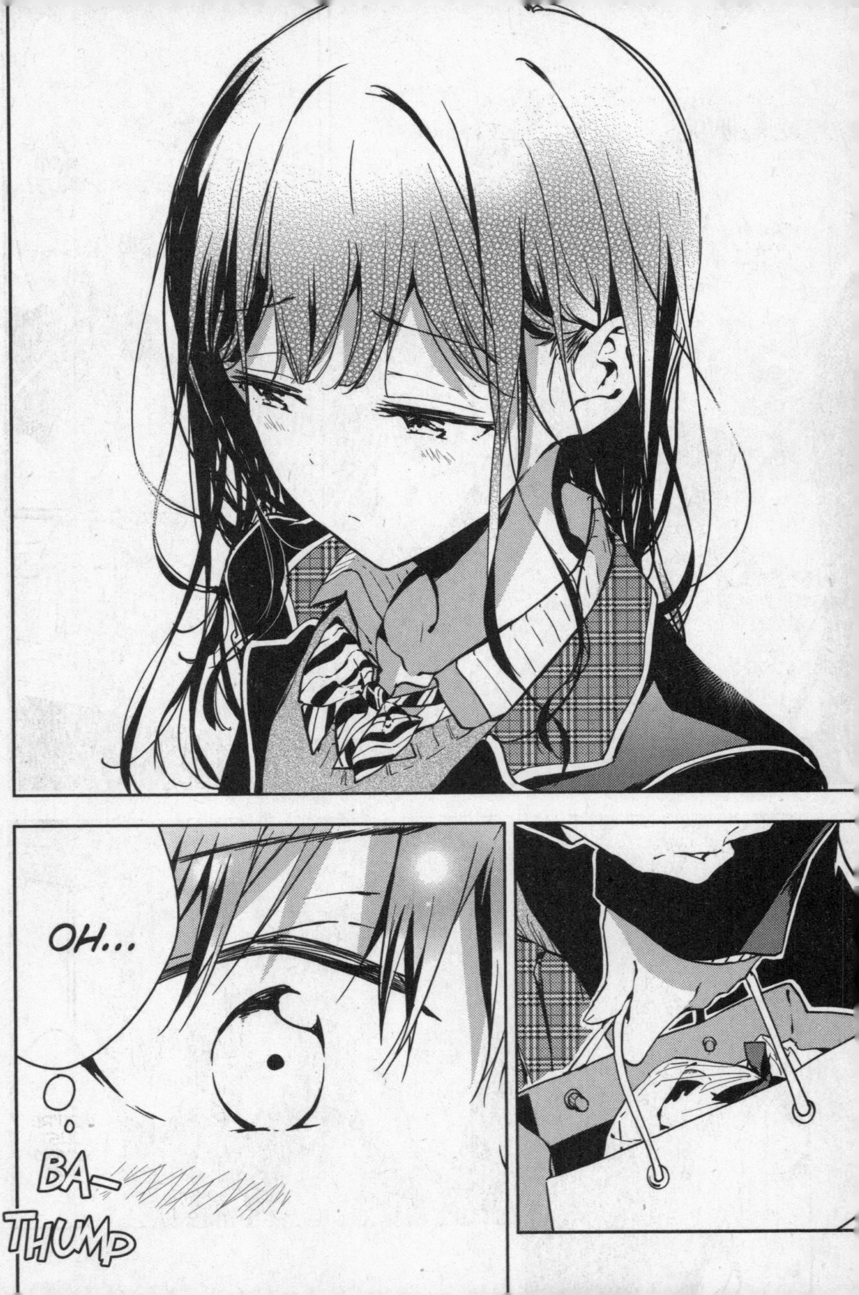
OH...
BA-THUMP

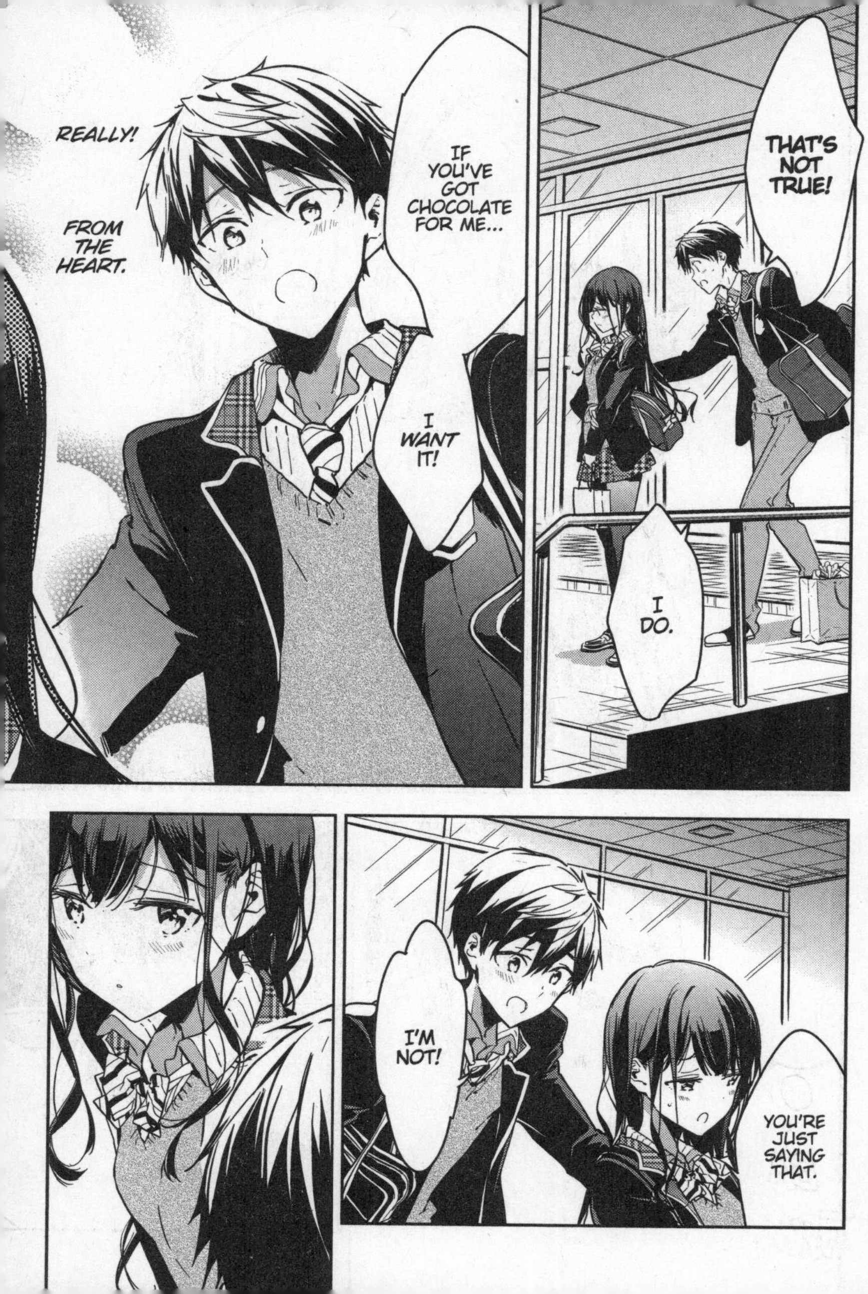
THAT'S NOT TRUE!
I DO.
IF YOU'VE GOT CHOCOLATE FOR ME...
I WANT IT!
REALLY!
FROM THE HEART.
YOU'RE JUST SAYING THAT.
I'M NOT!

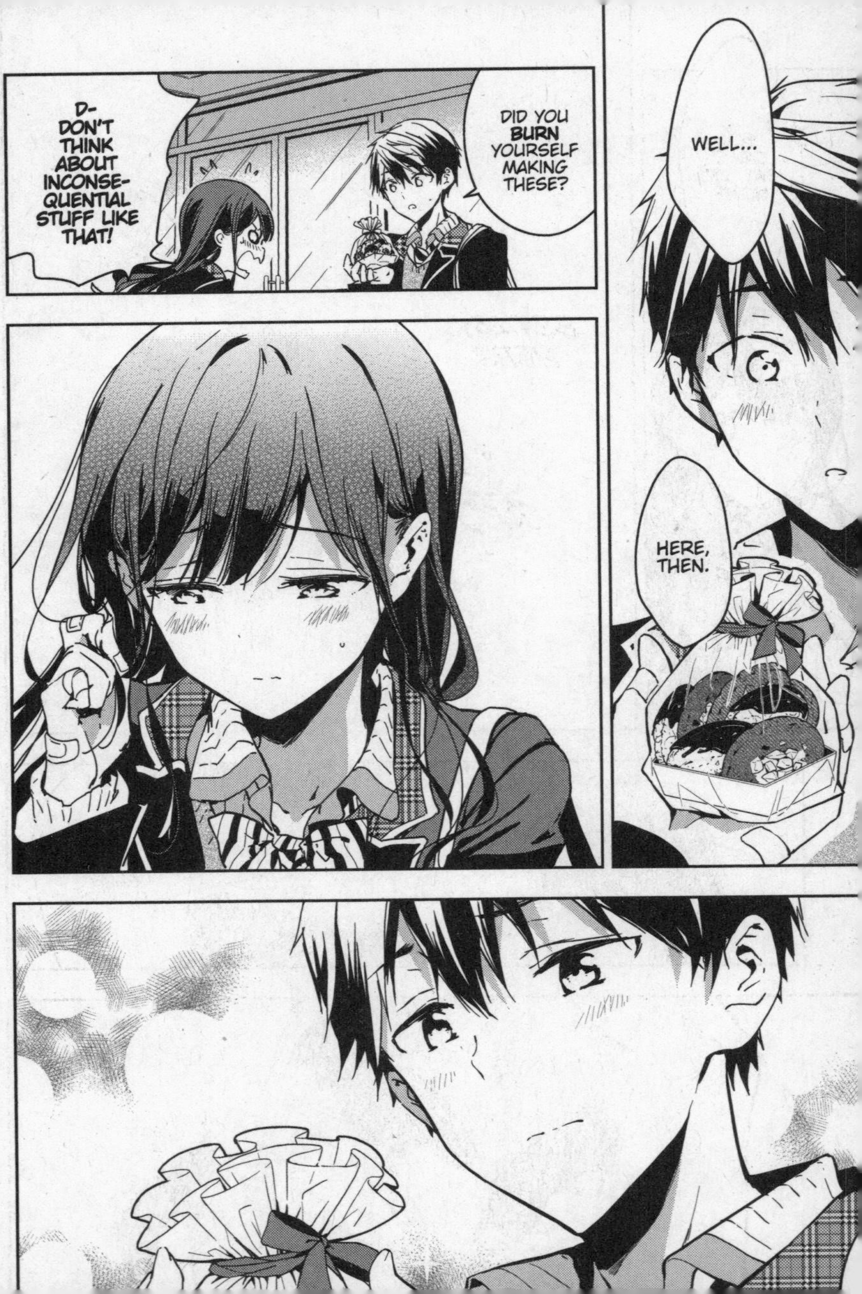
DID YOU BURN YOURSELF MAKING THESE?
D-DON'T THINK ABOUT INCONSE-QUENTIAL STUFF LIKE THAT!
WELL...
HERE, THEN.

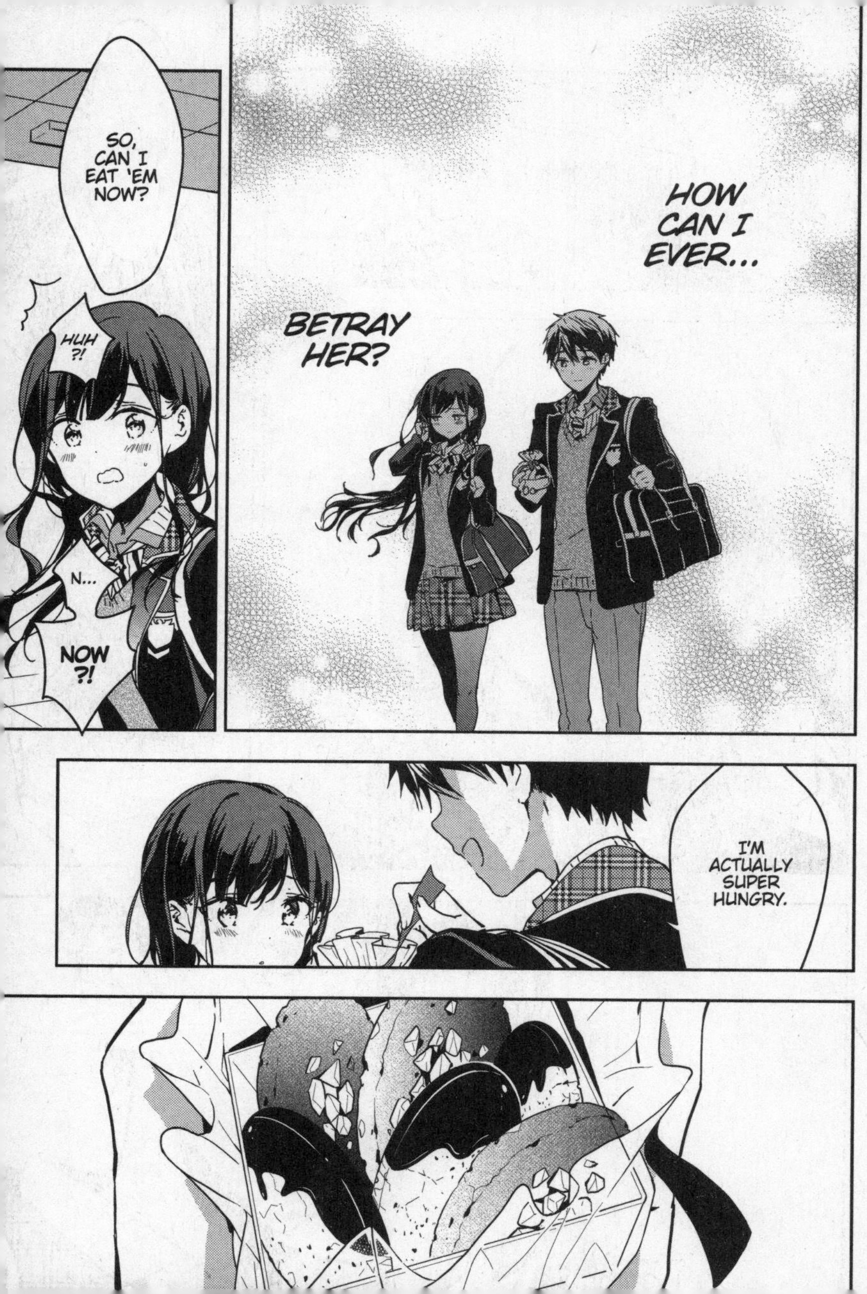
HOW CAN I EVER...
BETRAY HER?
SO, CAN I EAT 'EM NOW?
HUH ?!
N...
NOW ?!
I'M ACTUALLY SUPER HUNGRY.

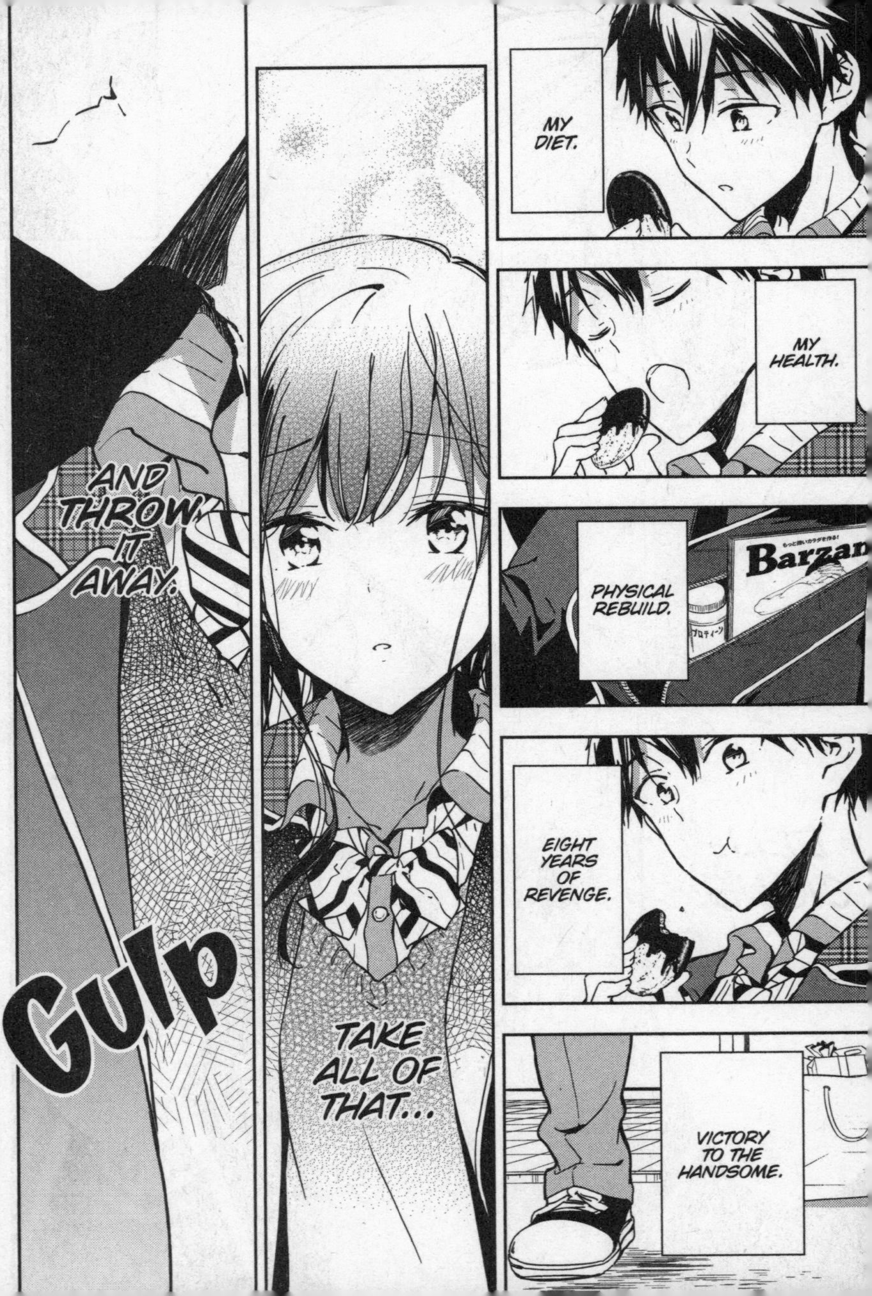
MY DIET.
MY HEALTH.
Barzan
PHYSICAL REBUILD.
EIGHT YEARS OF REVENGE.
VICTORY TO THE HANDSOME.
TAKE ALL OF THAT...
AND THROW IT AWAY.
Gulp

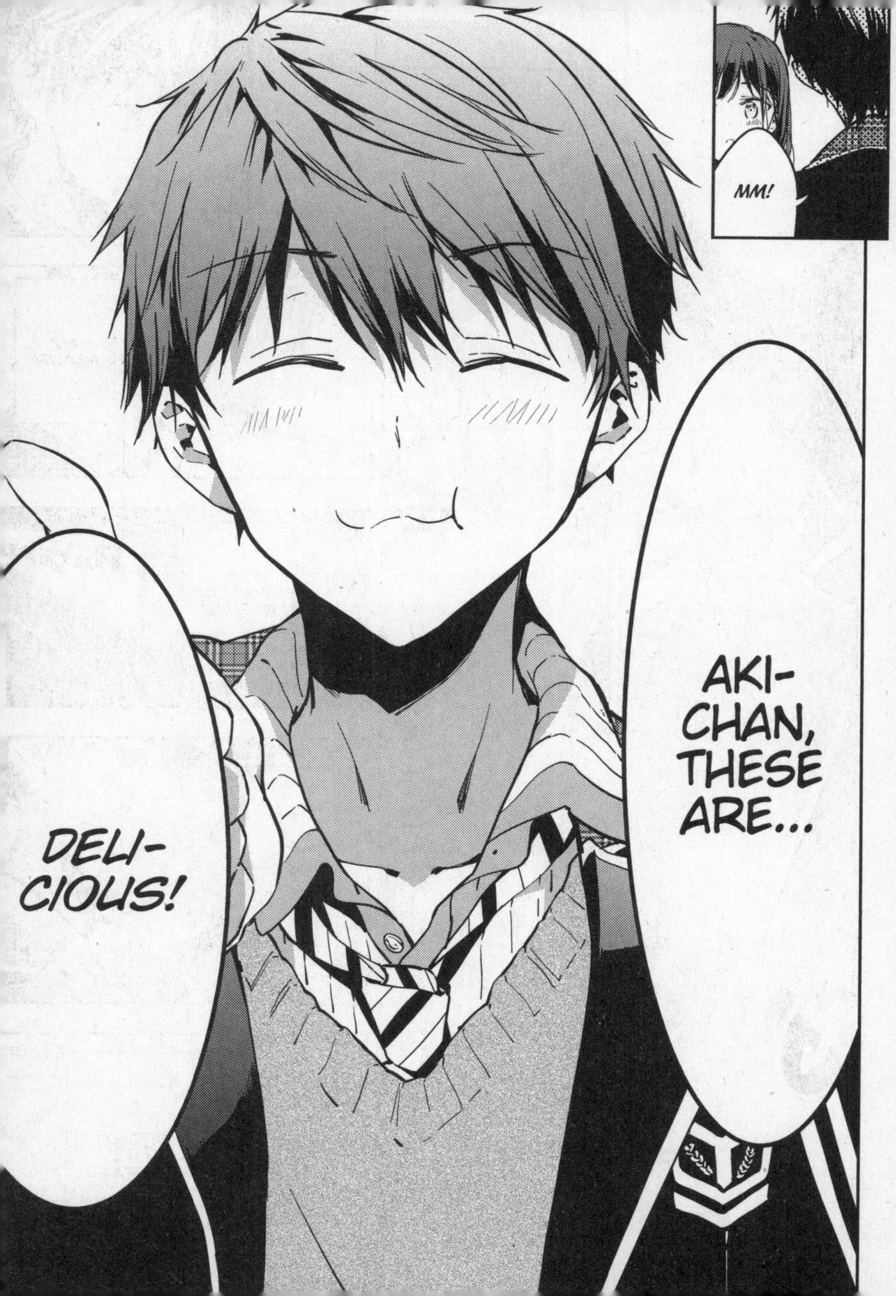
MM!
AKI-CHAN, THESE ARE...
DELI-CIOUS!

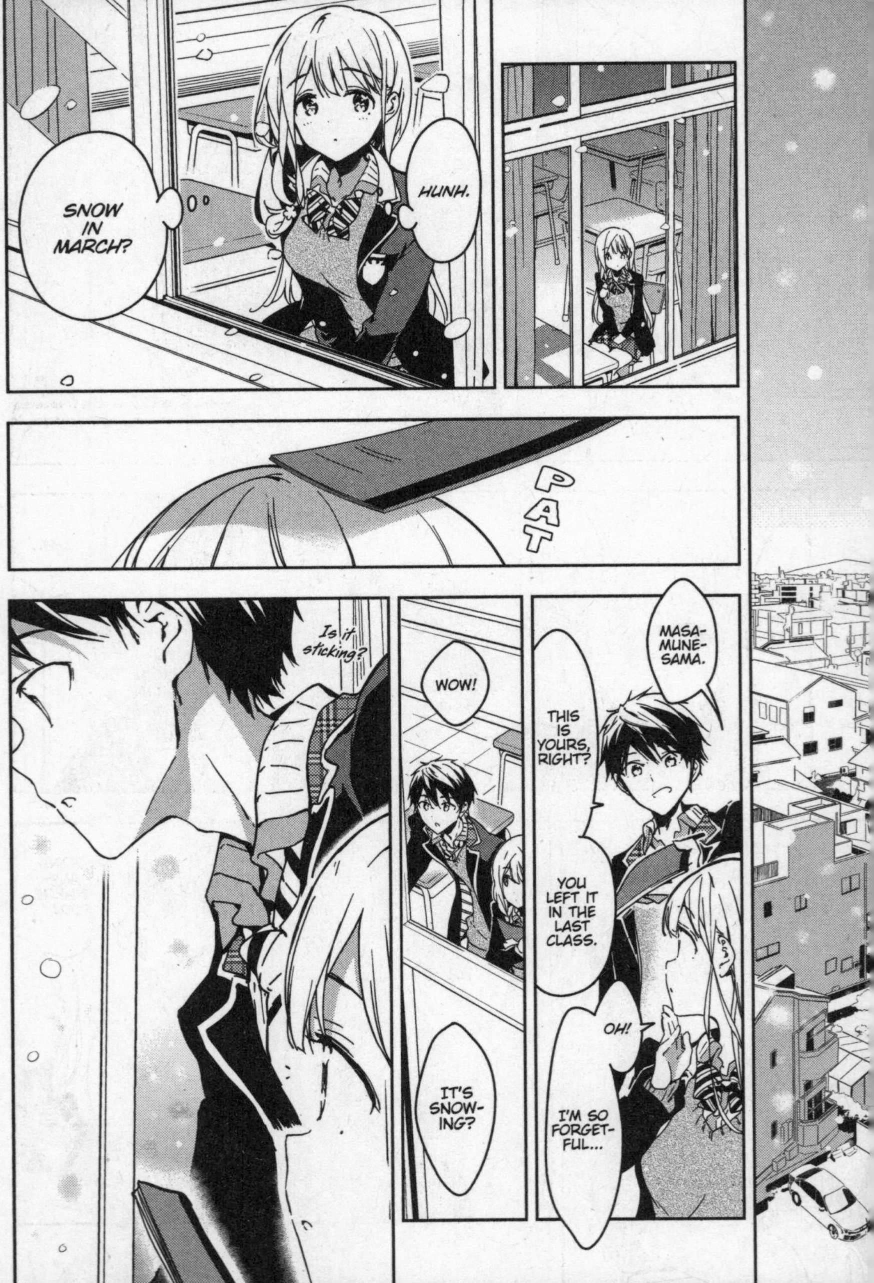
HUNH.
SNOW IN MARCH?
PAT
MASA-MUNE-SAMA.
THIS IS YOURS, RIGHT?
YOU LEFT IT IN THE LAST CLASS.
OH!
I'M SO FORGET-FUL...
WOW!
IT'S SNOW-ING?
Is it sticking?

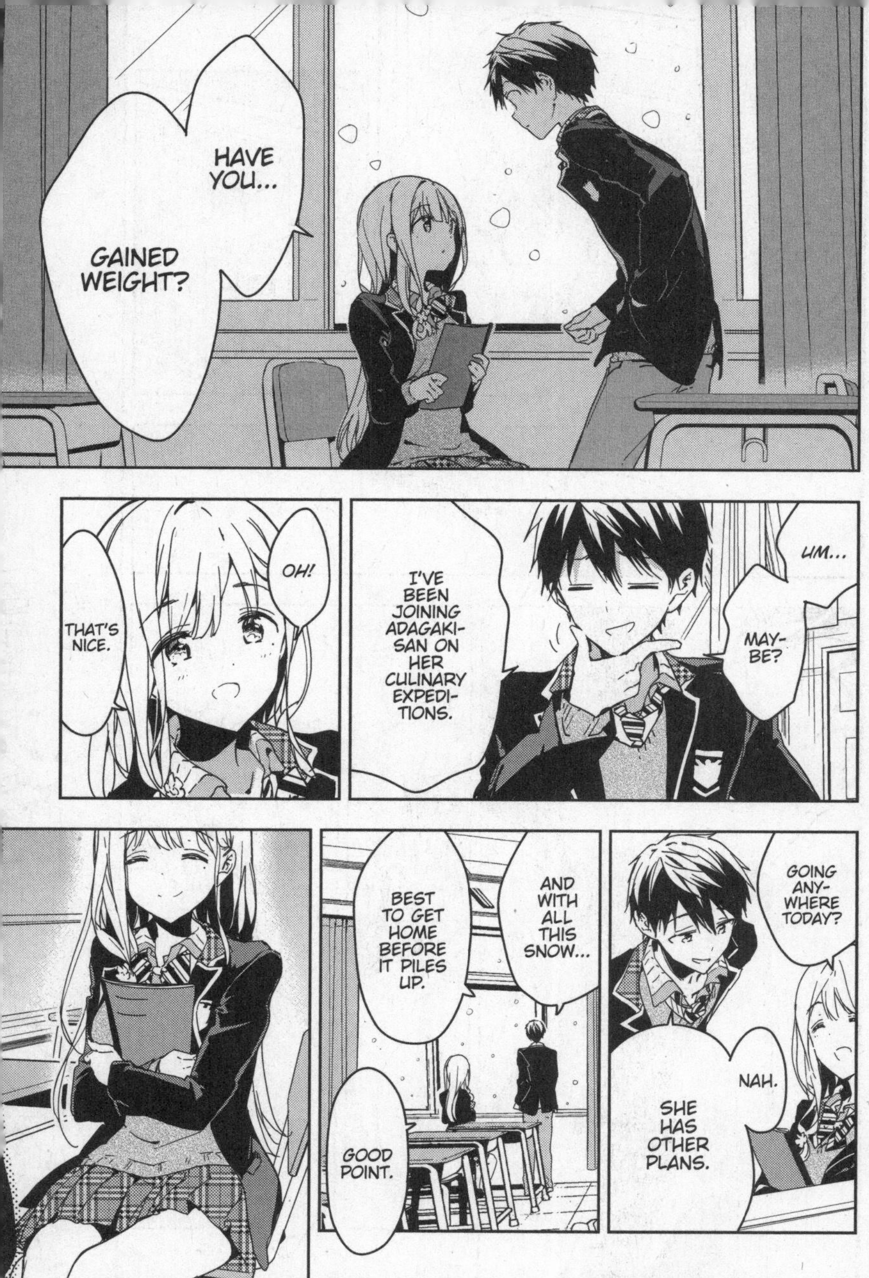
HAVE YOU...
GAINED WEIGHT?
UM...
MAY-BE?
I'VE BEEN JOINING ADAGAKI-SAN ON HER CULINARY EXPEDITIONS.
OH!
THAT'S NICE.
GOING ANY-WHERE TODAY?
NAH.
SHE HAS OTHER PLANS.
AND WITH ALL THIS SNOW...
BEST TO GET HOME BEFORE IT PILES UP.
GOOD POINT.

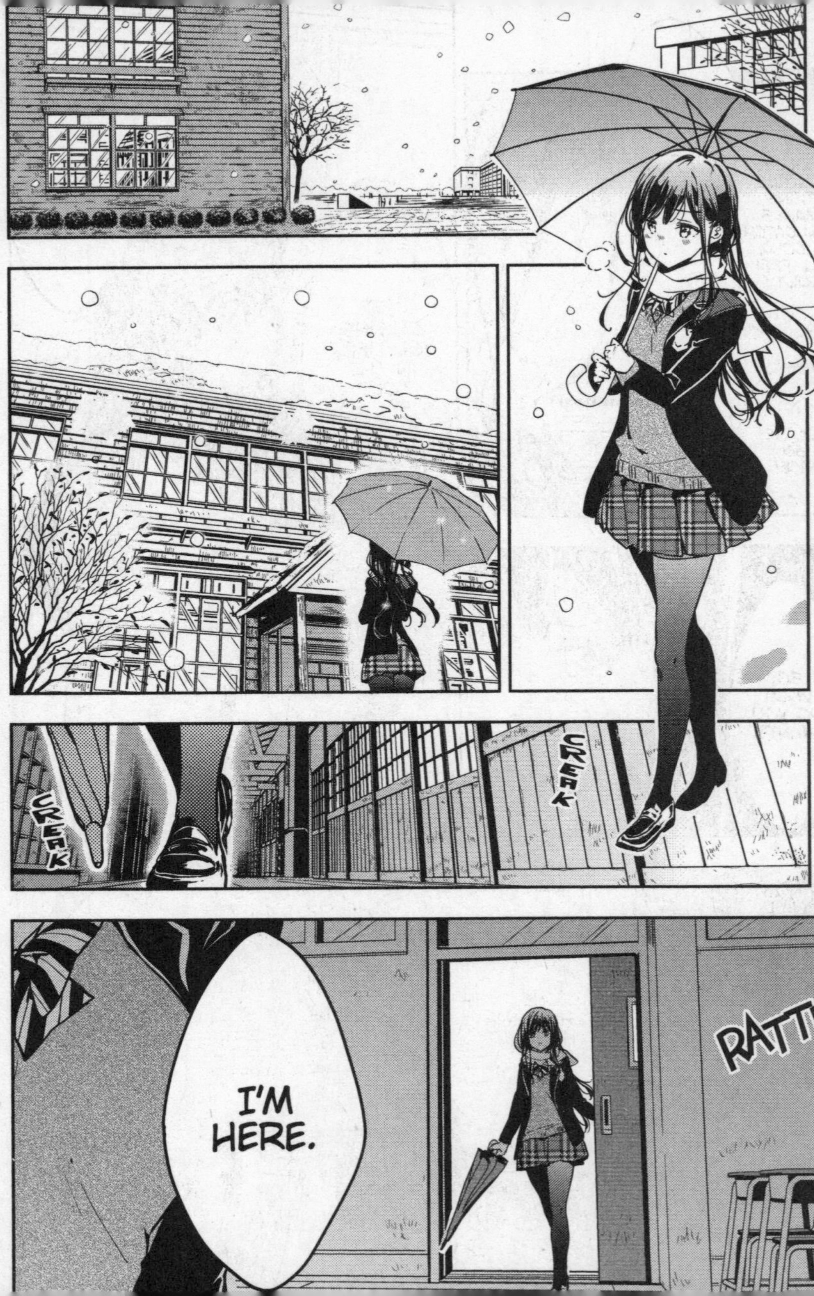
CREAK
CREAK
RATTLE
I'M HERE.

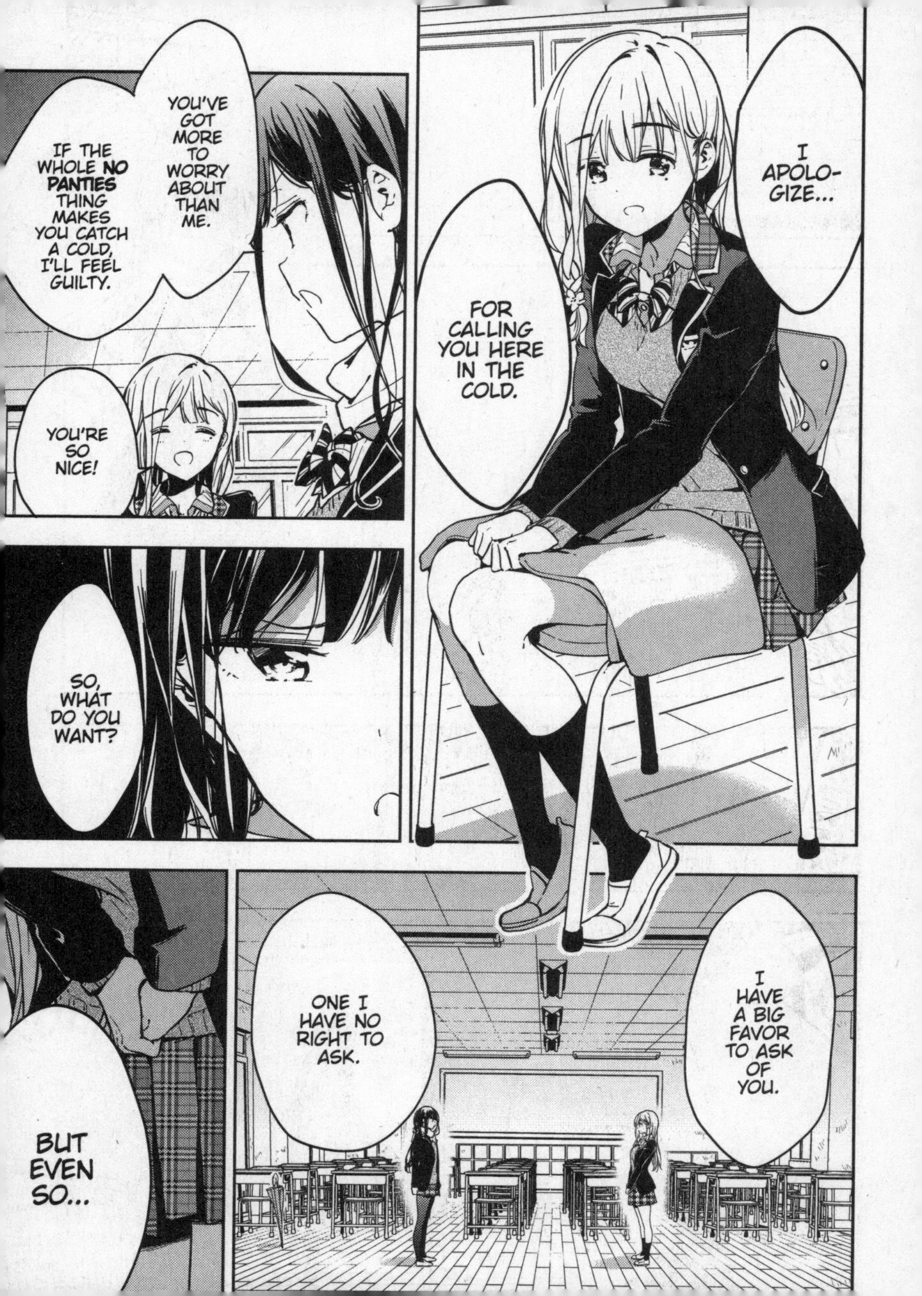
I APOLOGIZE...
FOR CALLING YOU HERE IN THE COLD.
YOU'VE GOT MORE TO WORRY ABOUT THAN ME.
IF THE WHOLE **NO PANTIES** THING MAKES YOU CATCH A COLD, I'LL FEEL GUILTY.
YOU'RE SO NICE!
SO, WHAT DO YOU WANT?
I HAVE A BIG FAVOR TO ASK OF YOU.
ONE I HAVE NO RIGHT TO ASK.
BUT EVEN SO...

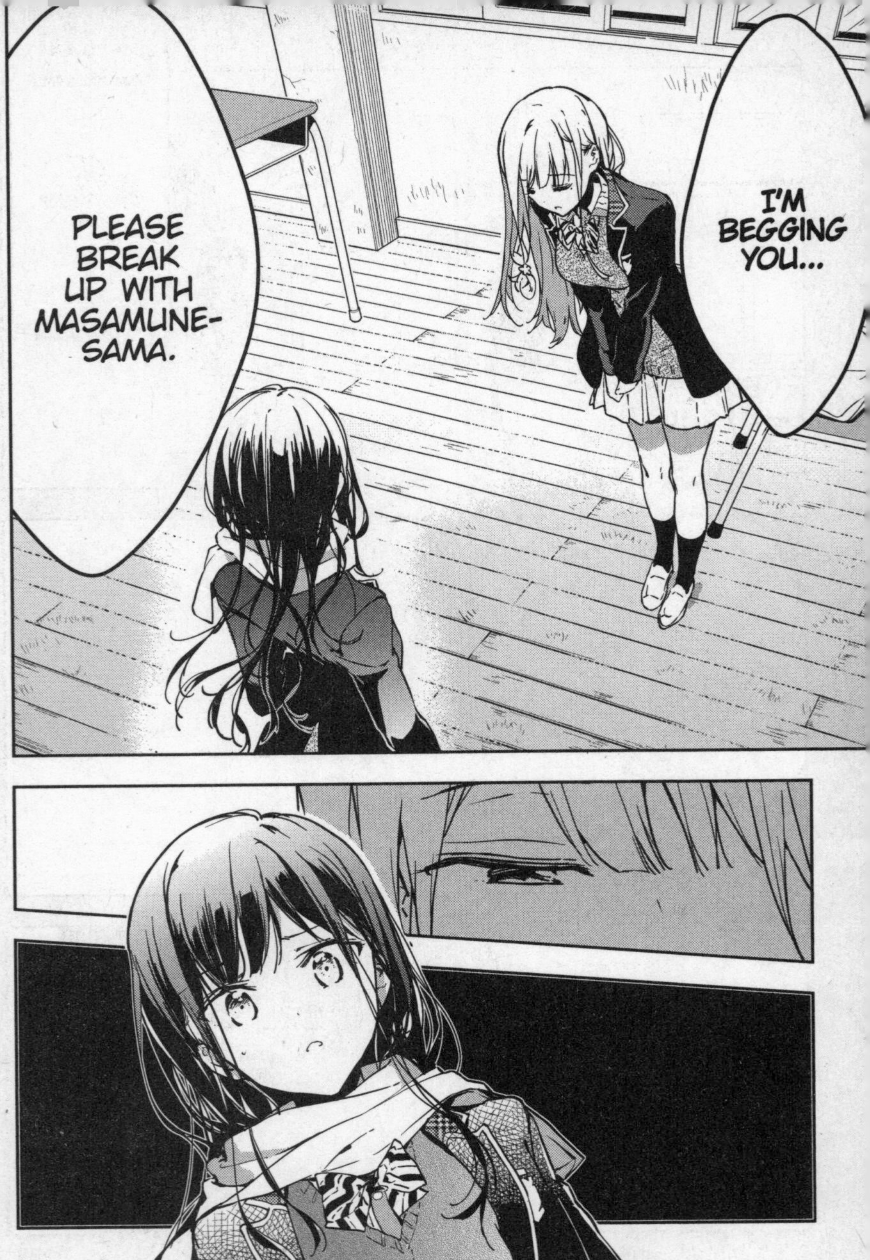
I'M BEGGING YOU...
PLEASE BREAK UP WITH MASAMUNE-SAMA.

# CHAPTER 46

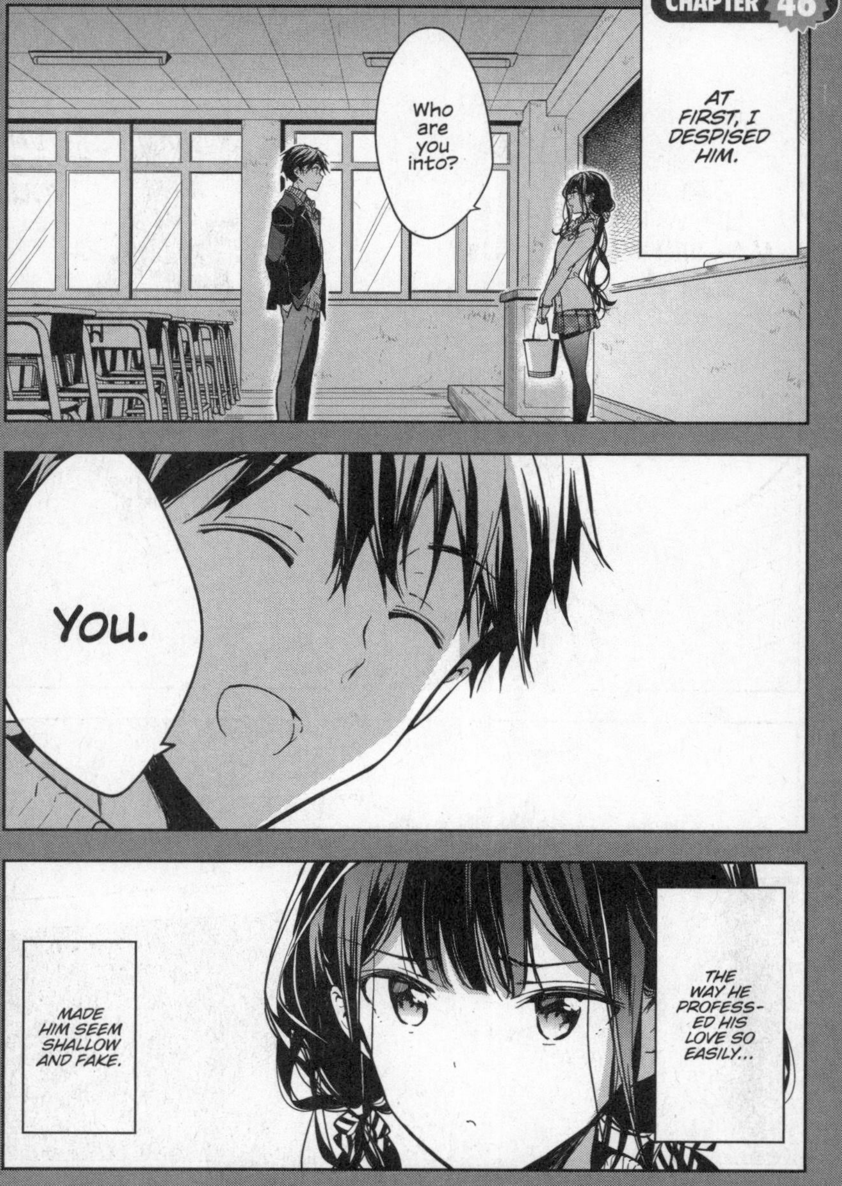
AT FIRST, I DESPISED HIM.
Who are you into?
YOU.
THE WAY HE PROFESS-ED HIS LOVE SO EASILY...
MADE HIM SEEM SHALLOW AND FAKE.

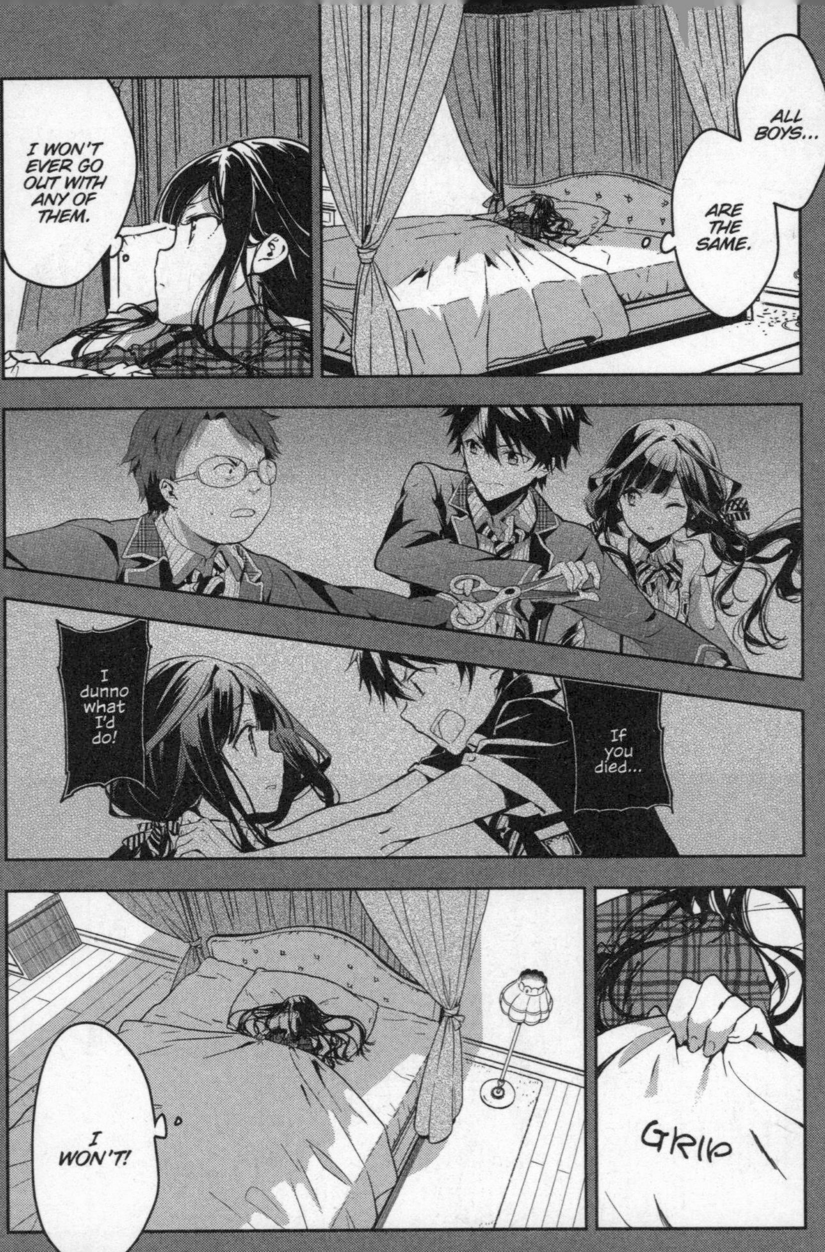
ALL BOYS... ARE THE SAME.
I WON'T EVER GO OUT WITH ANY OF THEM.
If you died...
I dunno what I'd do!
GRIP
I WON'T!

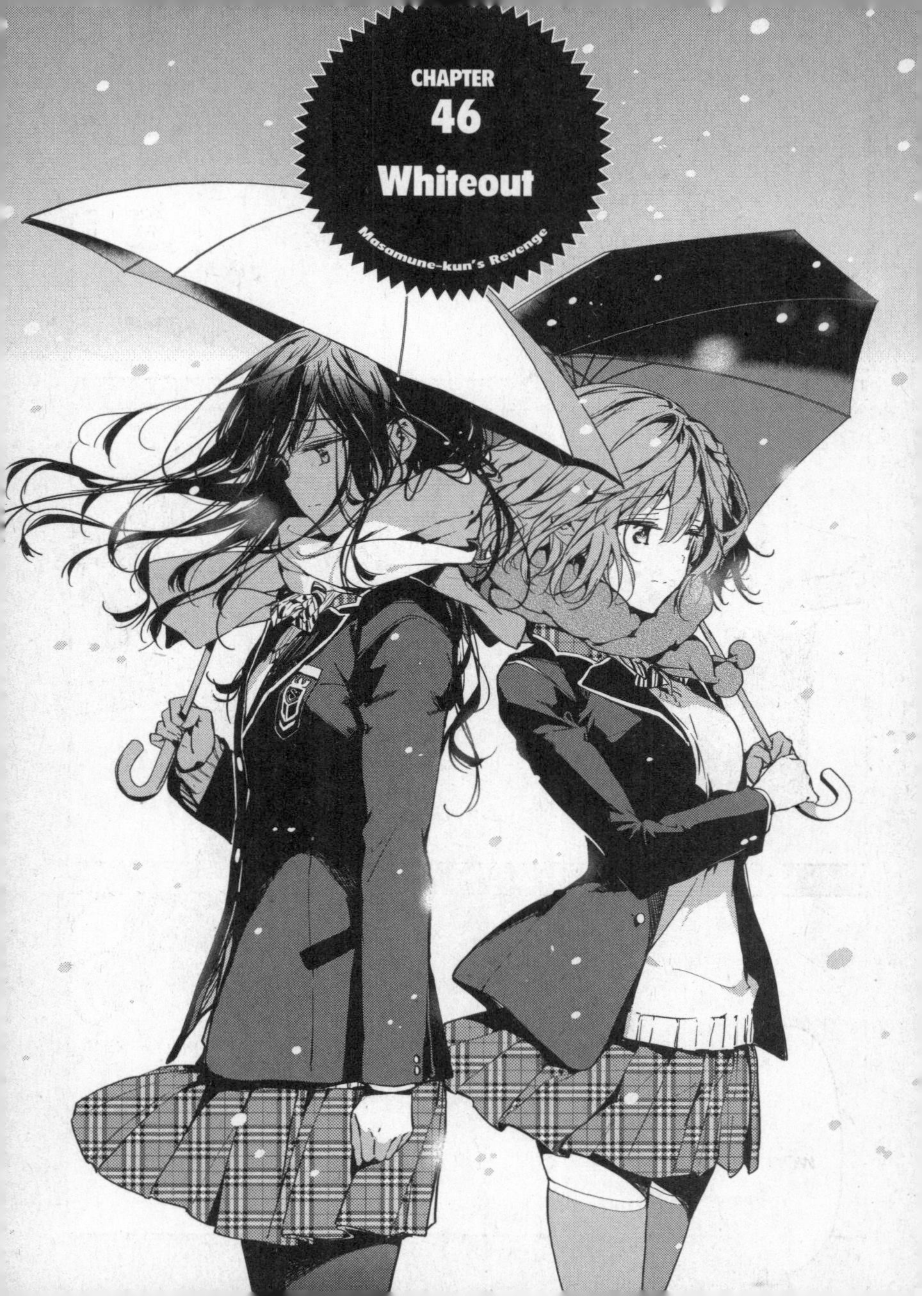
CHAPTER
46
Whiteout
Masamune-kun's Revenge

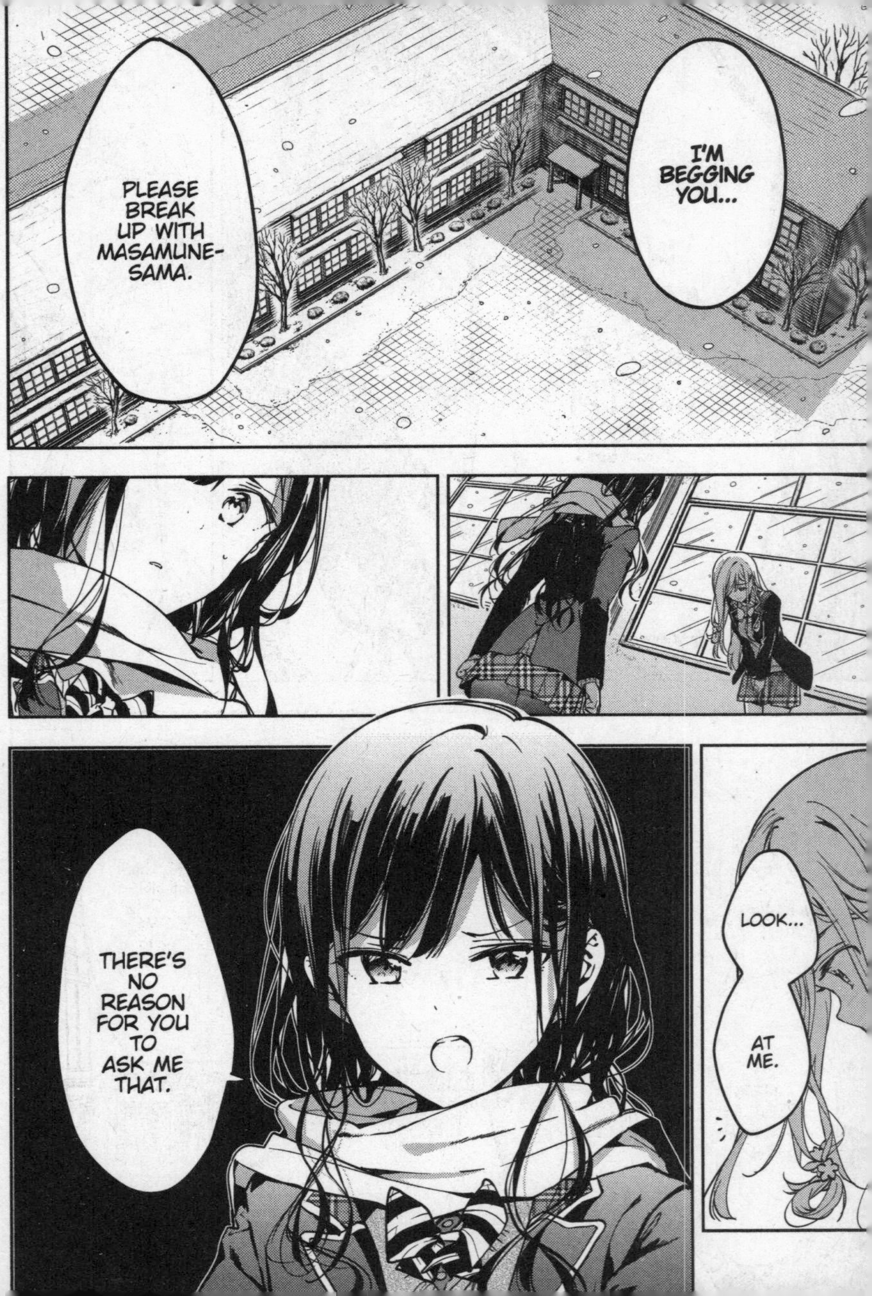
I'M BEGGING YOU...
PLEASE BREAK UP WITH MASAMUNE-SAMA.
LOOK... AT ME.
THERE'S NO REASON FOR YOU TO ASK ME THAT.

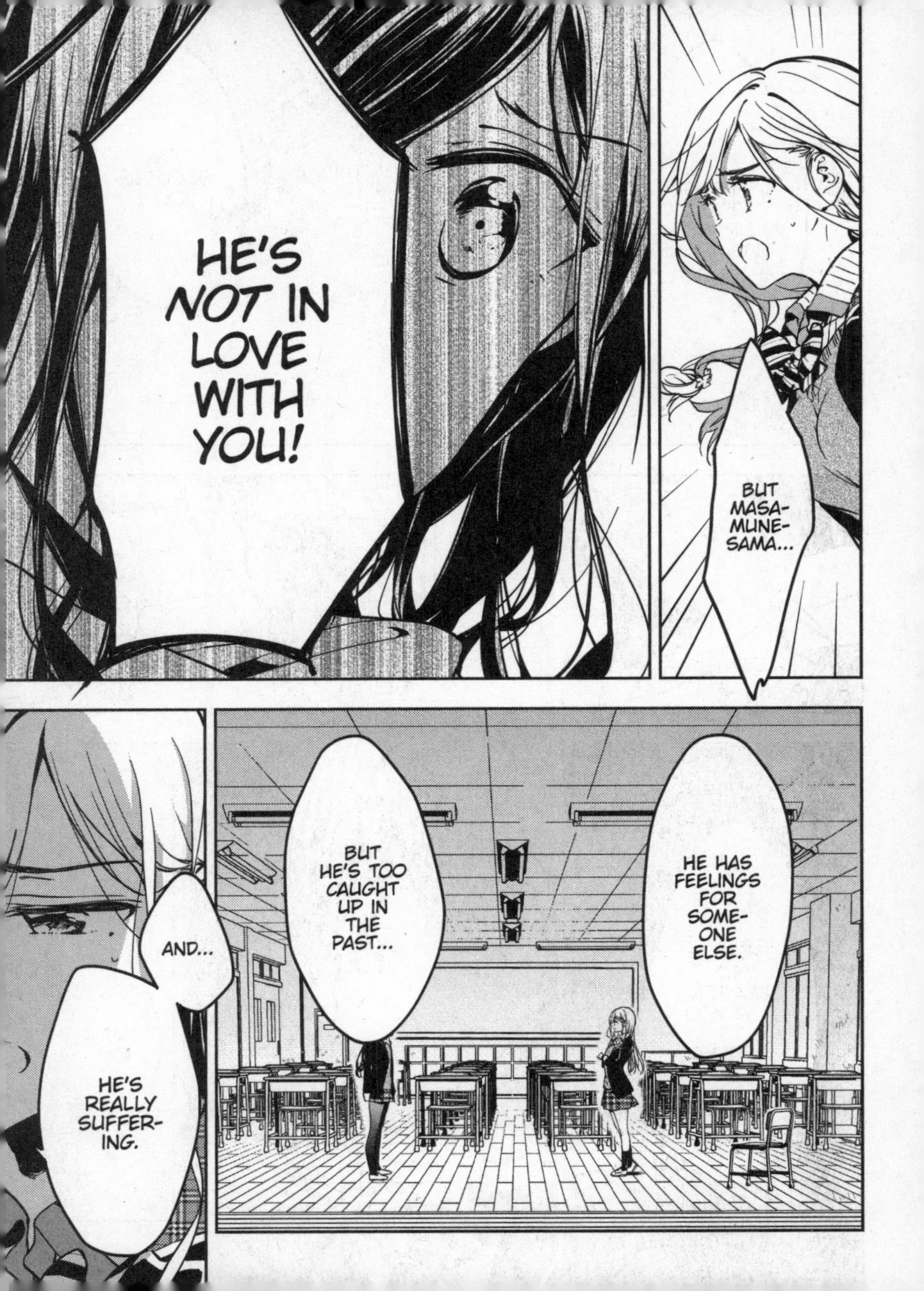
BUT MASAMUNE-SAMA...
HE'S *NOT* IN LOVE WITH YOU!
HE HAS FEELINGS FOR SOMEONE ELSE.
BUT HE'S TOO CAUGHT UP IN THE PAST...
AND...
HE'S REALLY SUFFERING.

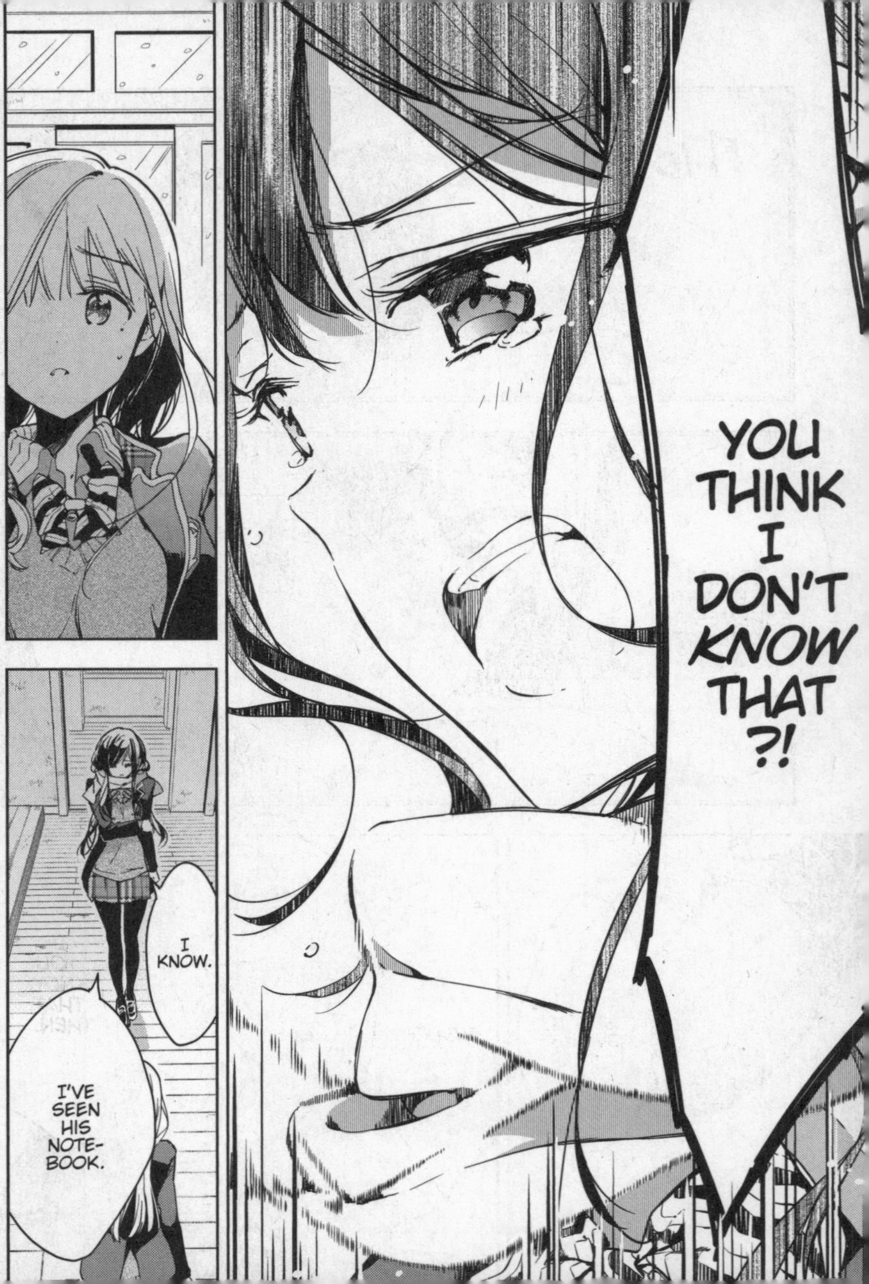
YOU THINK I DON'T KNOW THAT?!
I KNOW.
I'VE SEEN HIS NOTE-BOOK.

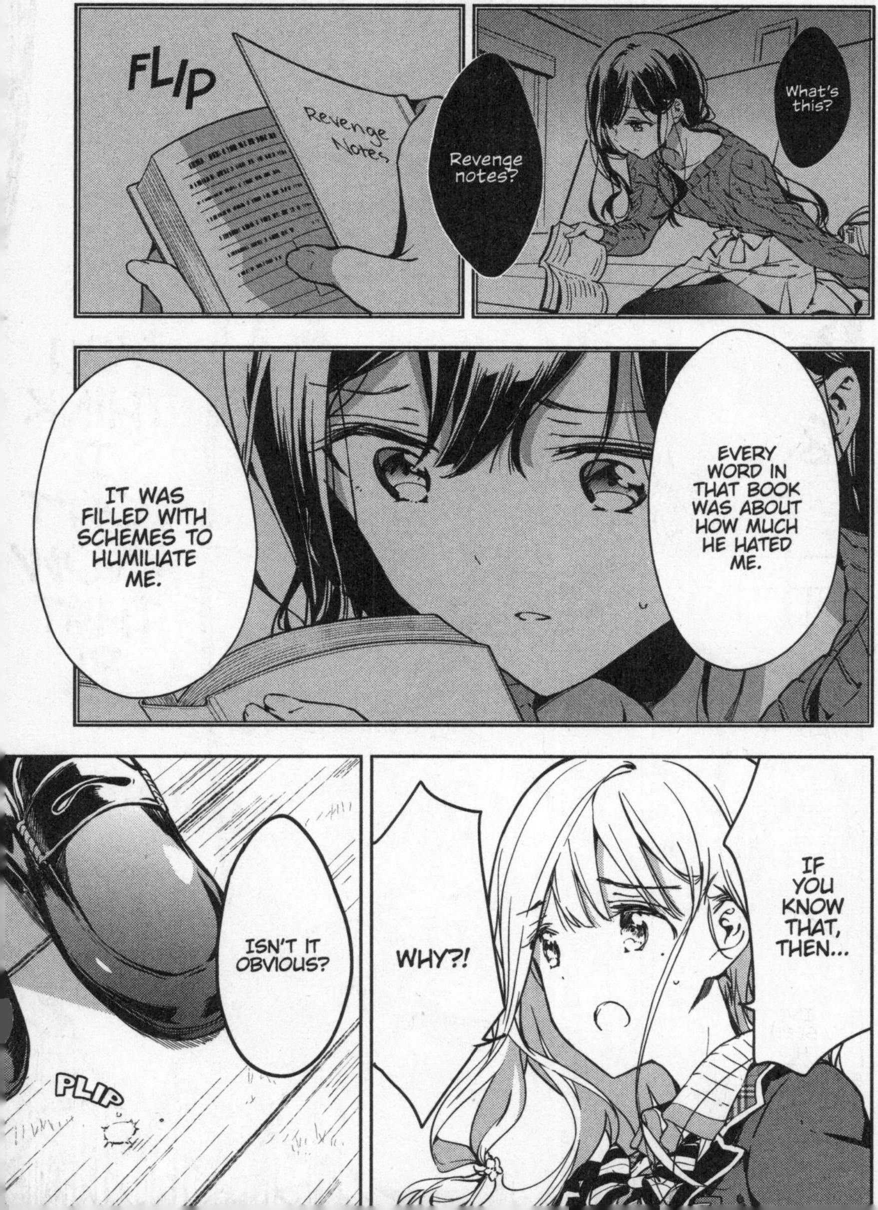
What's this?
FLIP
Revenge Notes
Revenge notes?
EVERY WORD IN THAT BOOK WAS ABOUT HOW MUCH HE HATED ME.
IT WAS FILLED WITH SCHEMES TO HUMILIATE ME.
IF YOU KNOW THAT, THEN...
WHY?!
ISN'T IT OBVIOUS?
PLIP

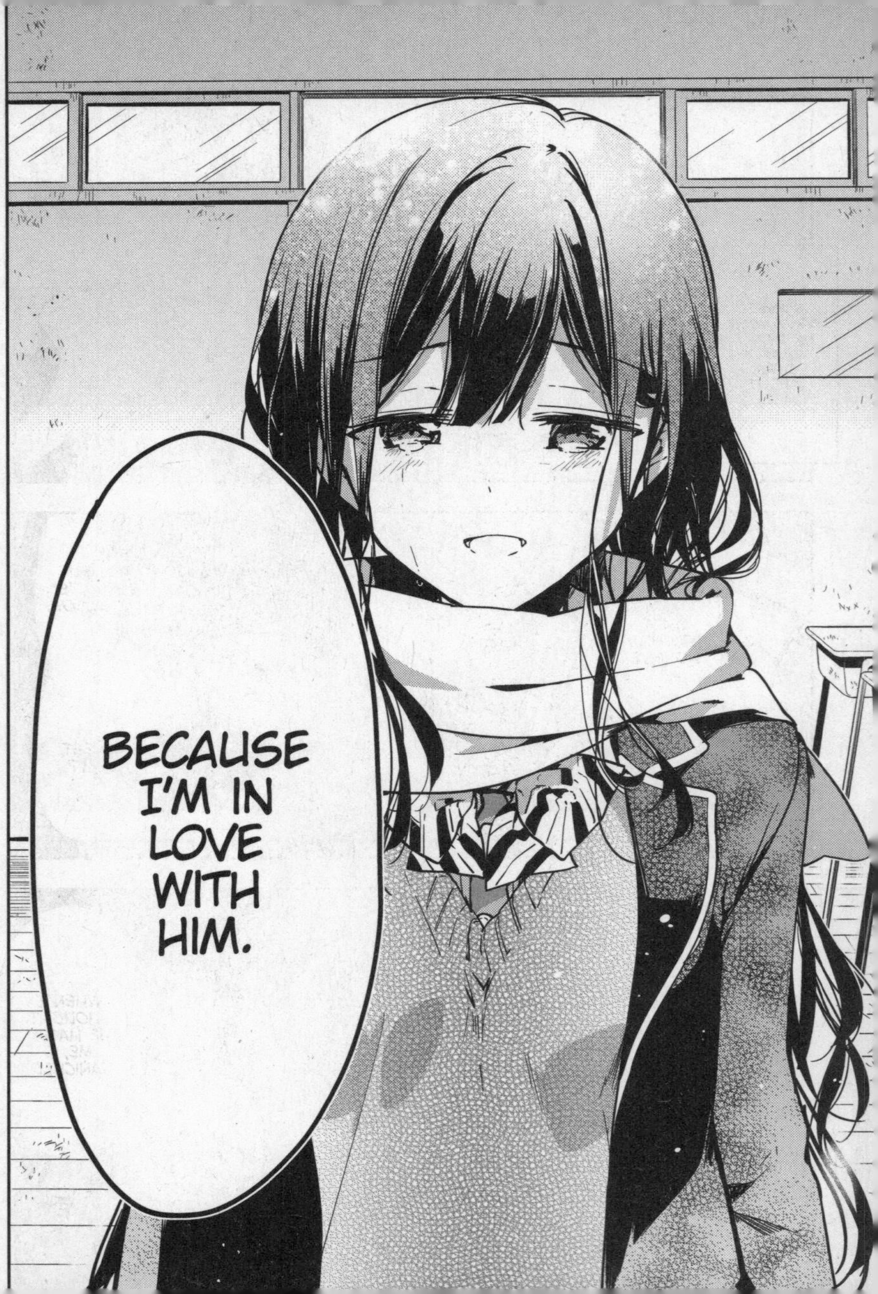
BECAUSE I'M IN LOVE WITH HIM.

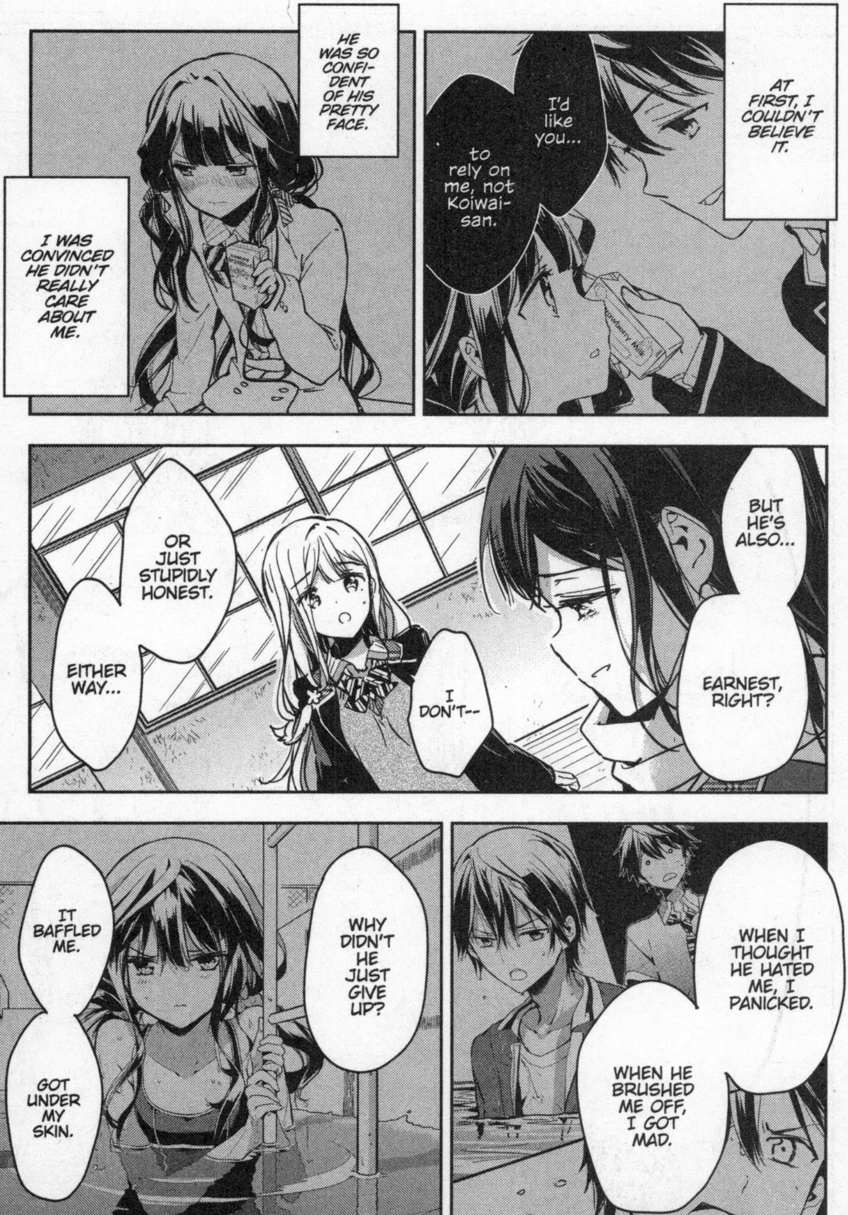
AT FIRST, I COULDN'T BELIEVE IT.
I'd like you...
to rely on me, not Koiwai-san.
HE WAS SO CONFIDENT OF HIS PRETTY FACE.
I WAS CONVINCED HE DIDN'T REALLY CARE ABOUT ME.
BUT HE'S ALSO...
EARNEST, RIGHT?
OR JUST STUPIDLY HONEST.
EITHER WAY...
I DON'T--
WHEN I THOUGHT HE HATED ME, I PANICKED.
WHEN HE BRUSHED ME OFF, I GOT MAD.
WHY DIDN'T HE JUST GIVE UP?
IT BAFFLED ME.
GOT UNDER MY SKIN.

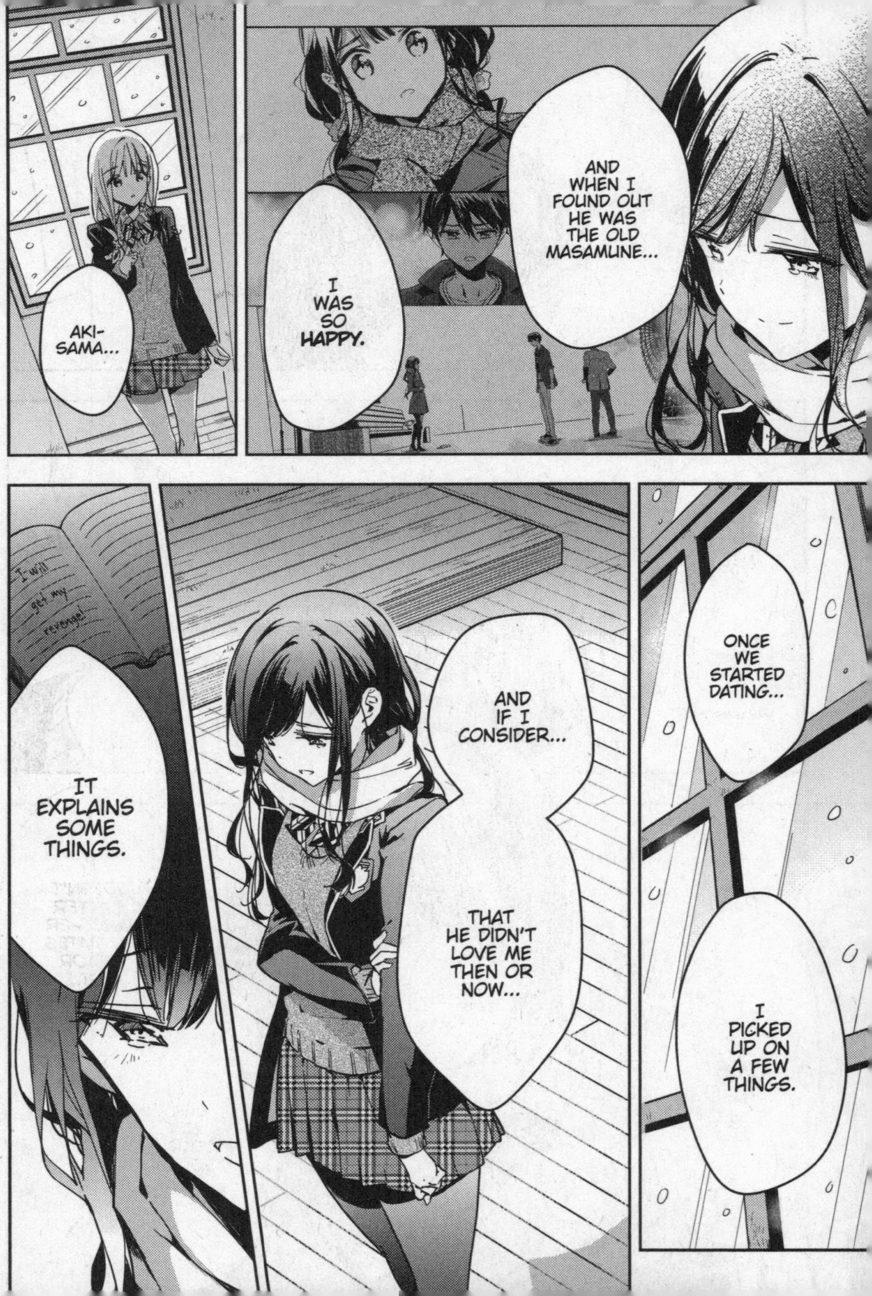
AND WHEN I FOUND OUT HE WAS THE OLD MASAMUNE...
I WAS SO HAPPY.
AKI-SAMA...
ONCE WE STARTED DATING...
I PICKED UP ON A FEW THINGS.
AND IF I CONSIDER...
THAT HE DIDN'T LOVE ME THEN OR NOW...
I will get my revenge!
IT EXPLAINS SOME THINGS.

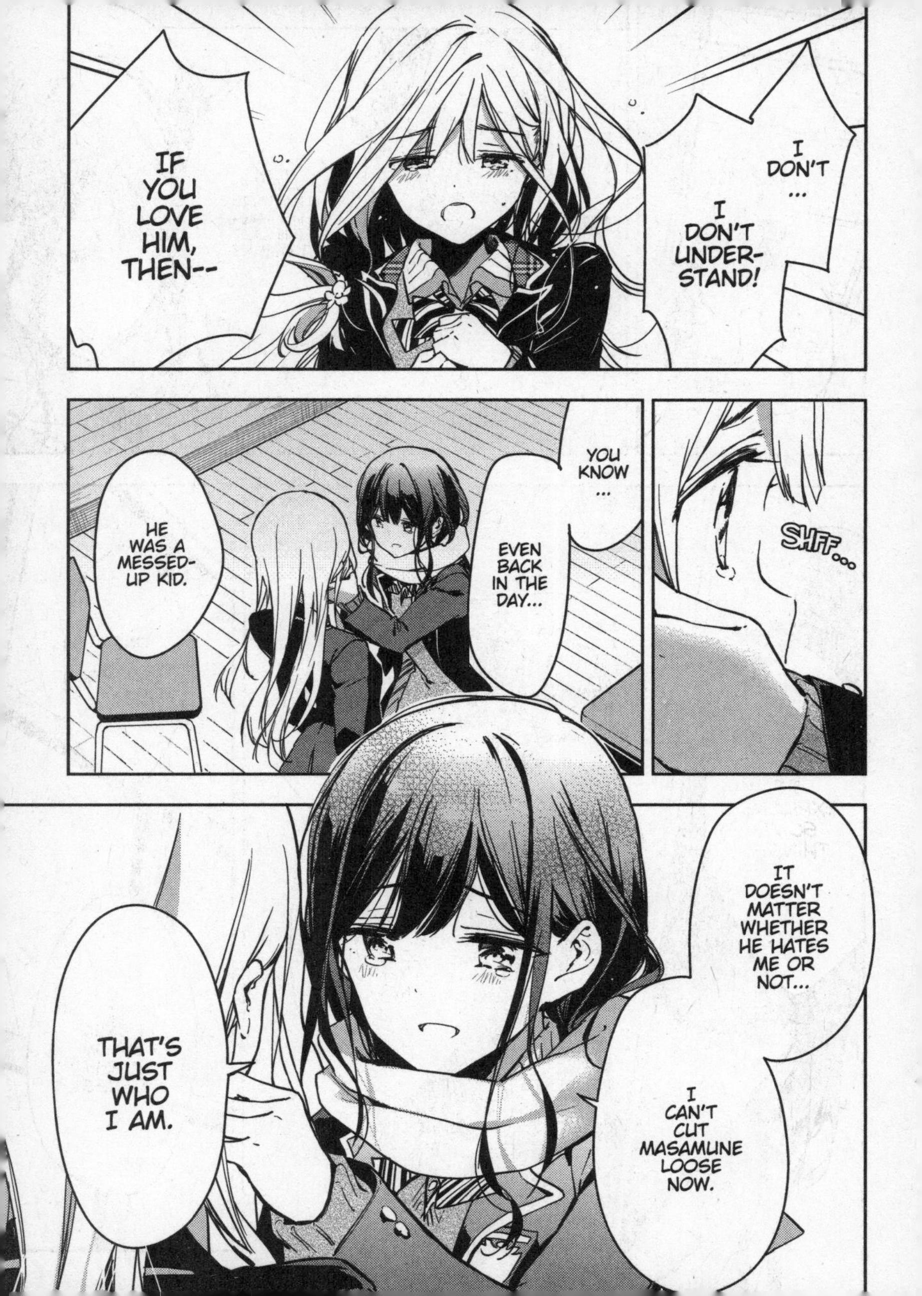
I DON'T ...
I DON'T UNDERSTAND!
IF YOU LOVE HIM, THEN--
SHFF...
YOU KNOW ...
EVEN BACK IN THE DAY...
HE WAS A MESSED-UP KID.
IT DOESN'T MATTER WHETHER HE HATES ME OR NOT...
I CAN'T CUT MASAMUNE LOOSE NOW.
THAT'S JUST WHO I AM.

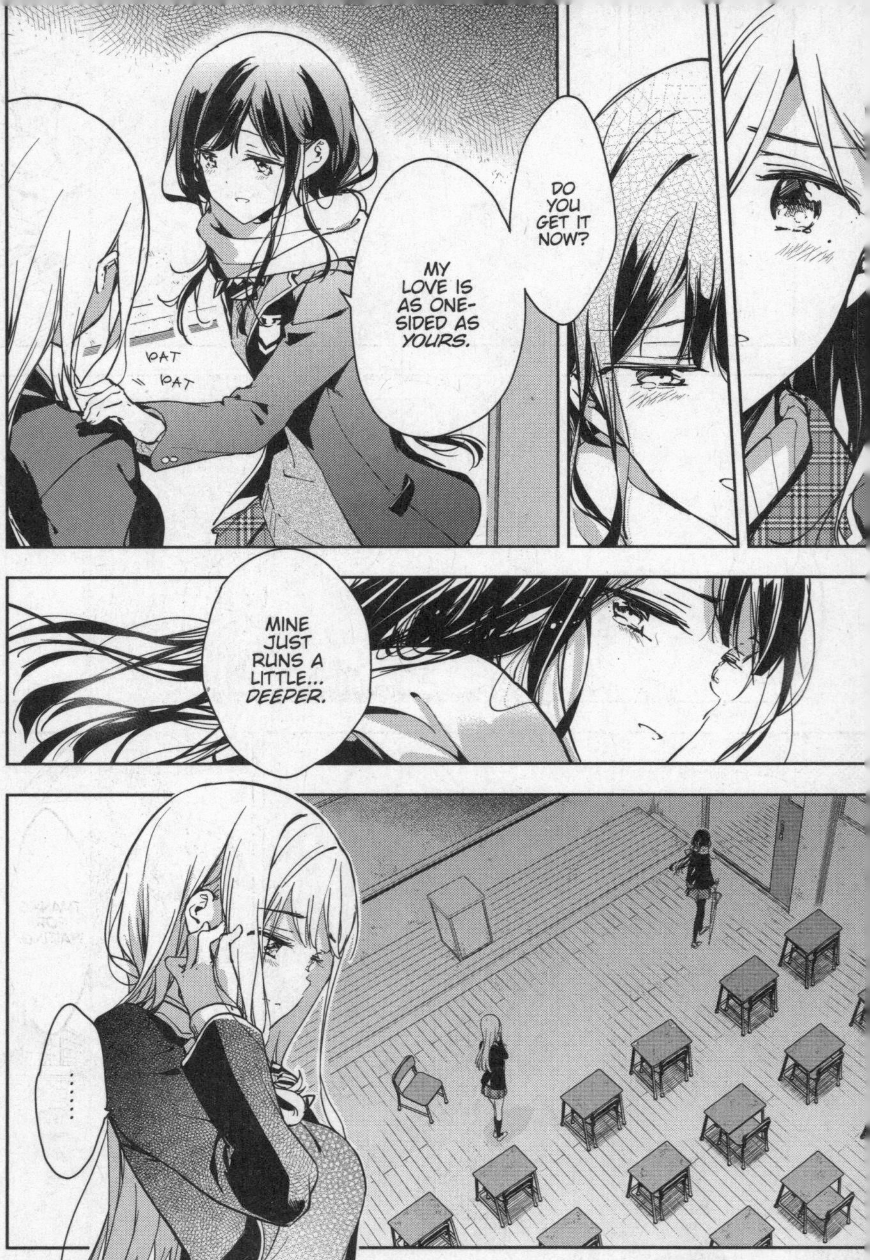
DO YOU GET IT NOW?
MY LOVE IS AS ONE-SIDED AS *YOURS.*
PAT PAT
MINE JUST RUNS A LITTLE... *DEEPER.*
......

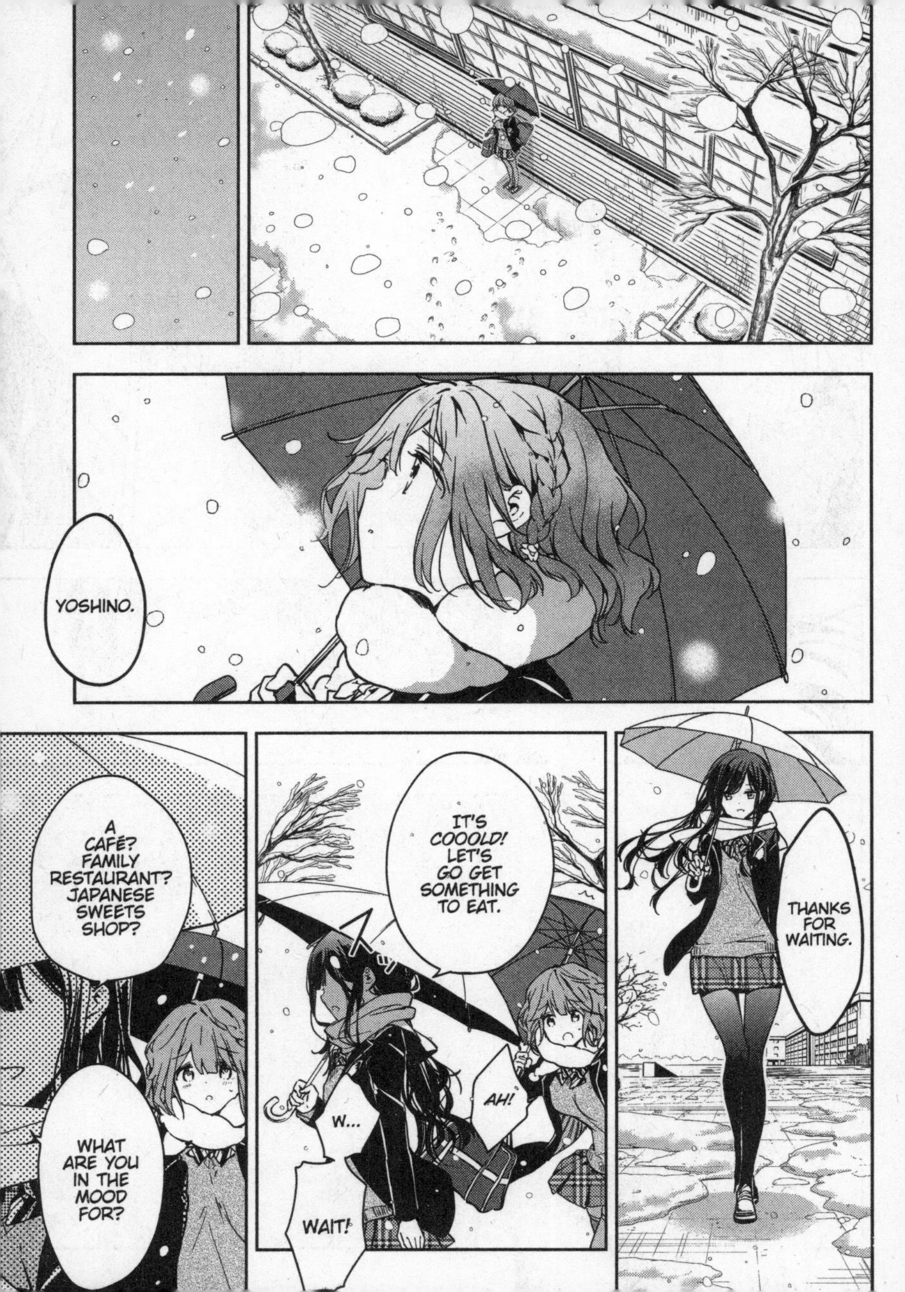
YOSHINO.
THANKS FOR WAITING.
IT'S COOOLD! LET'S GO GET SOMETHING TO EAT.
AH!
W...
WAIT!
A CAFÉ? FAMILY RESTAURANT? JAPANESE SWEETS SHOP?
WHAT ARE YOU IN THE MOOD FOR?

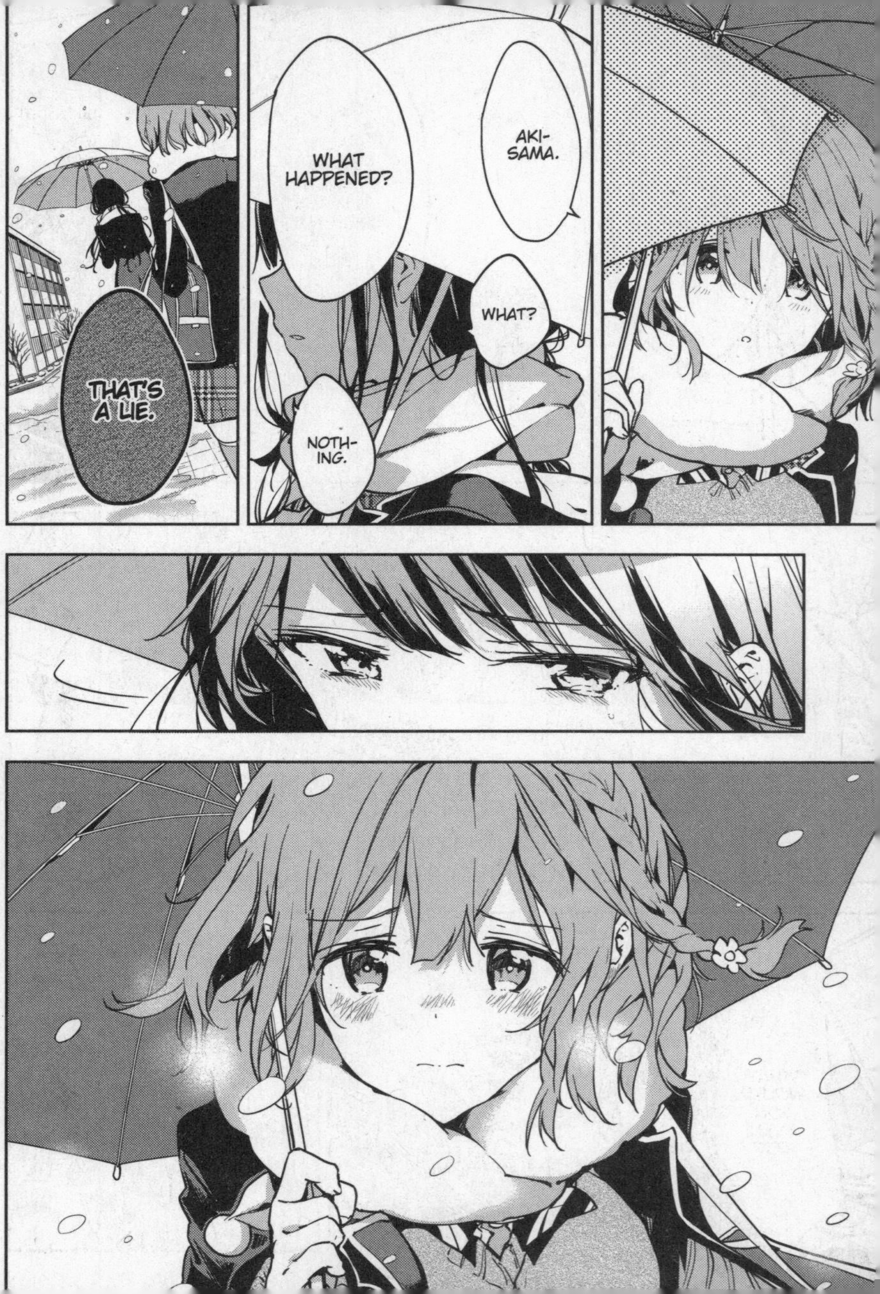
AKI-SAMA.
WHAT?
WHAT HAPPENED?
NOTH-ING.
THAT'S A LIE.

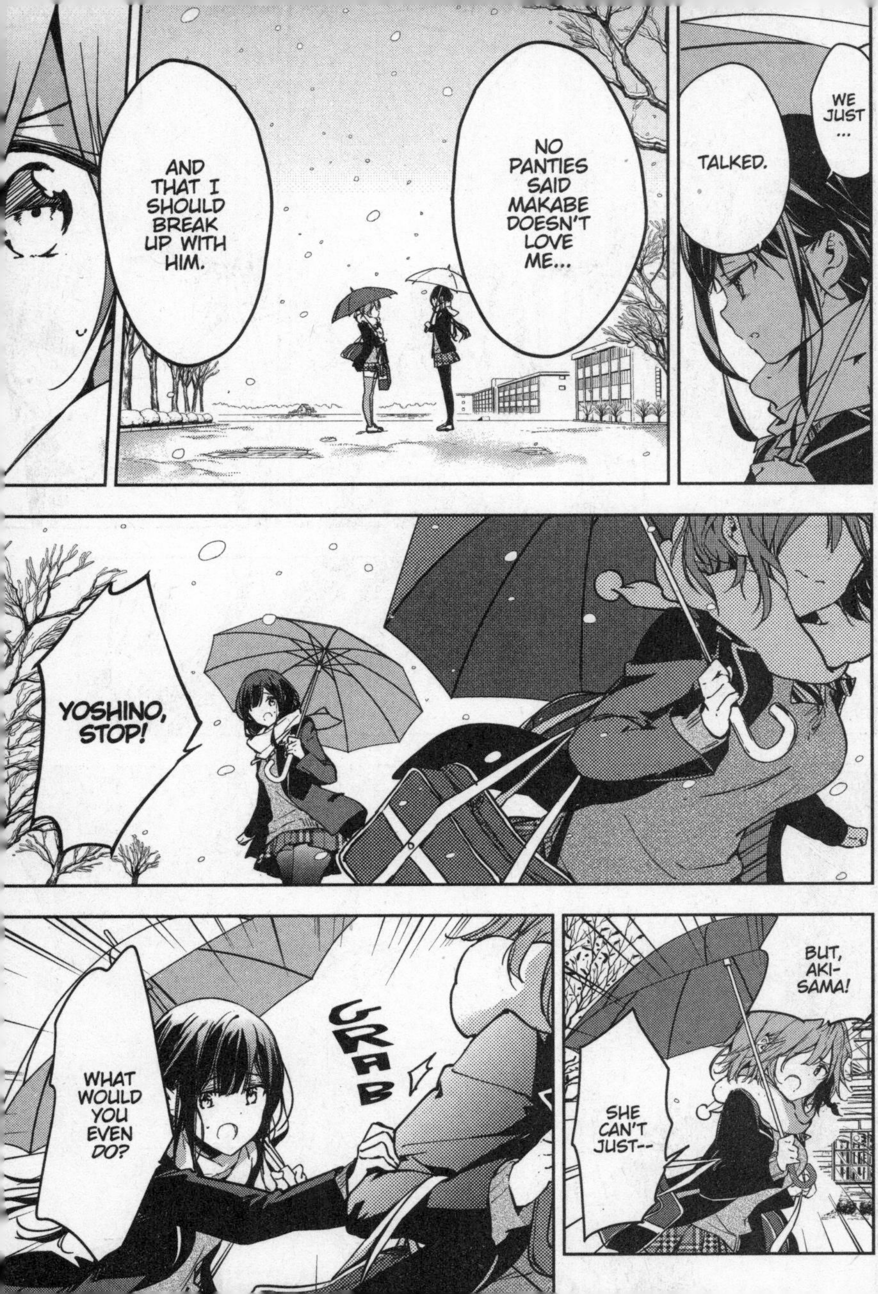
WE JUST ...
TALKED.
NO PANTIES SAID MAKABE DOESN'T LOVE ME...
AND THAT I SHOULD BREAK UP WITH HIM.
YOSHINO, STOP!
BUT, AKI-SAMA!
SHE CAN'T JUST--
GRAB
WHAT WOULD YOU EVEN *DO*?

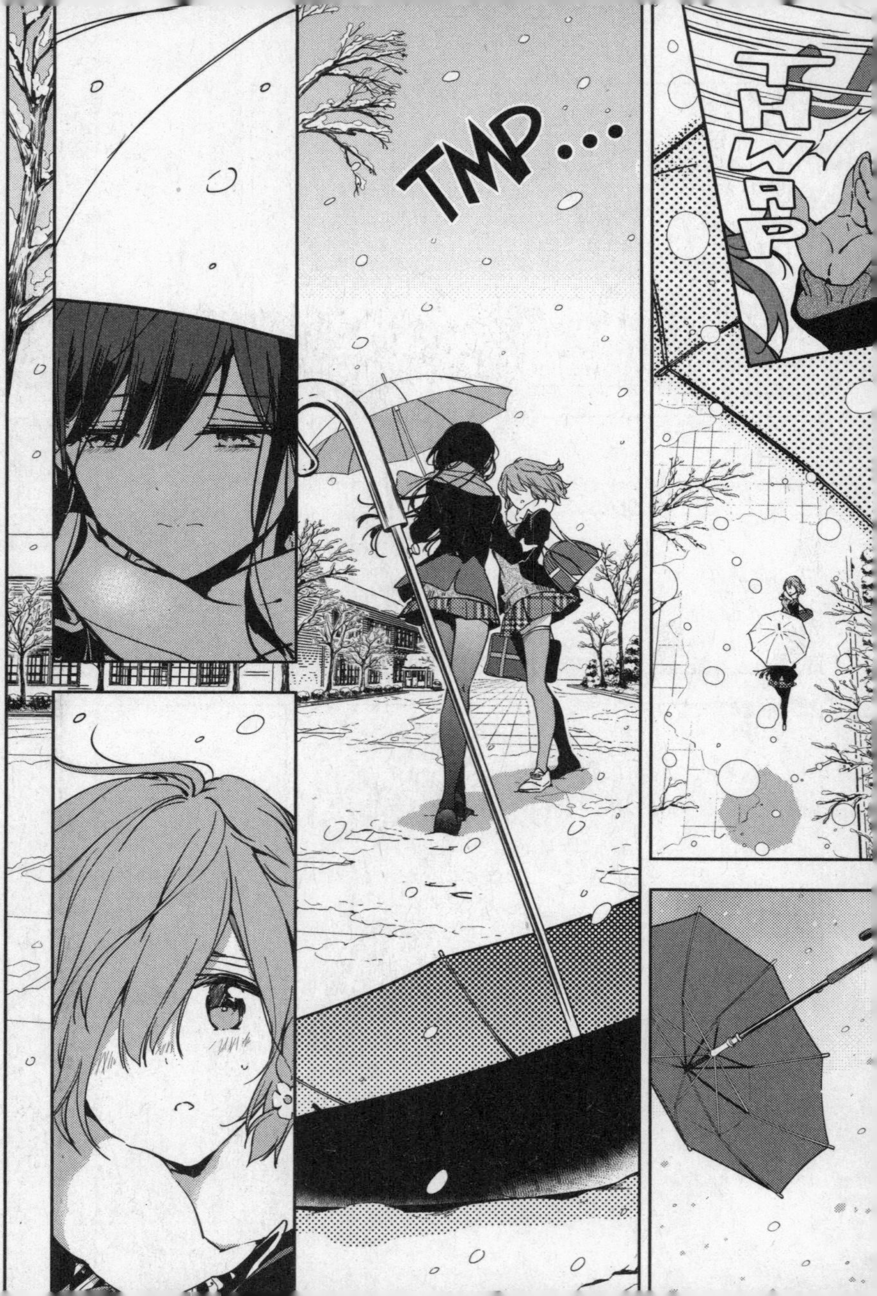
THWAP
TMP...

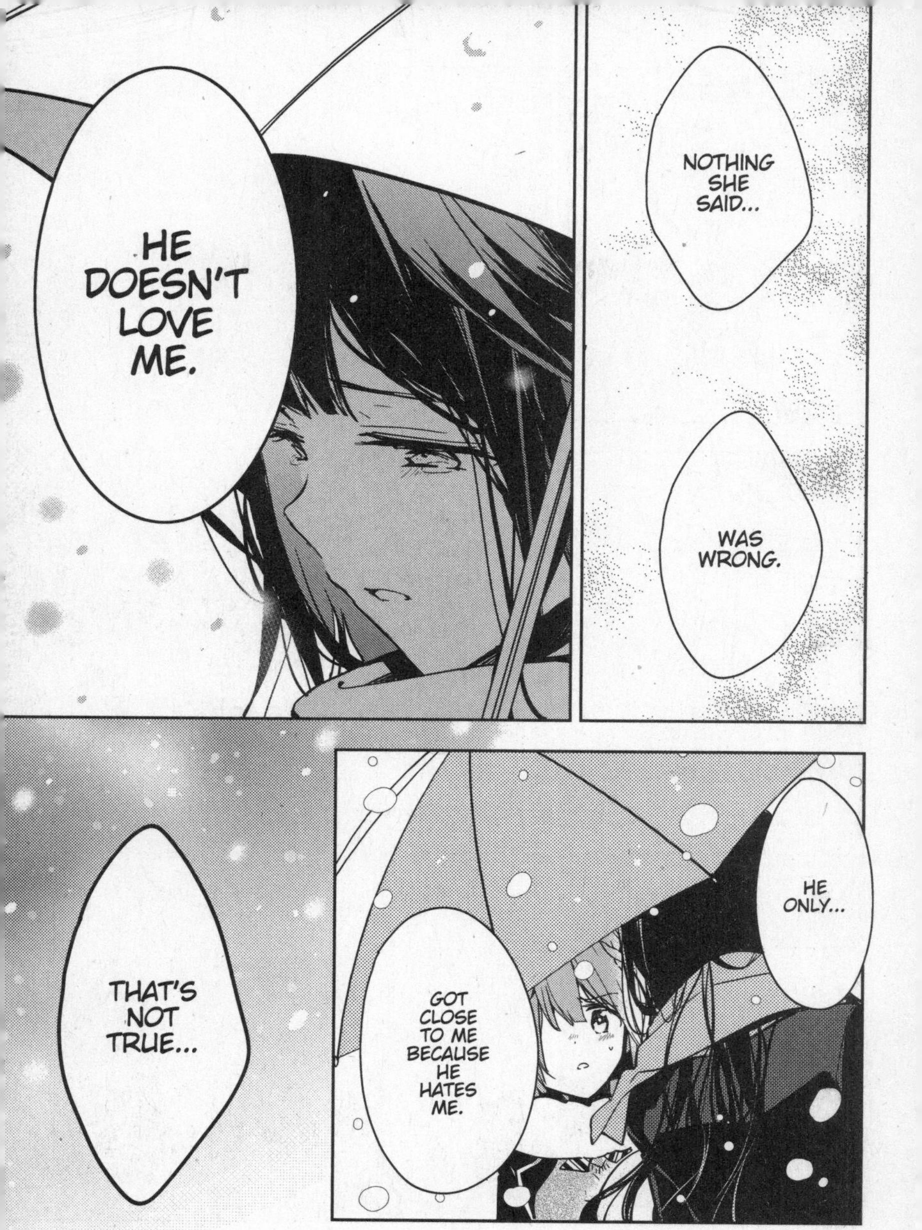
NOTHING SHE SAID...
WAS WRONG.
HE DOESN'T LOVE ME.
HE ONLY...
GOT CLOSE TO ME BECAUSE HE HATES ME.
THAT'S NOT TRUE...

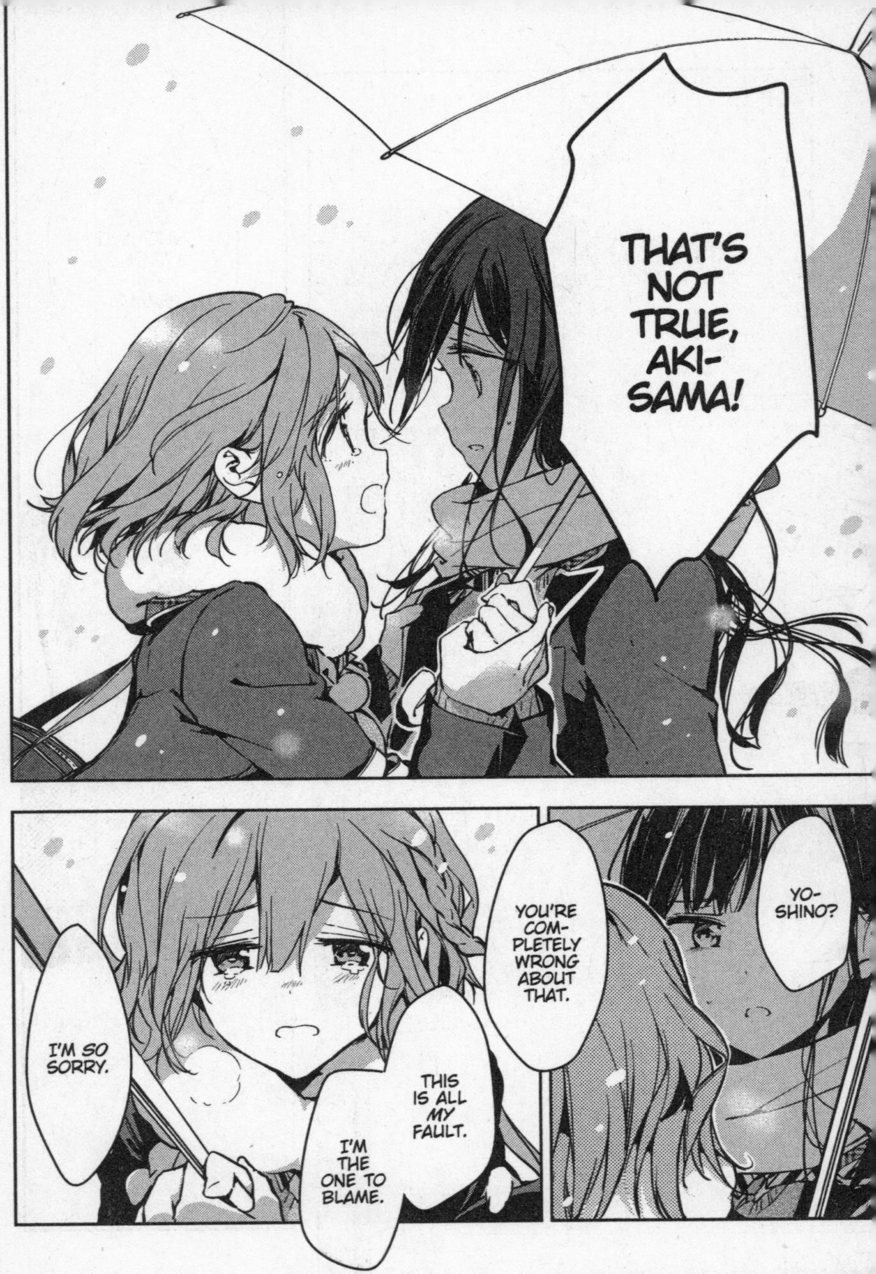
THAT'S NOT TRUE, AKI-SAMA!
YO-SHINO?
YOU'RE COM-PLETELY WRONG ABOUT THAT.
THIS IS ALL MY FAULT.
I'M THE ONE TO BLAME.
I'M SO SORRY.

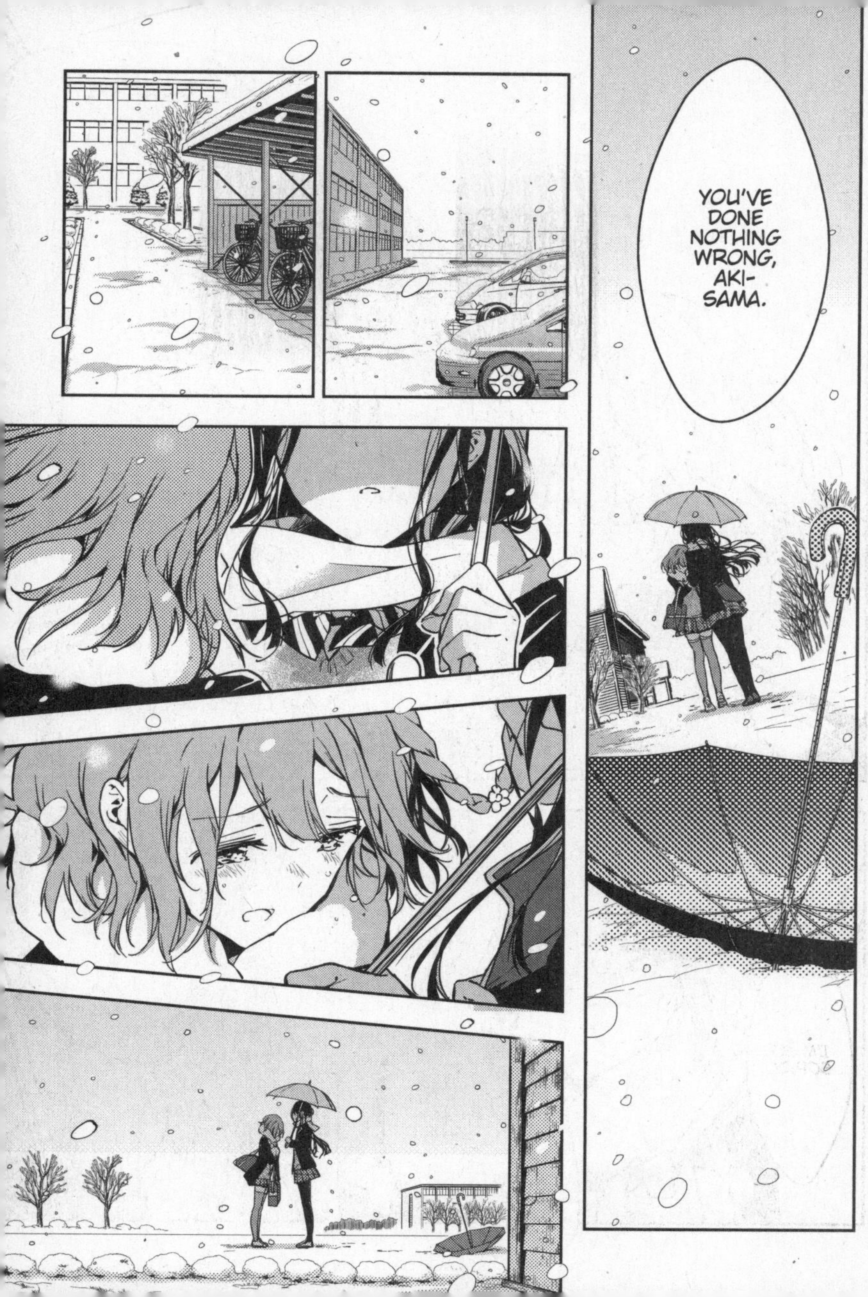
YOU'VE DONE NOTHING WRONG, AKI-SAMA.

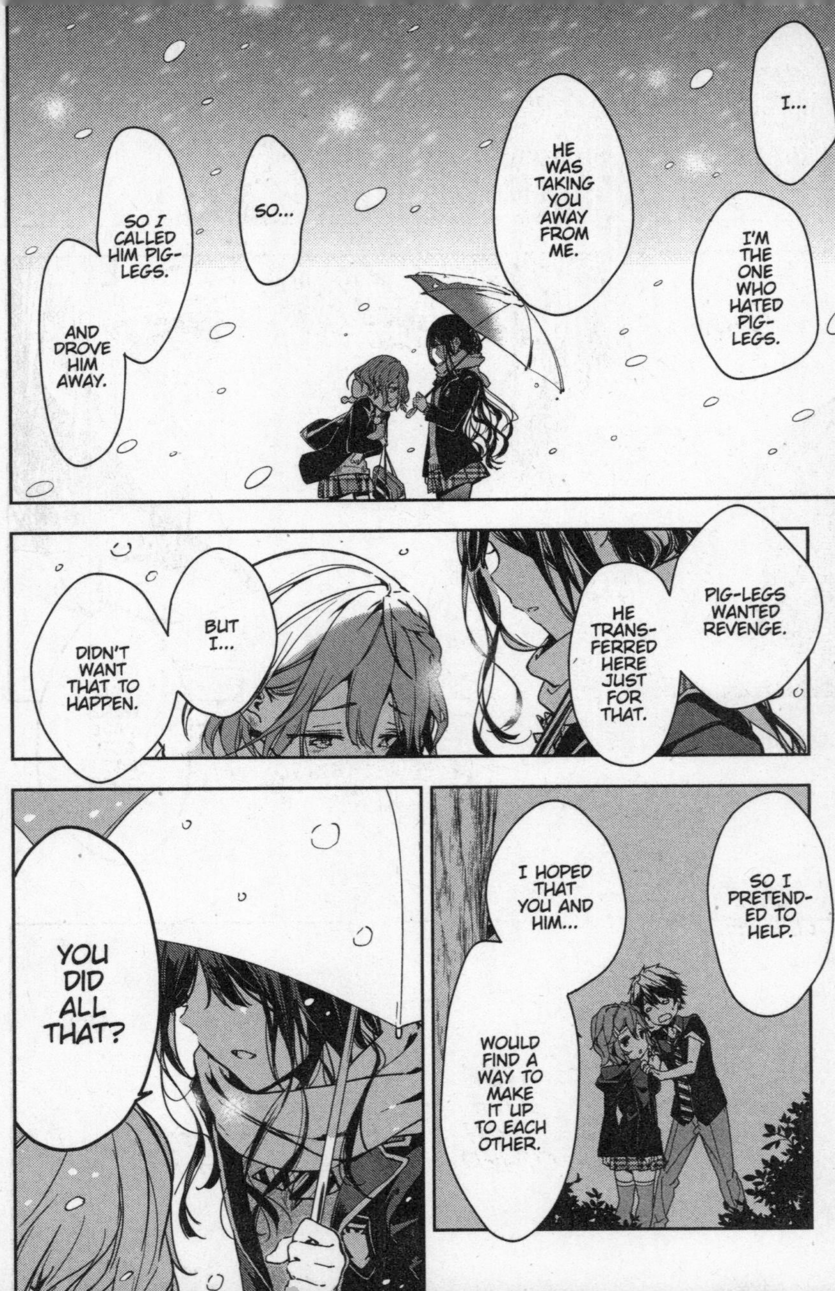
I...
I'M THE ONE WHO HATED PIG-LEGS.
HE WAS TAKING YOU AWAY FROM ME.
SO...
SO I CALLED HIM PIG-LEGS.
AND DROVE HIM AWAY.
PIG-LEGS WANTED REVENGE.
HE TRANSFERRED HERE JUST FOR THAT.
BUT I...
DIDN'T WANT THAT TO HAPPEN.
SO I PRETENDED TO HELP.
I HOPED THAT YOU AND HIM...
WOULD FIND A WAY TO MAKE IT UP TO EACH OTHER.
YOU DID ALL THAT?

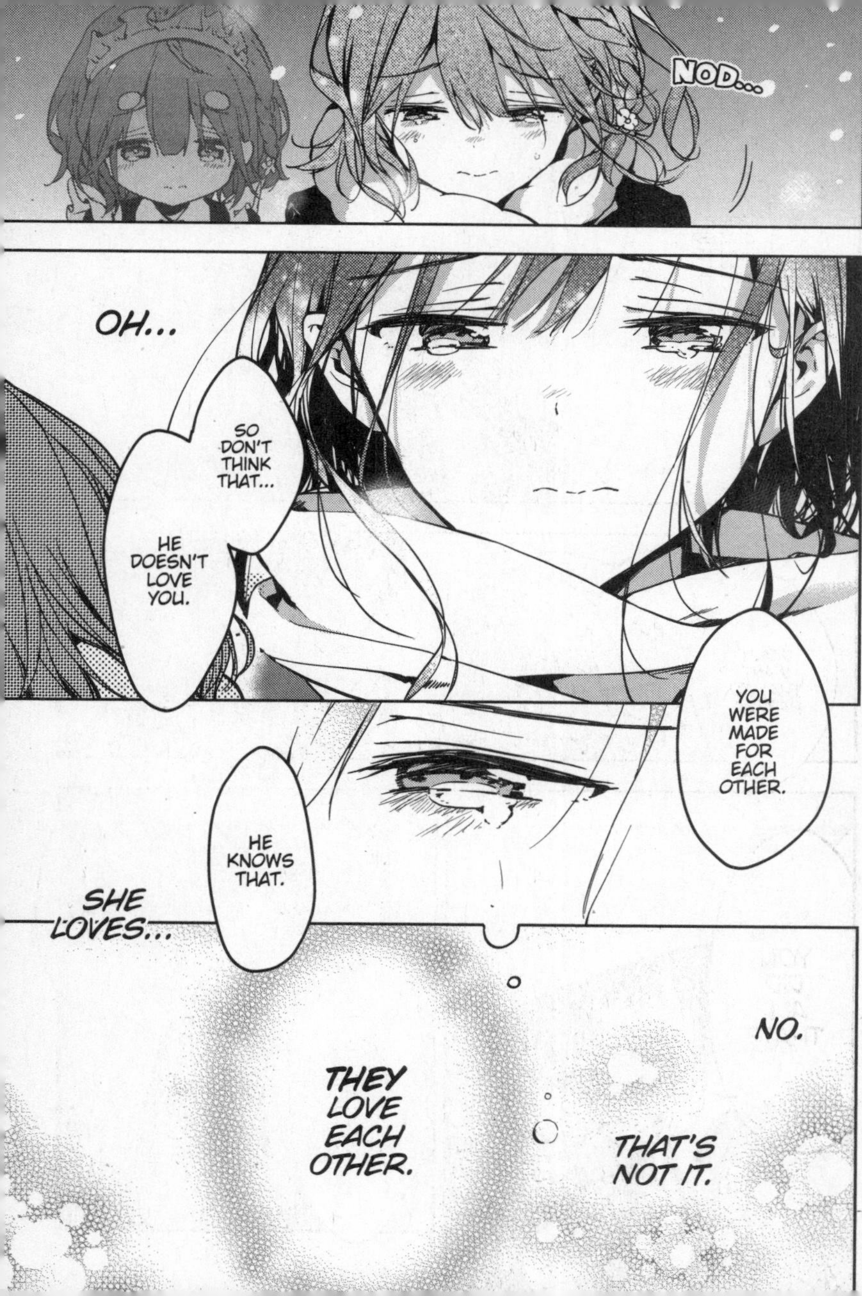
NOD...
OH...
SO DON'T THINK THAT...
HE DOESN'T LOVE YOU.
YOU WERE MADE FOR EACH OTHER.
HE KNOWS THAT.
SHE LOVES...
NO.
THAT'S NOT IT.
THEY LOVE EACH OTHER.

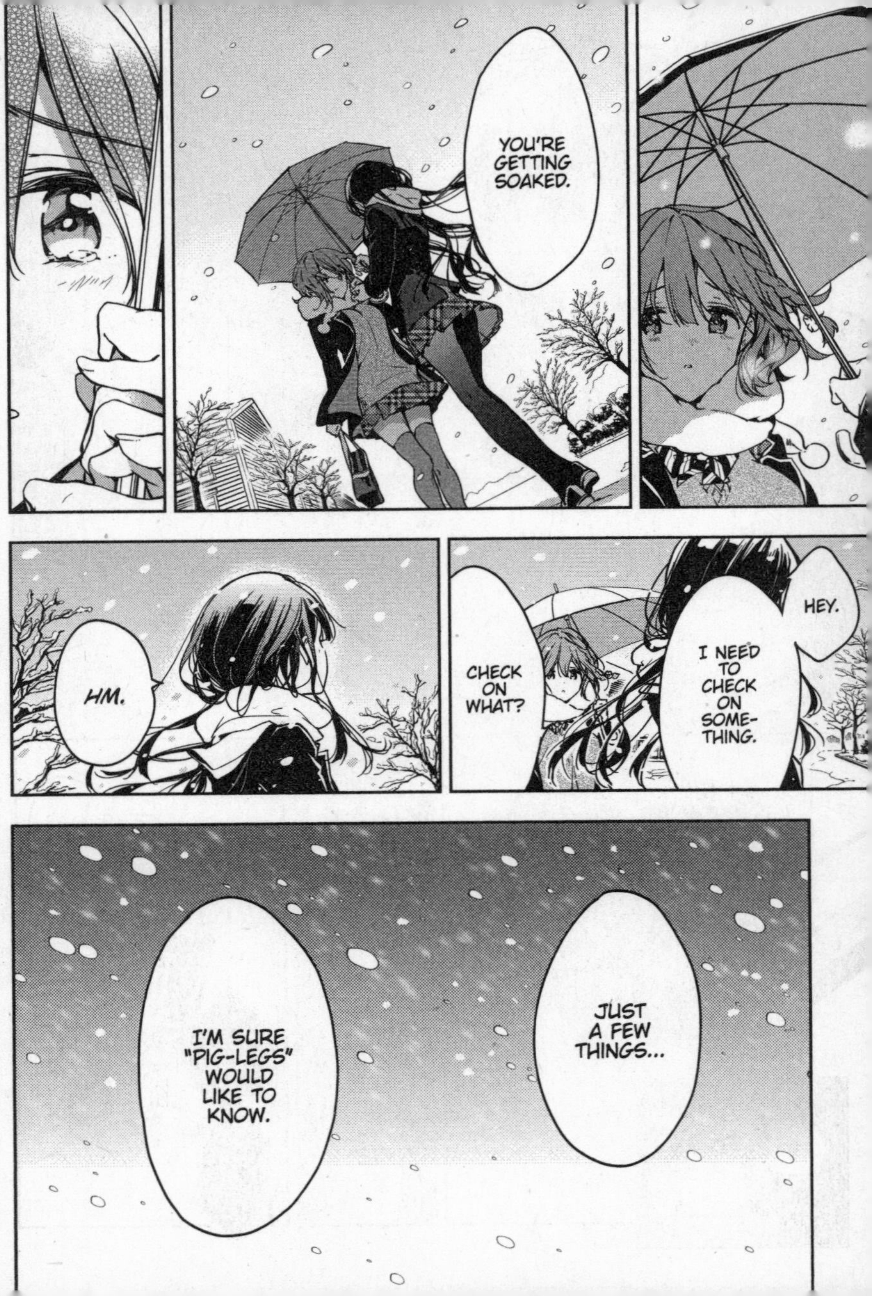
YOU'RE GETTING SOAKED.
HEY.
I NEED TO CHECK ON SOME-THING.
CHECK ON WHAT?
HM.
JUST A FEW THINGS...
I'M SURE "PIG-LEGS" WOULD LIKE TO KNOW.

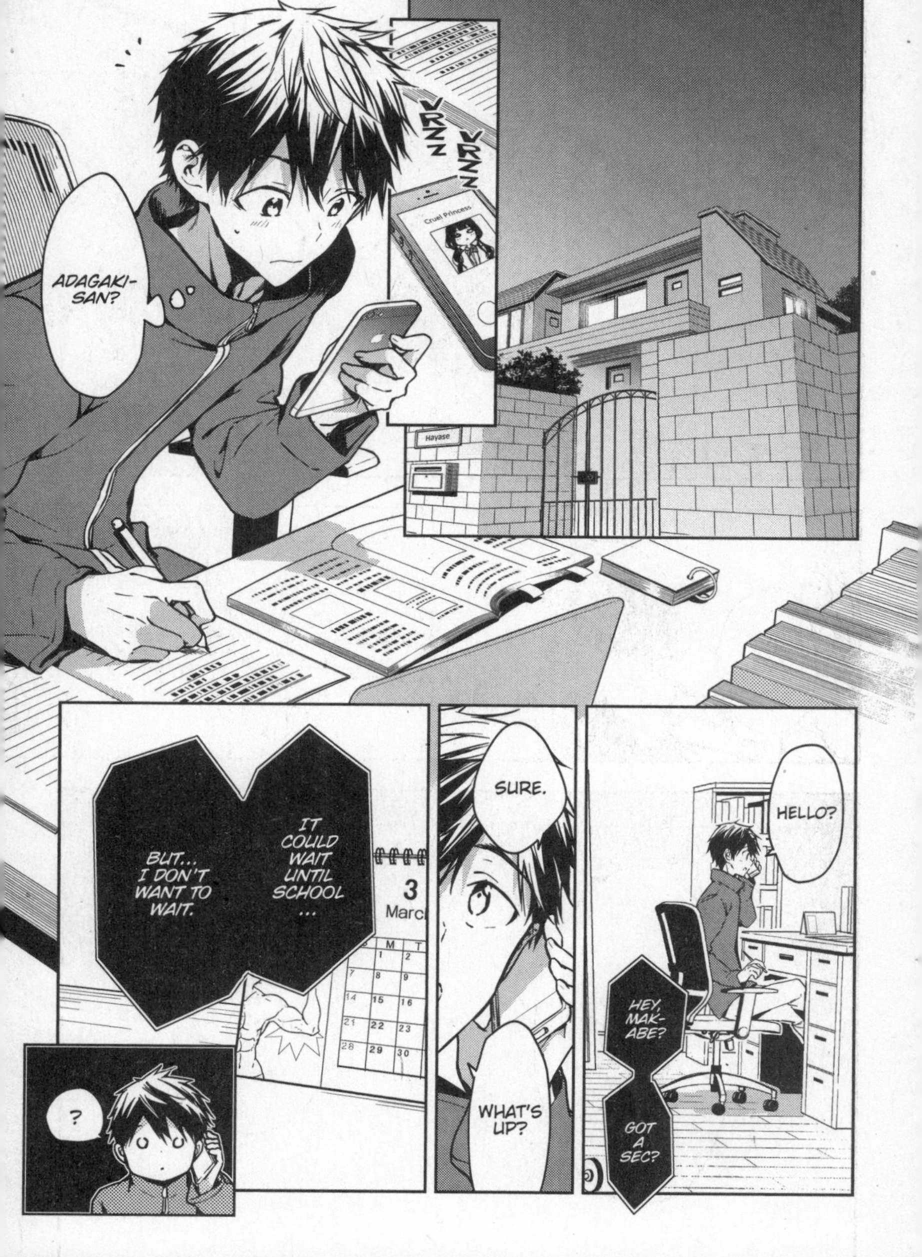

Hayase
VRZZ VRZZ
Cruel Princess
ADAGAKI-SAN?
HELLO?
HEY, MAK-ABE?
GOT A SEC?
SURE.
WHAT'S UP?
IT COULD WAIT UNTIL SCHOOL ...
BUT... I DON'T WANT TO WAIT.
3
March
?

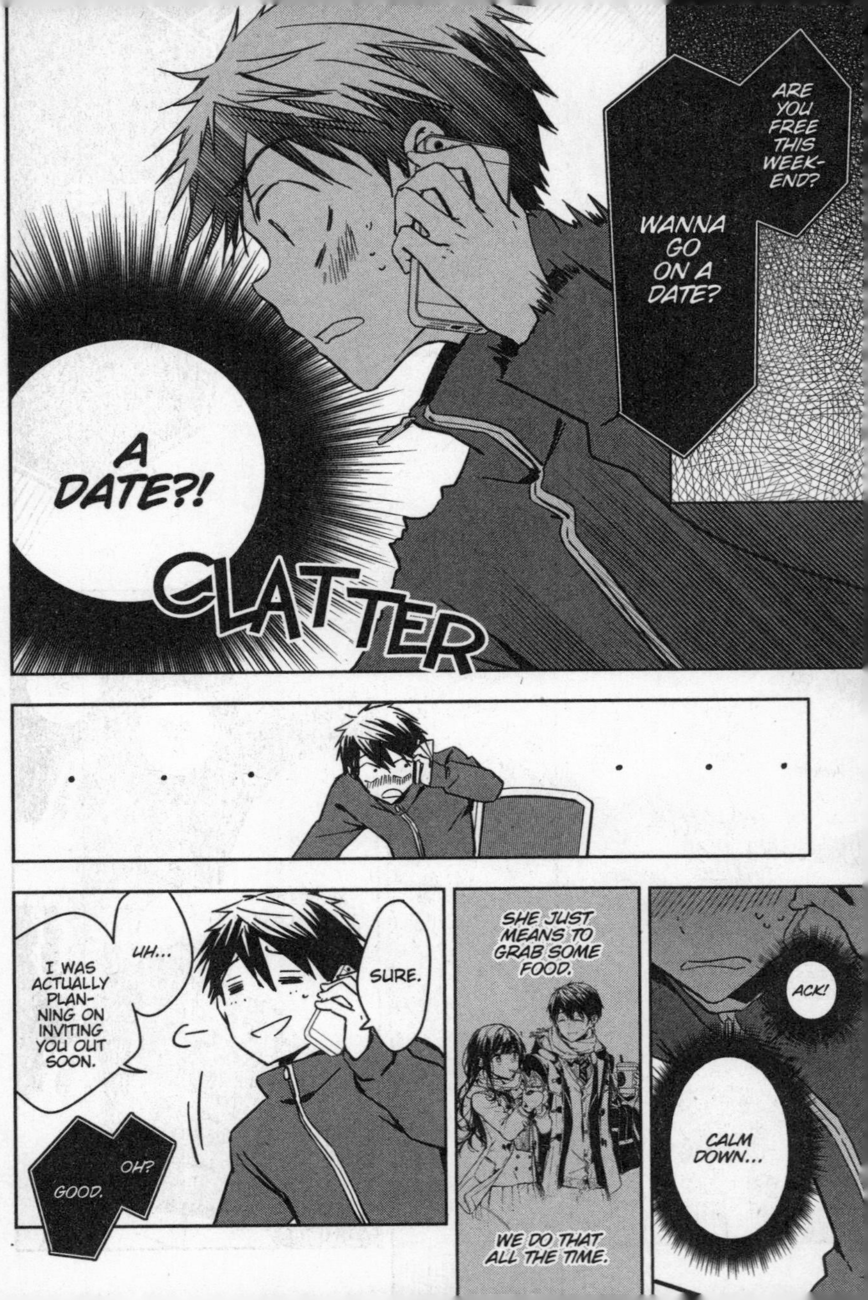
ARE YOU FREE THIS WEEK-END?
WANNA GO ON A DATE?
A DATE?!
CLATTER
. . . . . .
ACK!
CALM DOWN...
SHE JUST MEANS TO GRAB SOME FOOD.
WE DO THAT ALL THE TIME.
SURE.
UH...
I WAS ACTUALLY PLAN-NING ON INVITING YOU OUT SOON.
OH?
GOOD.

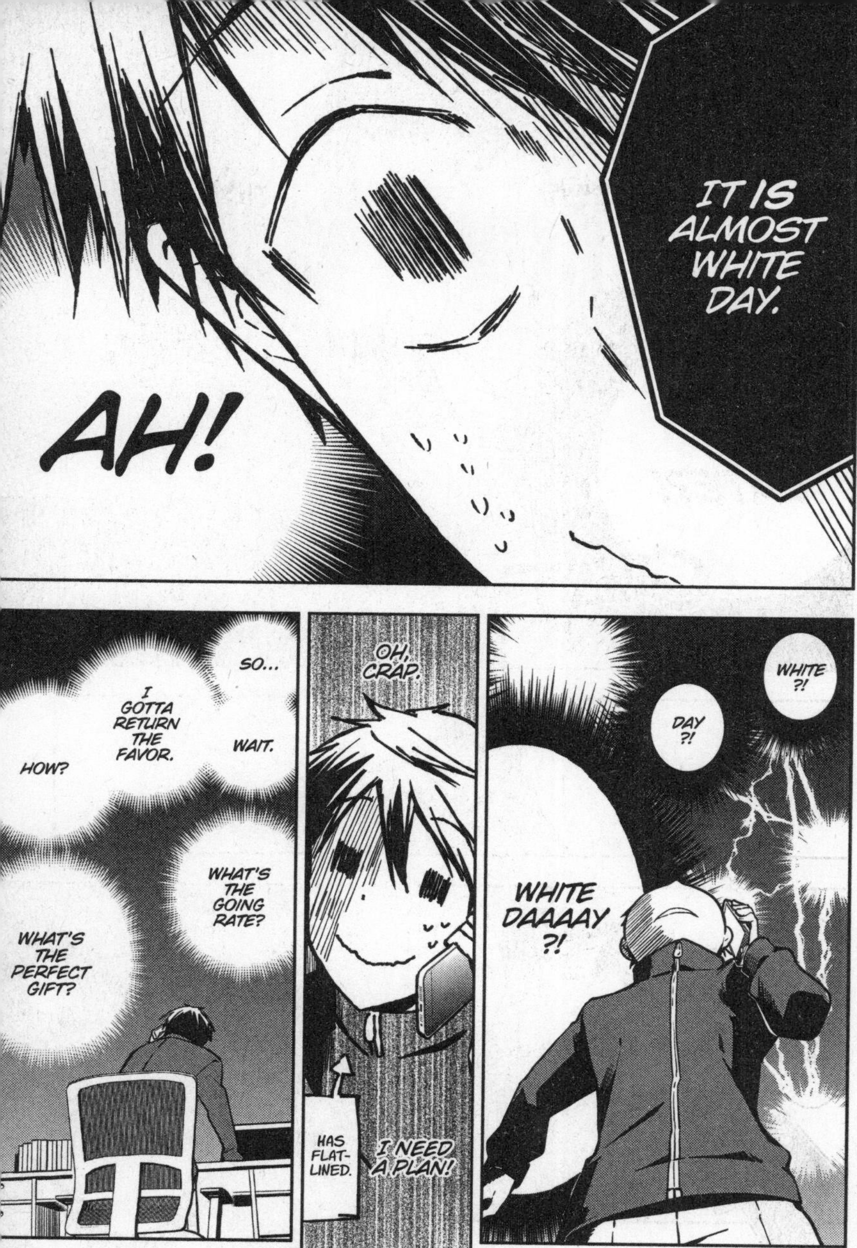
IT IS ALMOST WHITE DAY.
AH!
WHITE ?!
DAY ?!
WHITE DAAAAY ?!
OH, CRAP.
I NEED A PLAN!
HAS FLAT-LINED.
SO...
I GOTTA RETURN THE FAVOR.
WAIT.
HOW?
WHAT'S THE GOING RATE?
WHAT'S THE PERFECT GIFT?

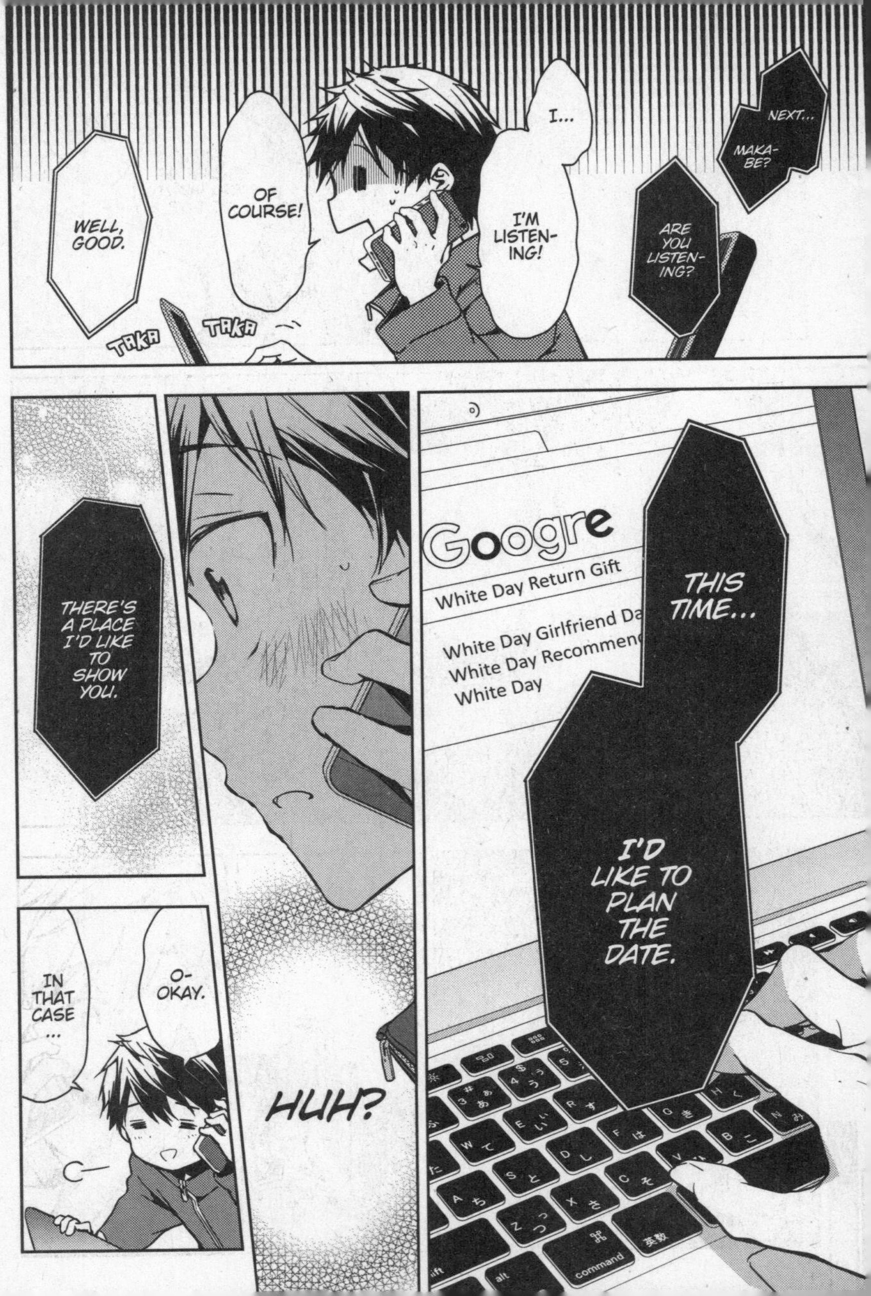
NEXT... MAKABE?
ARE YOU LISTENING?
I...
I'M LISTENING!
OF COURSE!
WELL, GOOD.
TAKA
TAKA
Googre
White Day Return Gift
White Day Girlfriend Da
White Day Recommend
White Day
THIS TIME...
I'D LIKE TO PLAN THE DATE.
HUH?
THERE'S A PLACE I'D LIKE TO SHOW YOU.
O-OKAY.
IN THAT CASE...

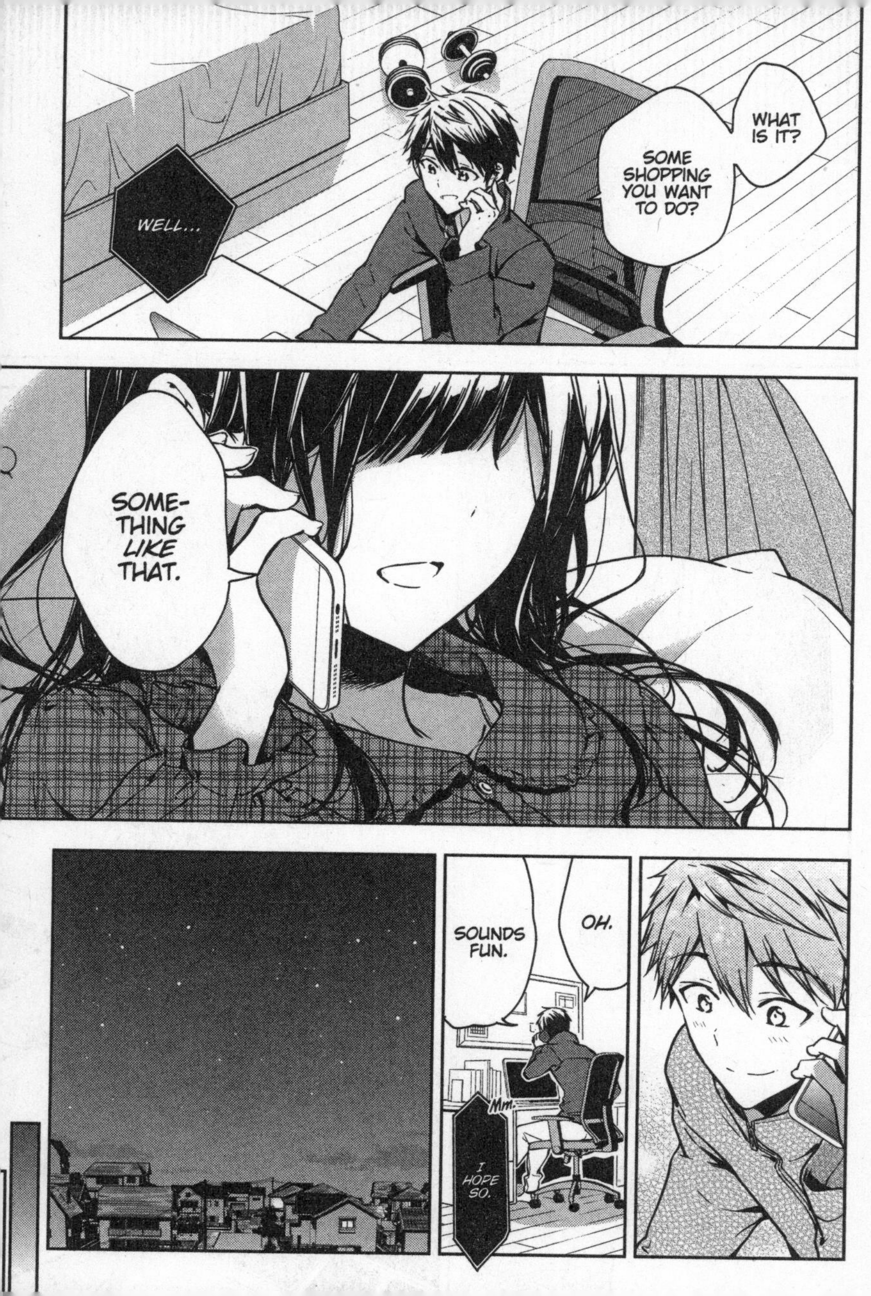
WHAT IS IT?
SOME SHOPPING YOU WANT TO DO?
WELL...
SOME-THING LIKE THAT.
OH.
SOUNDS FUN.
Mm.
I HOPE SO.

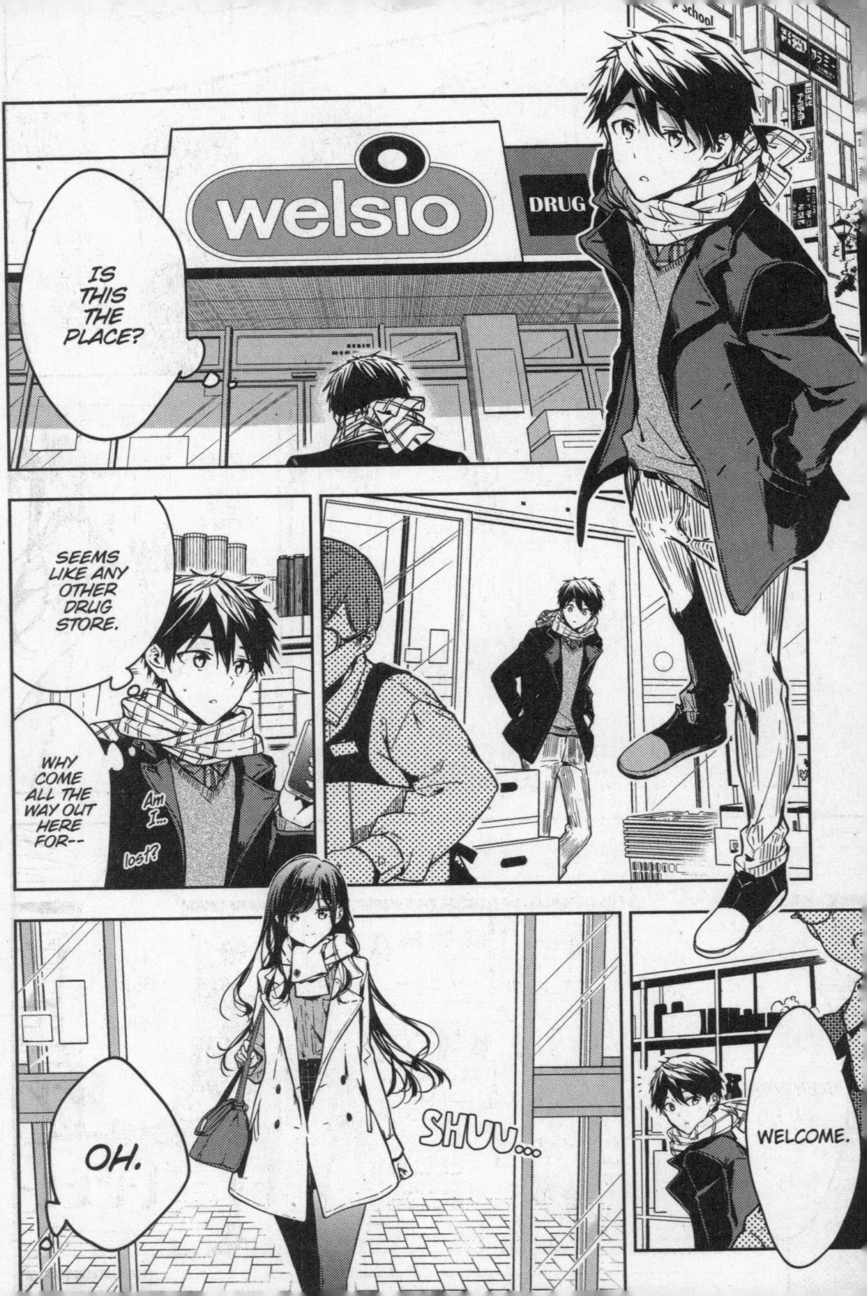
School
welsio
DRUG
IS THIS THE PLACE?
SEEMS LIKE ANY OTHER DRUG STORE.
WHY COME ALL THE WAY OUT HERE FOR--
Am I... lost?
WELCOME.
SHUU...
OH.

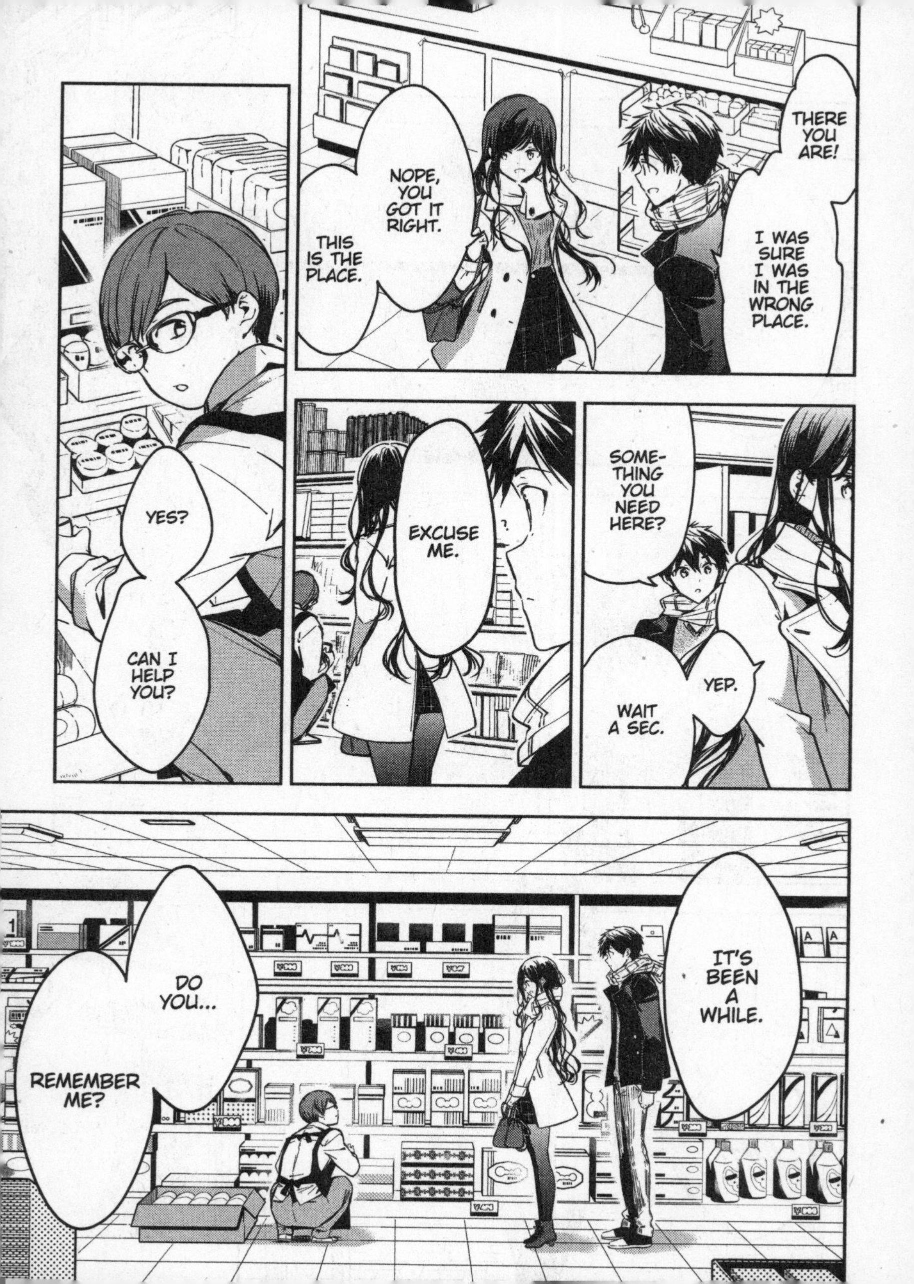
THERE YOU ARE!
I WAS SURE I WAS IN THE WRONG PLACE.
NOPE, YOU GOT IT RIGHT.
THIS IS THE PLACE.
SOME-THING YOU NEED HERE?
YEP.
WAIT A SEC.
EXCUSE ME.
YES?
CAN I HELP YOU?
IT'S BEEN A WHILE.
DO YOU...
REMEMBER ME?

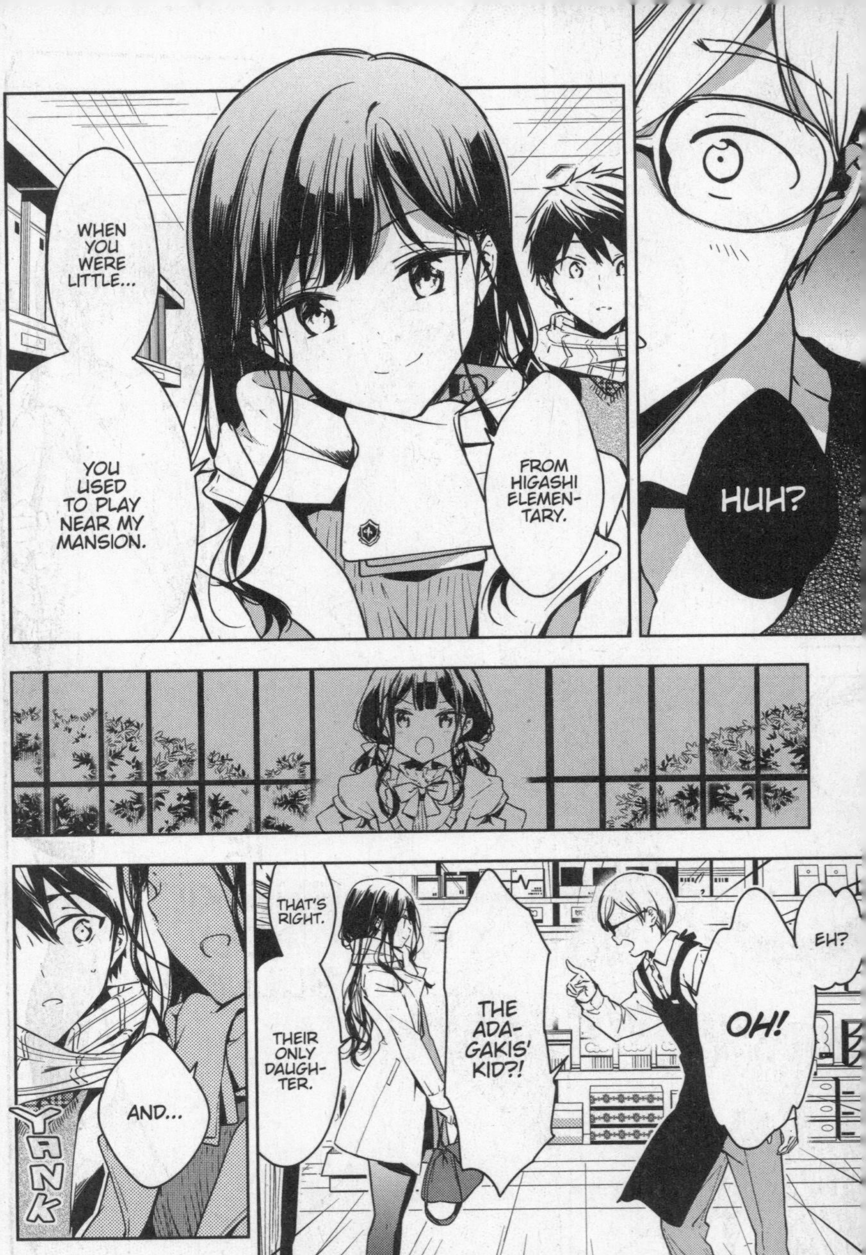
HUH?
FROM HIGASHI ELEMENTARY.
WHEN YOU WERE LITTLE...
YOU USED TO PLAY NEAR MY MANSION.
EH?
OH!
THE ADAGAKIS' KID?!
THAT'S RIGHT.
THEIR ONLY DAUGHTER.
AND...
YANK

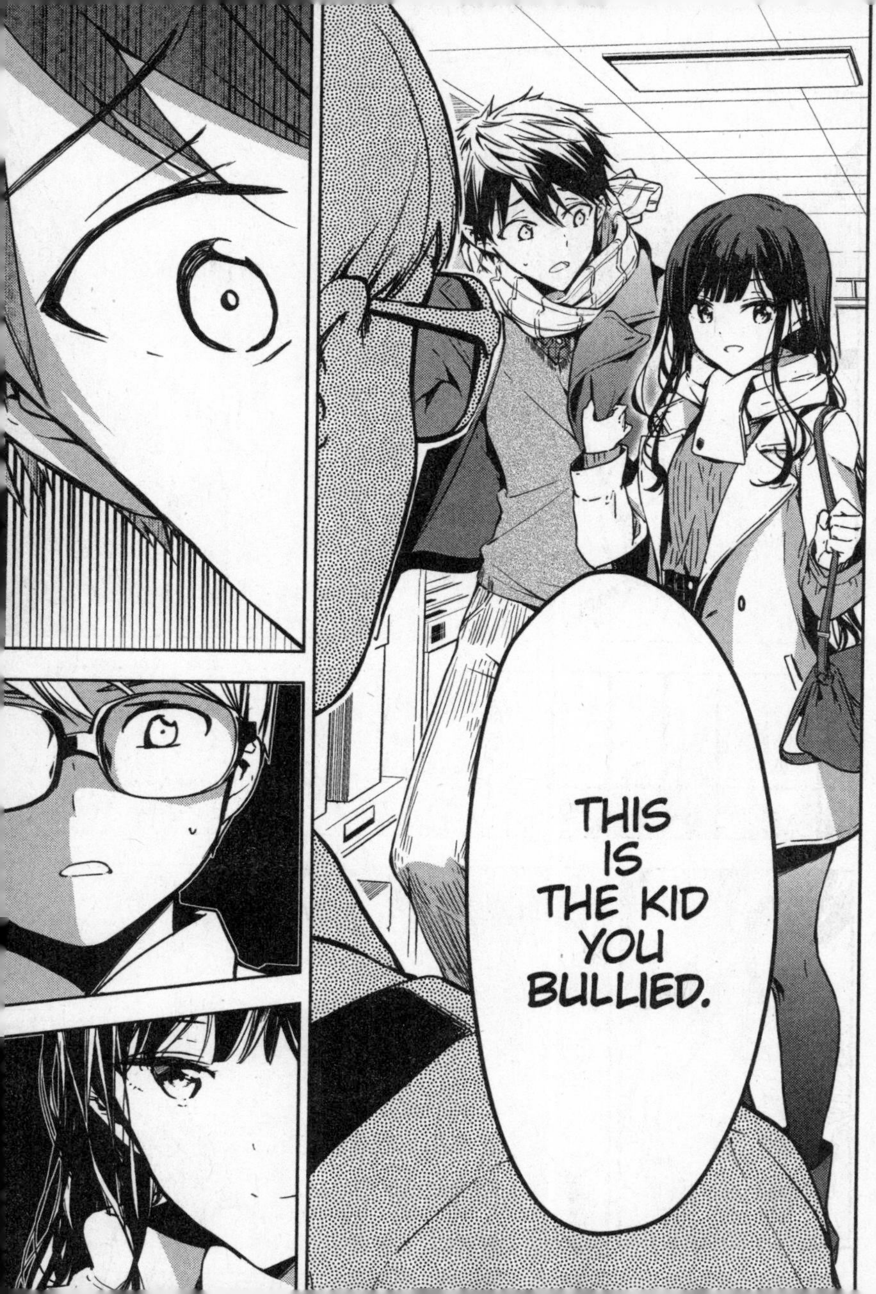
THIS IS THE KID YOU BULLIED.

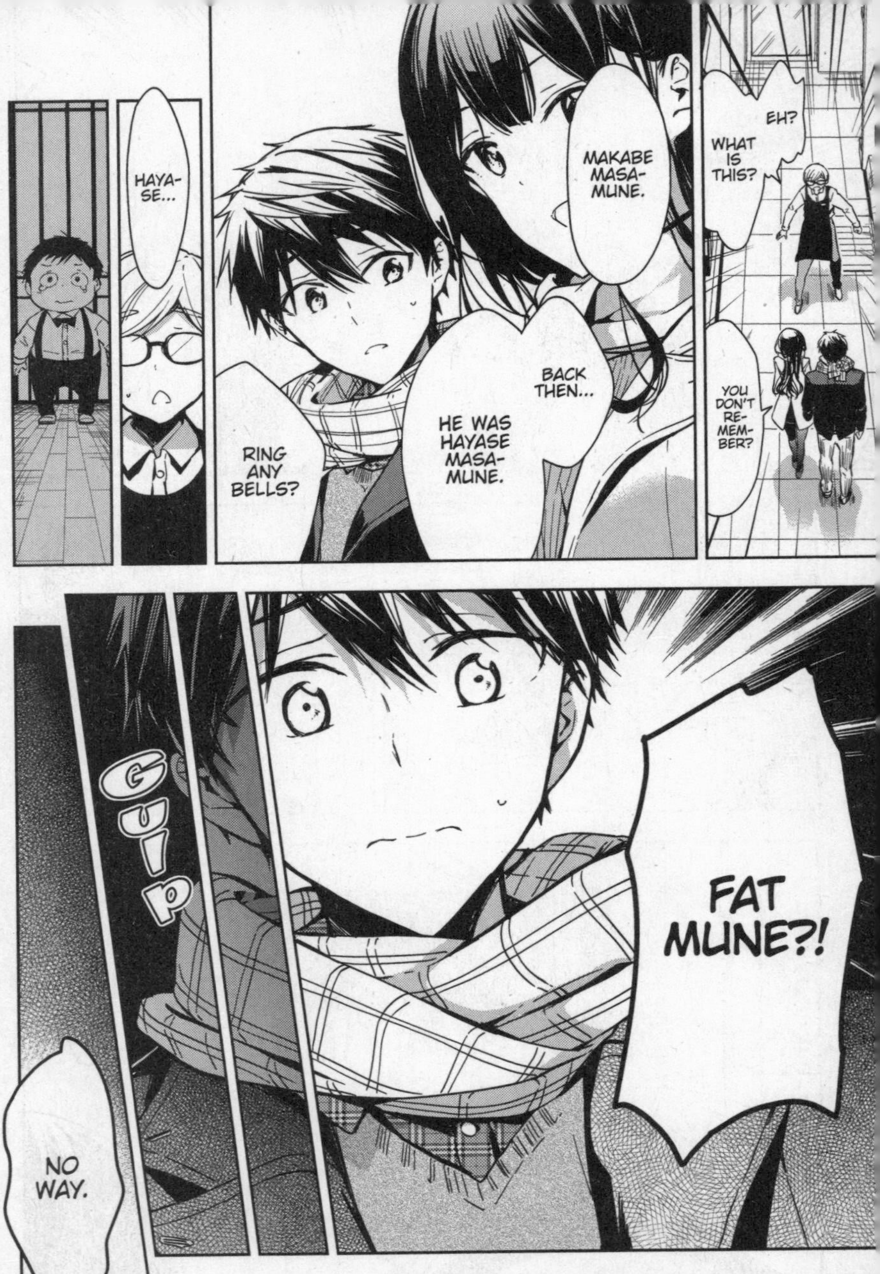
EH?
WHAT IS THIS?
YOU DON'T RE-MEM-BER?
MAKABE MASA-MUNE.
BACK THEN...
HE WAS HAYASE MASA-MUNE.
RING ANY BELLS?
HAYA-SE...
FAT MUNE?!
GULP
NO WAY.

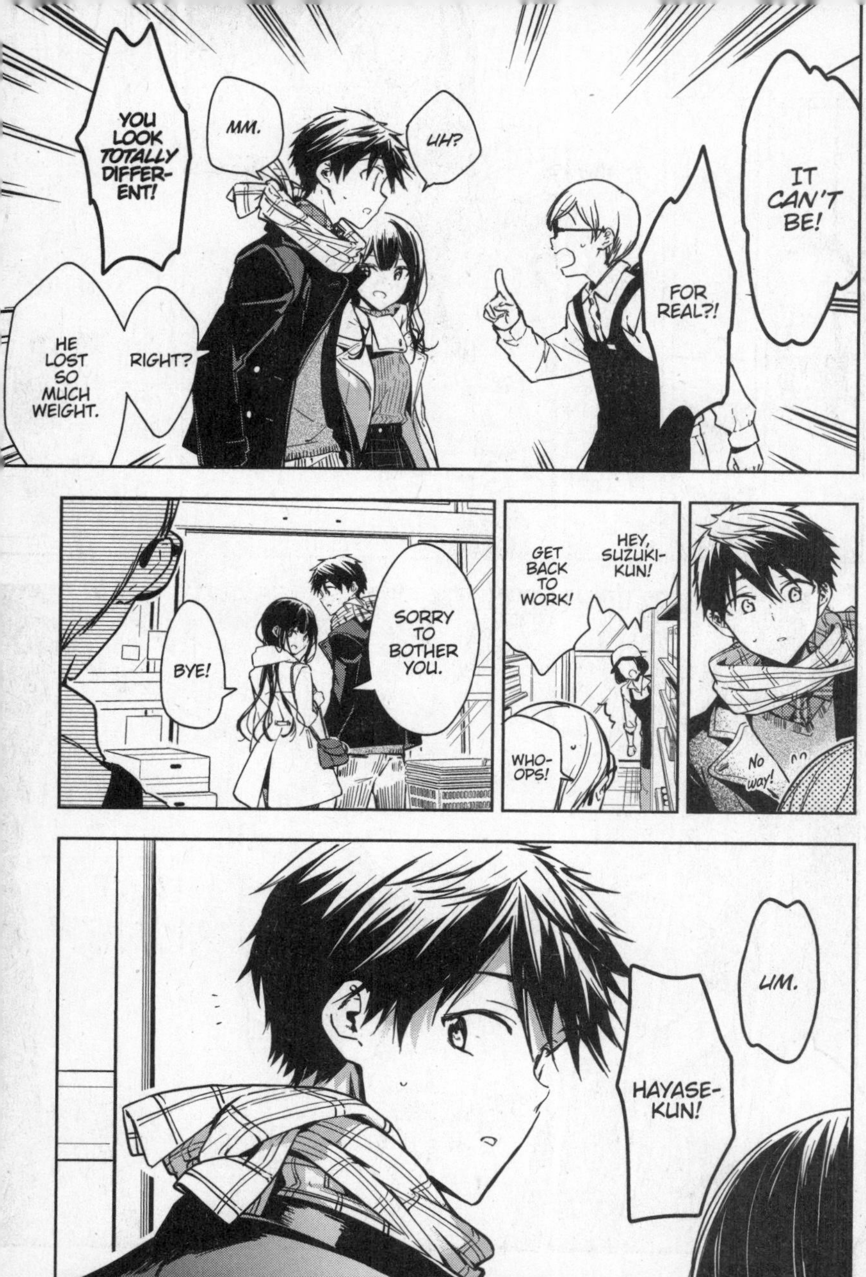
IT CAN'T BE!
FOR REAL?!
UH?
MM.
YOU LOOK TOTALLY DIFFERENT!
RIGHT?
HE LOST SO MUCH WEIGHT.
No way!
HEY, SUZUKI-KUN!
GET BACK TO WORK!
WHO-OPS!
SORRY TO BOTHER YOU.
BYE!
UM.
HAYASE-KUN!

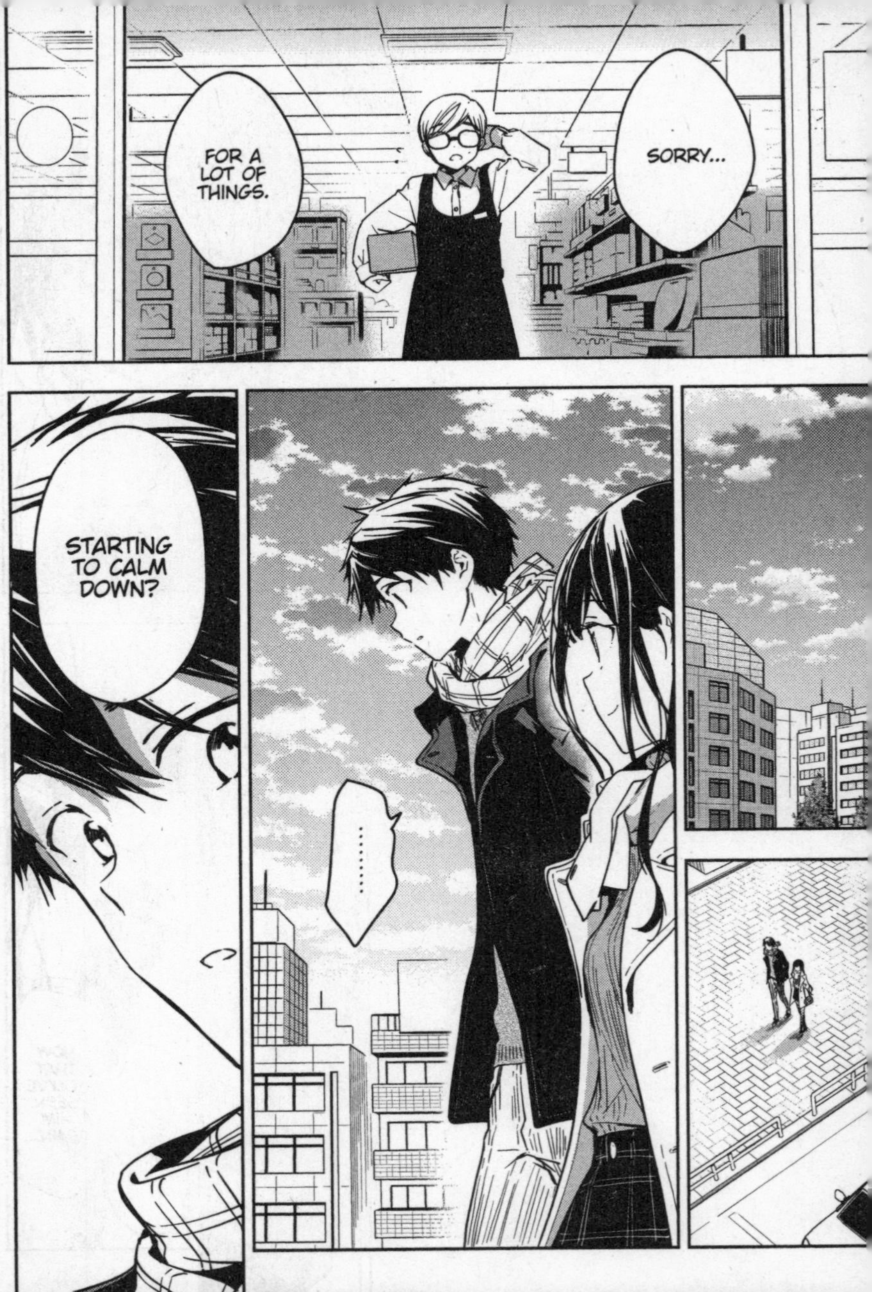
SORRY...
FOR A LOT OF THINGS.
......
STARTING TO CALM DOWN?

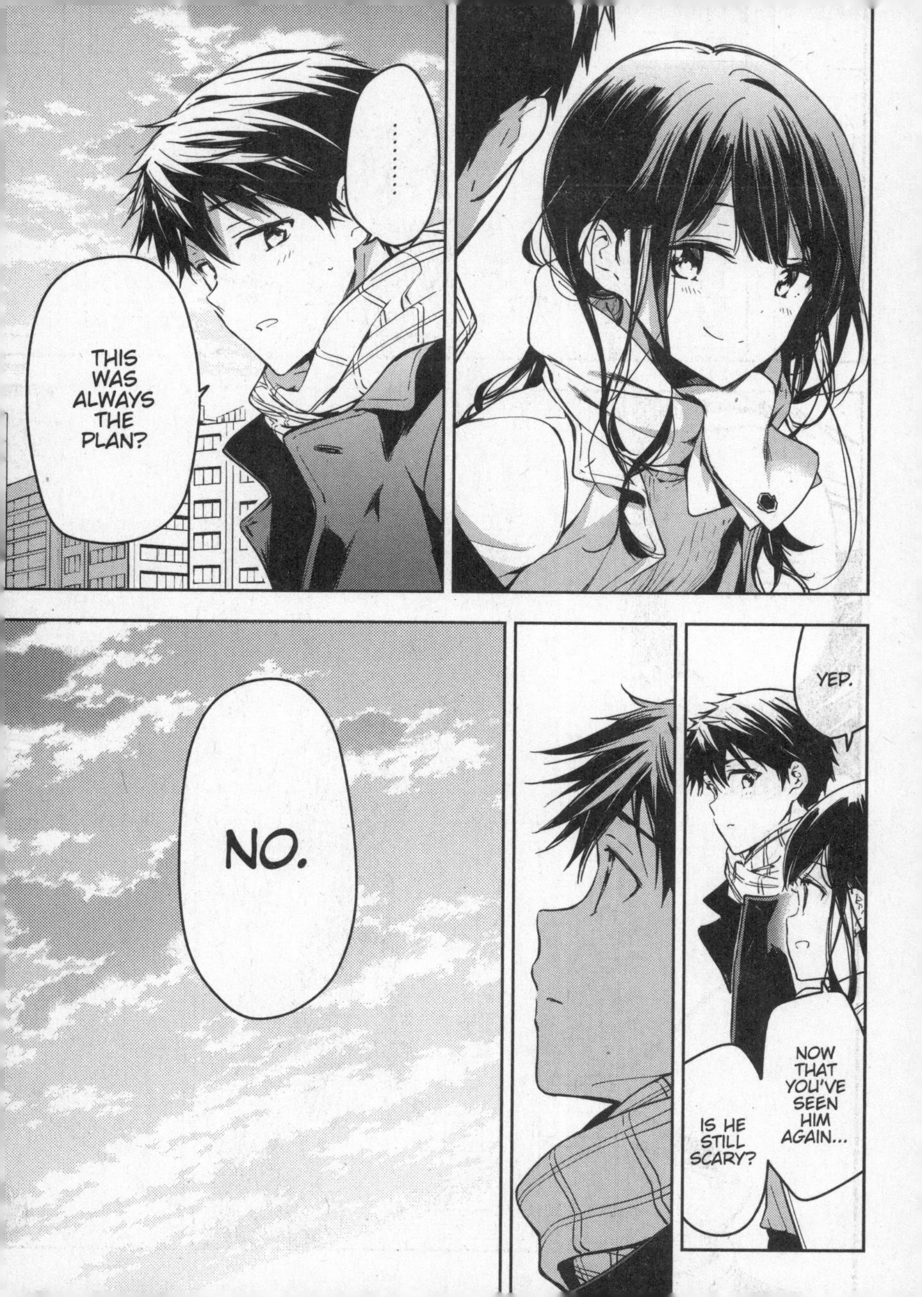
......
THIS WAS ALWAYS THE PLAN?
YEP.
NOW THAT YOU'VE SEEN HIM AGAIN...
IS HE STILL SCARY?
NO.

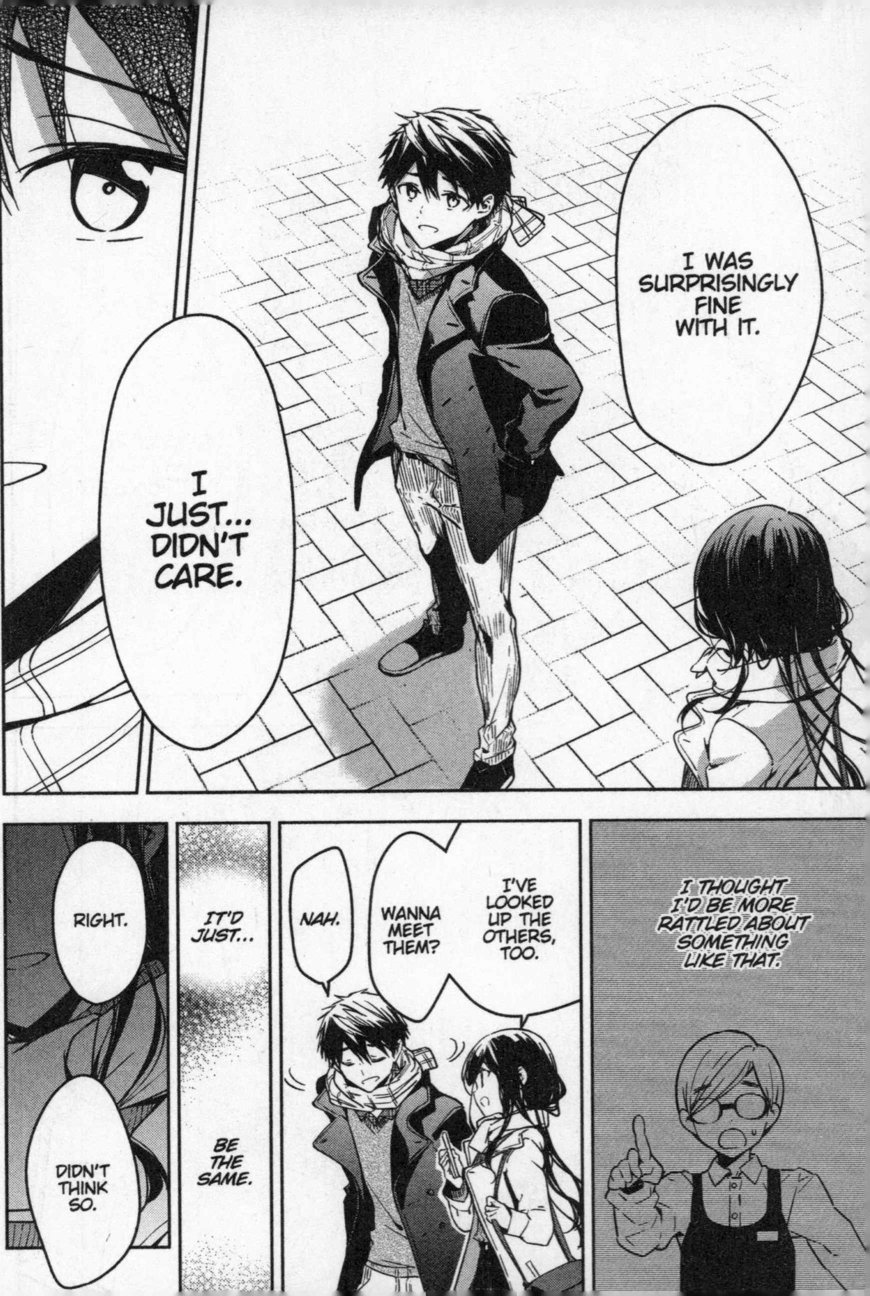
I WAS SURPRISINGLY FINE WITH IT.
I JUST... DIDN'T CARE.
I THOUGHT I'D BE MORE RATTLED ABOUT SOMETHING LIKE THAT.
I'VE LOOKED UP THE OTHERS, TOO.
WANNA MEET THEM?
NAH.
IT'D JUST...
BE THE SAME.
RIGHT.
DIDN'T THINK SO.

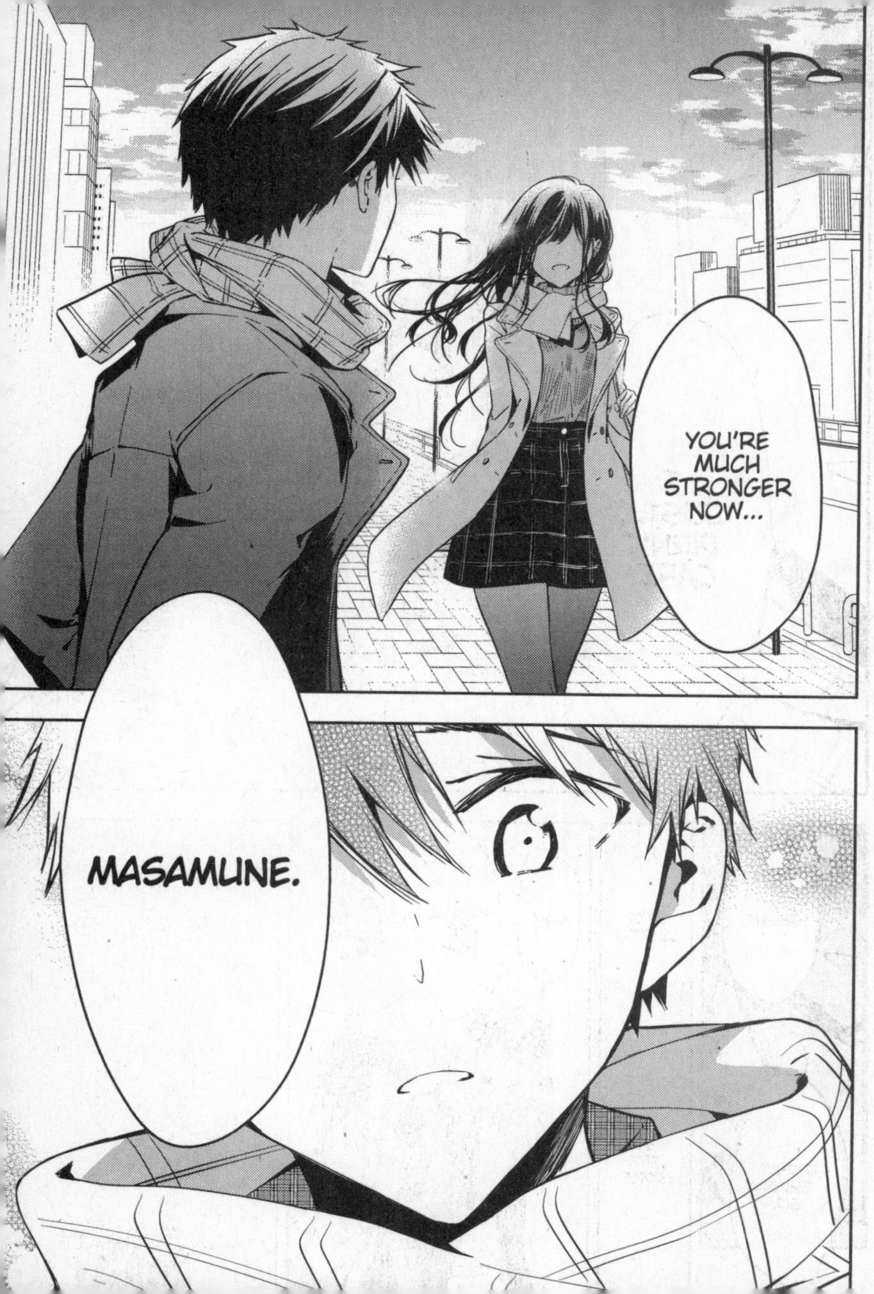
YOU'RE MUCH STRONGER NOW...
MASAMUNE.

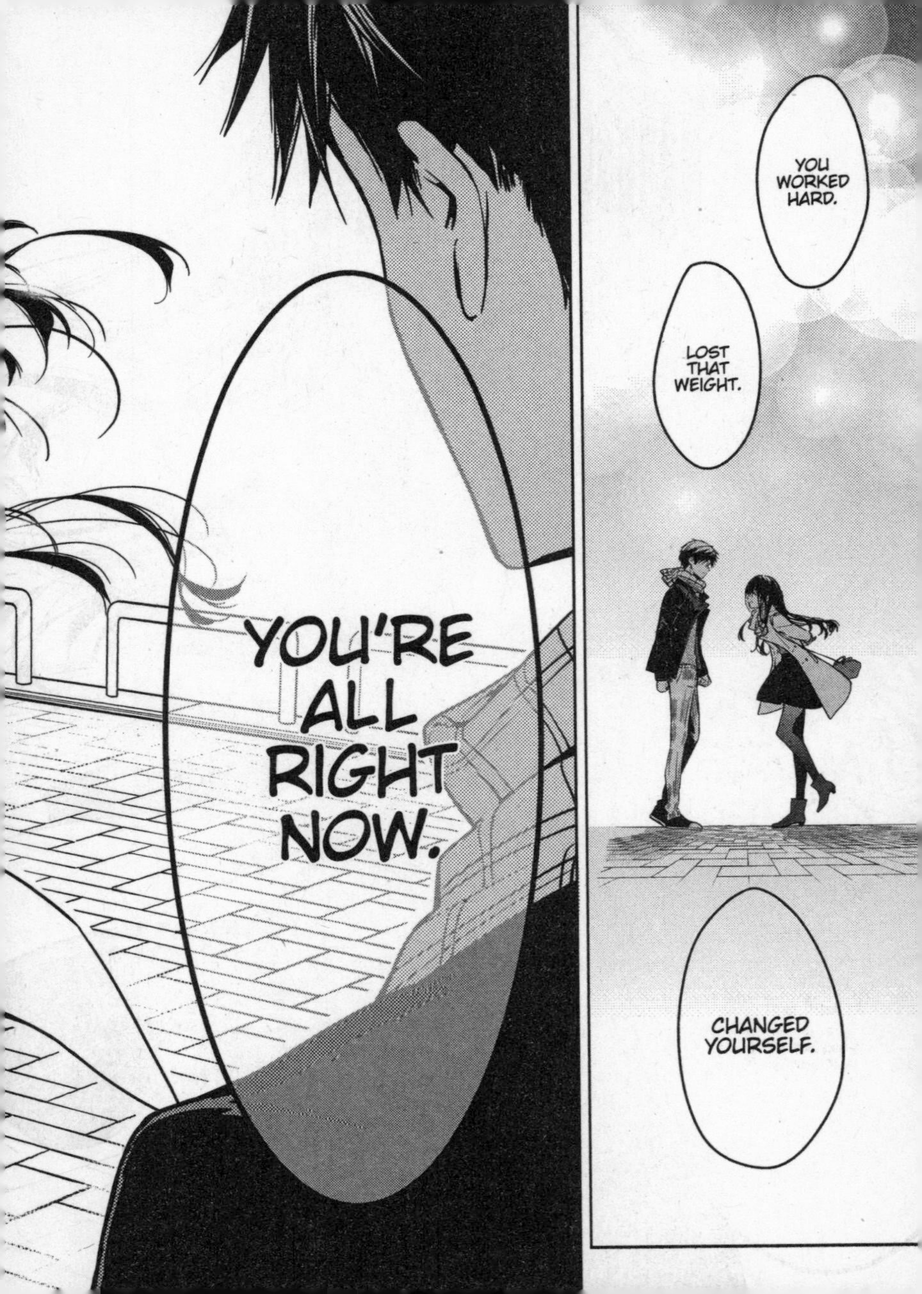
YOU WORKED HARD.
LOST THAT WEIGHT.
CHANGED YOURSELF.
YOU'RE ALL RIGHT NOW.

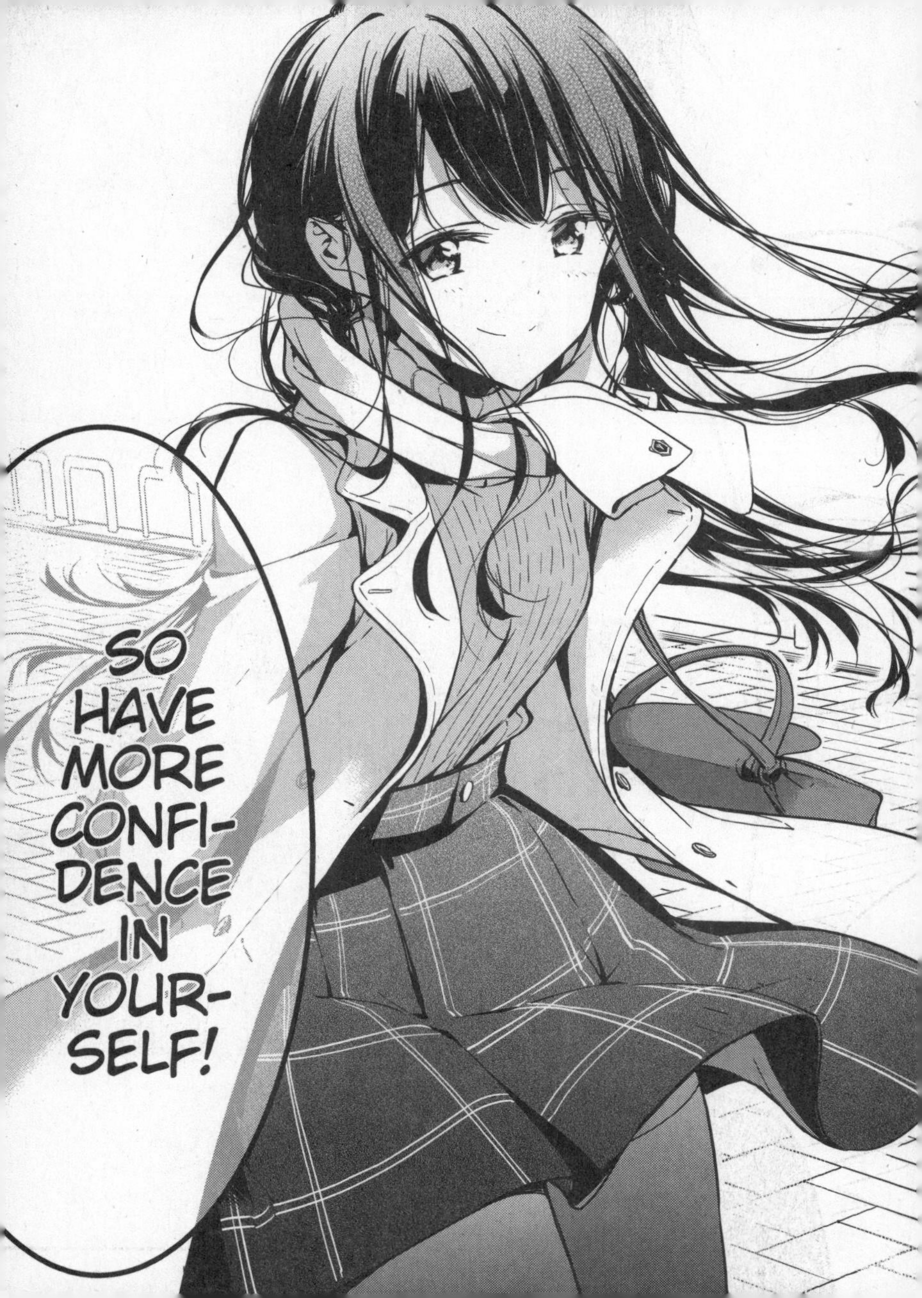
SO HAVE MORE CONFI- DENCE IN YOUR- SELF!

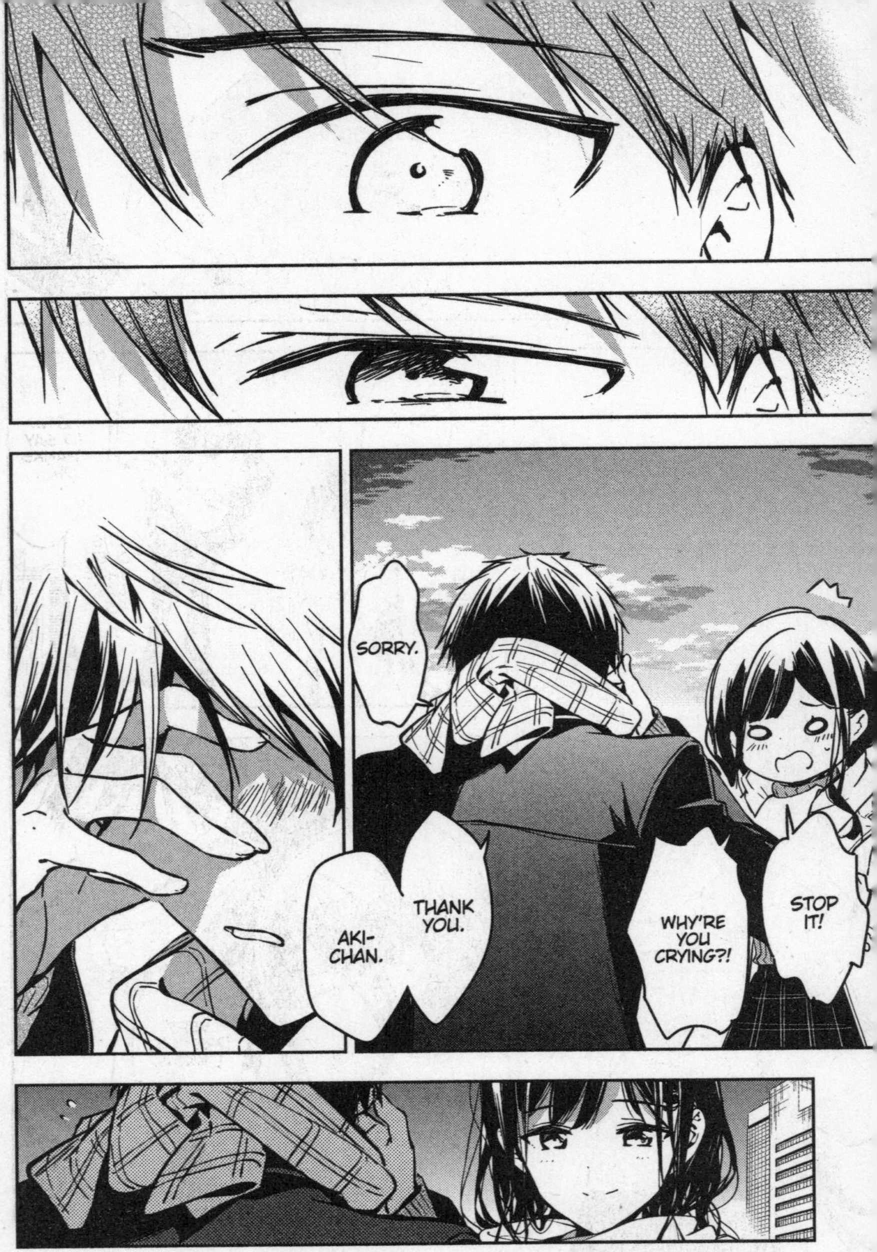
STOP IT!
WHY'RE YOU CRYING?!
SORRY.
THANK YOU.
AKI-CHAN.

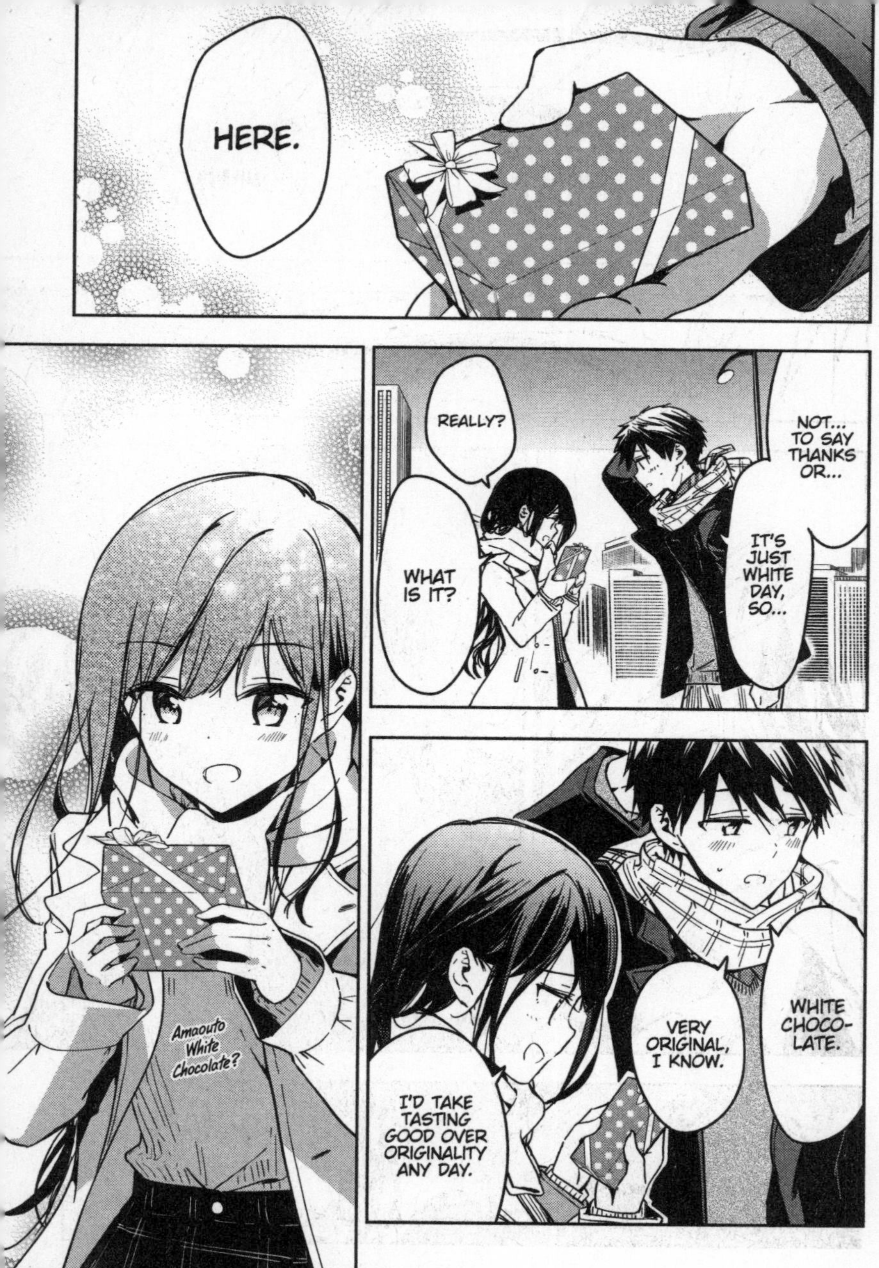
HERE.
NOT... TO SAY THANKS OR...
IT'S JUST WHITE DAY, SO...
REALLY?
WHAT IS IT?
WHITE CHOCO-LATE.
VERY ORIGINAL, I KNOW.
I'D TAKE TASTING GOOD OVER ORIGINALITY ANY DAY.
Amaouto White Chocolate?

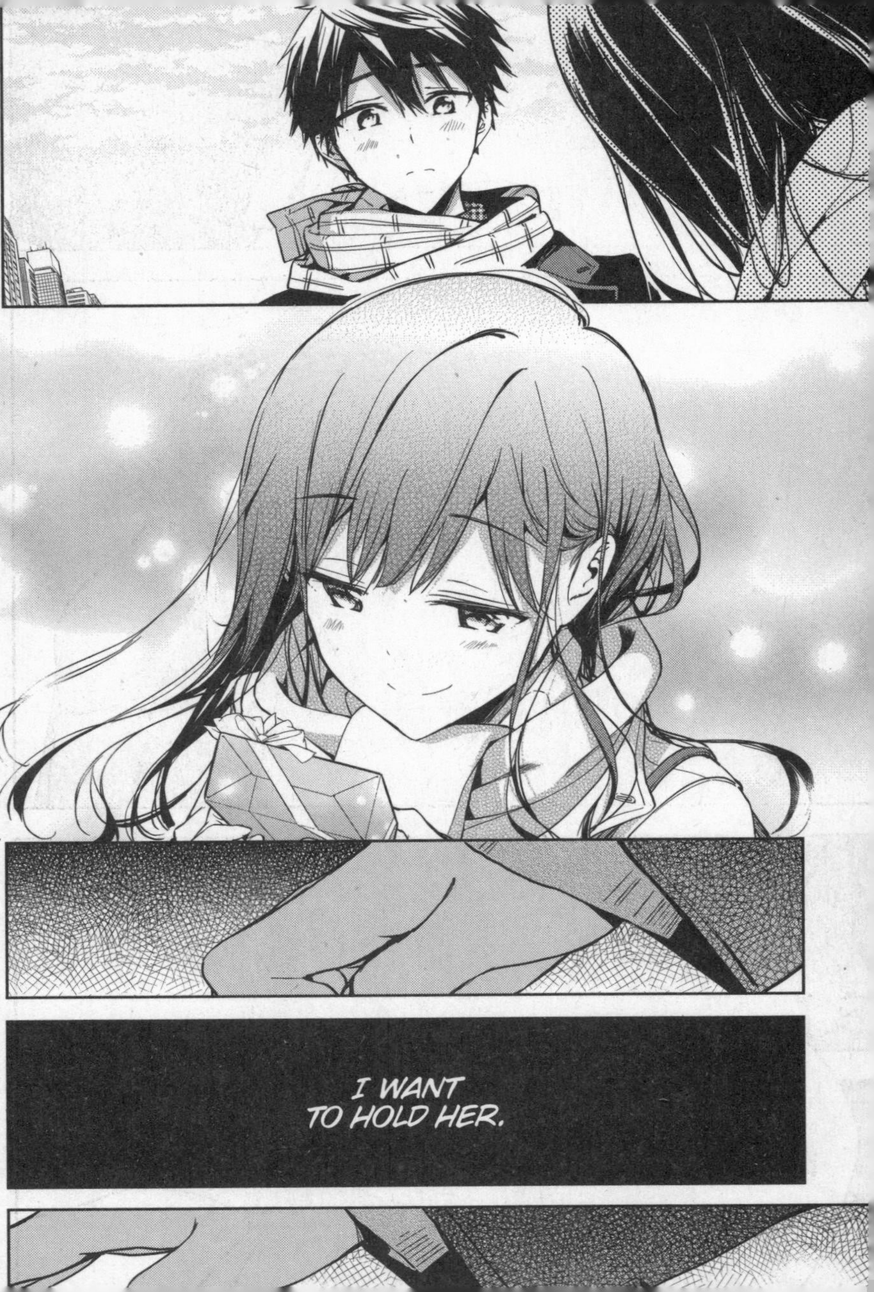
I WANT TO HOLD HER.

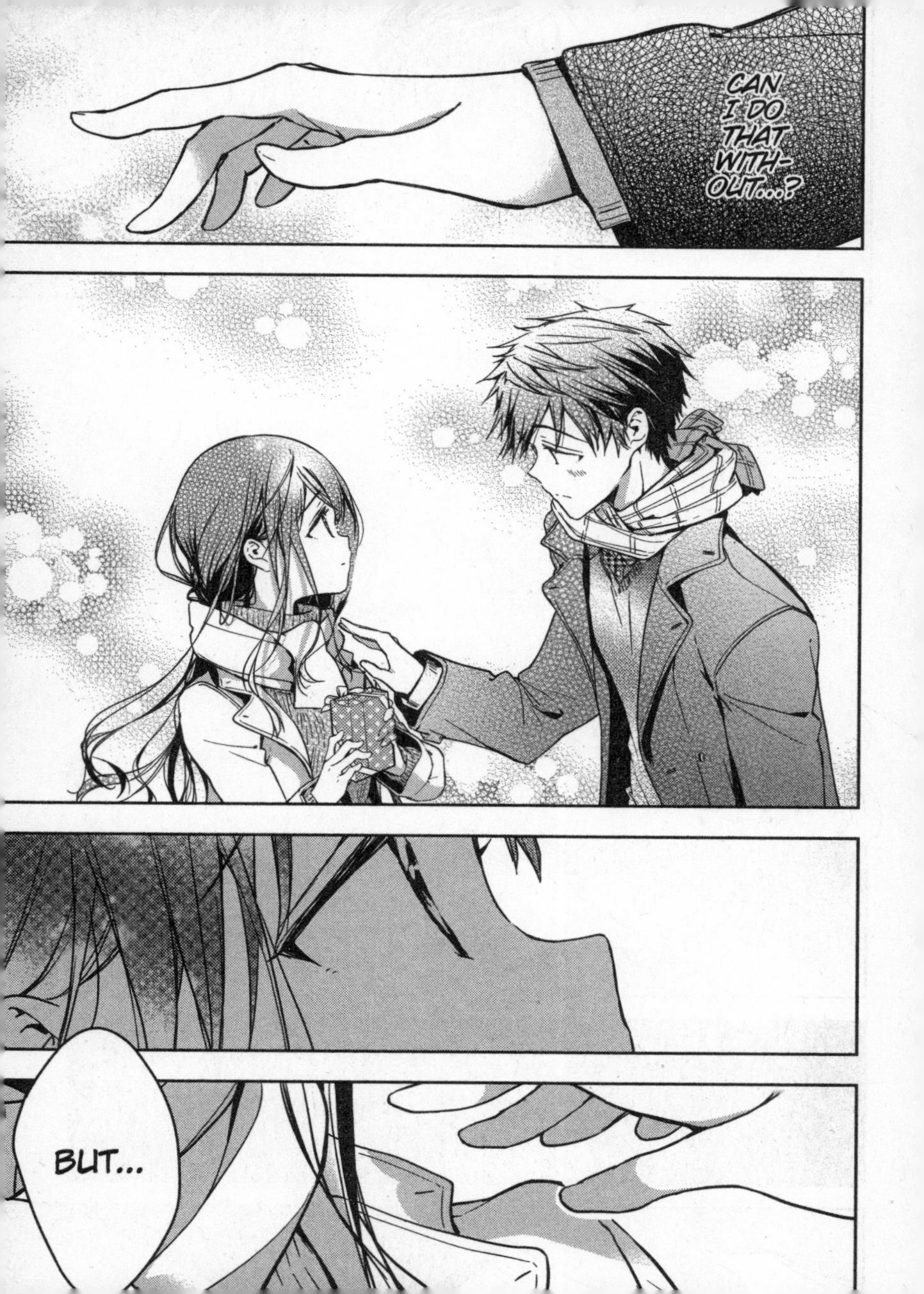
CAN I DO THAT WITH-OUT...?
BUT...

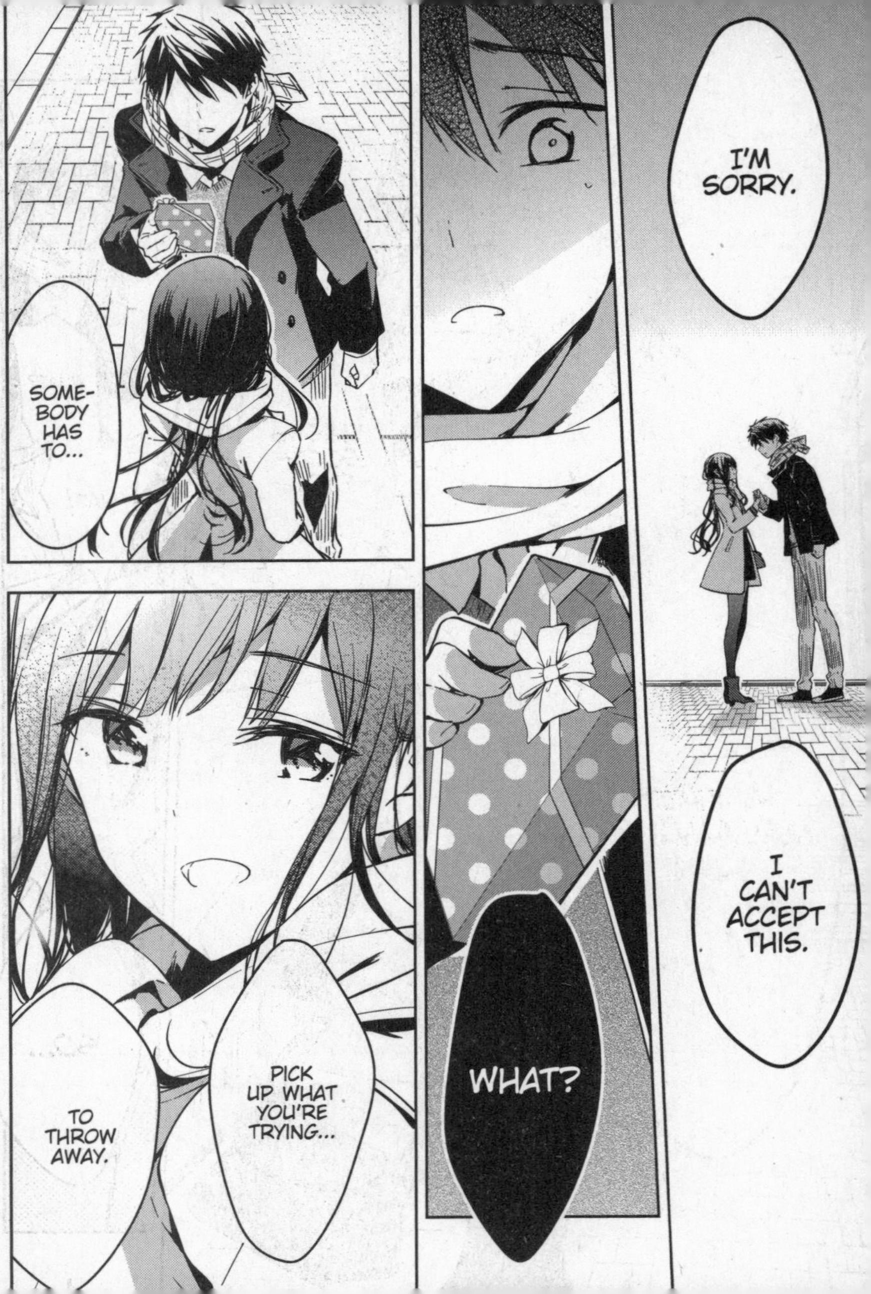
I'M SORRY.
I CAN'T ACCEPT THIS.
WHAT?
SOMEBODY HAS TO...
PICK UP WHAT YOU'RE TRYING...
TO THROW AWAY.

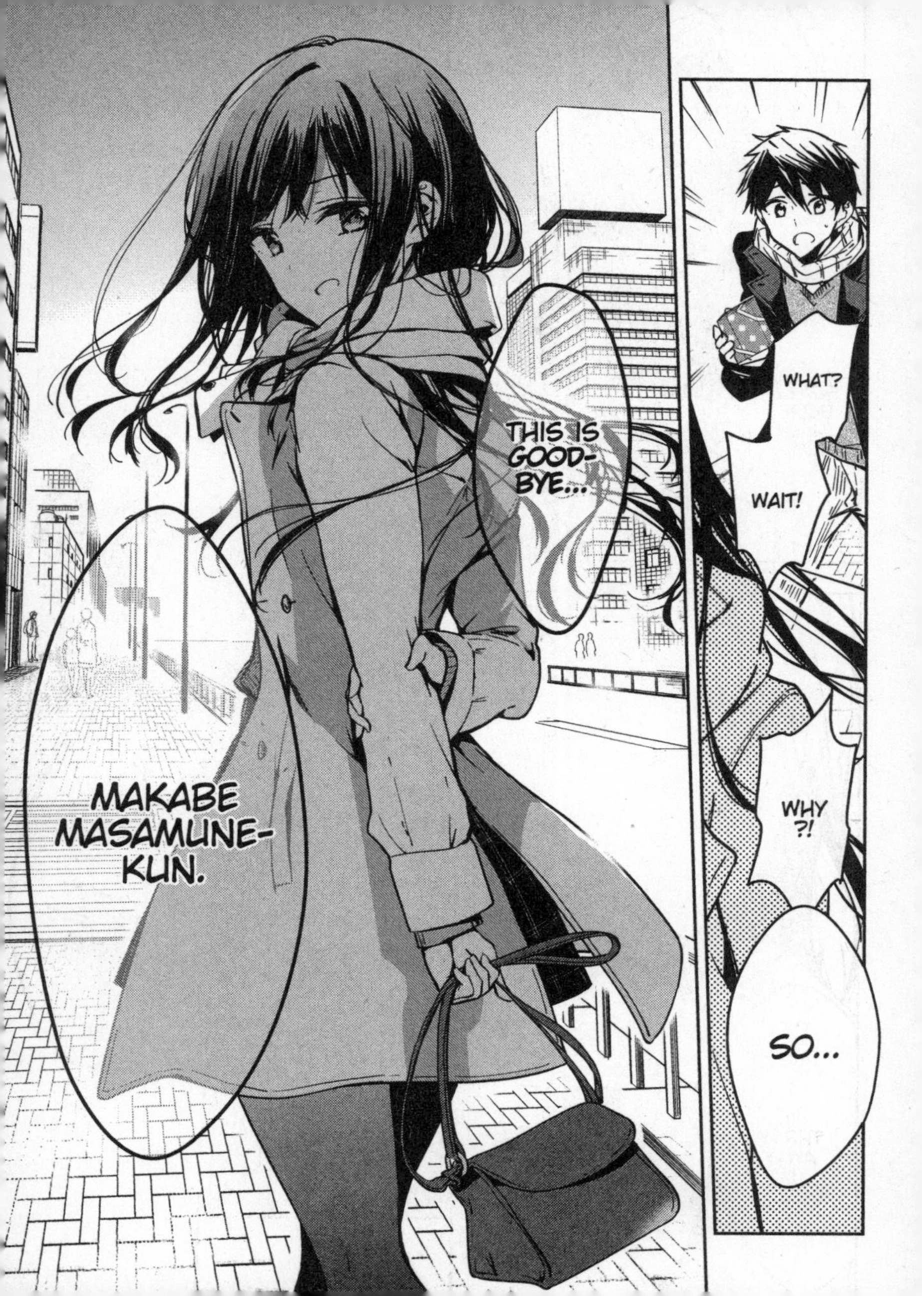
THIS IS GOOD-BYE...
MAKABE MASAMUNE-KUN.
WHAT?
WAIT!
WHY ?!
SO...

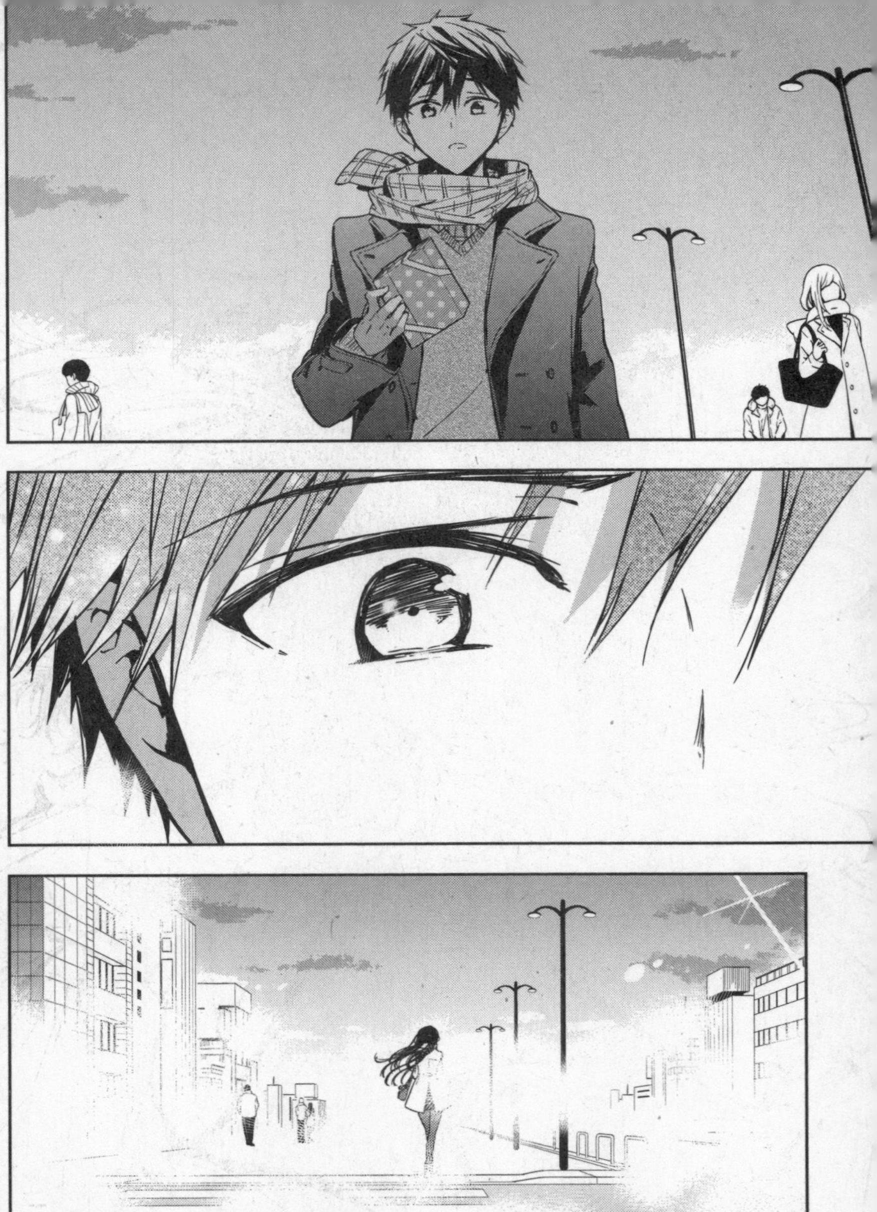

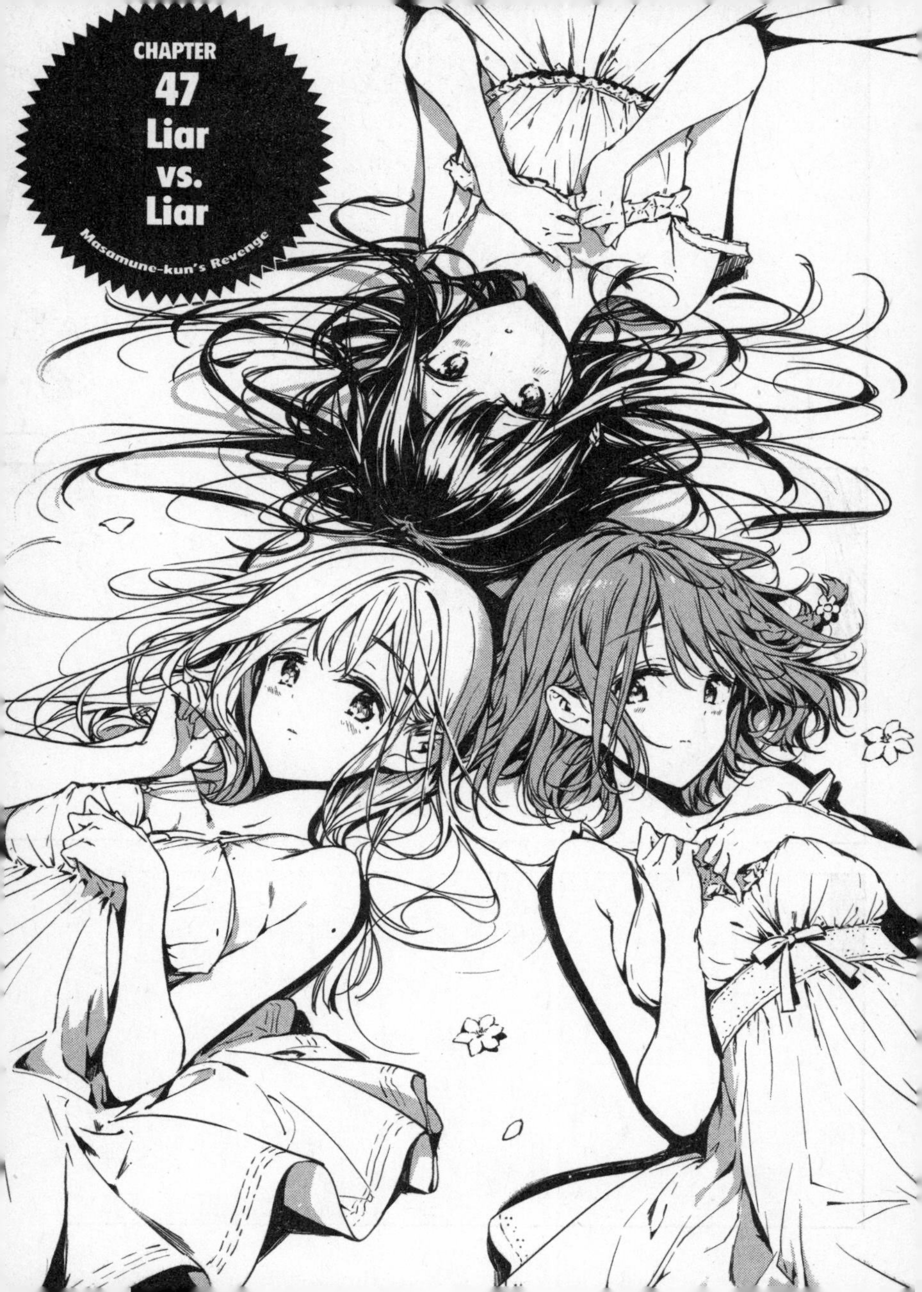
CHAPTER
47
Liar
vs.
Liar
Masamune-kun's Revenge

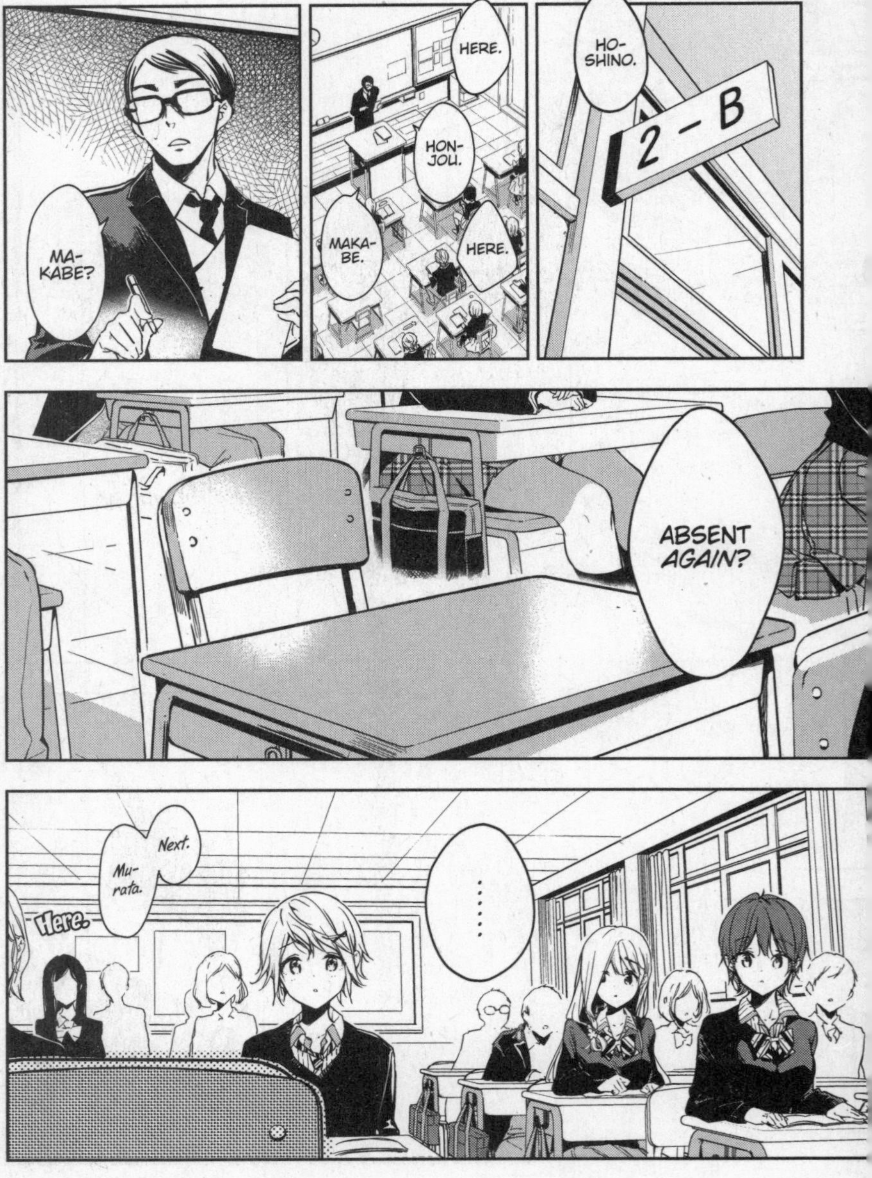
HO-SHINO.
2 - B
HERE.
HON-JOU.
HERE.
MAKA-BE.
MA-KABE?
ABSENT AGAIN?
......
Next. Mu-rata.
Here.

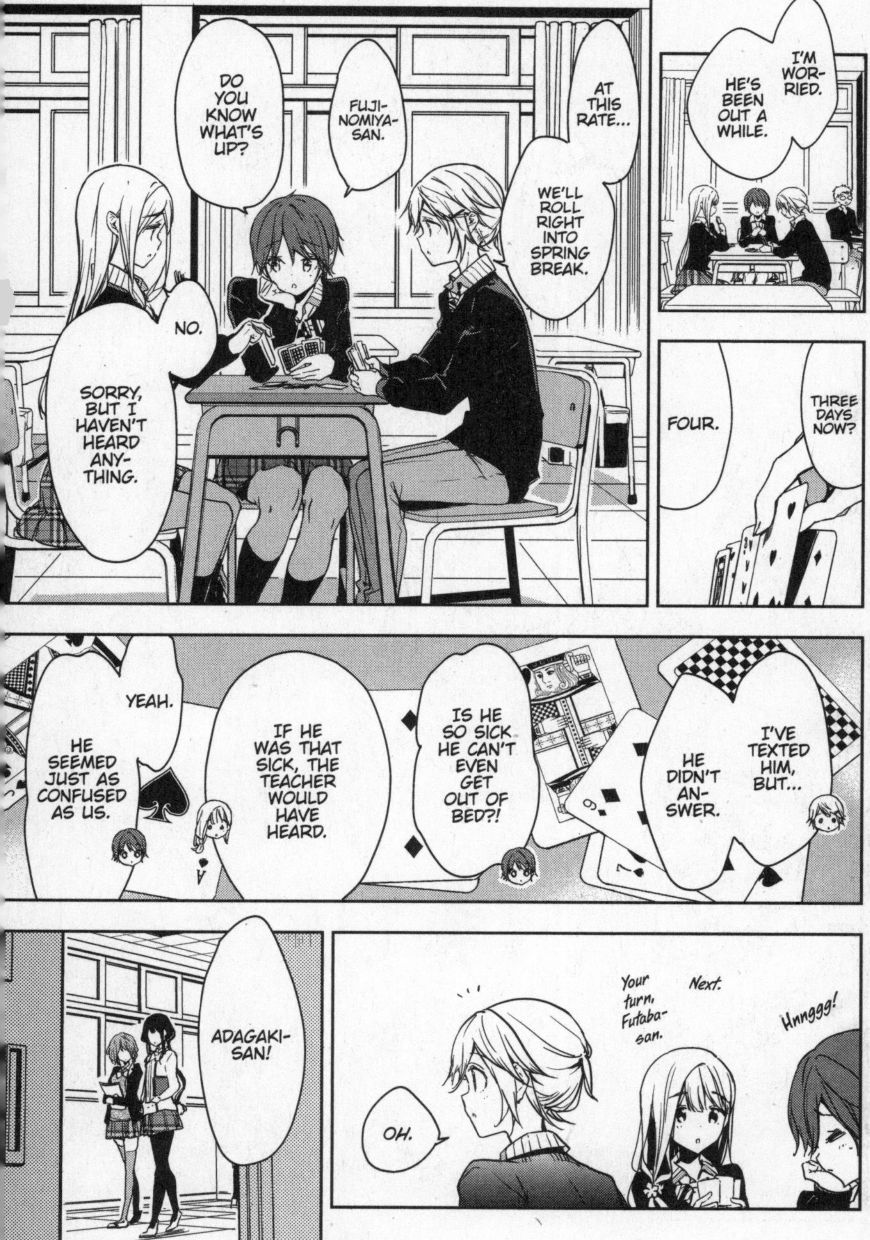
I'M WOR-RIED.
HE'S BEEN OUT A WHILE.
THREE DAYS NOW?
FOUR.
AT THIS RATE...
WE'LL ROLL RIGHT INTO SPRING BREAK.
FUJI-NOMIYA-SAN.
DO YOU KNOW WHAT'S UP?
NO.
SORRY, BUT I HAVEN'T HEARD ANY-THING.
I'VE TEXTED HIM, BUT...
HE DIDN'T AN-SWER.
IS HE SO SICK HE CAN'T EVEN GET OUT OF BED?!
IF HE WAS THAT SICK, THE TEACHER WOULD HAVE HEARD.
YEAH.
HE SEEMED JUST AS CONFUSED AS US.
Hnnggg!
Next.
Your turn, Futaba-san.
OH.
ADAGAKI-SAN!

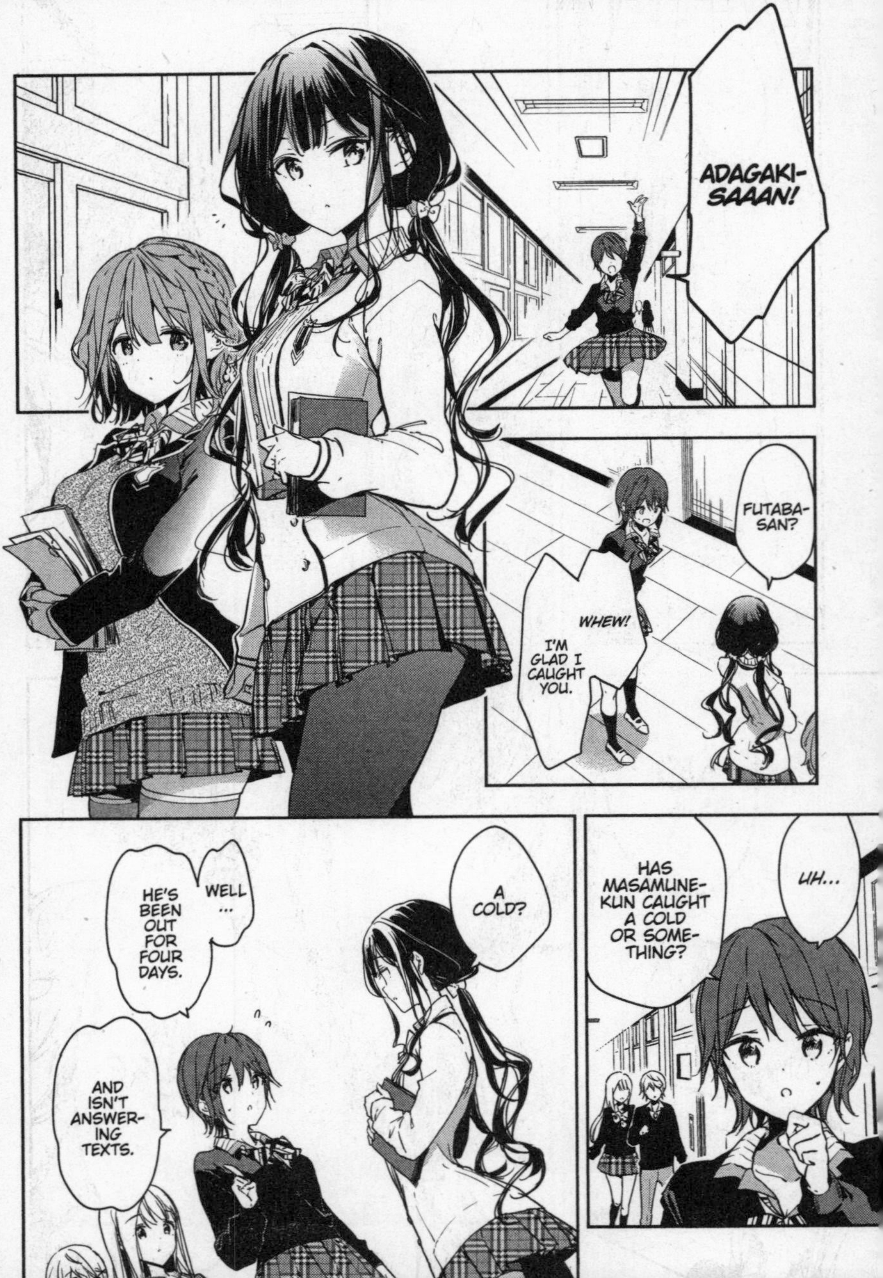
ADAGAKI-SAAAN!
FUTABA-SAN?
WHEW! I'M GLAD I CAUGHT YOU.
UH...
HAS MASAMUNE-KUN CAUGHT A COLD OR SOME-THING?
A COLD?
WELL...
HE'S BEEN OUT FOR FOUR DAYS.
AND ISN'T ANSWER-ING TEXTS.

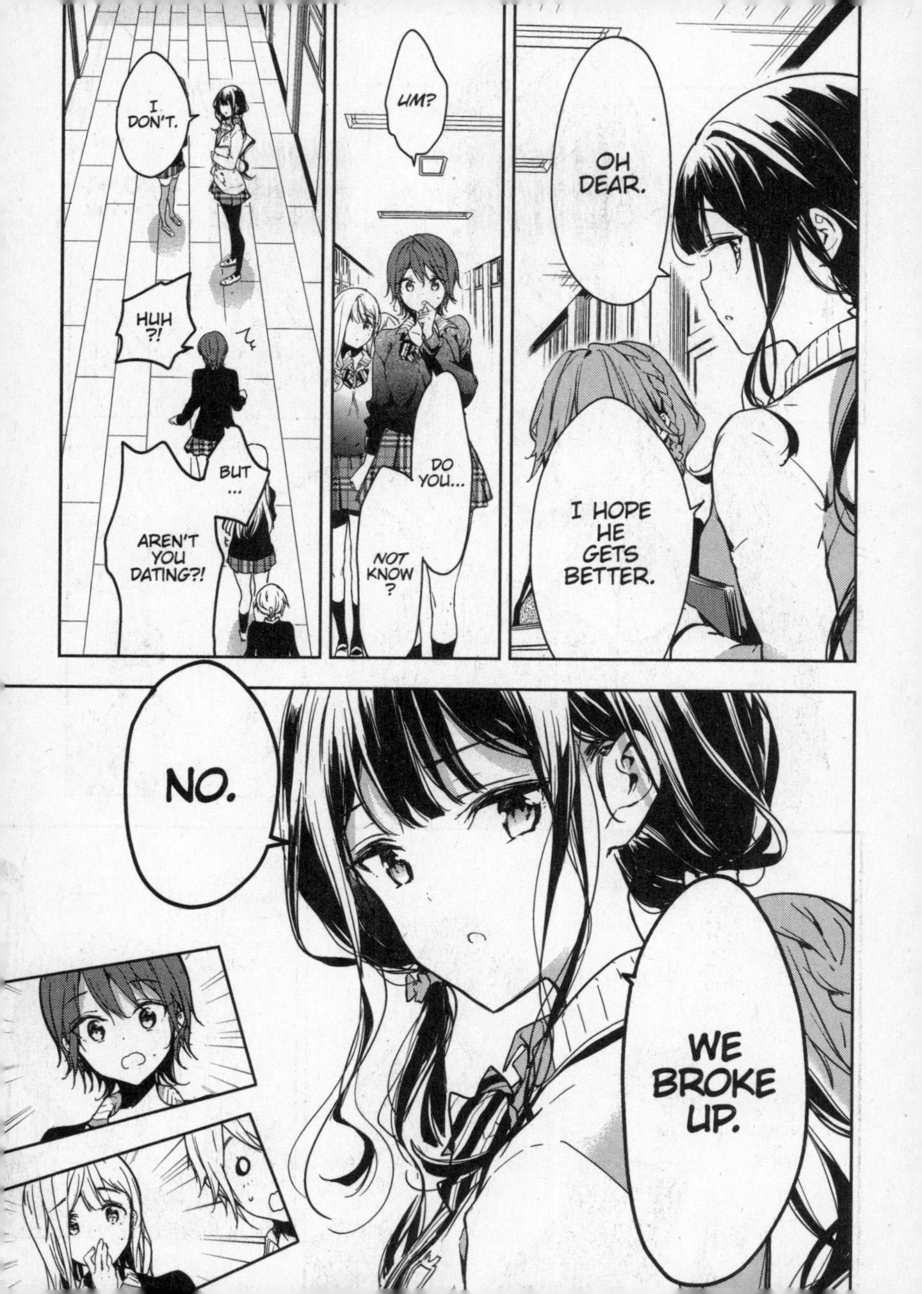
OH DEAR.
I HOPE HE GETS BETTER.
UM?
DO YOU... NOT KNOW?
I DON'T.
HUH?!
BUT... AREN'T YOU DATING?!
NO.
WE BROKE UP.

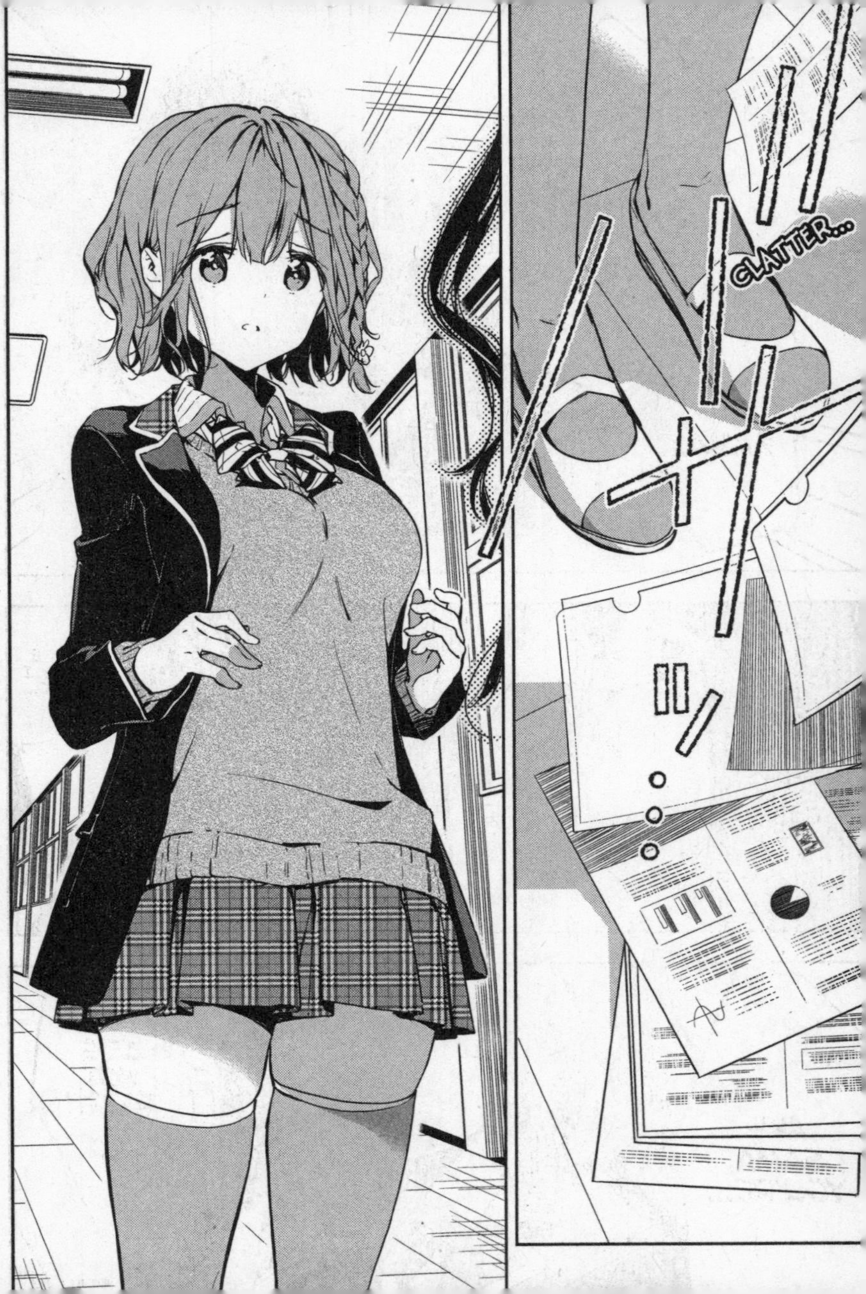
CLATTER...

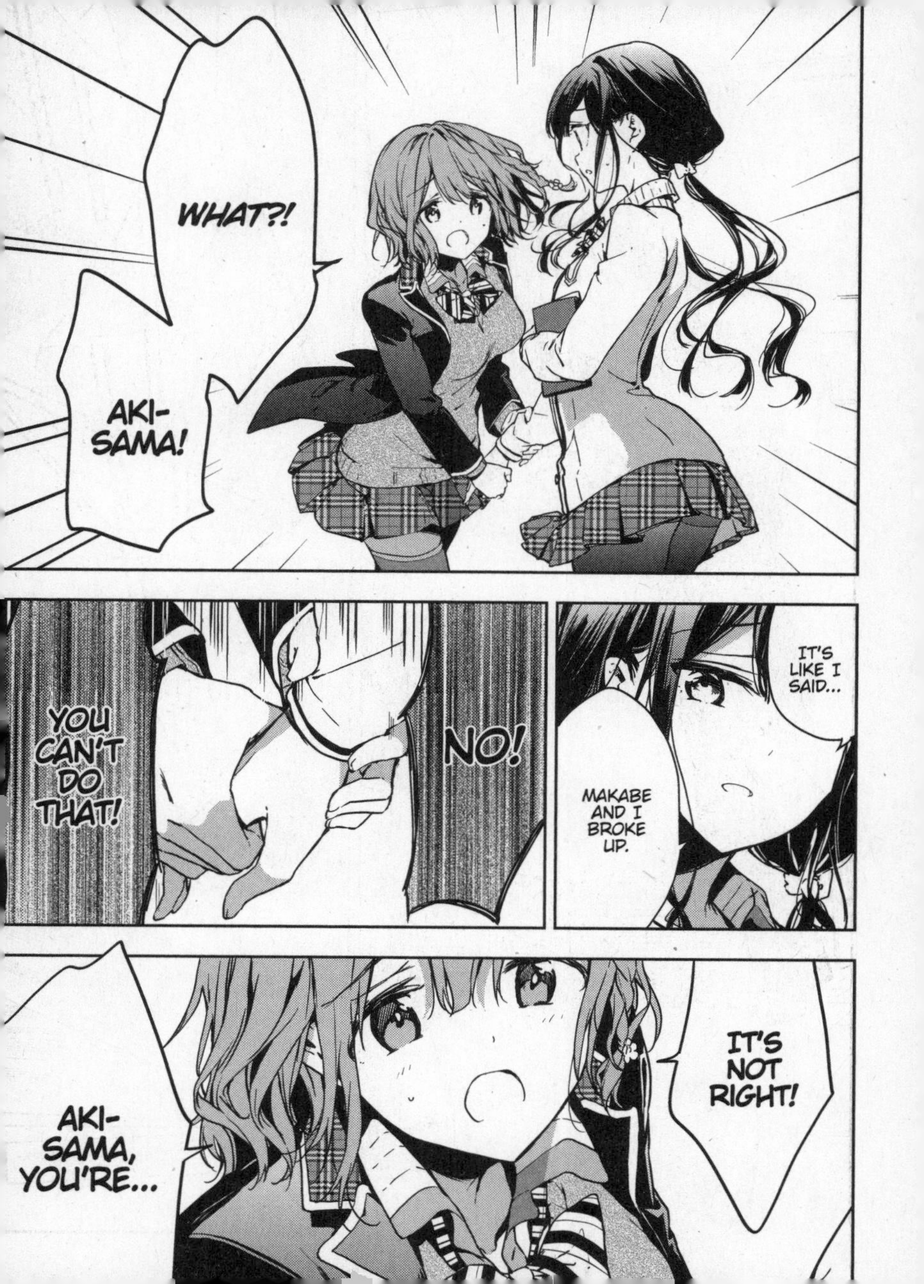
WHAT?!
AKI-SAMA!
IT'S LIKE I SAID...
MAKABE AND I BROKE UP.
NO!
YOU CAN'T DO THAT!
IT'S NOT RIGHT!
AKI-SAMA, YOU'RE...

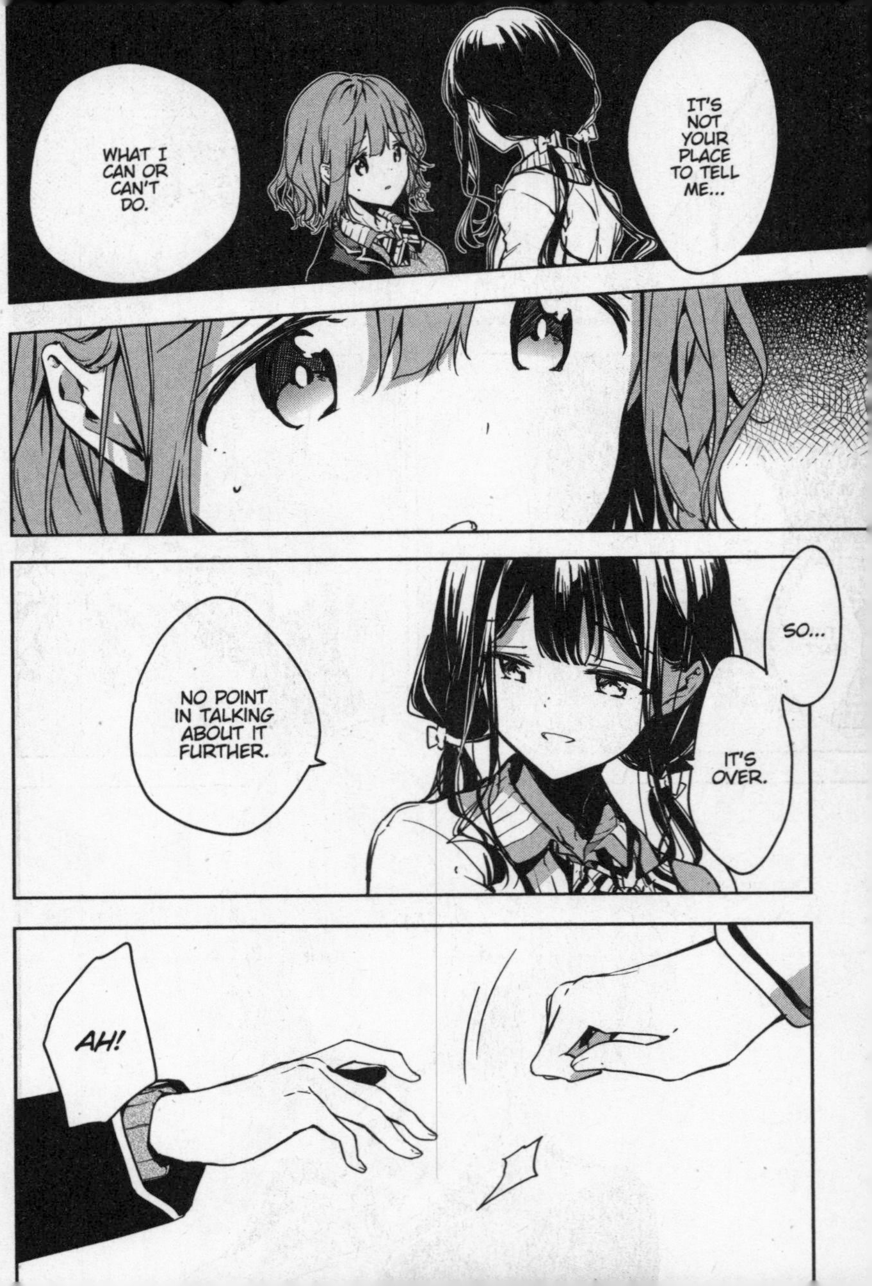
IT'S NOT YOUR PLACE TO TELL ME...
WHAT I CAN OR CAN'T DO.
SO...
IT'S OVER.
NO POINT IN TALKING ABOUT IT FURTHER.
AH!

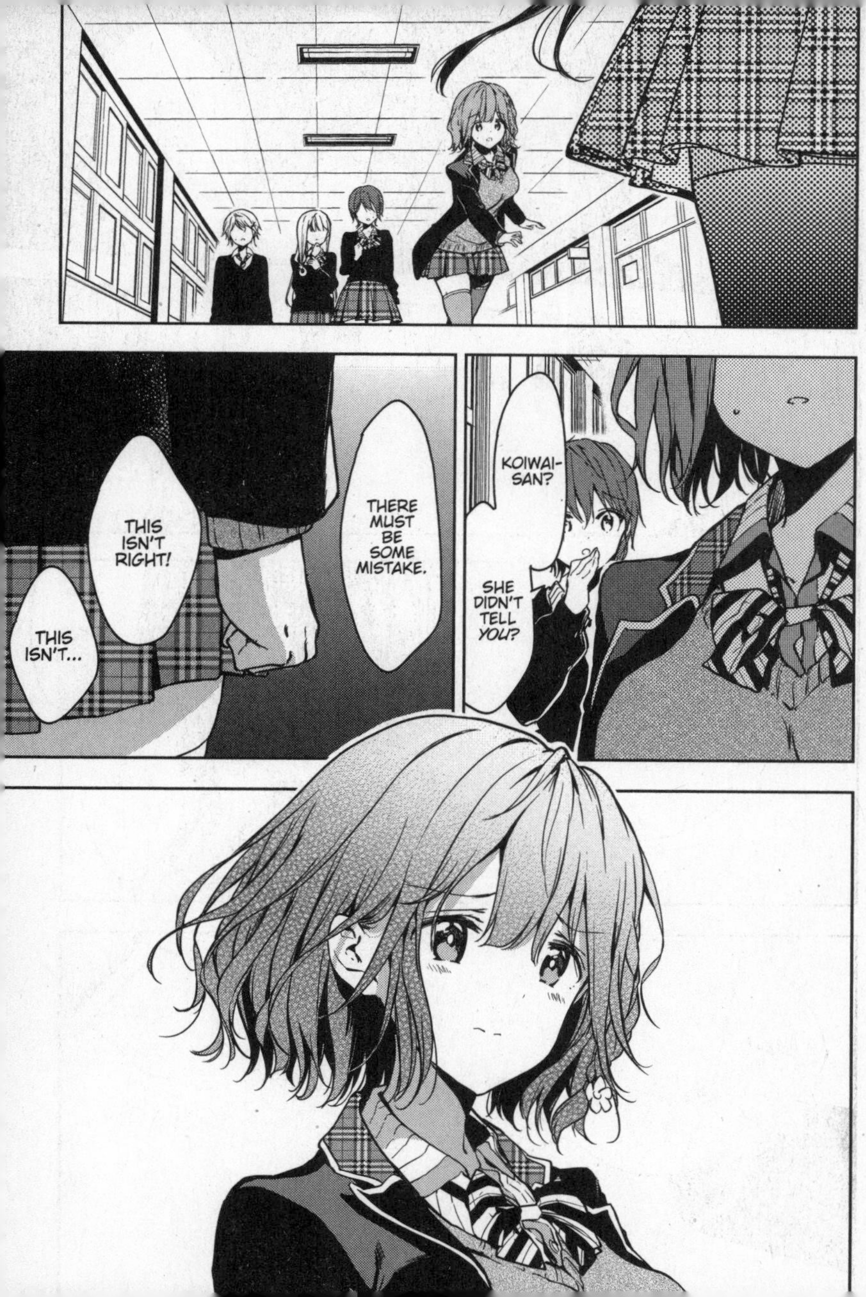
KOIWAI-SAN?
SHE DIDN'T TELL YOU?
THERE MUST BE SOME MISTAKE.
THIS ISN'T RIGHT!
THIS ISN'T...

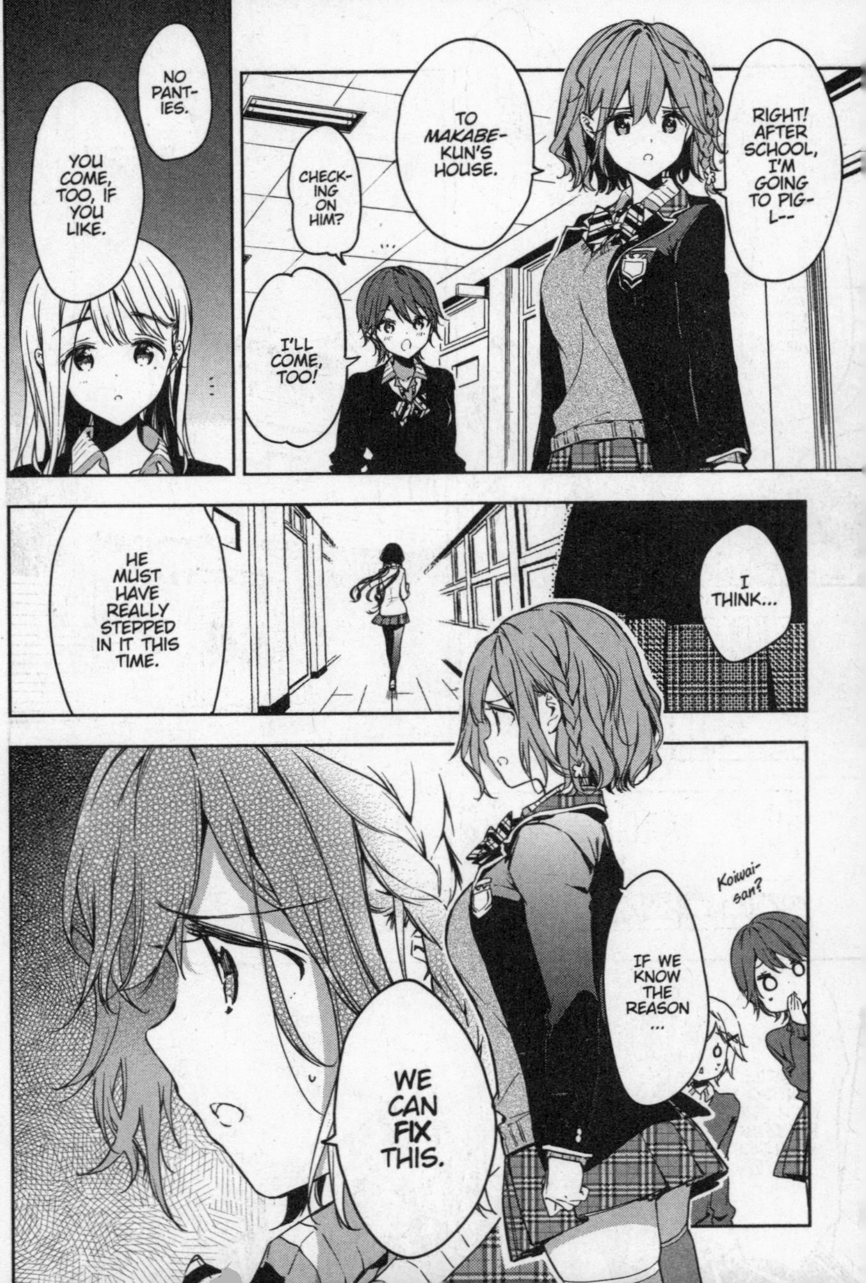
RIGHT! AFTER SCHOOL, I'M GOING TO PIGL--
TO MAKABE-KUN'S HOUSE.
CHECKING ON HIM?
...
I'LL COME, TOO!
NO PANTIES.
YOU COME, TOO, IF YOU LIKE.
...
HE MUST HAVE REALLY STEPPED IN IT THIS TIME.
I THINK...
Koiwai-san?
IF WE KNOW THE REASON...
WE CAN FIX THIS.

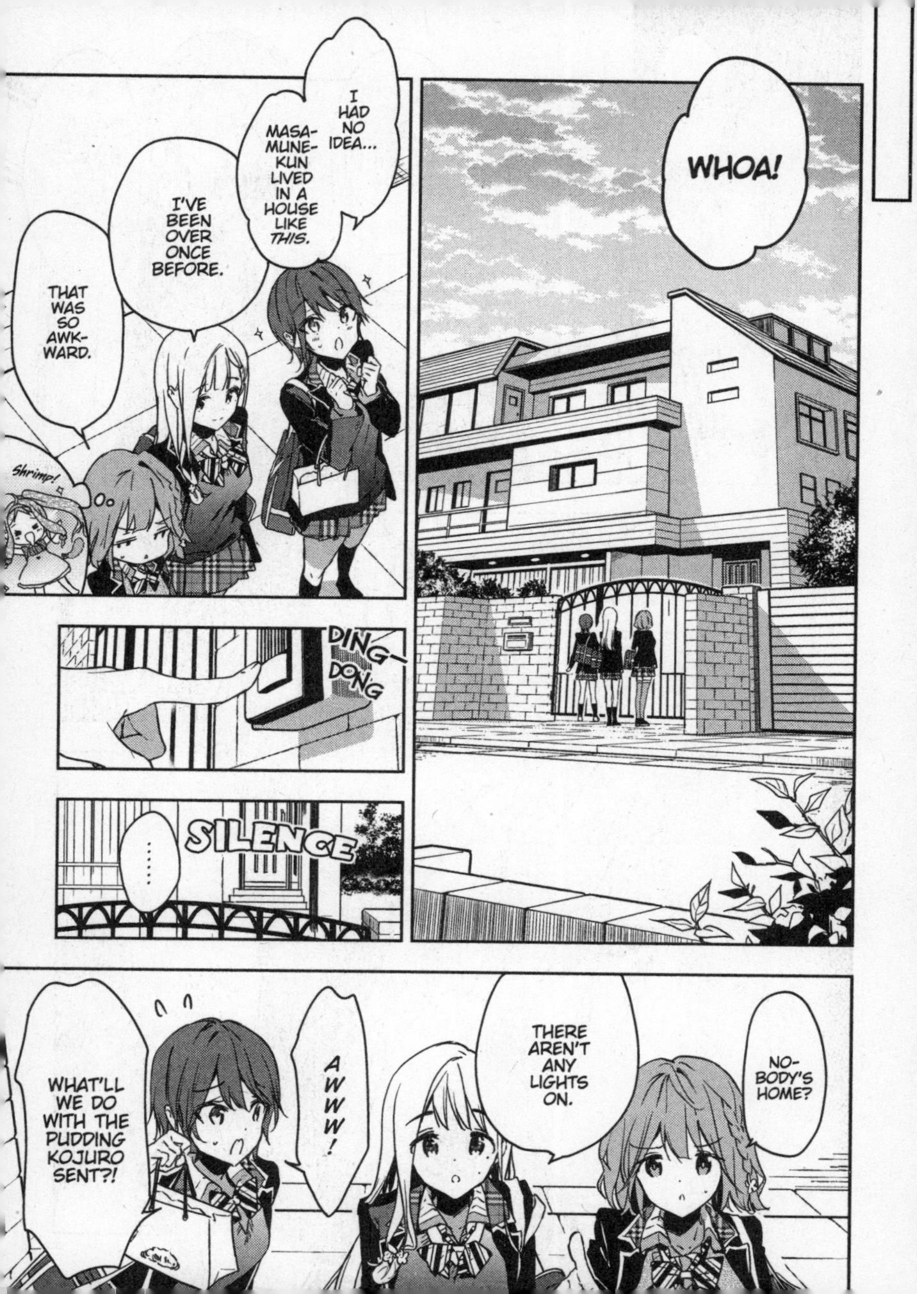
WHOA!
I HAD NO IDEA... MASAMUNE-KUN LIVED IN A HOUSE LIKE *THIS*.
I'VE BEEN OVER ONCE BEFORE.
THAT WAS SO AWKWARD.
Shrimp!
Oo
DING-DONG
SILENCE
......
NO-BODY'S HOME?
THERE AREN'T ANY LIGHTS ON.
AWWW!
WHAT'LL WE DO WITH THE PUDDING KOJURO SENT?!

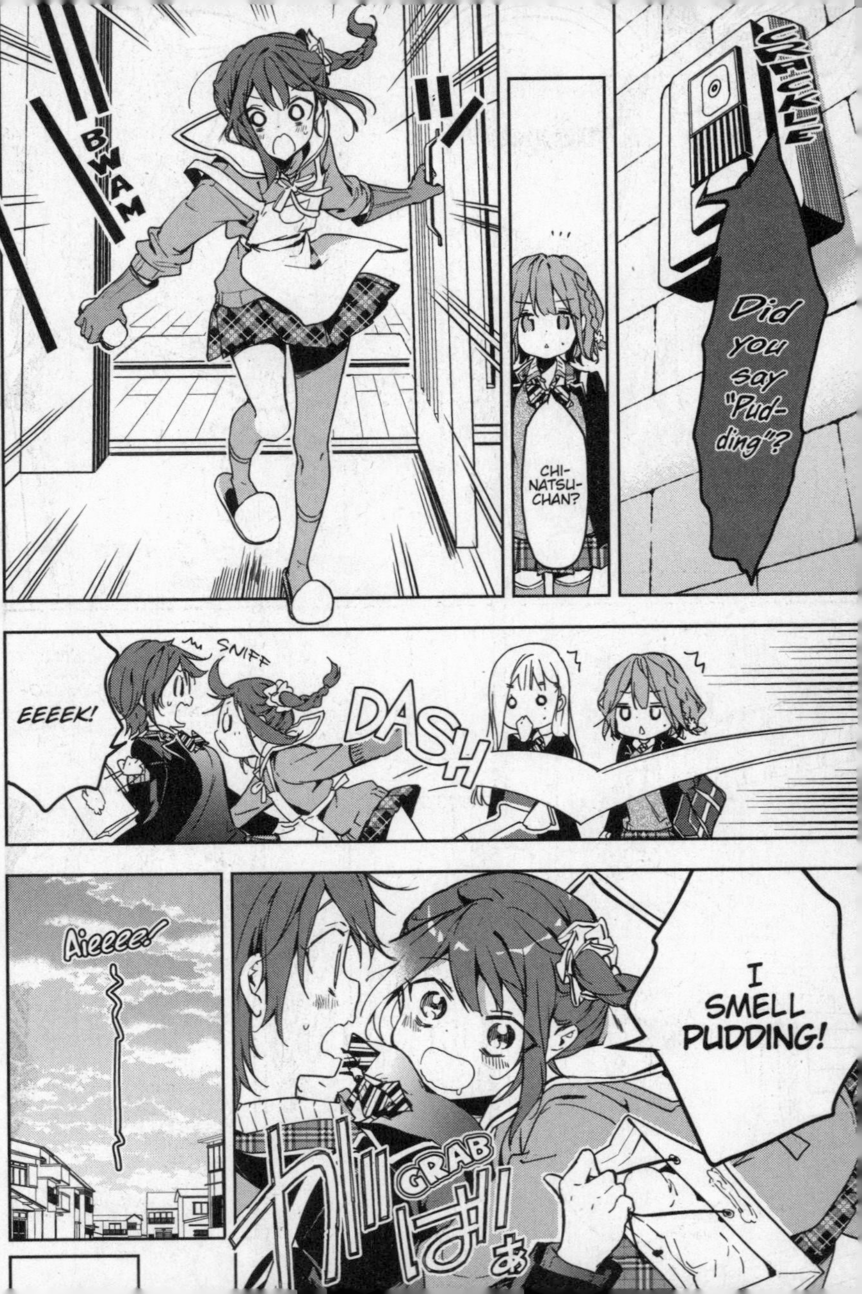
CRACKLE
Did you say "Pud-ding"?
CHI-NATSU-CHAN?
!!
BWAM
DASH
SNIFF
EEEEK!
I SMELL PUDDING!
GRAB
Aieeee!

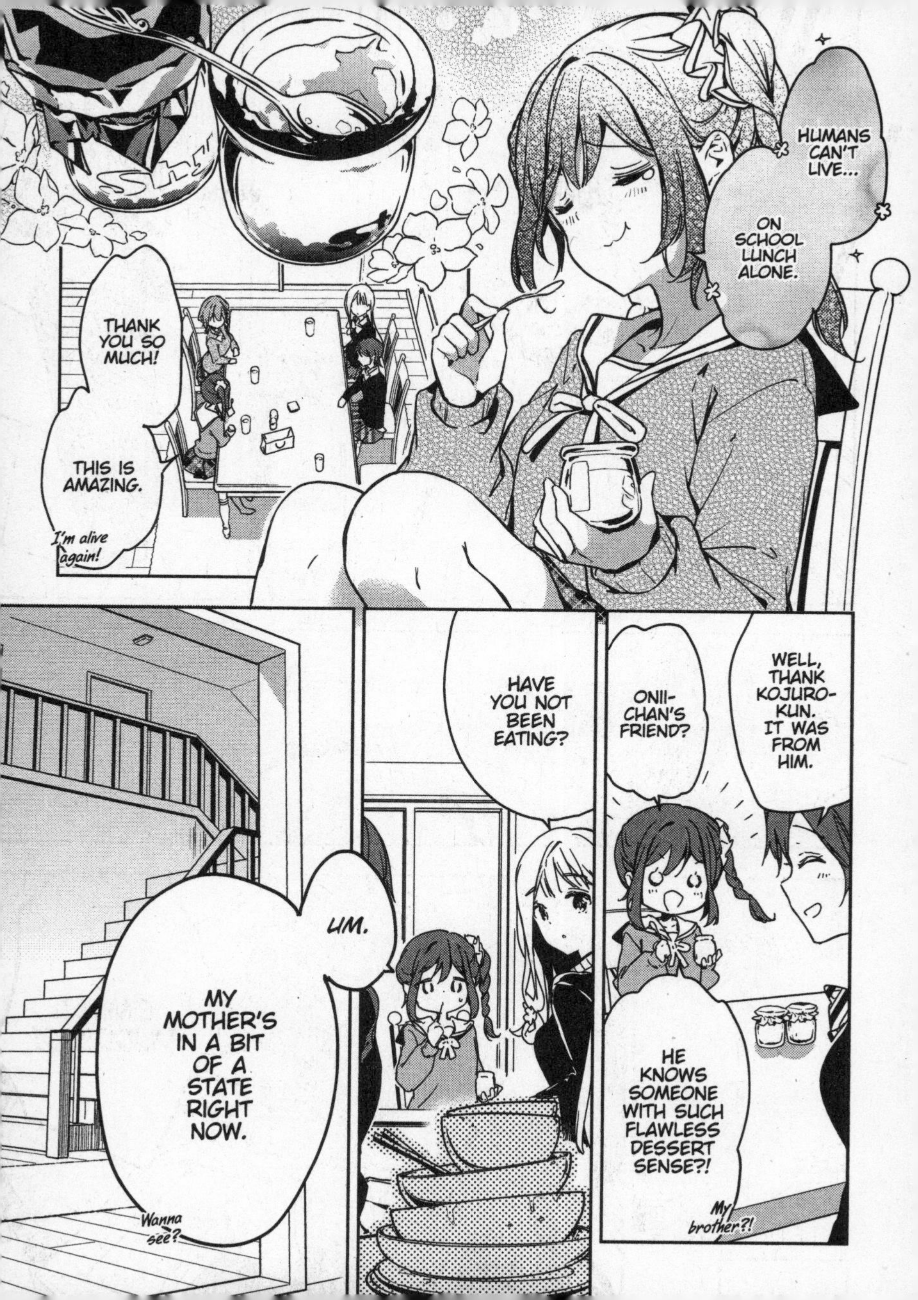
HUMANS CAN'T LIVE...
ON SCHOOL LUNCH ALONE.
THANK YOU SO MUCH!
THIS IS AMAZING.
I'm alive again!
WELL, THANK KOJURO-KUN. IT WAS FROM HIM.
ONII-CHAN'S FRIEND?
HE KNOWS SOMEONE WITH SUCH FLAWLESS DESSERT SENSE?!
My brother?!
HAVE YOU NOT BEEN EATING?
UM.
MY MOTHER'S IN A BIT OF A STATE RIGHT NOW.
Wanna see?

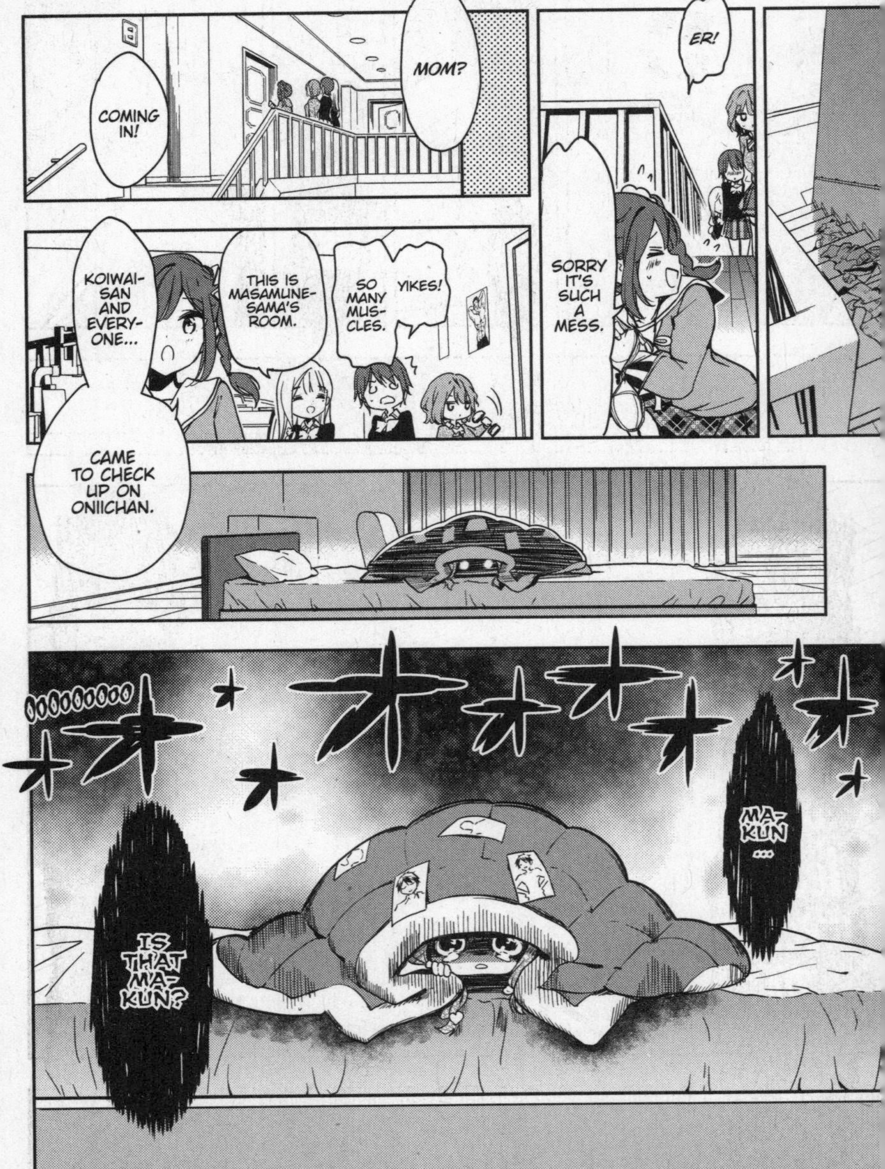
ER!
SORRY IT'S SUCH A MESS.
MOM?
COMING IN!
YIKES!
SO MANY MUS-CLES.
THIS IS MASAMUNE-SAMA'S ROOM.
KOIWAI-SAN AND EVERY-ONE... CAME TO CHECK UP ON ONIICHAN.
MA-KUN...
IS THAT MA-KUN?

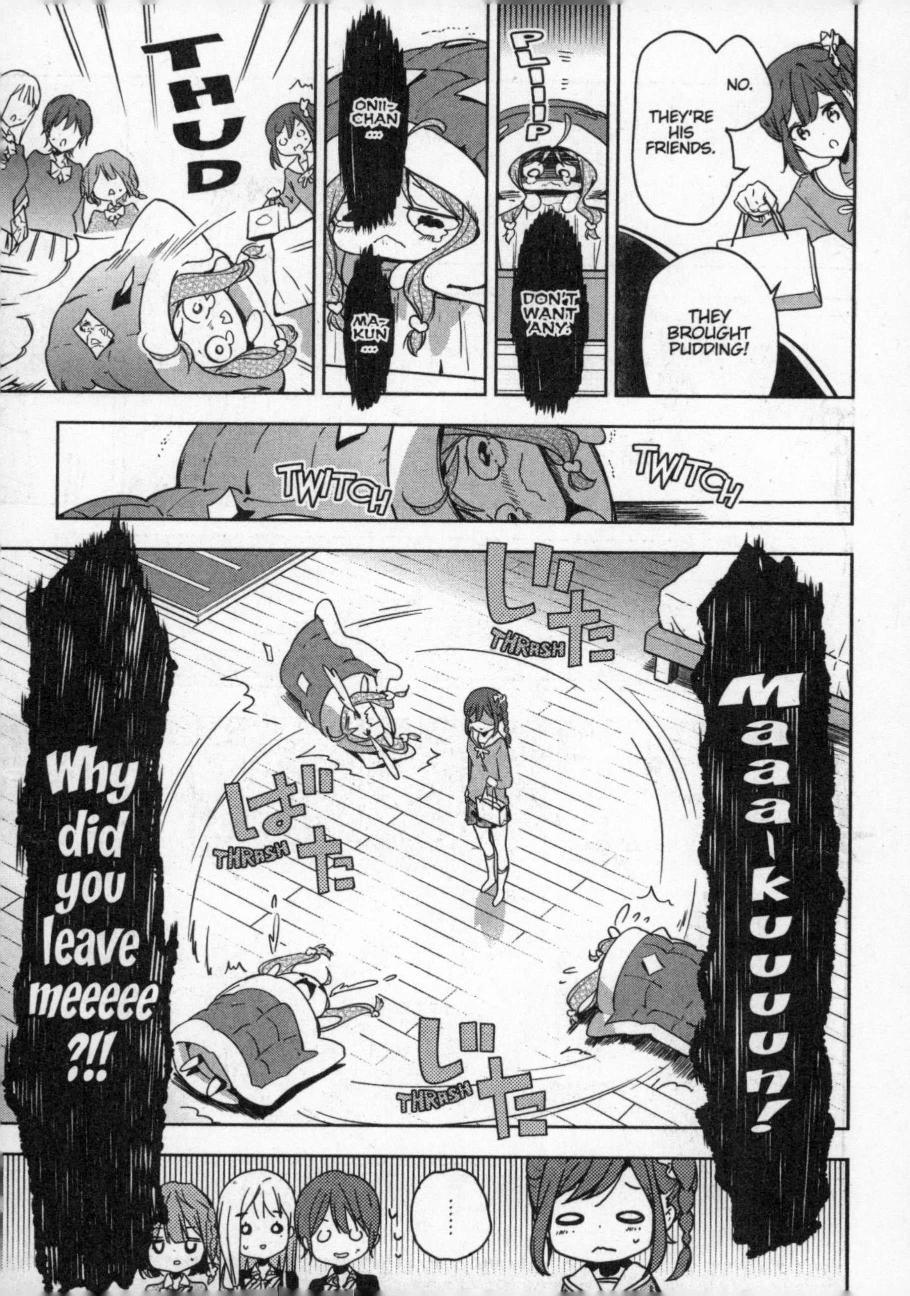
NO.
THEY'RE HIS FRIENDS.
THEY BROUGHT PUDDING!
PLIIIP
DON'T WANT ANY.
ONII-CHAN...
MA-KUN...
THUD
TWITCH
TWITCH
Maaa-kuuuun!
じた THRASH
ばた THRASH
じた THRASH
Why did you leave meeeee?!!
......

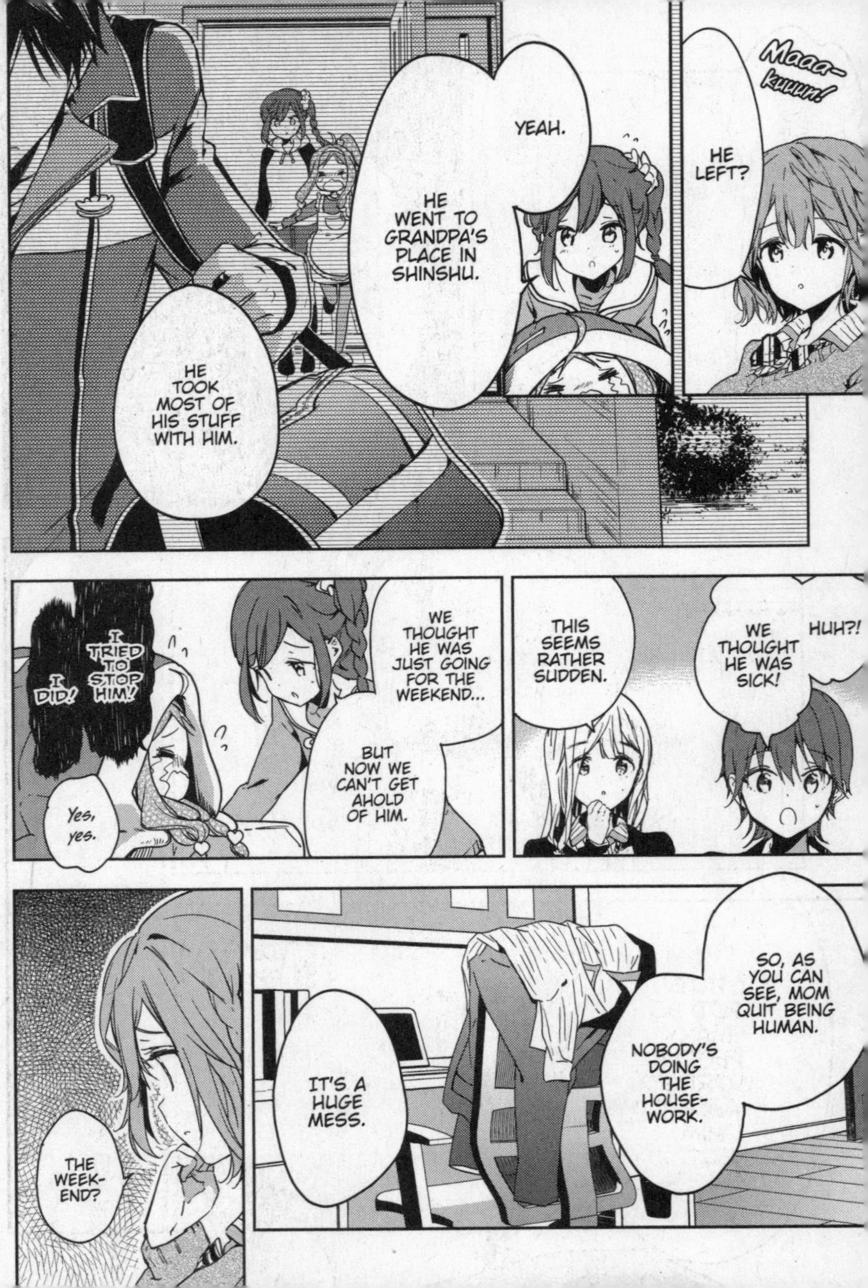
Maaa-kuuun!
HE LEFT?
YEAH.
HE WENT TO GRANDPA'S PLACE IN SHINSHU.
HE TOOK MOST OF HIS STUFF WITH HIM.
HUH?!
WE THOUGHT HE WAS SICK!
THIS SEEMS RATHER SUDDEN.
WE THOUGHT HE WAS JUST GOING FOR THE WEEKEND...
BUT NOW WE CAN'T GET AHOLD OF HIM.
I TRIED TO STOP HIM!
I DID!
Yes, yes.
SO, AS YOU CAN SEE, MOM QUIT BEING HUMAN.
NOBODY'S DOING THE HOUSE-WORK.
IT'S A HUGE MESS.
THE WEEK-END?

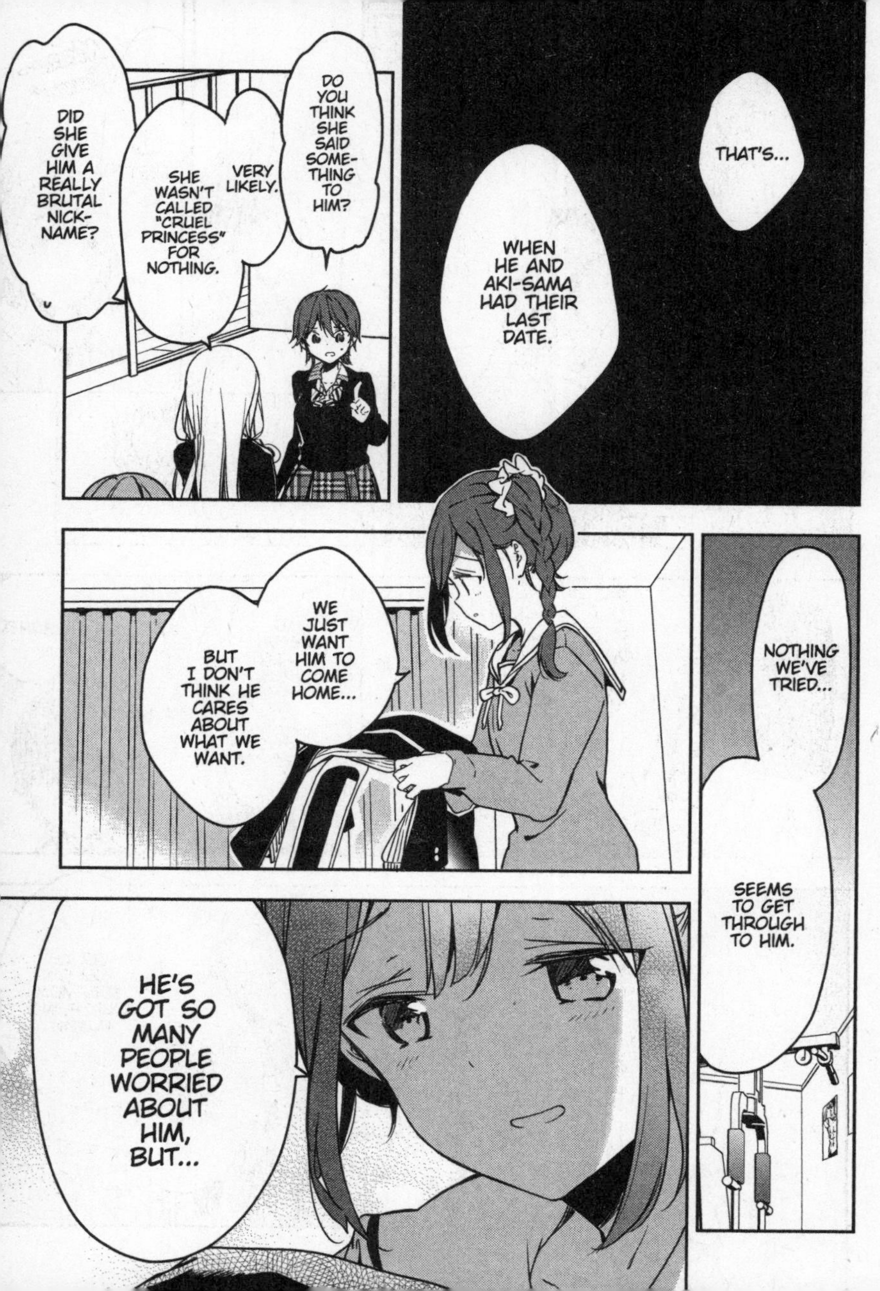
THAT'S...
WHEN HE AND AKI-SAMA HAD THEIR LAST DATE.
DO YOU THINK SHE SAID SOMETHING TO HIM?
VERY LIKELY.
SHE WASN'T CALLED "CRUEL PRINCESS" FOR NOTHING.
DID SHE GIVE HIM A REALLY BRUTAL NICK-NAME?
NOTHING WE'VE TRIED...
SEEMS TO GET THROUGH TO HIM.
WE JUST WANT HIM TO COME HOME...
BUT I DON'T THINK HE CARES ABOUT WHAT WE WANT.
HE'S GOT SO MANY PEOPLE WORRIED ABOUT HIM, BUT...

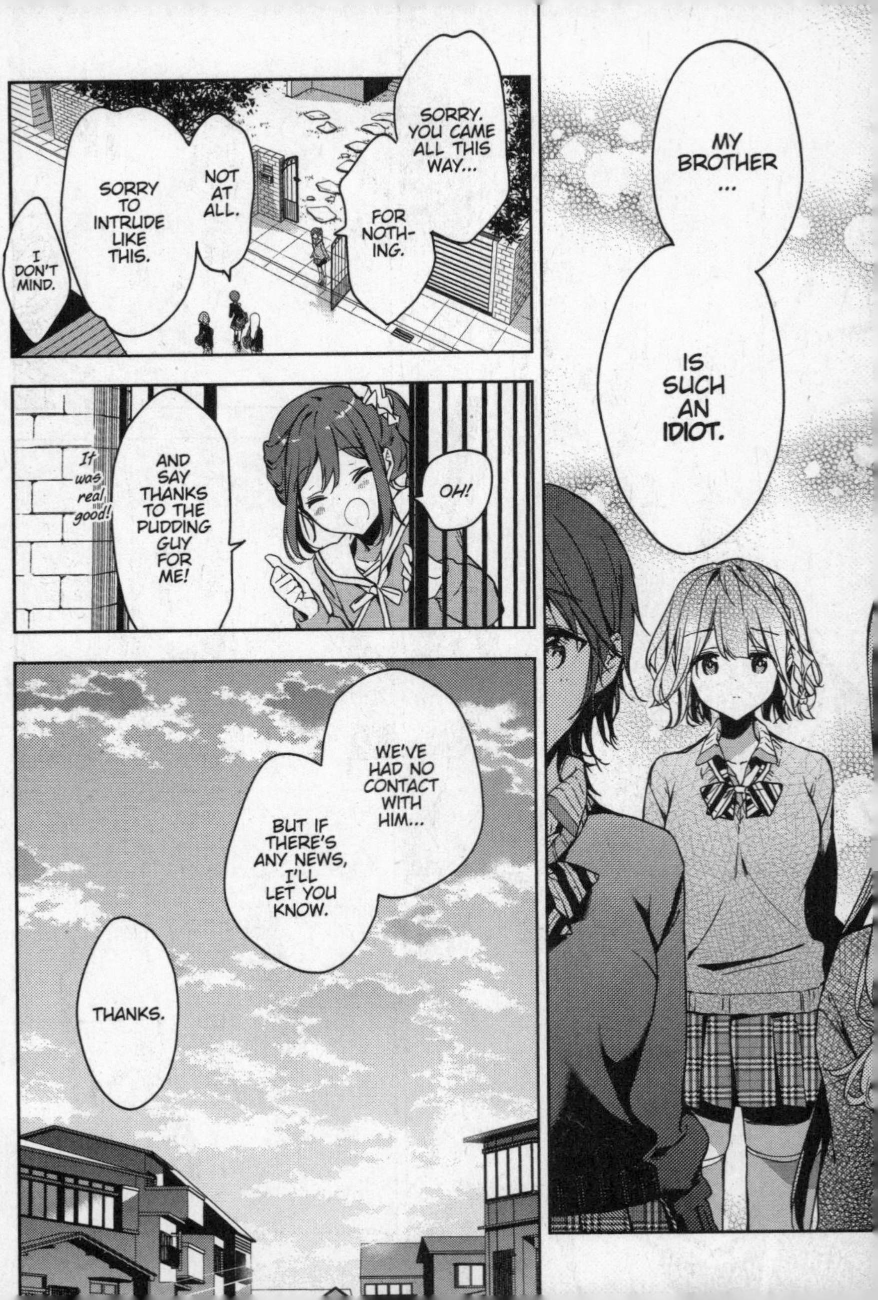
MY BROTHER ...
IS SUCH AN IDIOT.
SORRY. YOU CAME ALL THIS WAY...
FOR NOTHING.
NOT AT ALL.
SORRY TO INTRUDE LIKE THIS.
I DON'T MIND.
OH!
AND SAY THANKS TO THE PUDDING GUY FOR ME!
It was real good!
WE'VE HAD NO CONTACT WITH HIM...
BUT IF THERE'S ANY NEWS, I'LL LET YOU KNOW.
THANKS.

WELL, THAT GOT US NO-WHERE.

AT LEAST WE KNOW WHERE HE IS.

BUT I'M WORRIED.

WORRIED ABOUT WHAT?

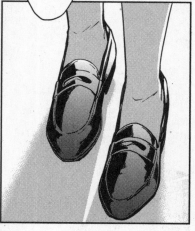

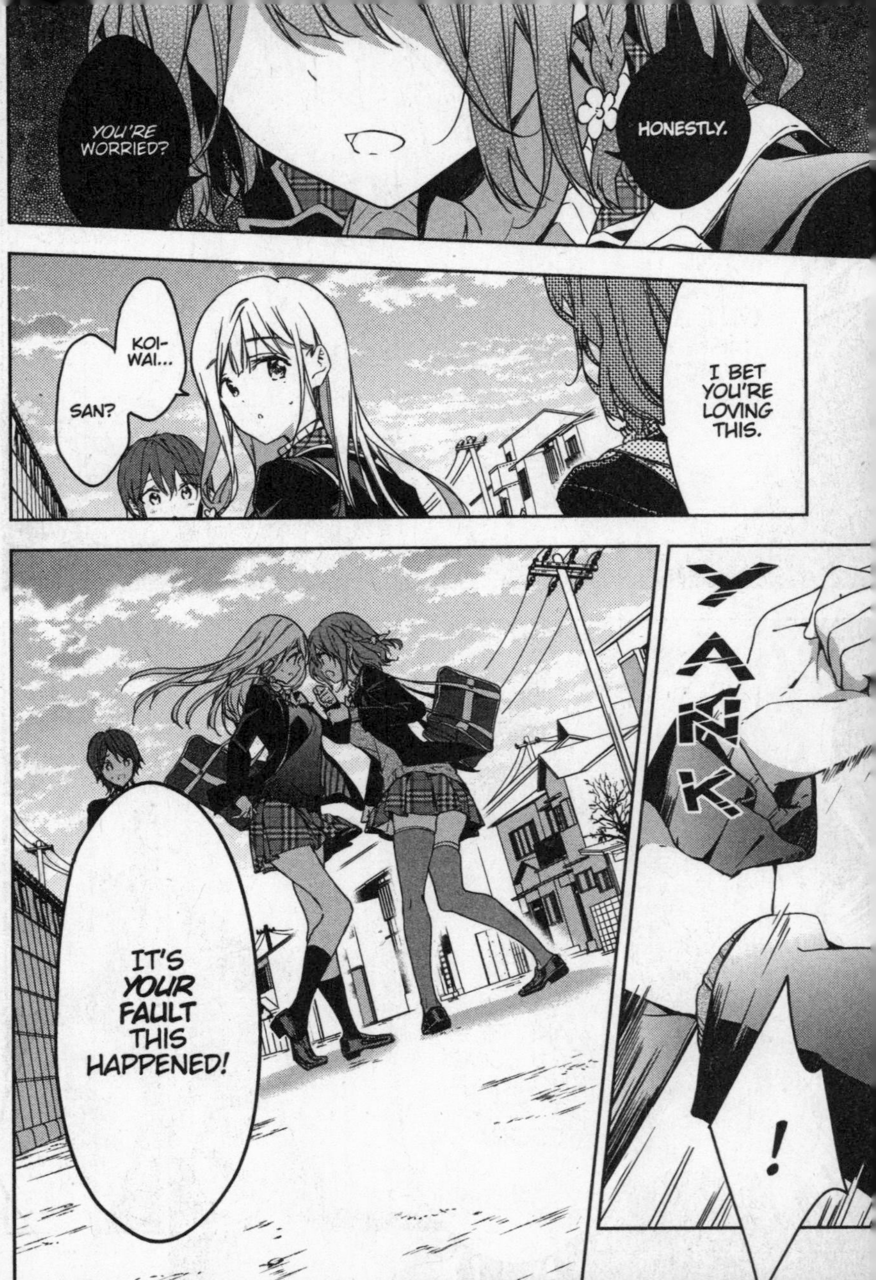
HONESTLY.
YOU'RE WORRIED?
I BET YOU'RE LOVING THIS.
KOI-WAI... SAN?
YANK
!
IT'S *YOUR* FAULT THIS HAPPENED!

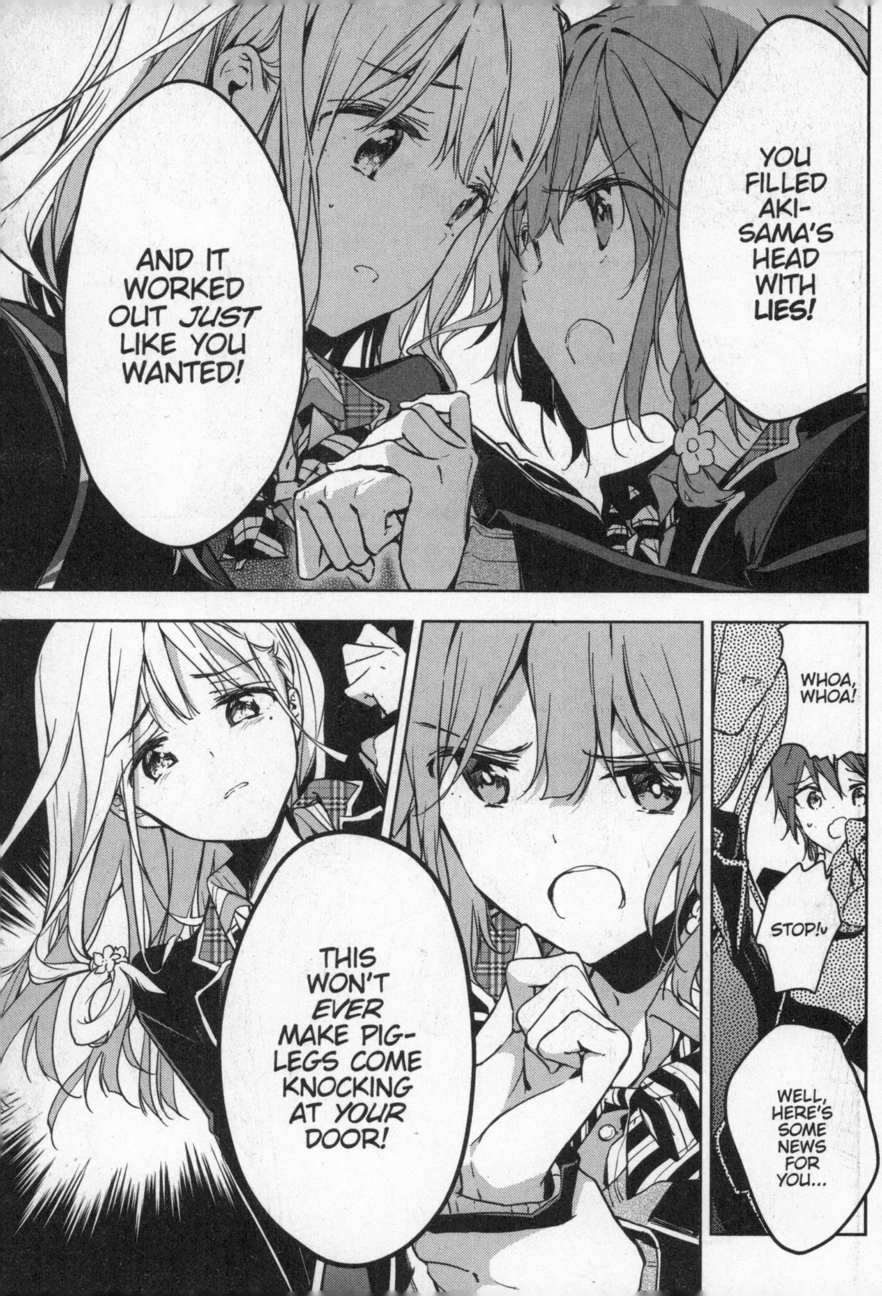
YOU FILLED AKI-SAMA'S HEAD WITH LIES!
AND IT WORKED OUT JUST LIKE YOU WANTED!
WHOA, WHOA!
STOP!
WELL, HERE'S SOME NEWS FOR YOU...
THIS WON'T EVER MAKE PIG-LEGS COME KNOCKING AT YOUR DOOR!

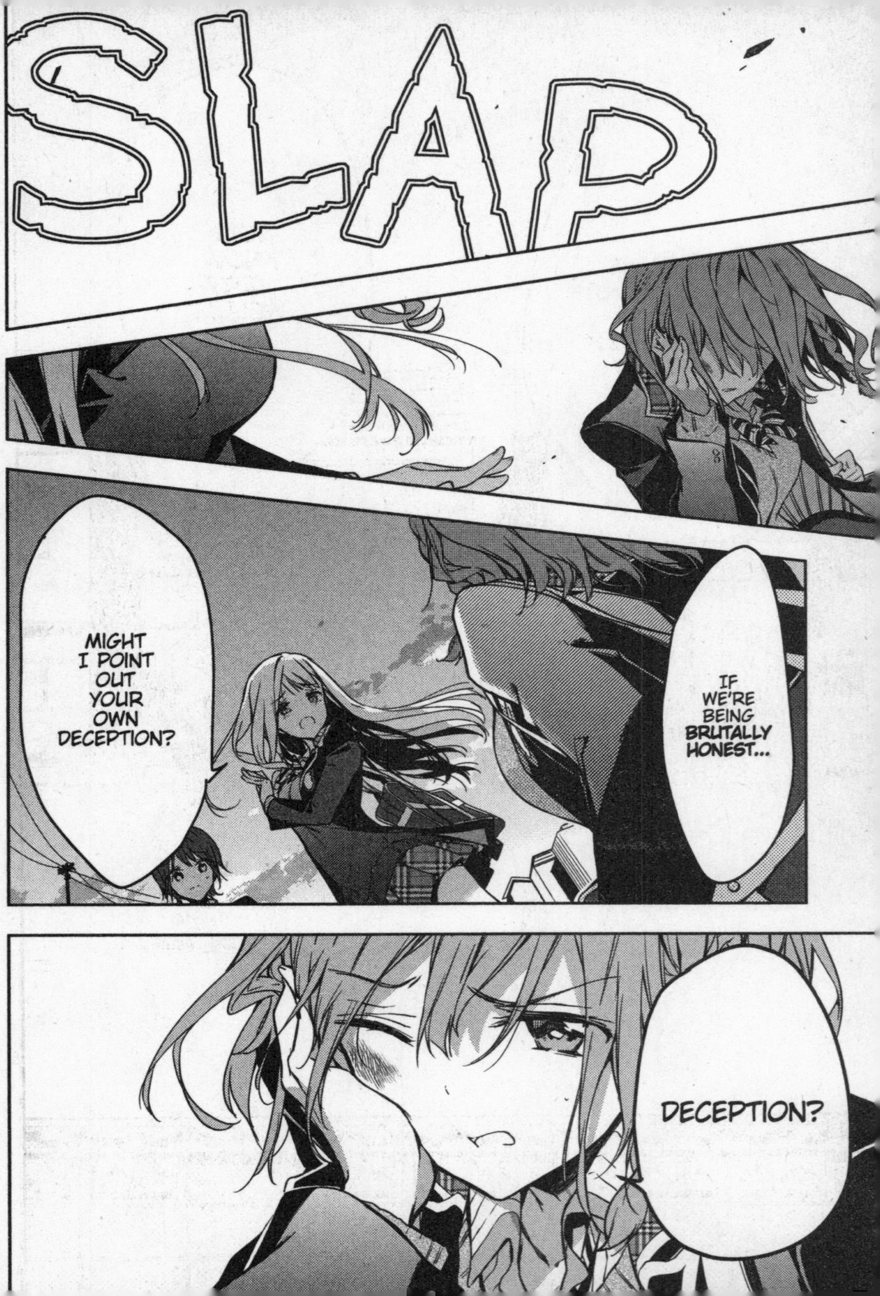
SLAP
IF WE'RE BEING BRUTALLY HONEST...
MIGHT I POINT OUT YOUR OWN DECEPTION?
DECEPTION?

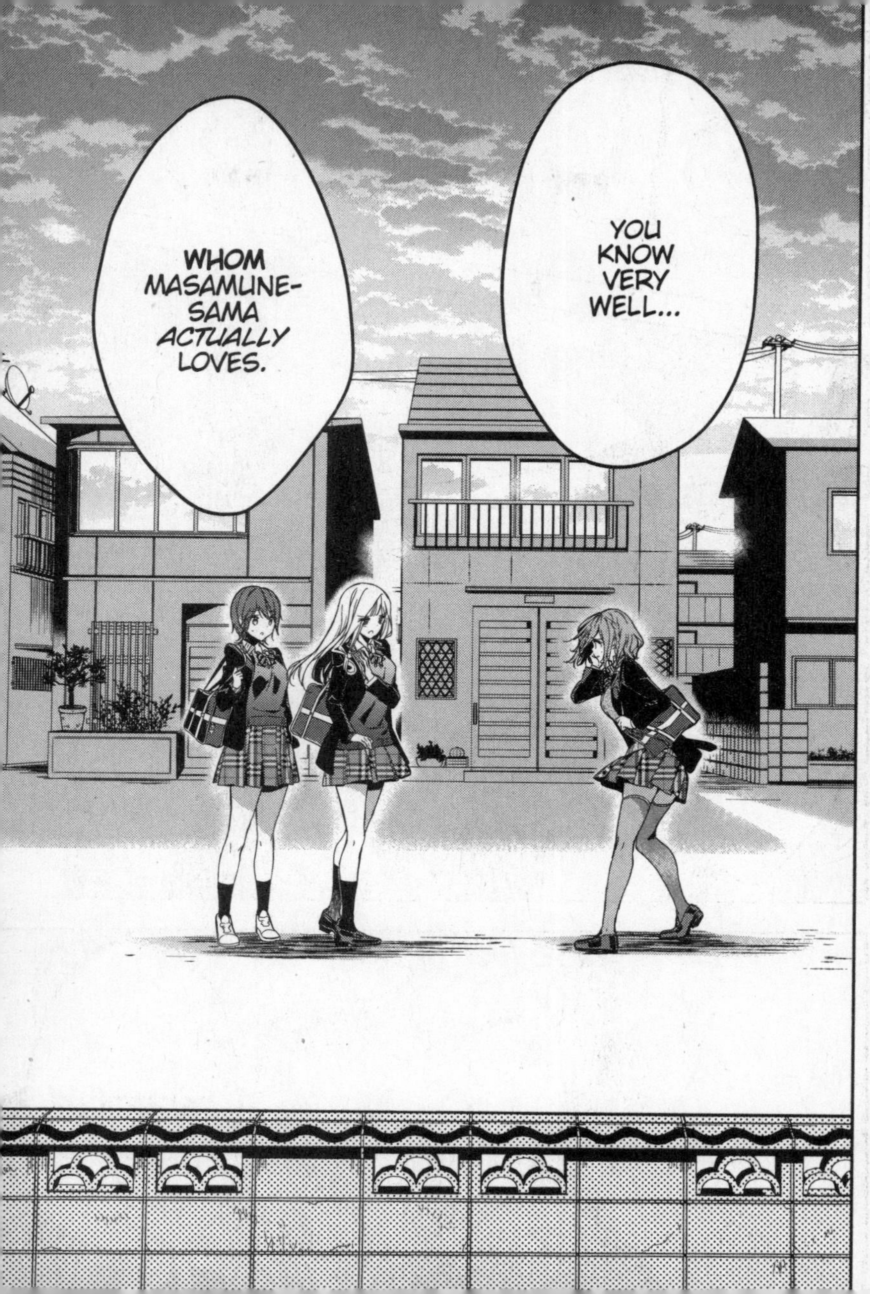
YOU KNOW VERY WELL...
WHOM MASAMUNE-SAMA ACTUALLY LOVES.

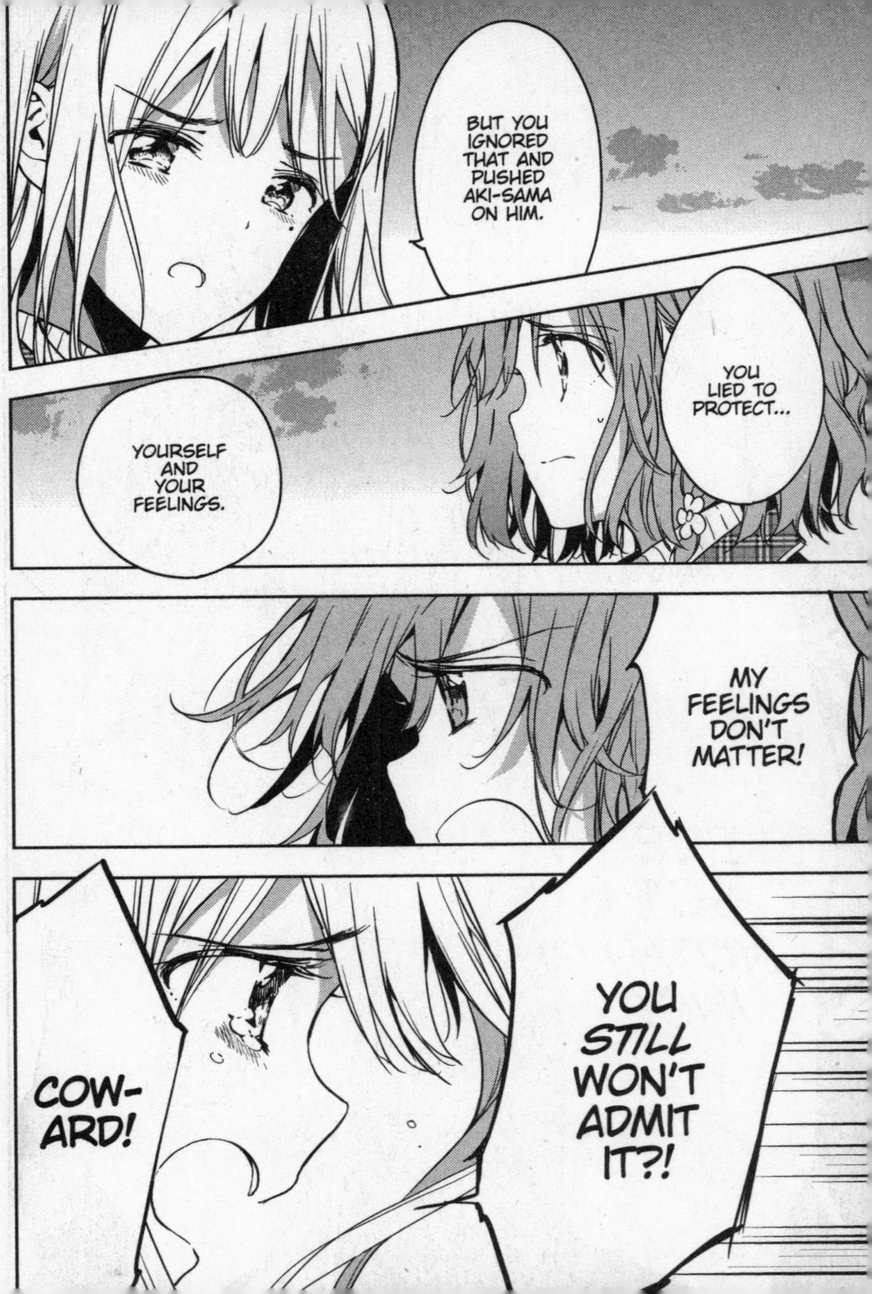
BUT YOU IGNORED THAT AND PUSHED AKI-SAMA ON HIM.
YOU LIED TO PROTECT...
YOURSELF AND YOUR FEELINGS.
MY FEELINGS DON'T MATTER!
YOU STILL WON'T ADMIT IT?!
COW-ARD!

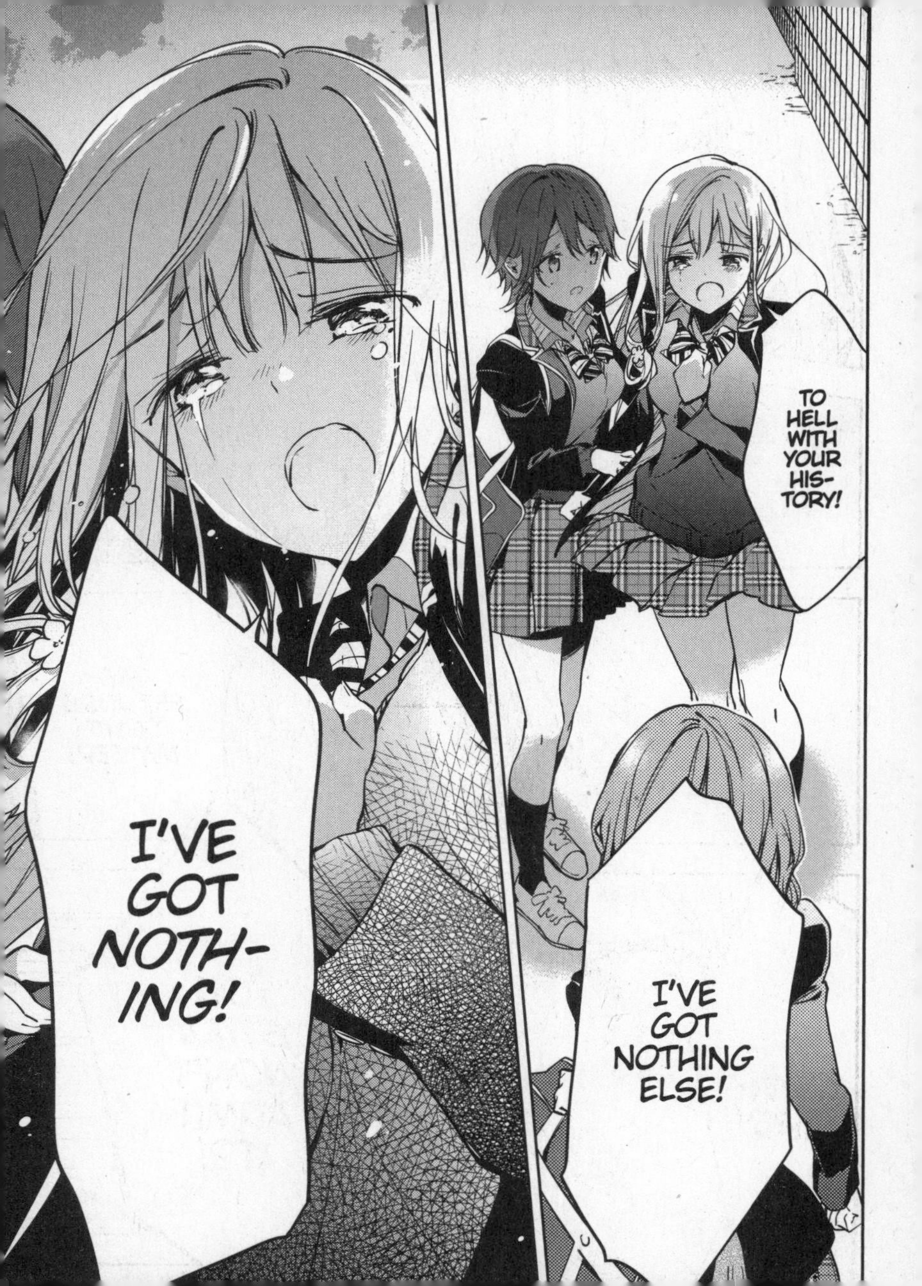
TO HELL WITH YOUR HIS-TORY!
I'VE GOT NOTHING ELSE!
I'VE GOT NOTH-ING!

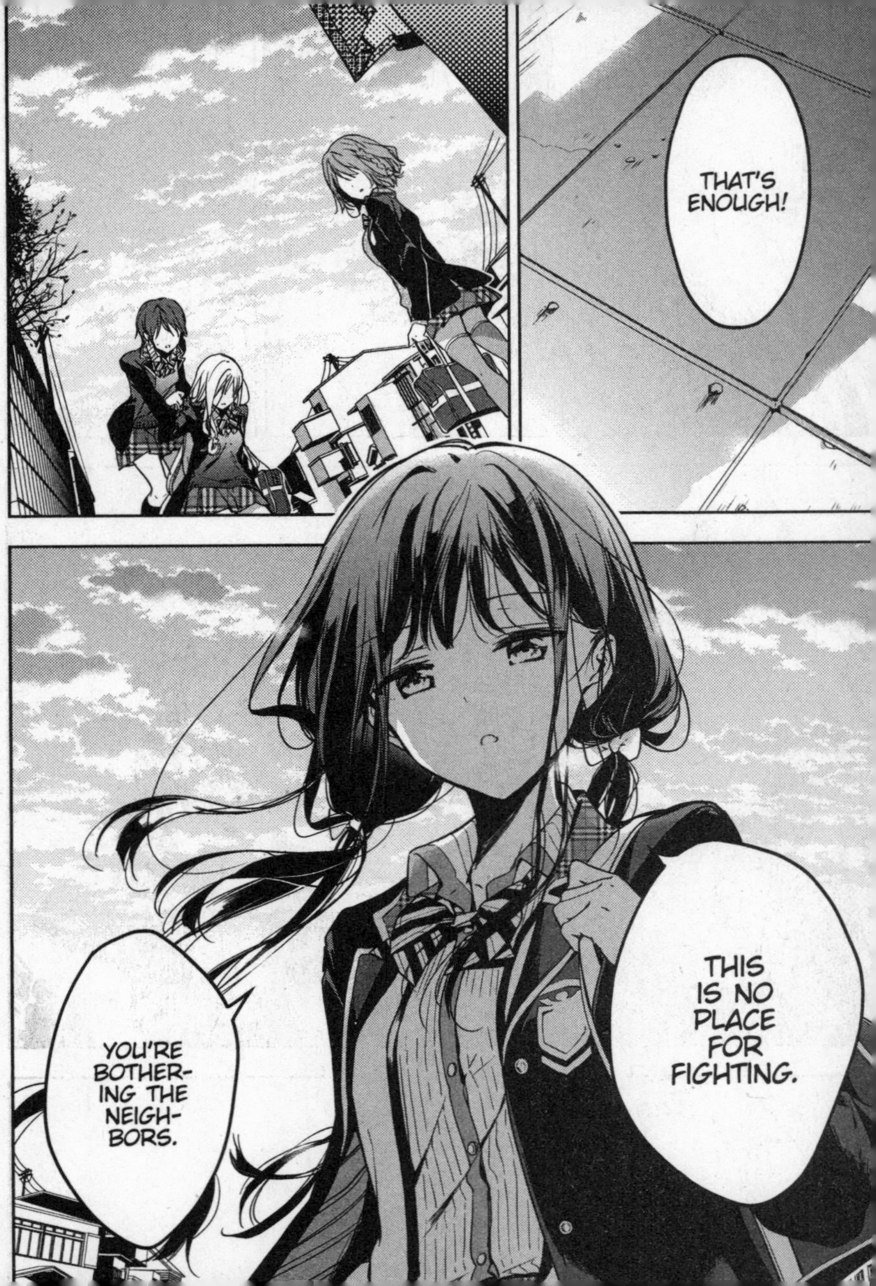
THAT'S ENOUGH!
THIS IS NO PLACE FOR FIGHTING.
YOU'RE BOTHER-ING THE NEIGH-BORS.

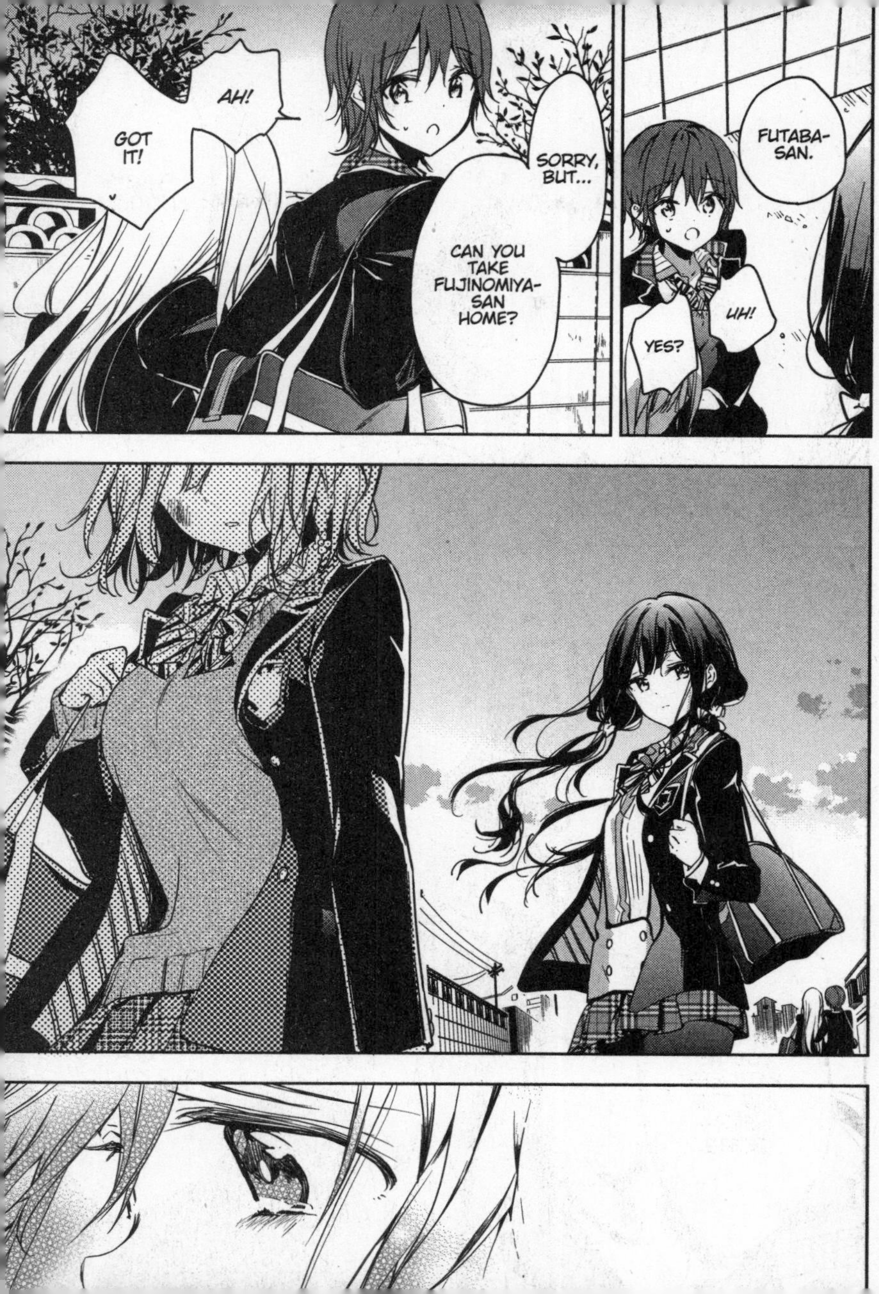
FUTABA-SAN.
UH!
YES?
SORRY, BUT...
CAN YOU TAKE FUJINOMIYA-SAN HOME?
AH!
GOT IT!

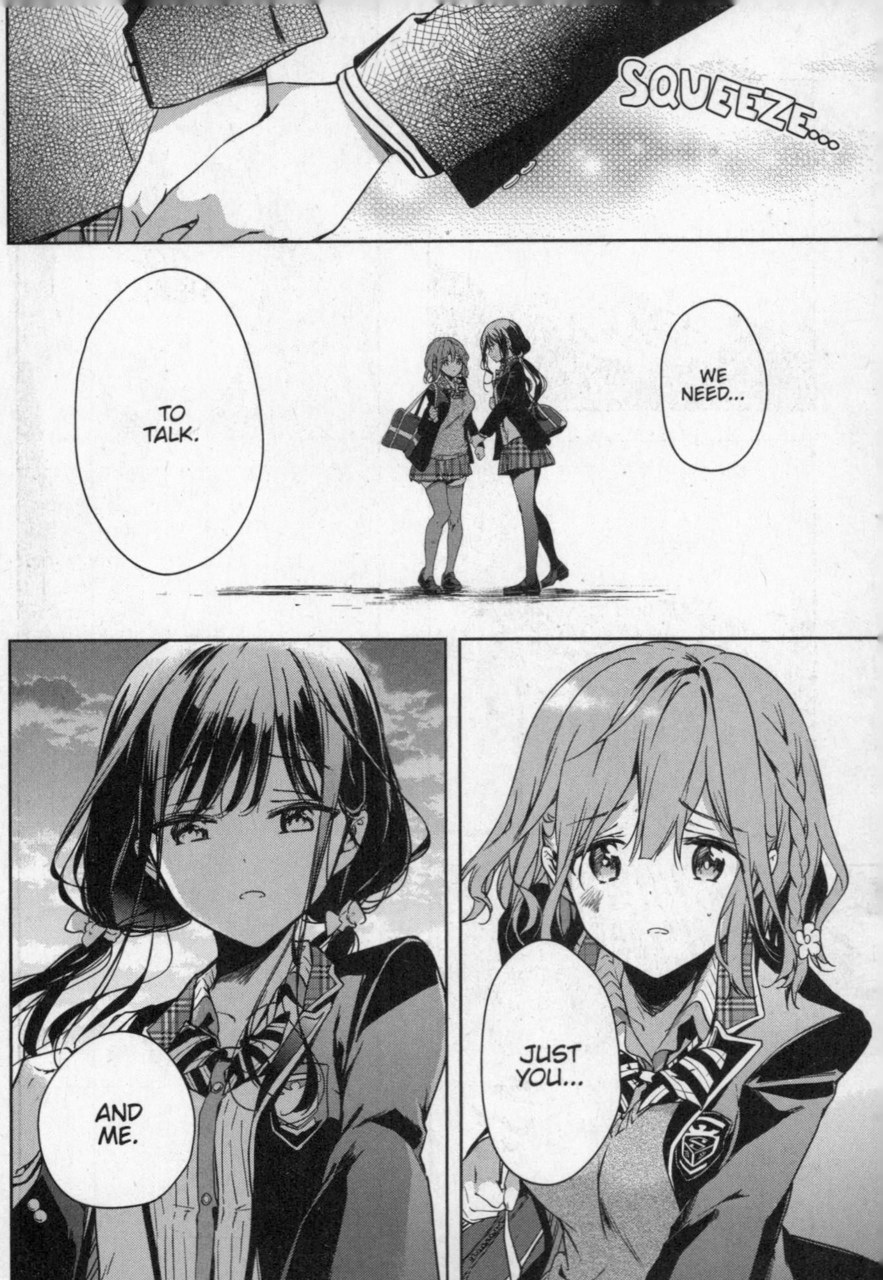
SQUEEZE...
WE NEED...
TO TALK.
JUST YOU...
AND ME.

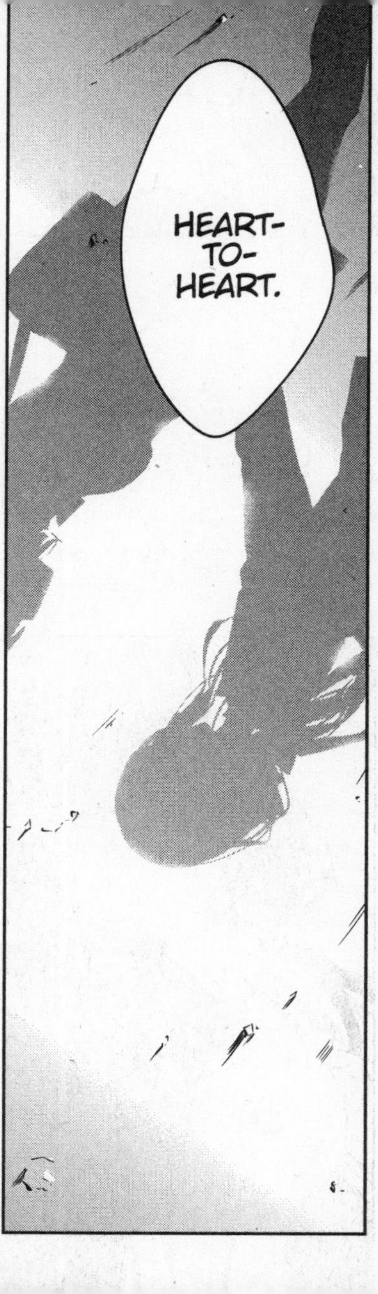
HEART-
TO-
HEART.
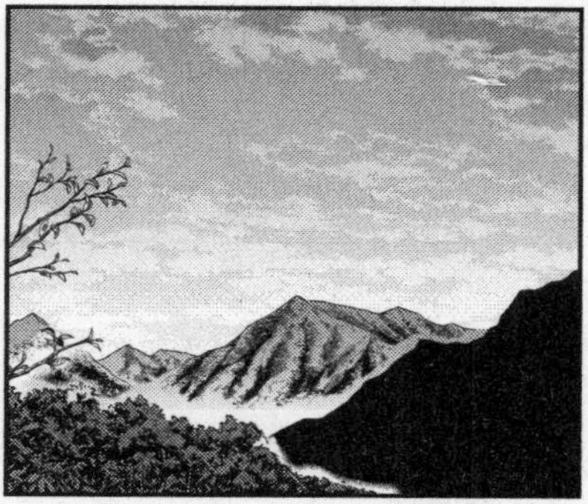
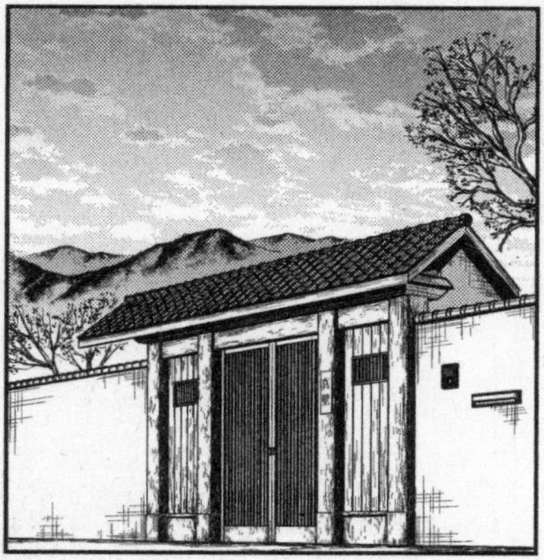
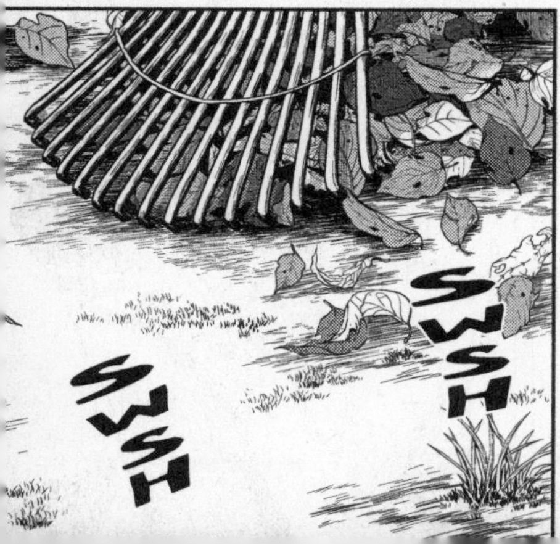
SWSH
SWSH

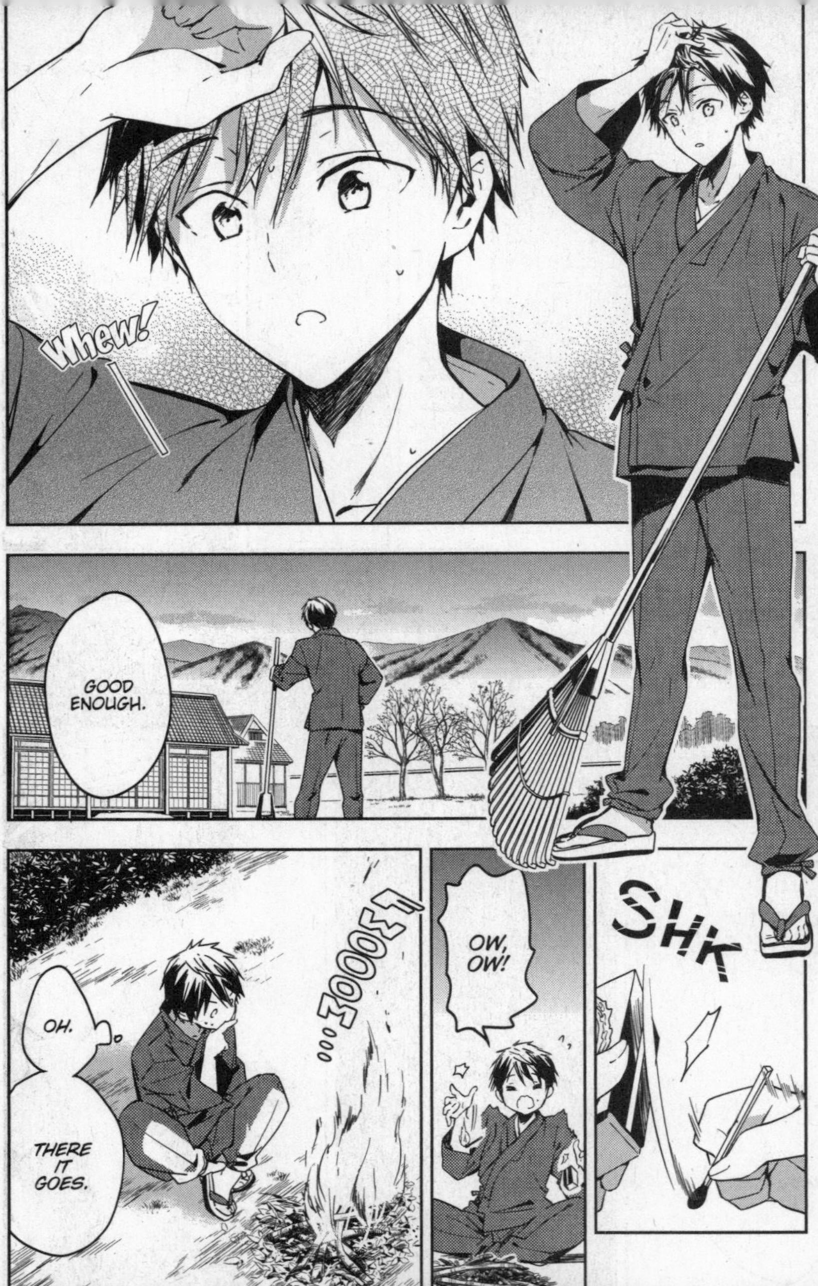
Whew!
GOOD ENOUGH.
SHK
OW, OW!
FWOOOM...
OH.
THERE IT GOES.

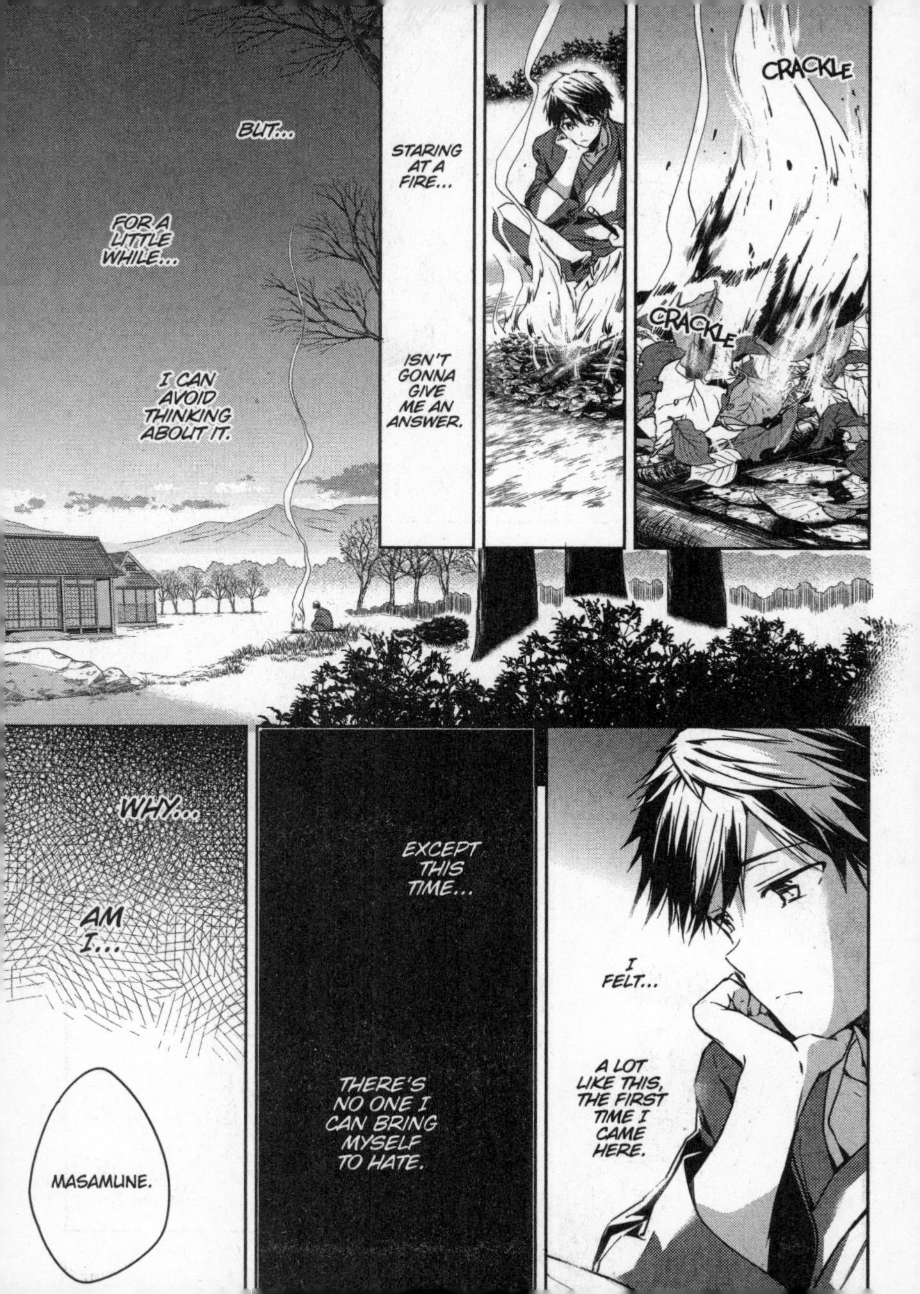
CRACKLE
CRACKLE
STARING AT A FIRE...
ISN'T GONNA GIVE ME AN ANSWER.
BUT...
FOR A LITTLE WHILE...
I CAN AVOID THINKING ABOUT IT.
I FELT...
A LOT LIKE THIS, THE FIRST TIME I CAME HERE.
EXCEPT THIS TIME...
THERE'S NO ONE I CAN BRING MYSELF TO HATE.
WHY...
AM I...
MASAMUNE.

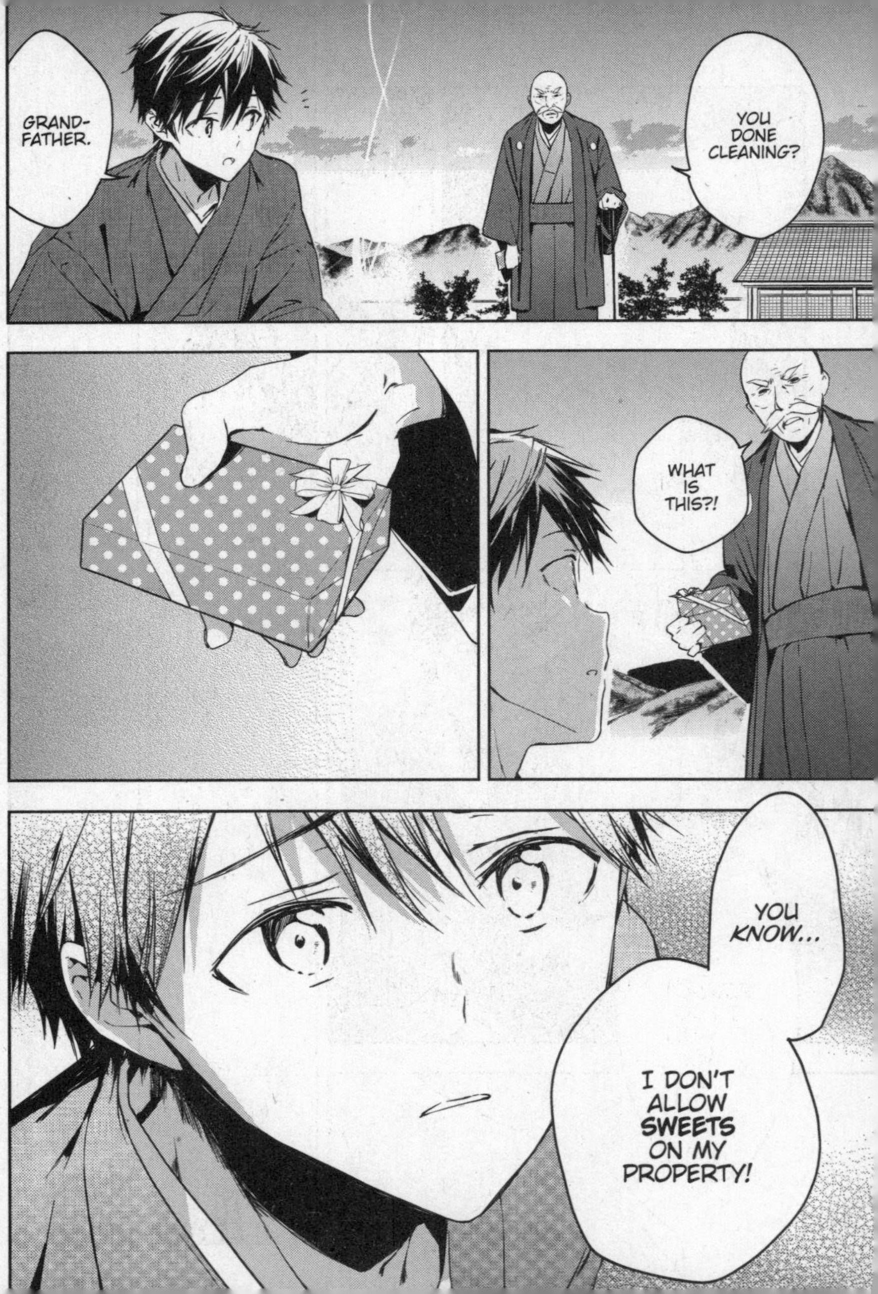
YOU DONE CLEANING?
GRAND-FATHER.
WHAT IS THIS?!
YOU KNOW...
I DON'T ALLOW SWEETS ON MY PROPERTY!

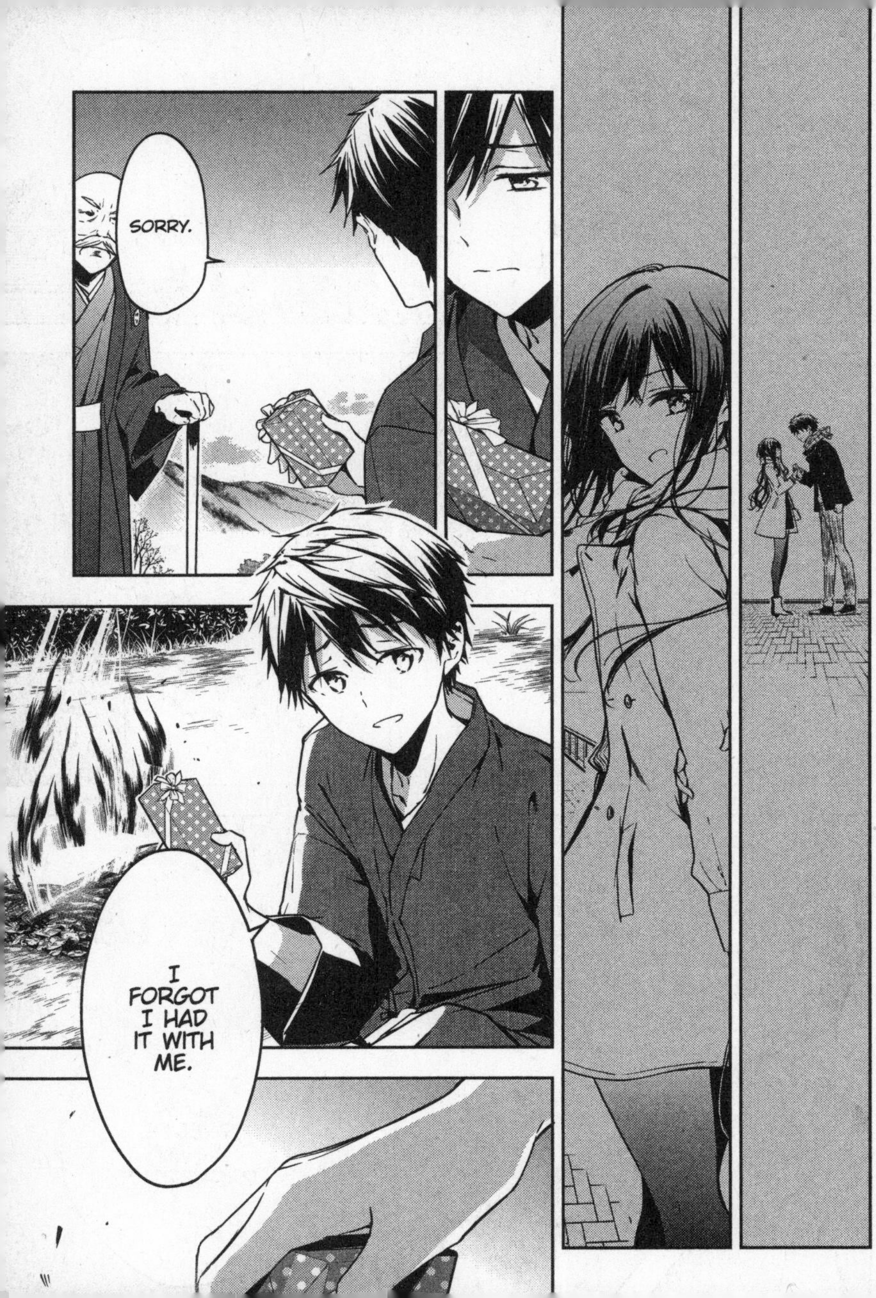
SORRY.
I FORGOT I HAD IT WITH ME.

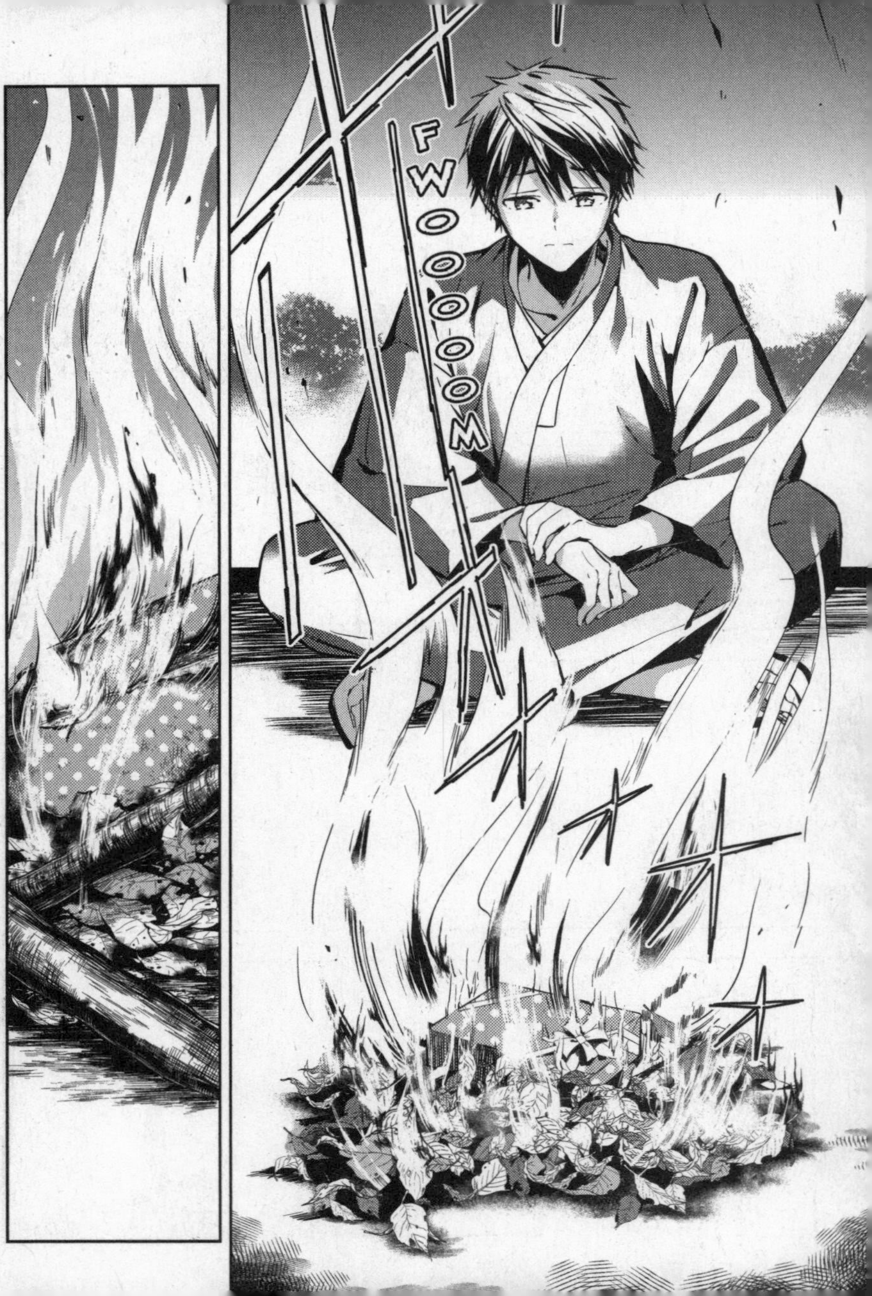
FWOOOOOOM

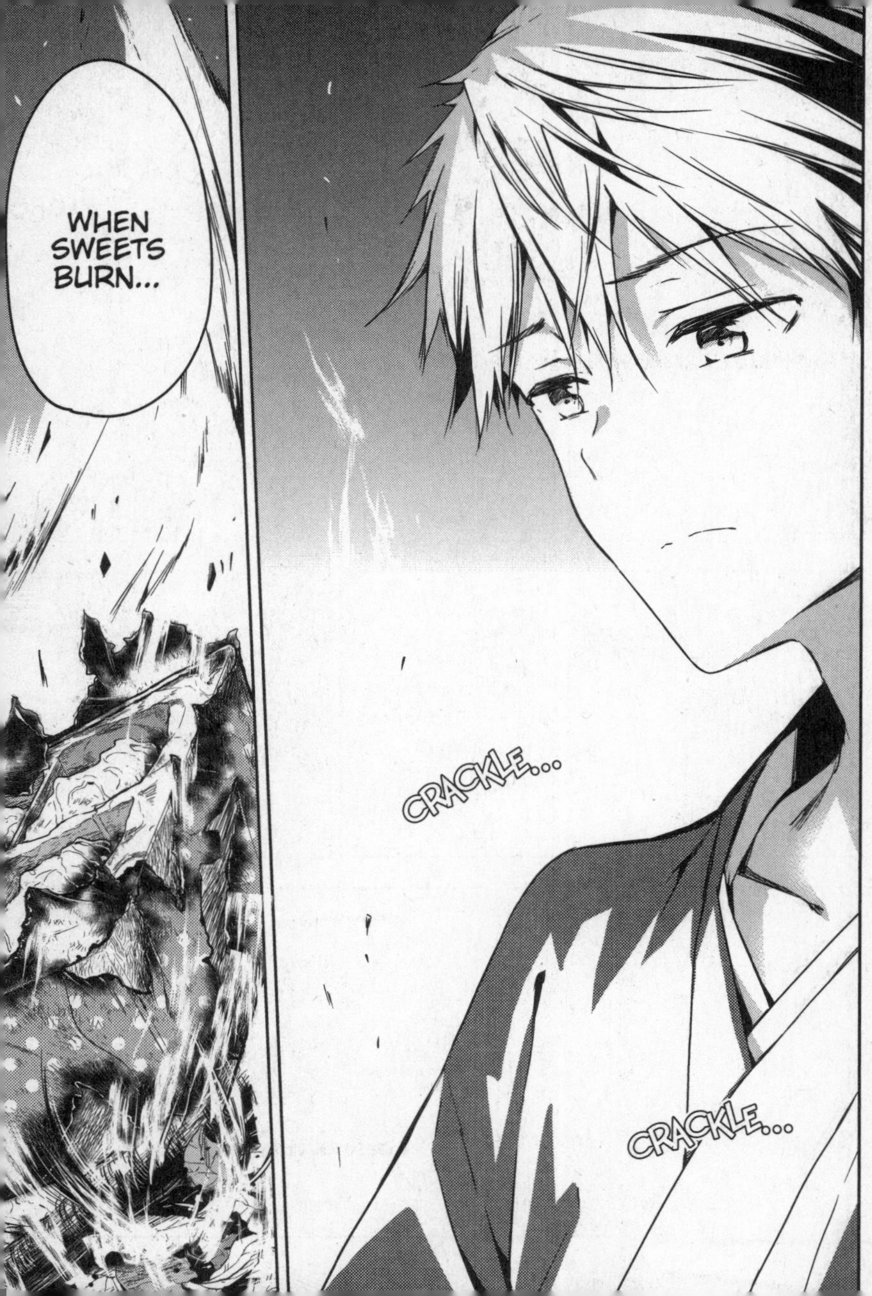
CRACKLE...
CRACKLE...
WHEN SWEETS BURN...

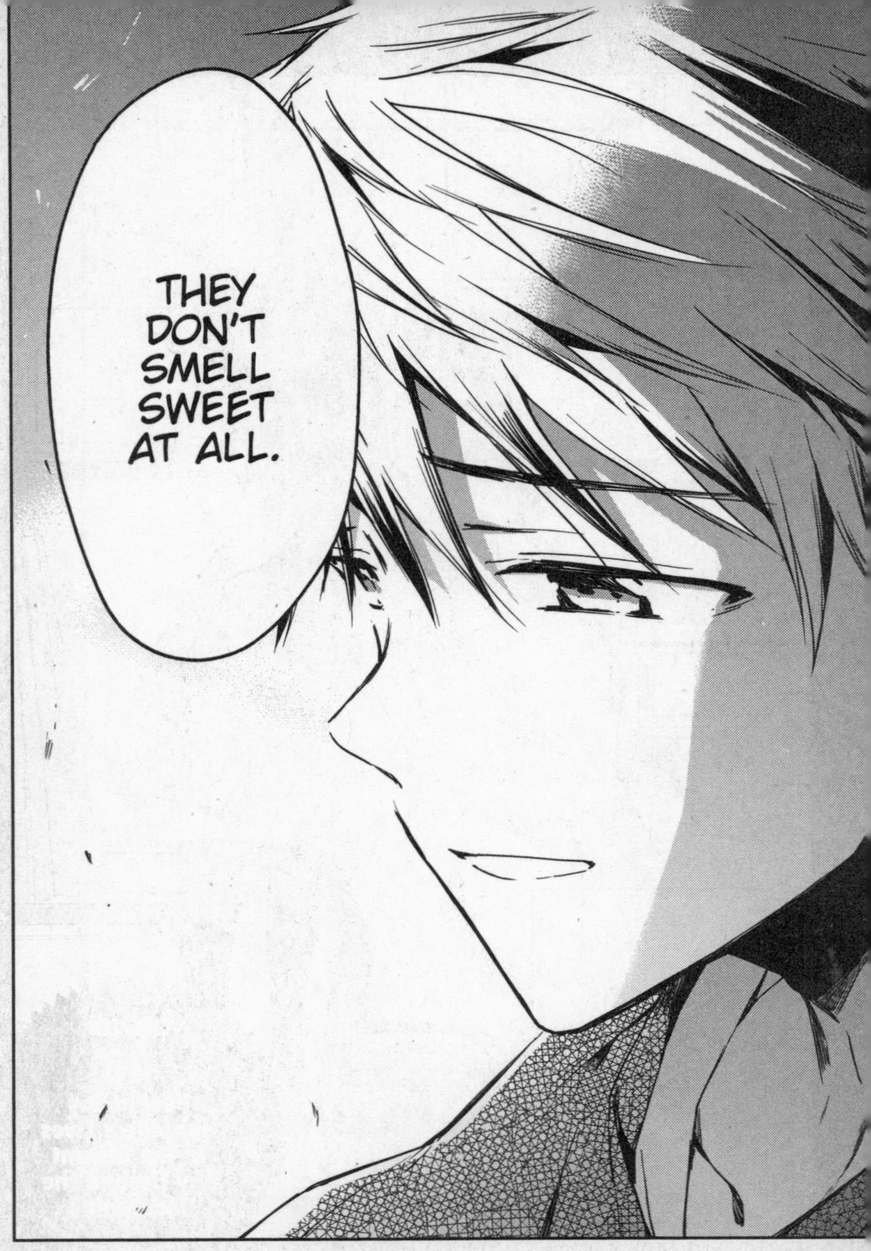
THEY DON'T SMELL SWEET AT ALL.

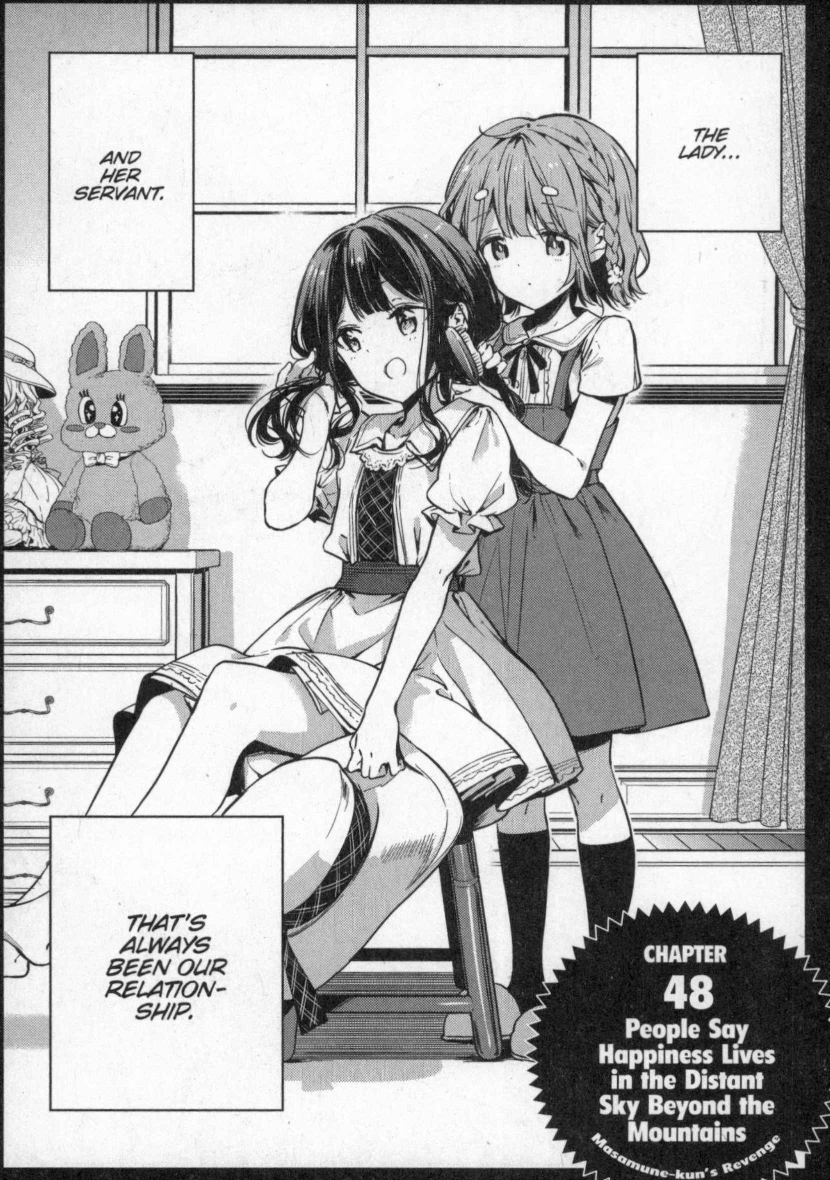
THE LADY...
AND HER SERVANT.
THAT'S ALWAYS BEEN OUR RELATION-SHIP.
CHAPTER 48
People Say Happiness Lives in the Distant Sky Beyond the Mountains
Masamune-kun's Revenge

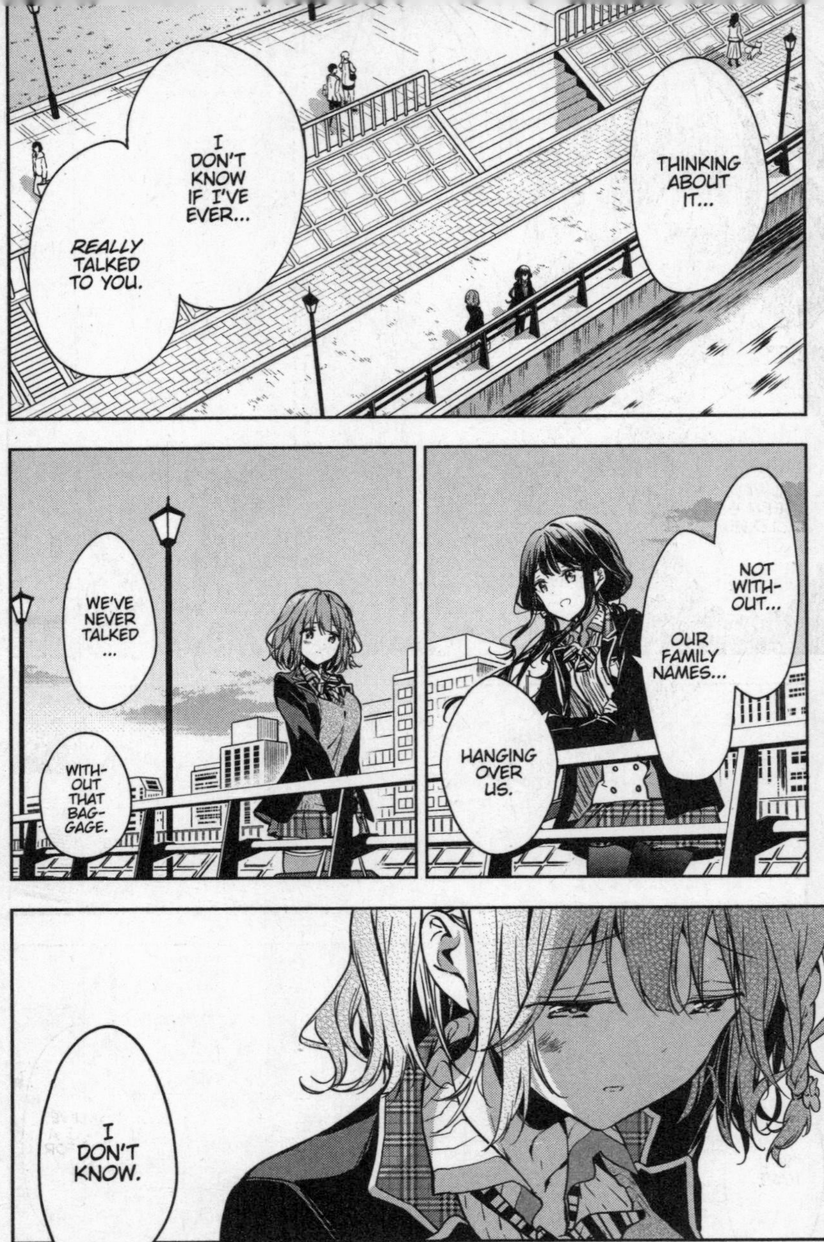
THINKING ABOUT IT...
I DON'T KNOW IF I'VE EVER...
*REALLY* TALKED TO YOU.
NOT WITH-OUT...
OUR FAMILY NAMES...
HANGING OVER US.
WE'VE NEVER TALKED...
WITH-OUT THAT BAG-GAGE.
I DON'T KNOW.

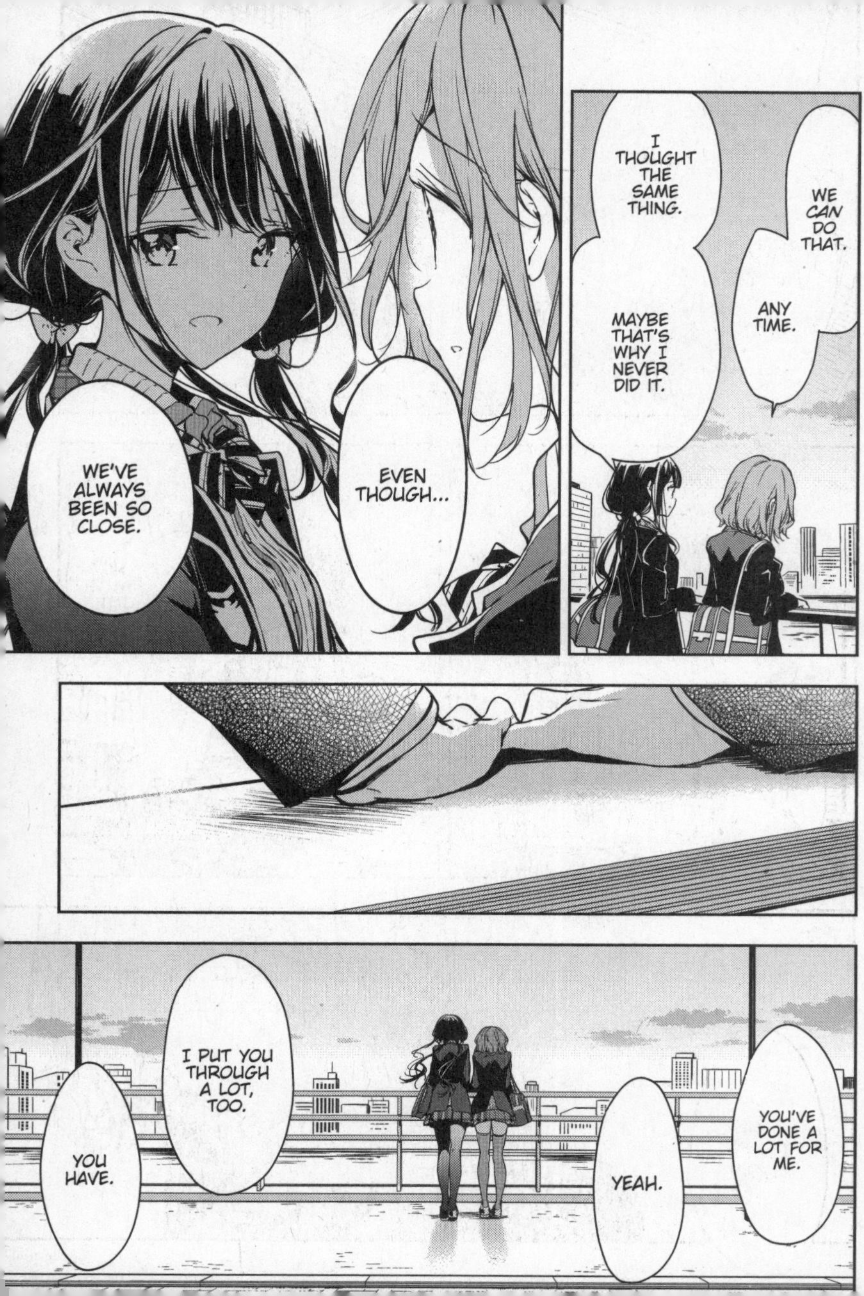
WE CAN DO THAT.
ANY TIME.
I THOUGHT THE SAME THING.
MAYBE THAT'S WHY I NEVER DID IT.
EVEN THOUGH...
WE'VE ALWAYS BEEN SO CLOSE.
YOU'VE DONE A LOT FOR ME.
YEAH.
I PUT YOU THROUGH A LOT, TOO.
YOU HAVE.

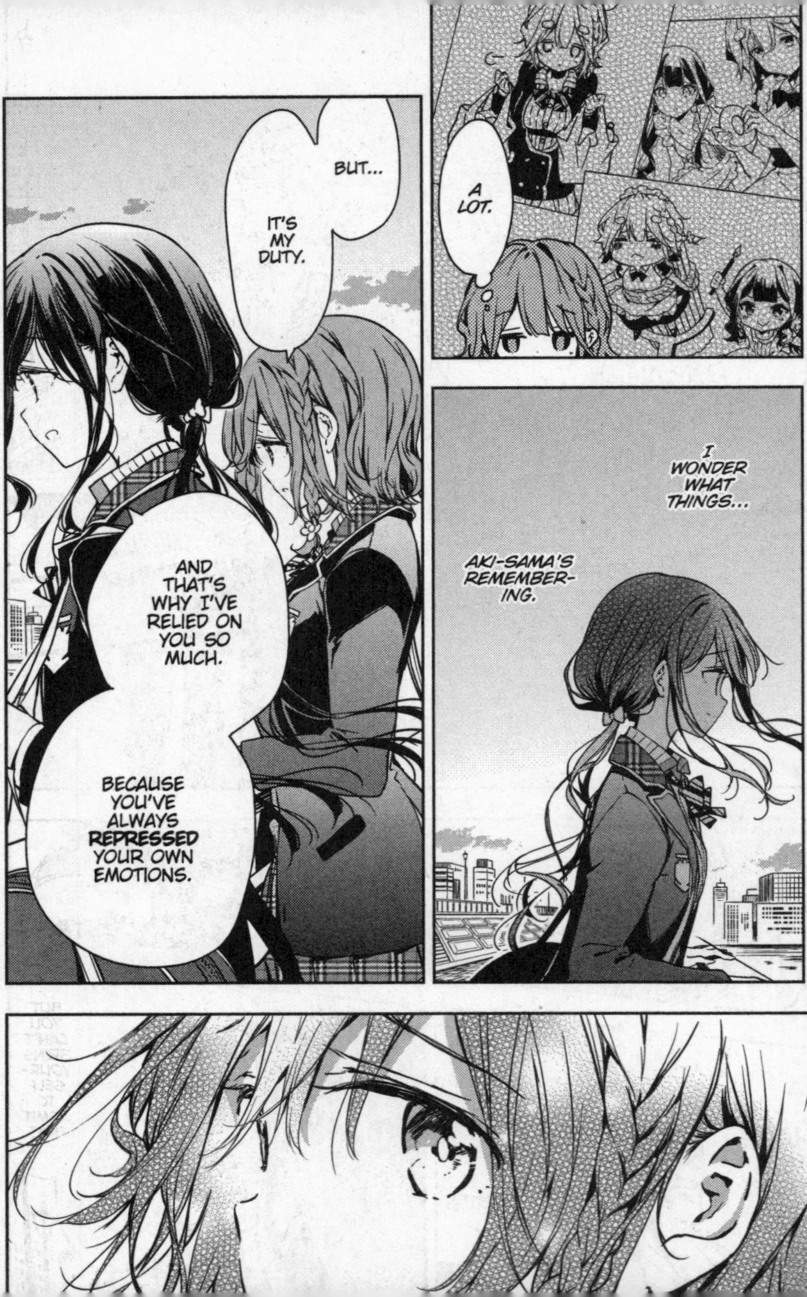
A LOT.
I WONDER WHAT THINGS...
AKI-SAMA'S REMEMBERING.
BUT...
IT'S MY DUTY.
AND THAT'S WHY I'VE RELIED ON YOU SO MUCH.
BECAUSE YOU'VE ALWAYS **REPRESSED** YOUR OWN EMOTIONS.

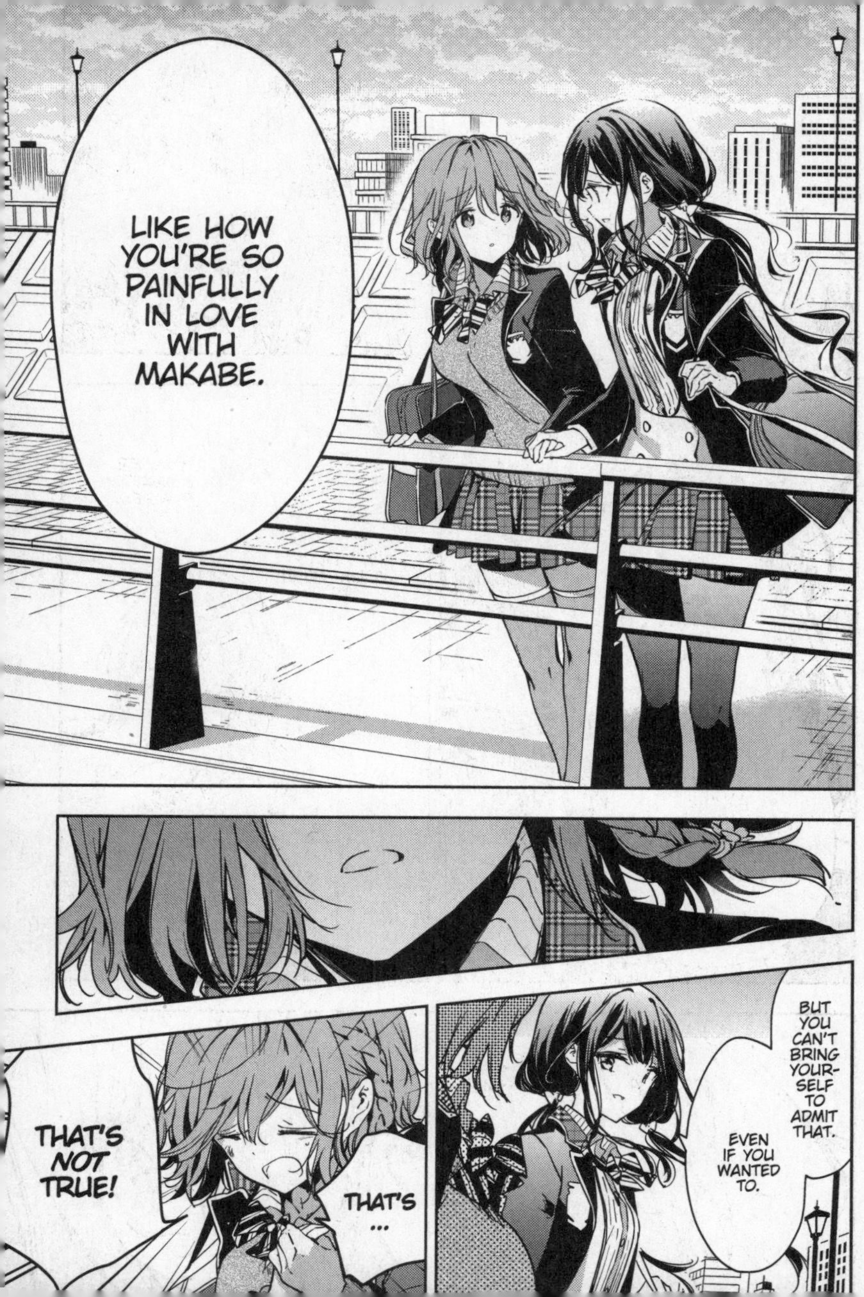
LIKE HOW YOU'RE SO PAINFULLY IN LOVE WITH MAKABE.
BUT YOU CAN'T BRING YOUR-SELF TO ADMIT THAT.
EVEN IF YOU WANTED TO.
THAT'S ...
THAT'S *NOT* TRUE!

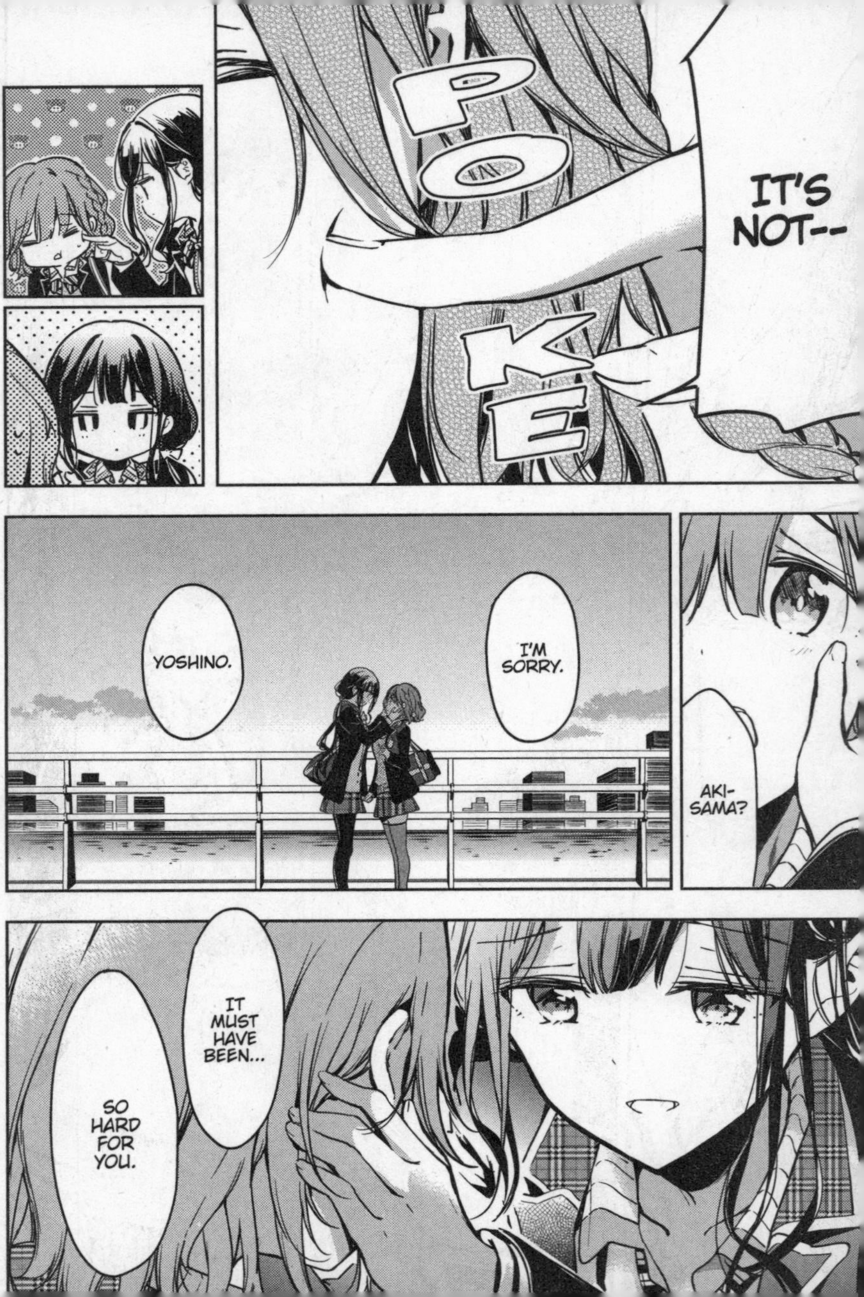
IT'S NOT--
POKE
AKI-SAMA?
I'M SORRY.
YOSHINO.
IT MUST HAVE BEEN...
SO HARD FOR YOU.

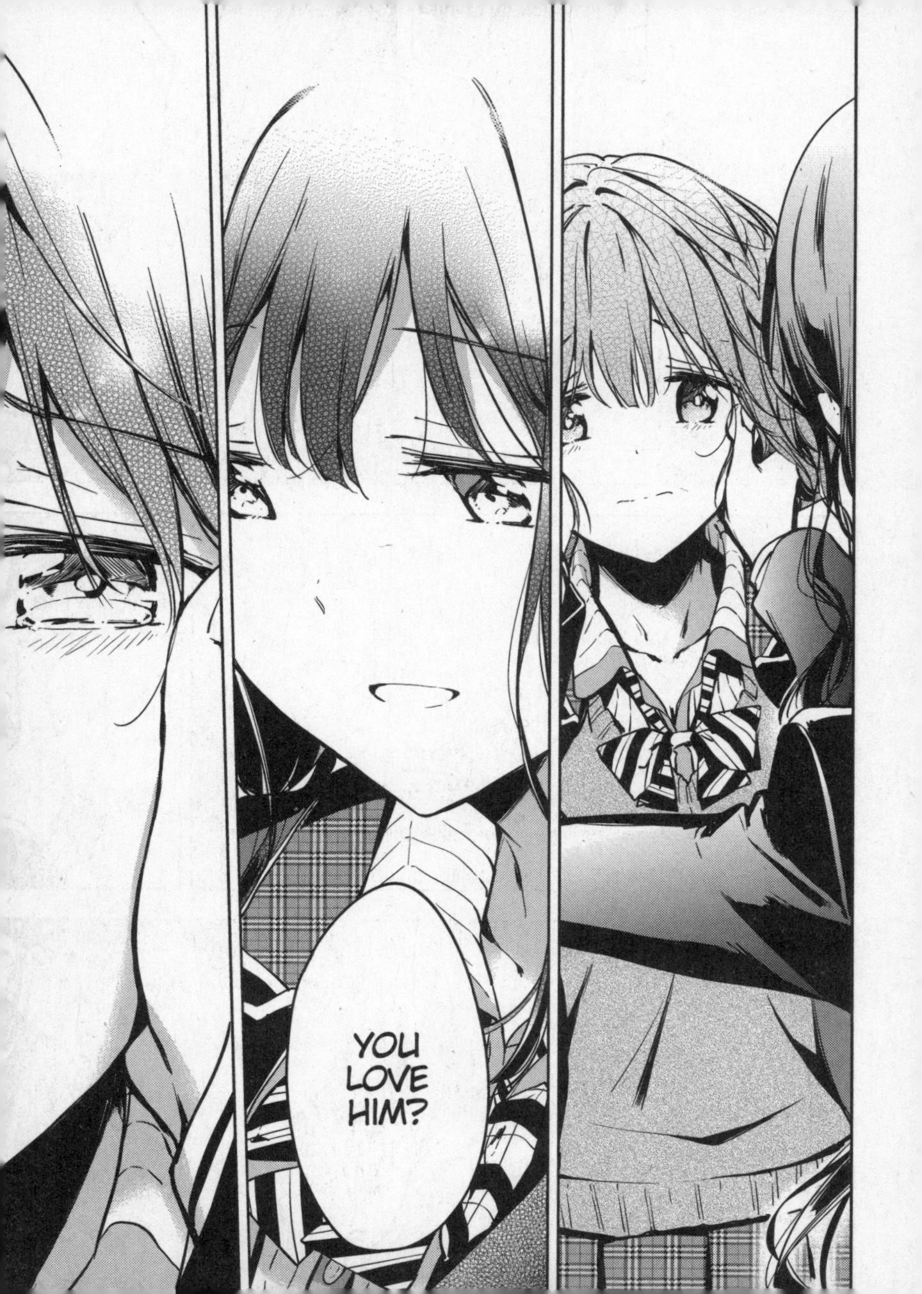
YOU LOVE HIM?

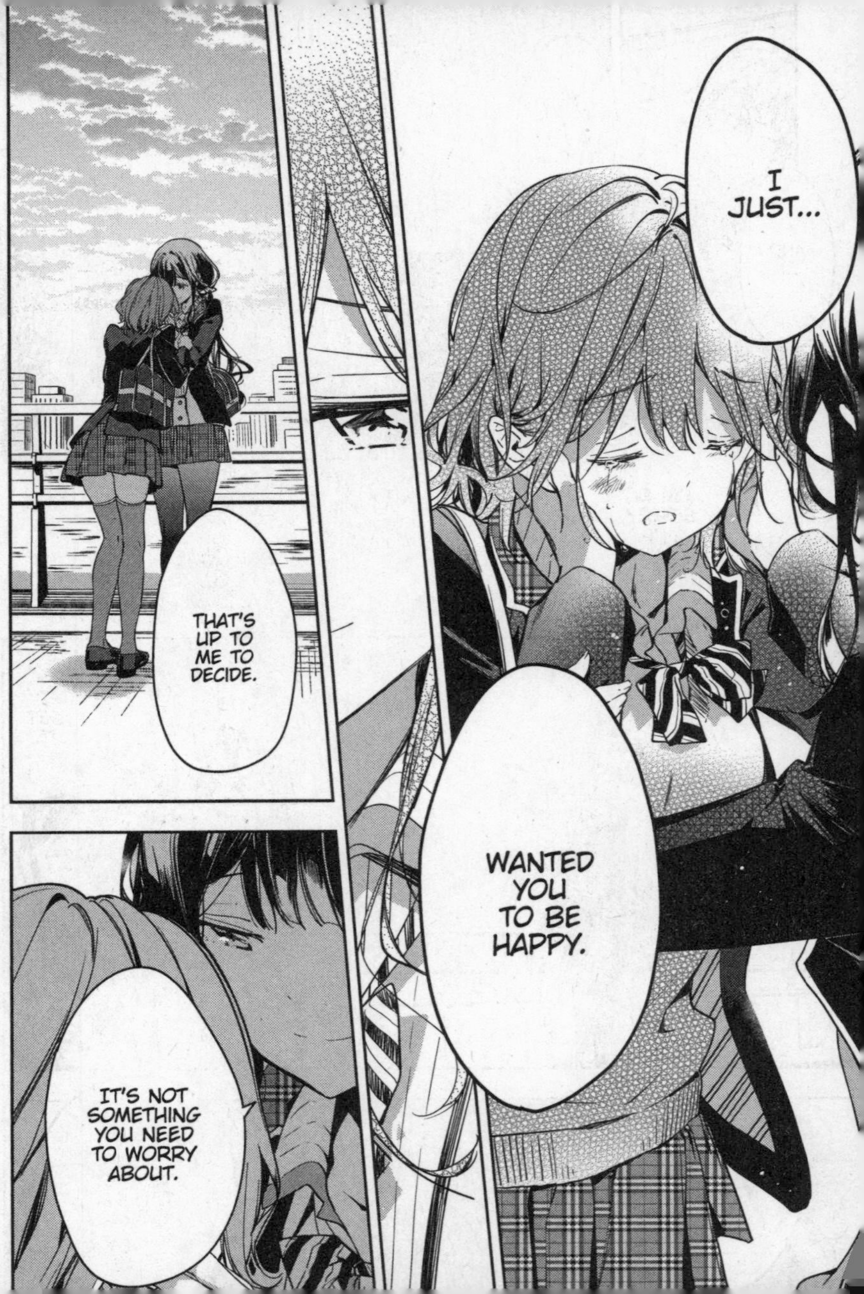
I JUST...
WANTED YOU TO BE HAPPY.
THAT'S UP TO ME TO DECIDE.
IT'S NOT SOMETHING YOU NEED TO WORRY ABOUT.

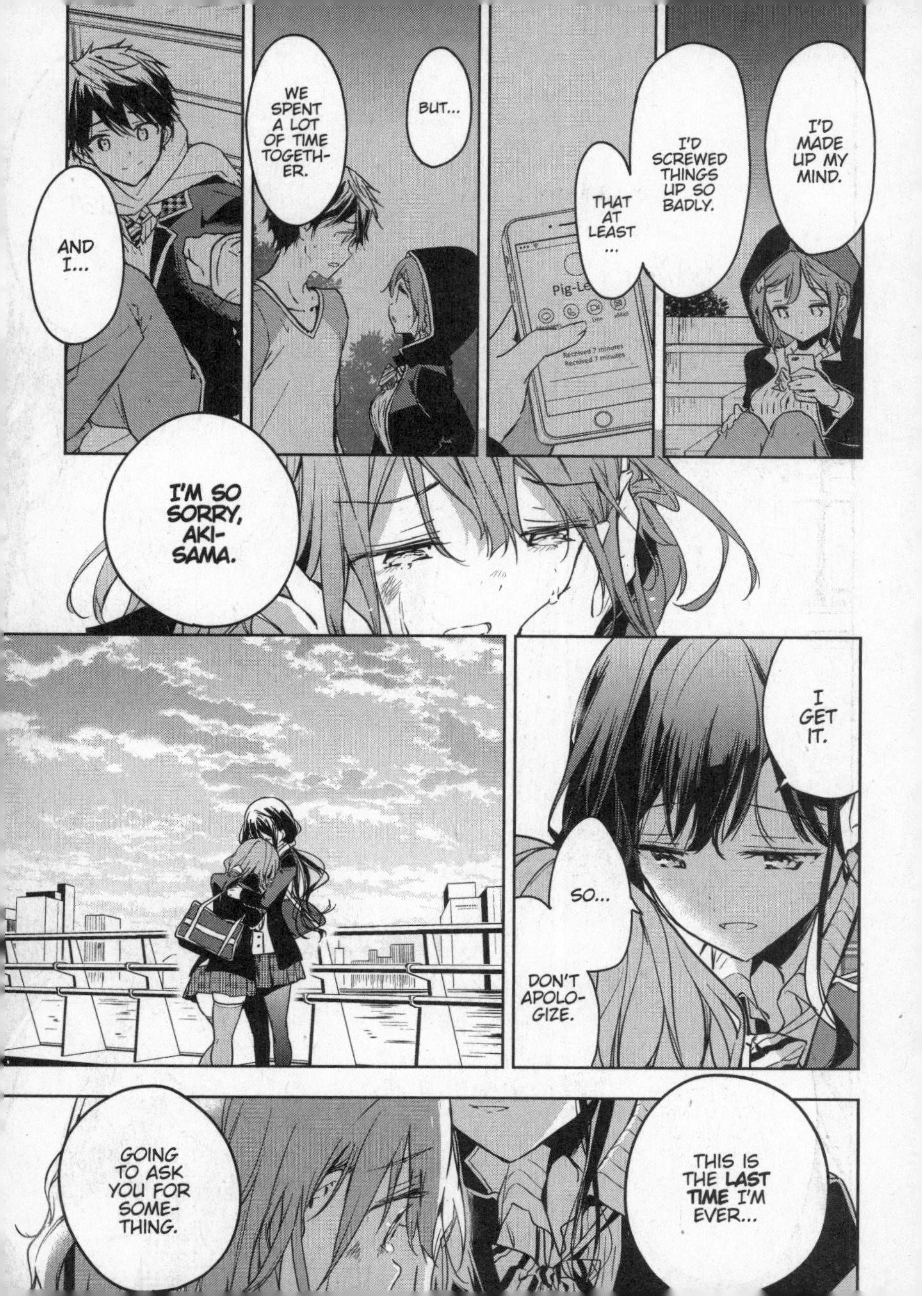
I'D MADE UP MY MIND.
I'D SCREWED THINGS UP SO BADLY.
THAT AT LEAST ...
WE SPENT A LOT OF TIME TOGETH-ER.
BUT...
AND I...
I'M SO SORRY, AKI-SAMA.
I GET IT.
SO...
DON'T APOLO-GIZE.
THIS IS THE LAST TIME I'M EVER...
GOING TO ASK YOU FOR SOME-THING.

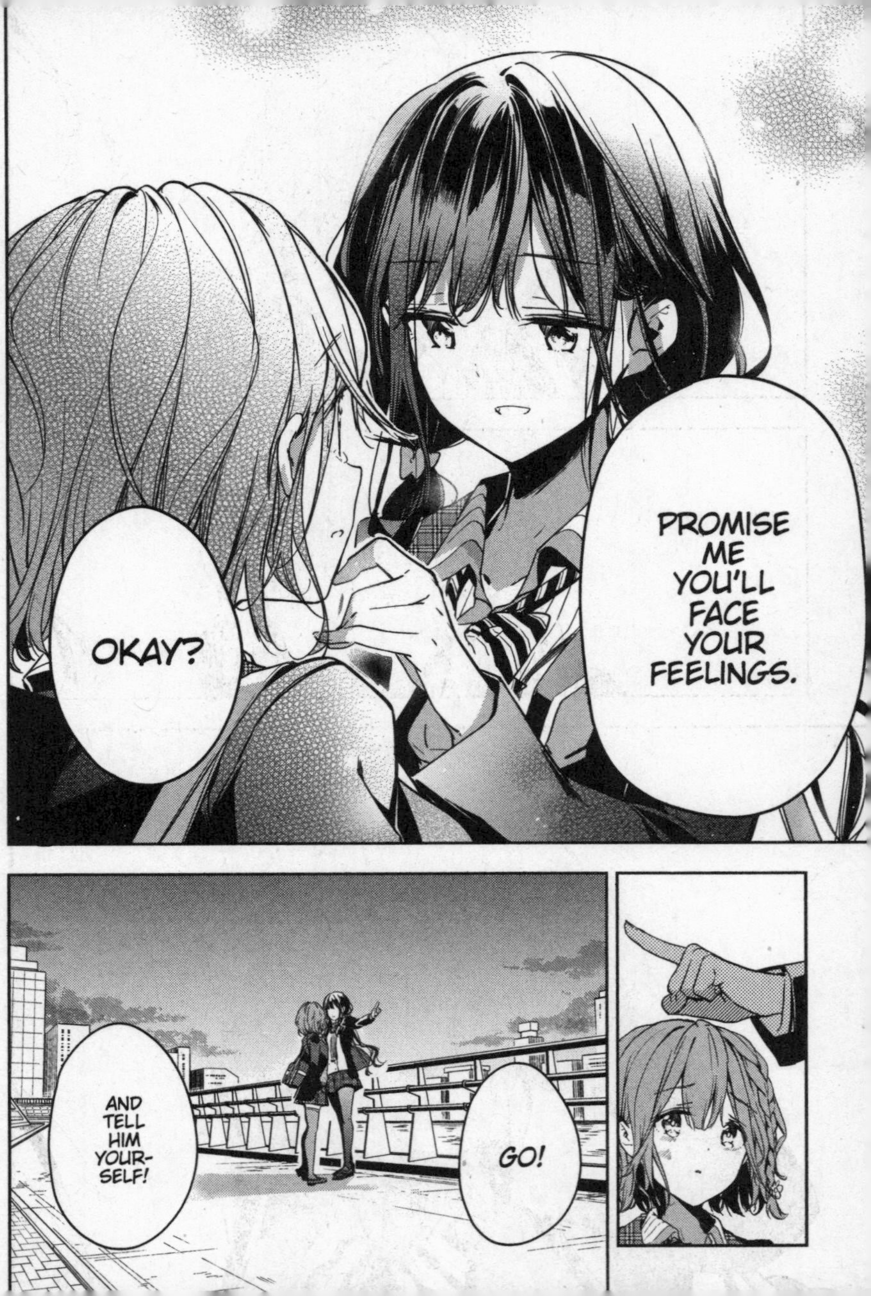
PROMISE ME YOU'LL FACE YOUR FEELINGS.
OKAY?
GO!
AND TELL HIM YOUR-SELF!

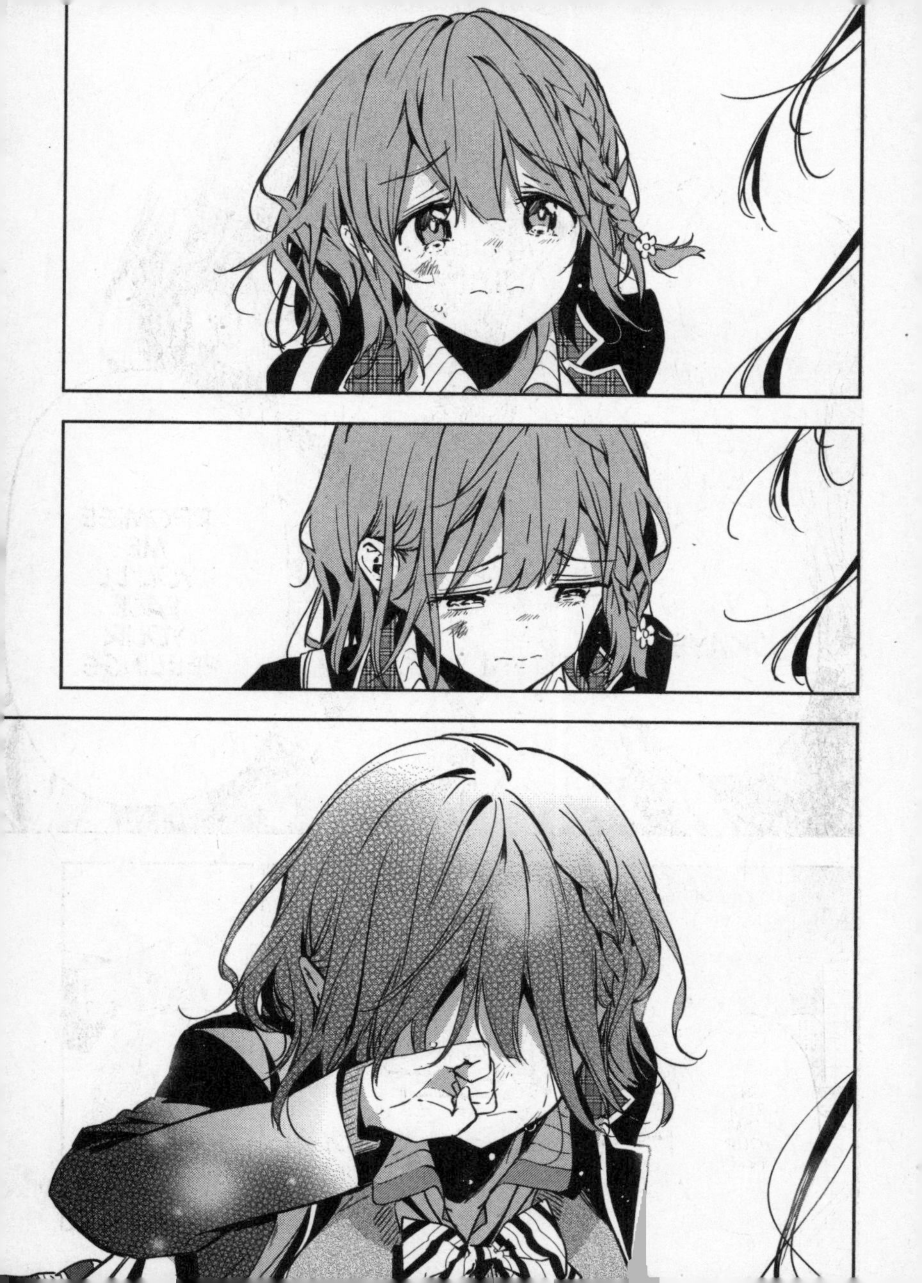

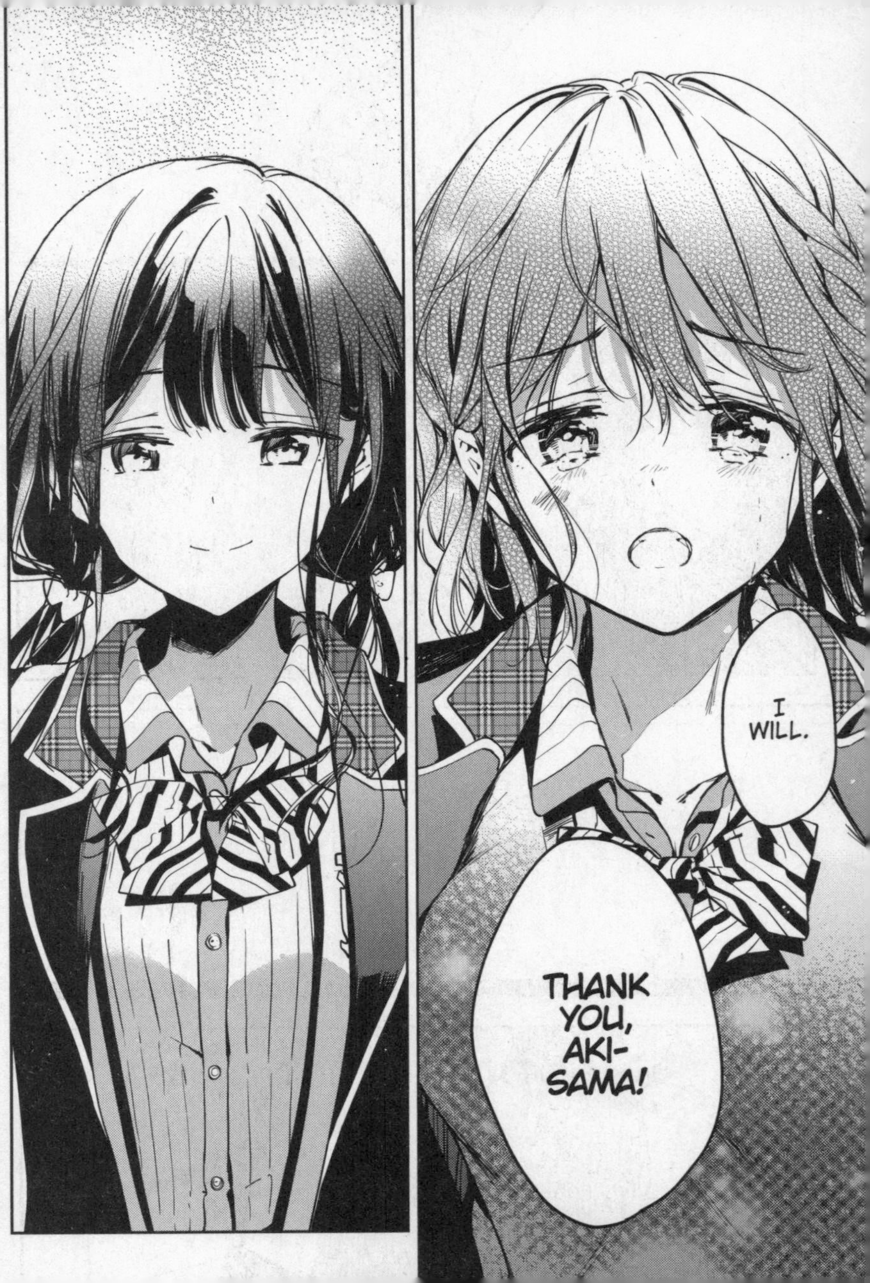
I WILL.
THANK YOU, AKI-SAMA!

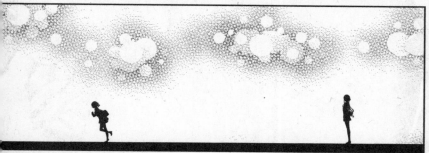

THE
NEXT
TIME WE
MEET...

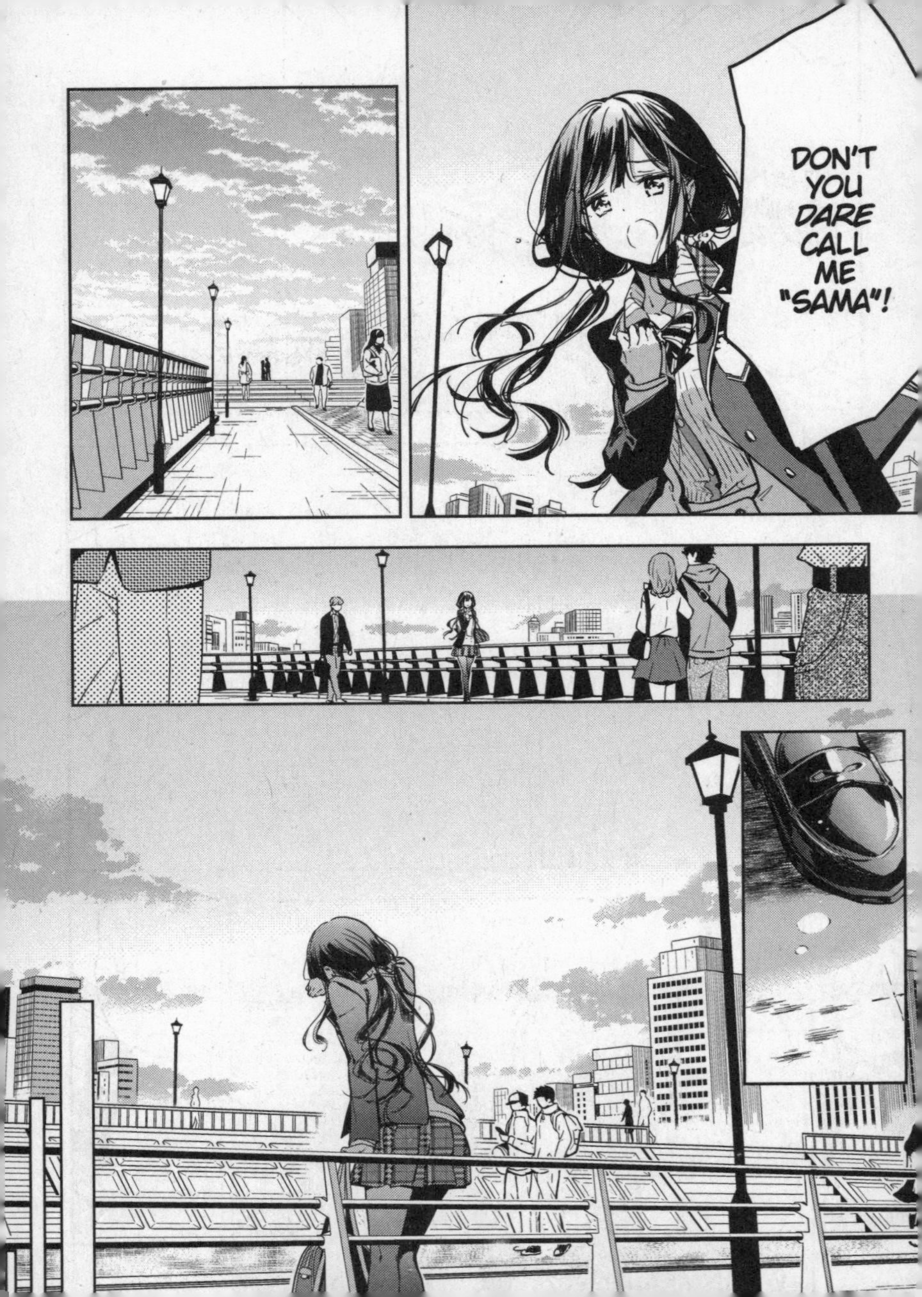
DON'T YOU DARE CALL ME "SAMA"!

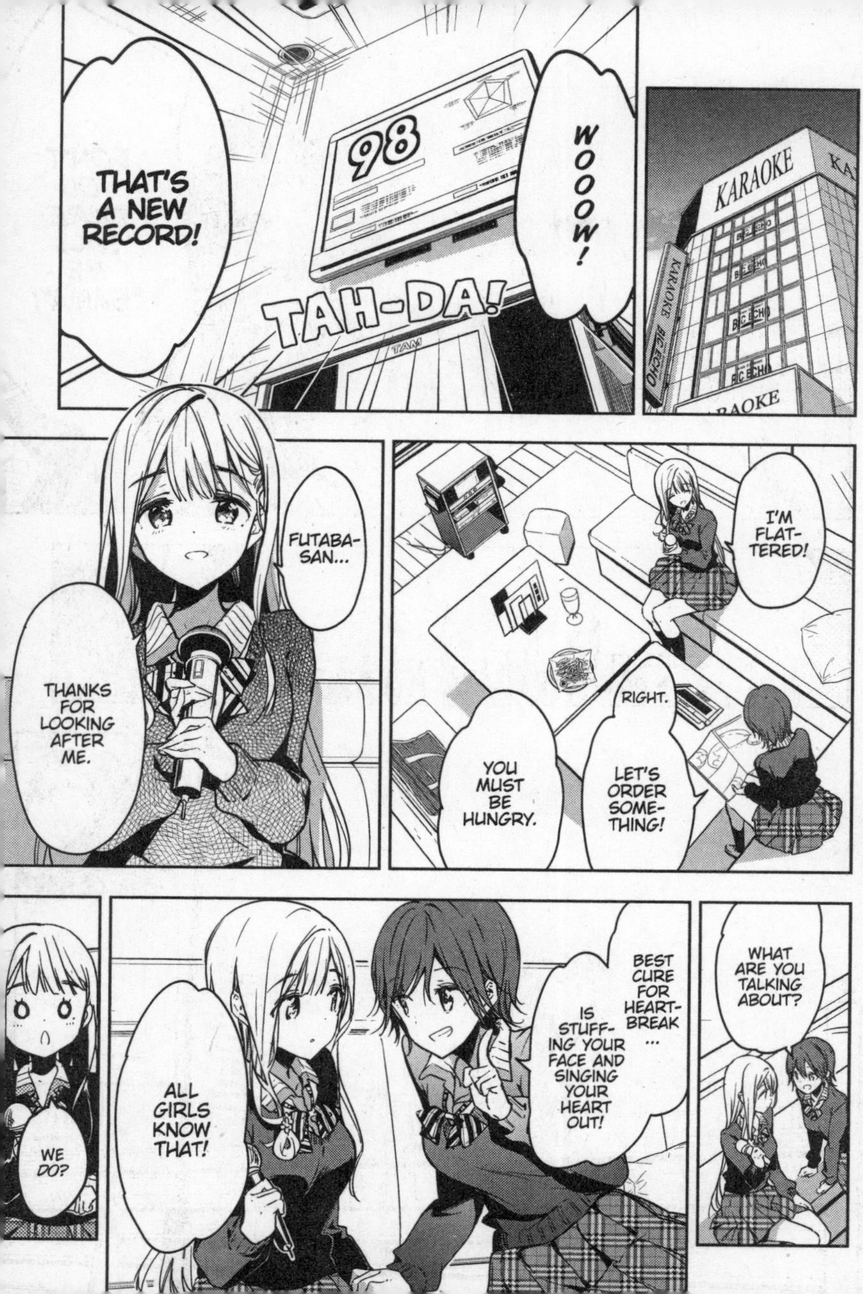
KARAOKE
KARAOKE BIG ECHO
BIG ECHO
KARAOKE
WOOOW!
98
TAH-DA!
THAT'S A NEW RECORD!
I'M FLAT-TERED!
RIGHT.
LET'S ORDER SOME-THING!
YOU MUST BE HUNGRY.
FUTABA-SAN...
THANKS FOR LOOKING AFTER ME.
WHAT ARE YOU TALKING ABOUT?
BEST CURE FOR HEART-BREAK ...
IS STUFF-ING YOUR FACE AND SINGING YOUR HEART OUT!
ALL GIRLS KNOW THAT!
WE DO?

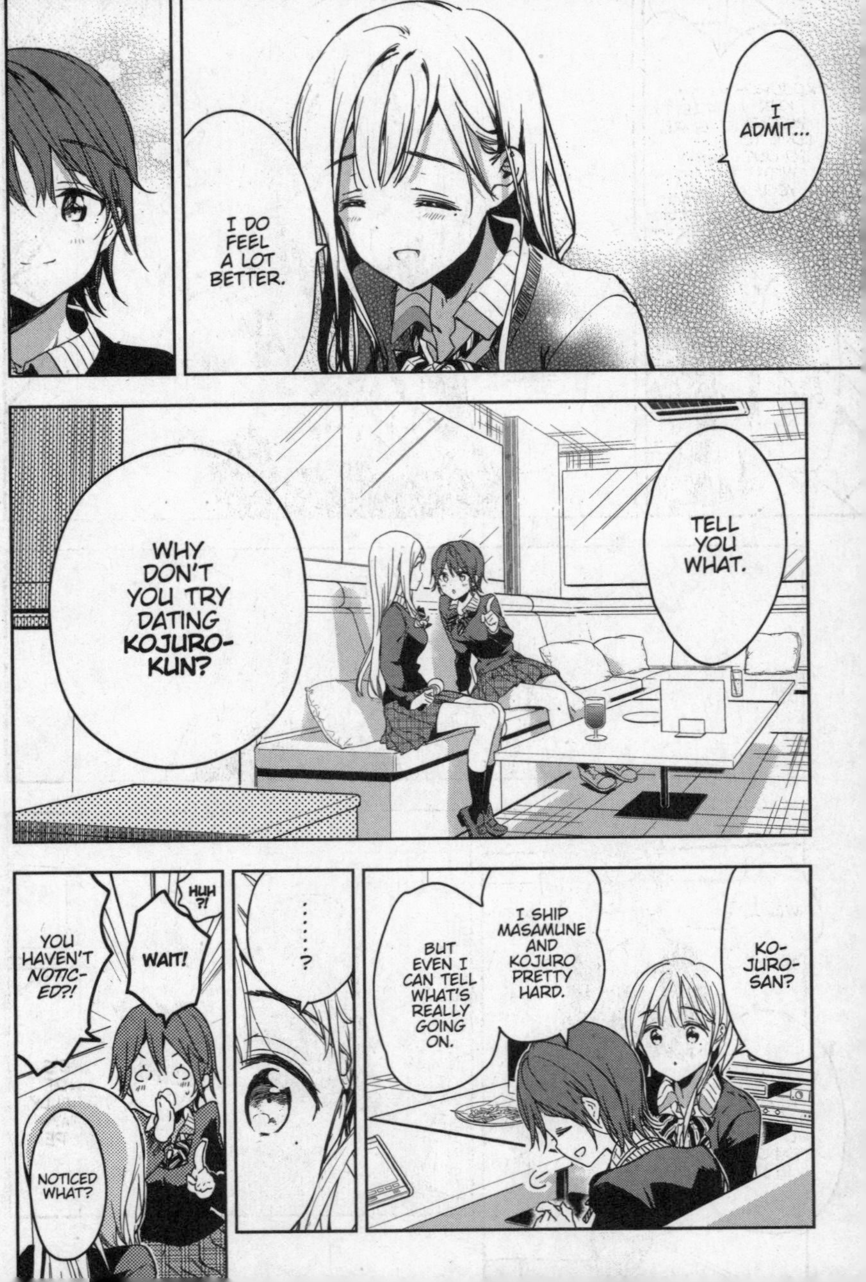
I ADMIT...
I DO FEEL A LOT BETTER.
TELL YOU WHAT.
WHY DON'T YOU TRY DATING KOJURO-KUN?
KO-JURO-SAN?
I SHIP MASAMUNE AND KOJURO PRETTY HARD.
BUT EVEN I CAN TELL WHAT'S REALLY GOING ON.
......?
HUH?!
WAIT!
YOU HAVEN'T NOTIC-ED?!
NOTICED WHAT?

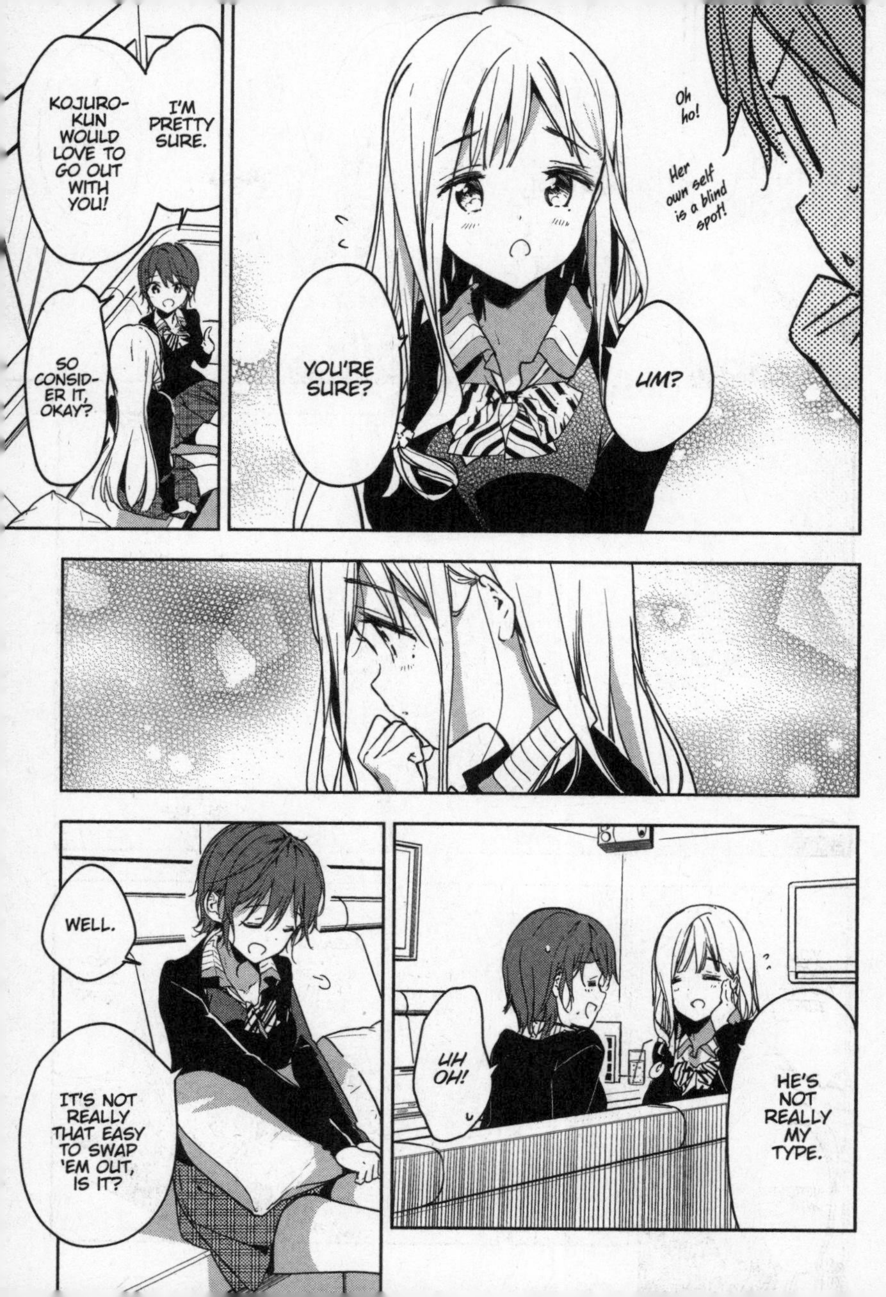
Oh ho! Her own self is a blind spot!
UM?
YOU'RE SURE?
I'M PRETTY SURE.
KOJURO-KUN WOULD LOVE TO GO OUT WITH YOU!
SO CONSIDER IT, OKAY?
HE'S NOT REALLY MY TYPE.
UH OH!
WELL.
IT'S NOT REALLY THAT EASY TO SWAP 'EM OUT, IS IT?

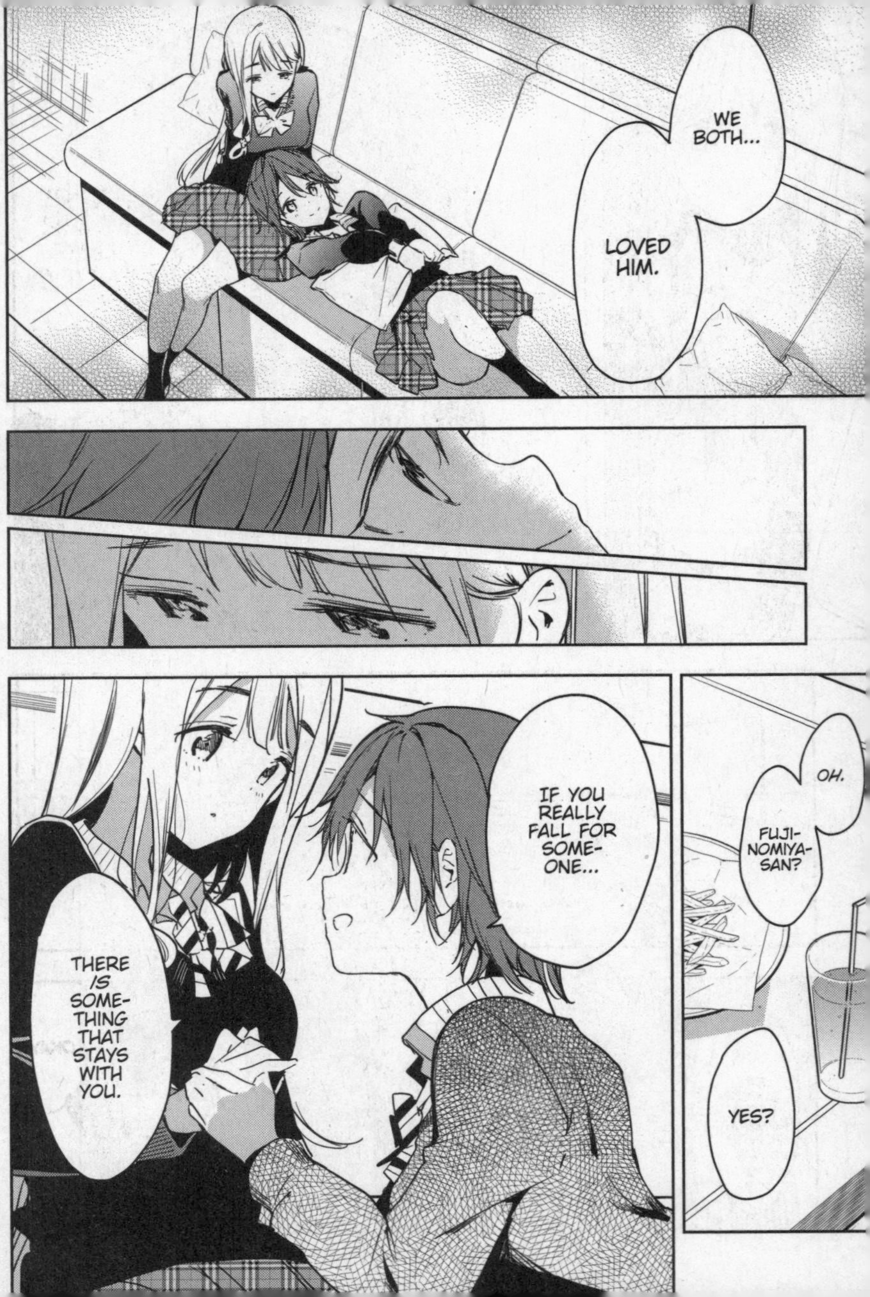
WE BOTH...
LOVED HIM.
OH.
FUJI-NOMIYA-SAN?
YES?
IF YOU REALLY FALL FOR SOME-ONE...
THERE IS SOME-THING THAT STAYS WITH YOU.

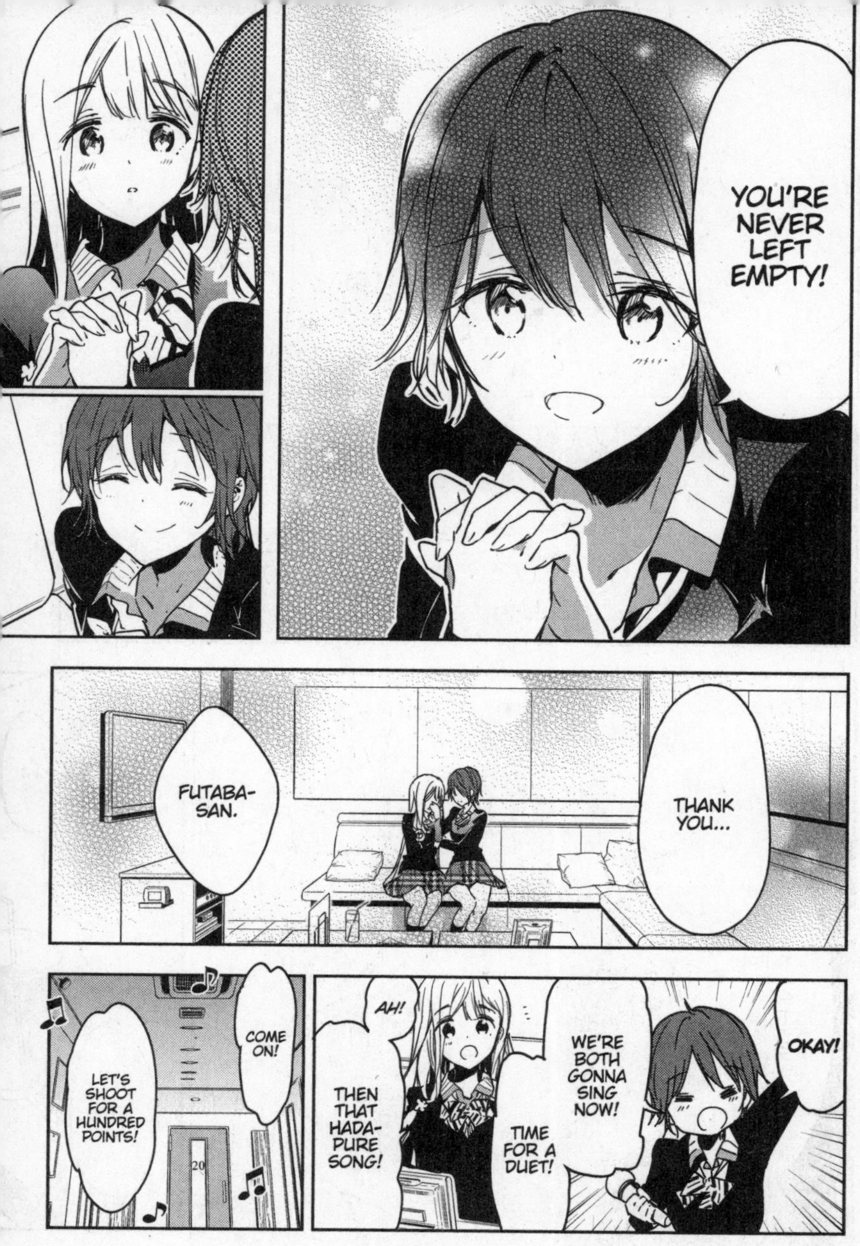

YOU'RE NEVER LEFT EMPTY!
THANK YOU...
FUTABA-SAN.
OKAY!
WE'RE BOTH GONNA SING NOW!
TIME FOR A DUET!
AH!
THEN THAT HADA-PURE SONG!
COME ON!
LET'S SHOOT FOR A HUNDRED POINTS!

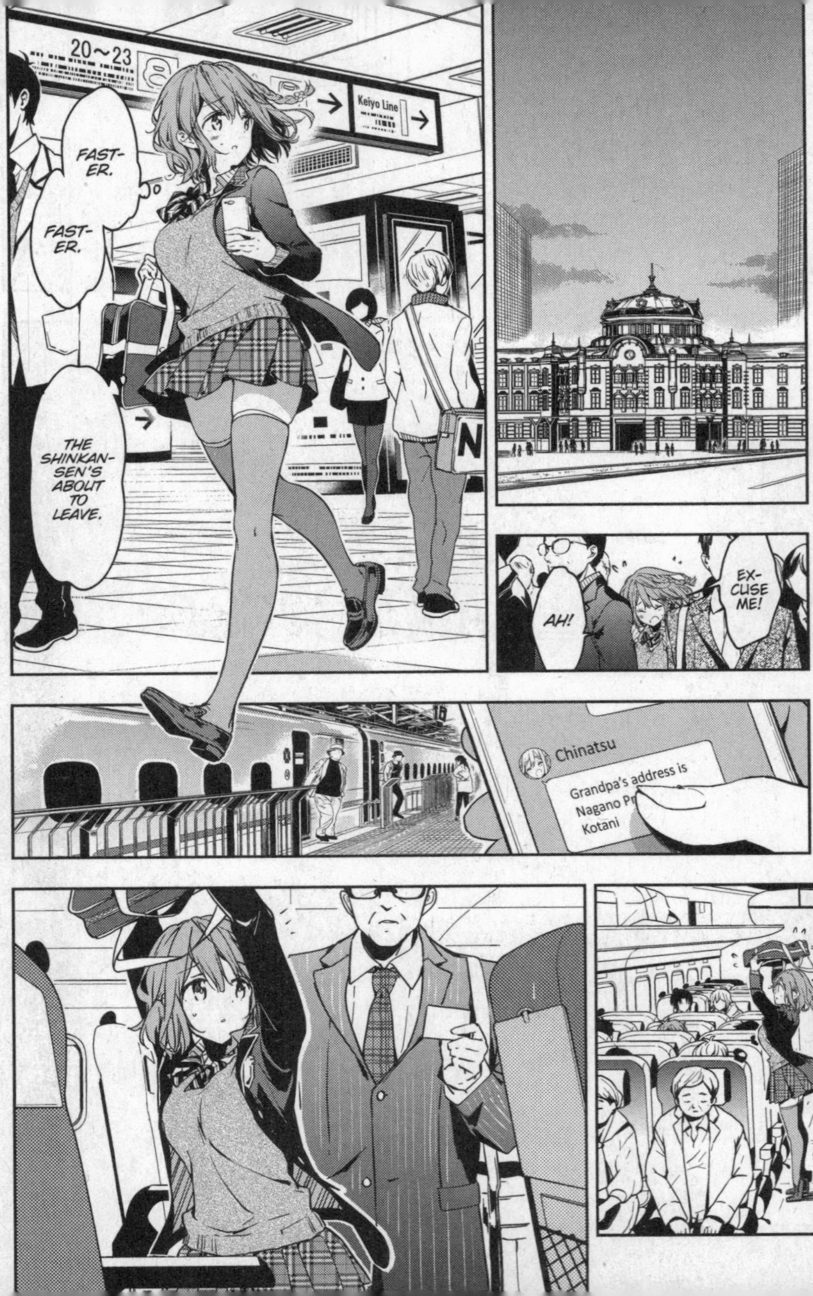
EX-CUSE ME!
AH!
20~23
Keiyo Line
FASTER. FASTER.
THE SHINKANSEN'S ABOUT TO LEAVE.
Chinatsu
Grandpa's address is Nagano Pr
Kotani

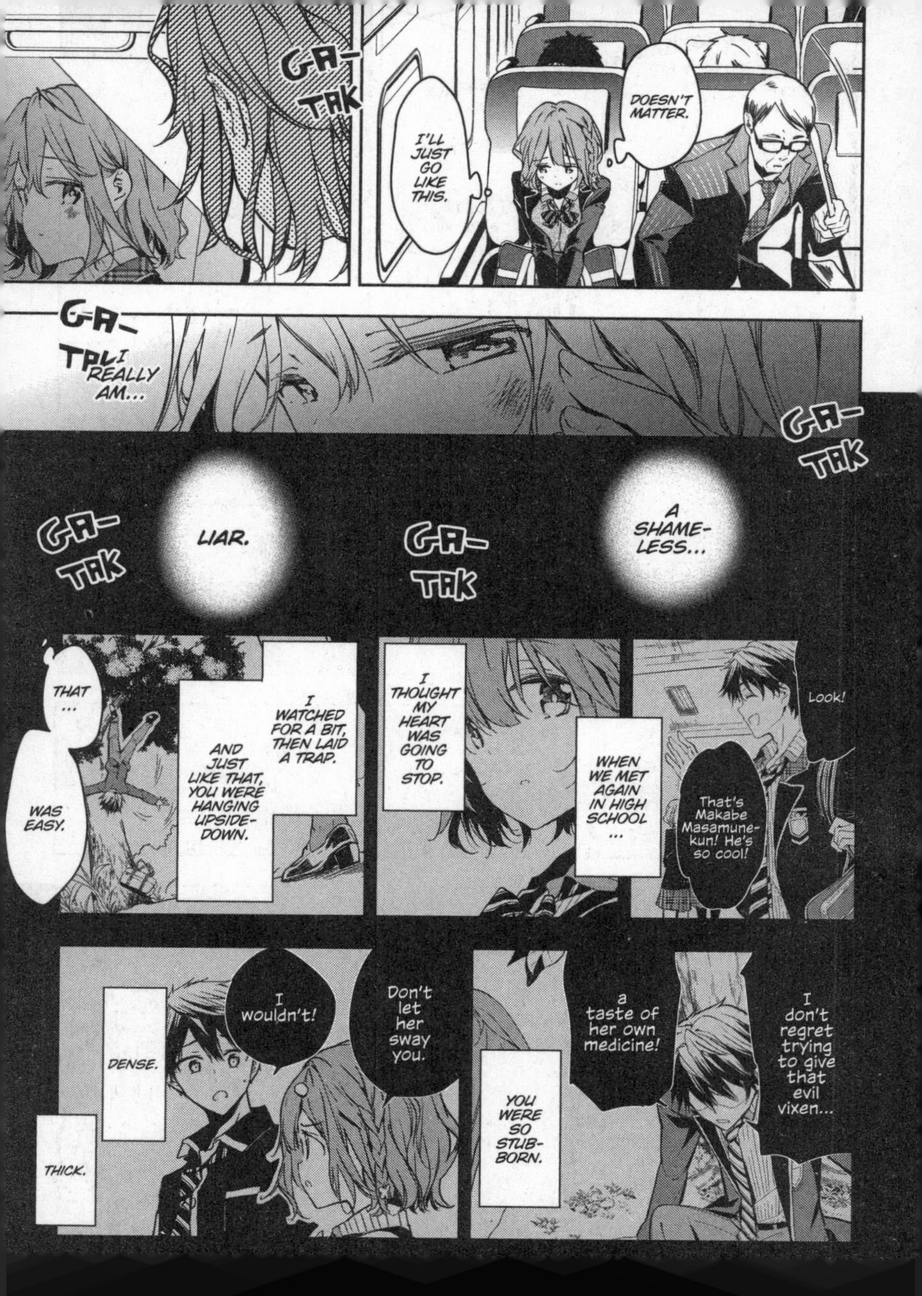
DOESN'T MATTER.
I'LL JUST GO LIKE THIS.
GA-TAK
GA-
I REALLY AM...
GA-TAK
A SHAME-LESS...
GA-TAK
LIAR.
GA-TAK
Look!
That's Makabe Masamune-kun! He's so cool!
WHEN WE MET AGAIN IN HIGH SCHOOL...
I THOUGHT MY HEART WAS GOING TO STOP.
I WATCHED FOR A BIT, THEN LAID A TRAP.
AND JUST LIKE THAT, YOU WERE HANGING UPSIDE-DOWN.
THAT... WAS EASY.
I don't regret trying to give that evil vixen...
a taste of her own medicine!
YOU WERE SO STUBBORN.
Don't let her sway you.
I wouldn't!
DENSE.
THICK.

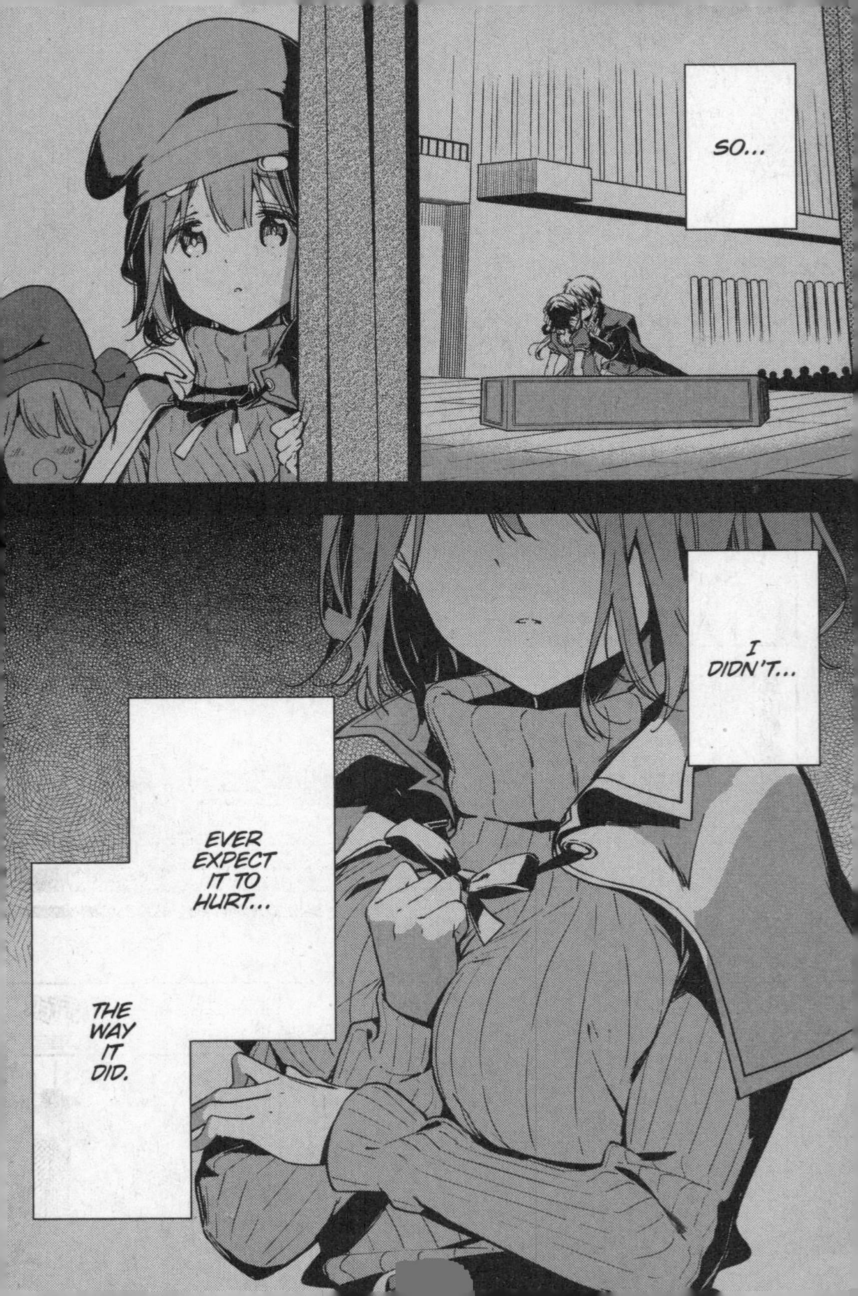
SO...
I DIDN'T...
EVER EXPECT IT TO HURT...
THE WAY IT DID.

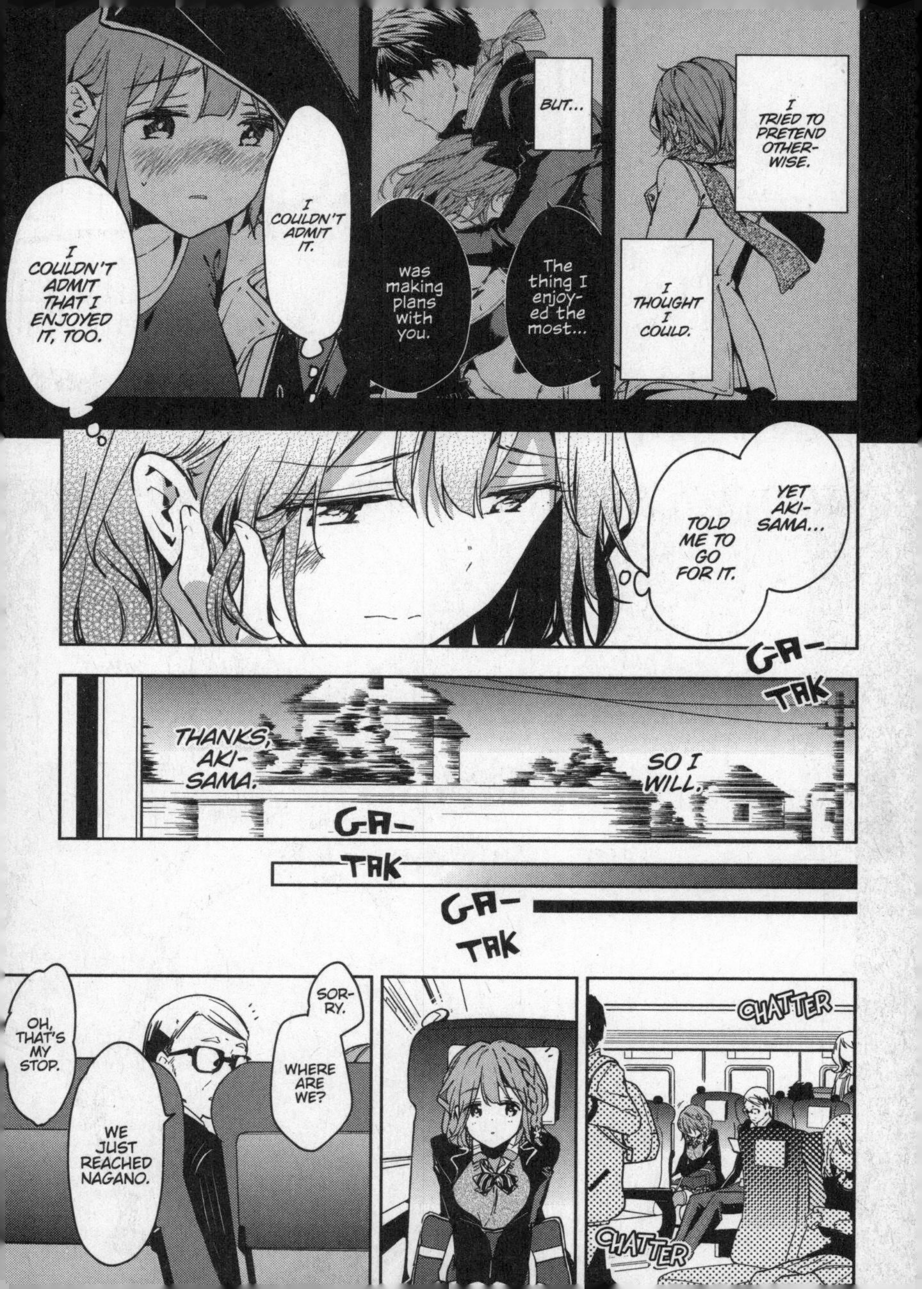
I TRIED TO PRETEND OTHER-WISE.
I THOUGHT I COULD.
BUT...
The thing I enjoy-ed the most...
was making plans with you.
I COULDN'T ADMIT IT.
I COULDN'T ADMIT THAT I ENJOYED IT, TOO.
YET AKI-SAMA...
TOLD ME TO GO FOR IT.
GA-TAK
SO I WILL.
THANKS, AKI-SAMA.
GA-TAK
GA-TAK
CHATTER
CHATTER
SOR-RY.
WHERE ARE WE?
OH, THAT'S MY STOP.
WE JUST REACHED NAGANO.

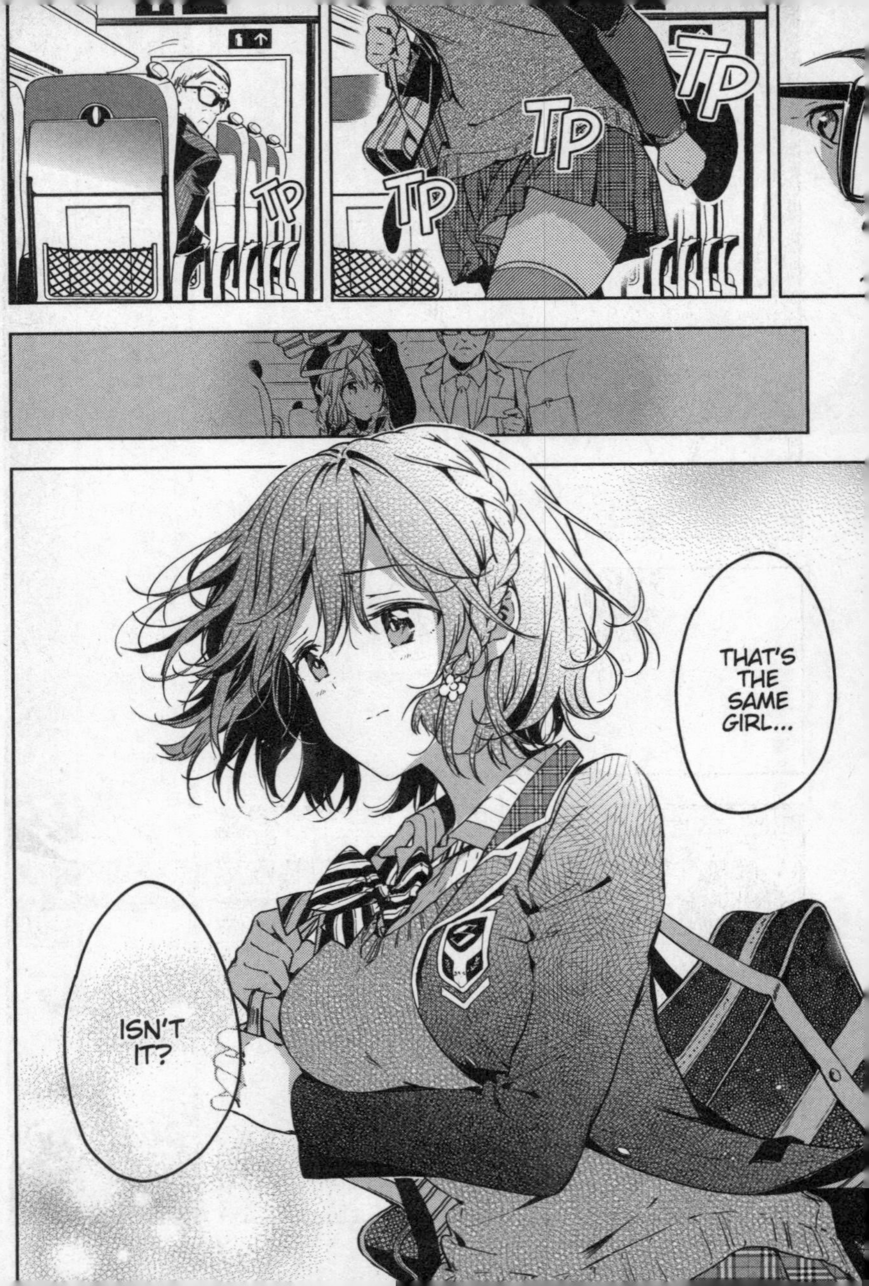
TP
TP
TP
TP
THAT'S THE SAME GIRL...
ISN'T IT?

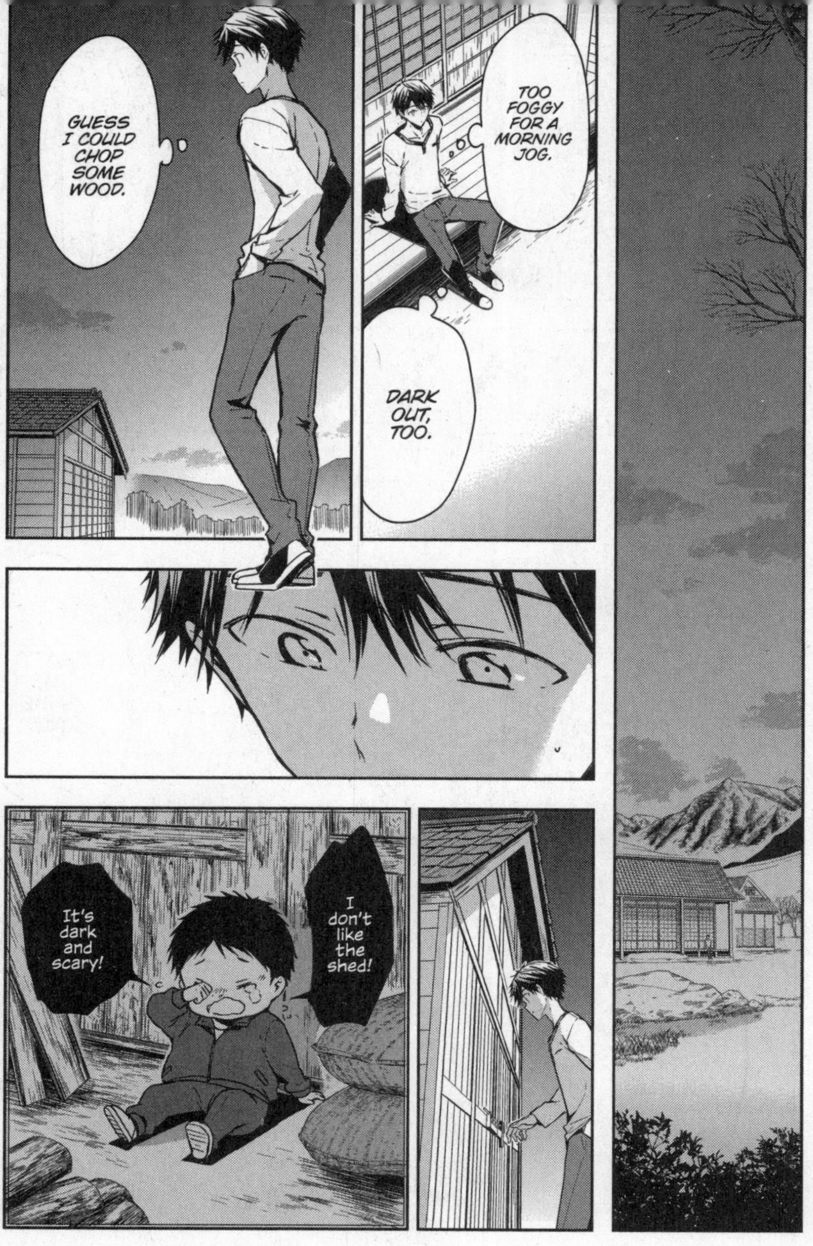
TOO FOGGY FOR A MORNING JOG.
DARK OUT, TOO.
GUESS I COULD CHOP SOME WOOD.
I don't like the shed!
It's dark and scary!

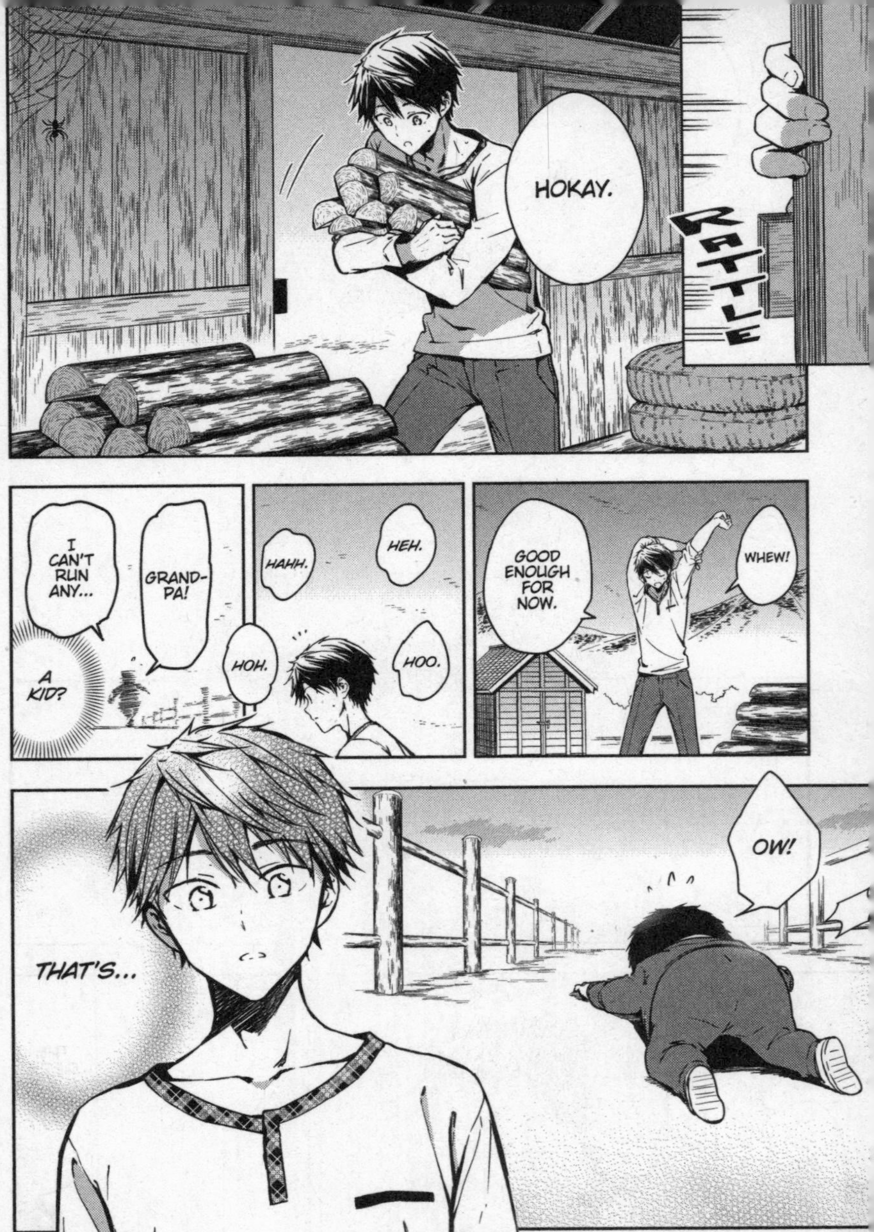
RATTLE
HOKAY.
WHEW!
GOOD ENOUGH FOR NOW.
HEH.
HAHH.
HOO.
HOH.
GRAND-PA!
I CAN'T RUN ANY...
A KID?
OW!
THAT'S...

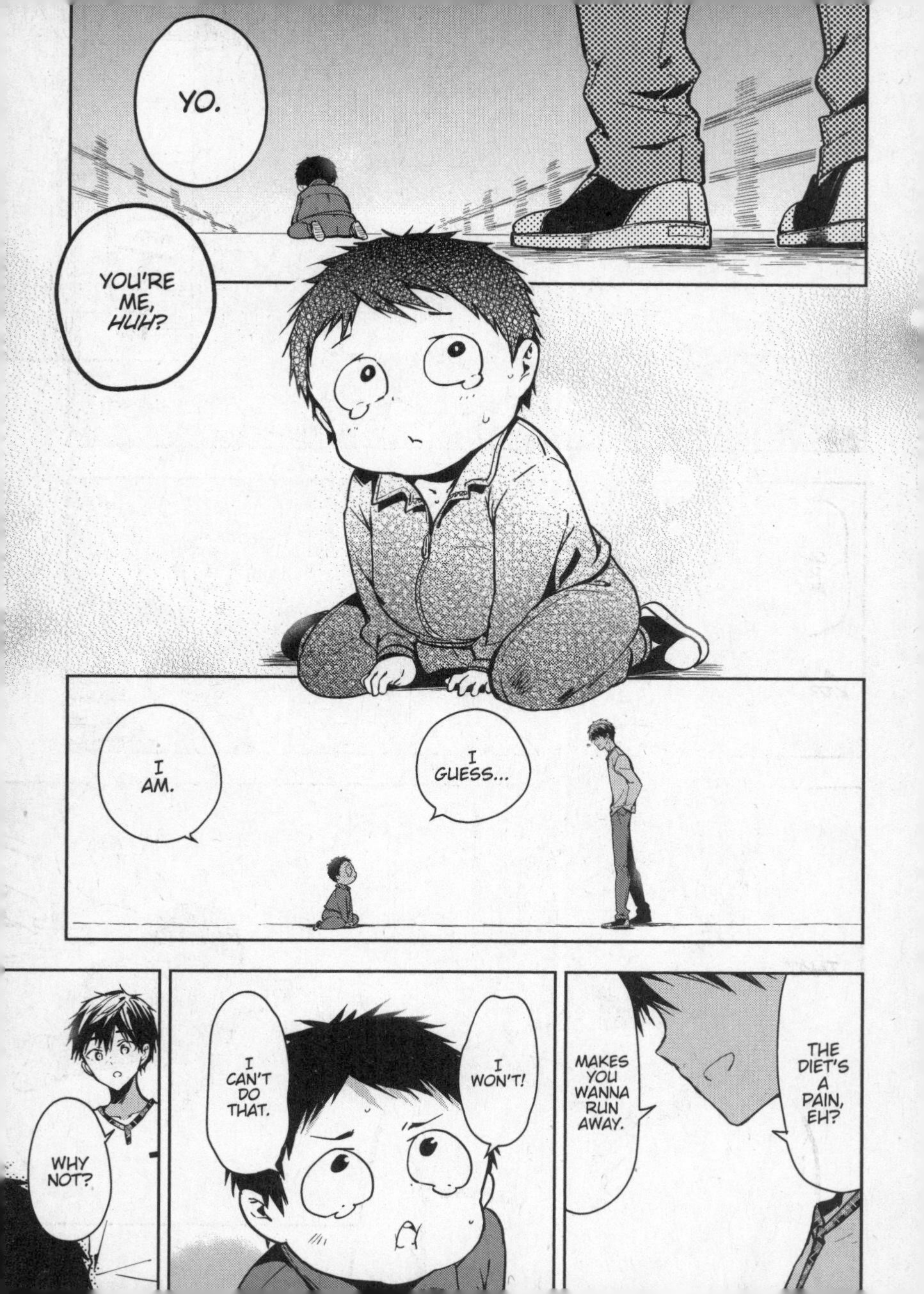
YO.
YOU'RE ME, HUH?
I GUESS...
I AM.
THE DIET'S A PAIN, EH?
MAKES YOU WANNA RUN AWAY.
I WON'T!
I CAN'T DO THAT.
WHY NOT?

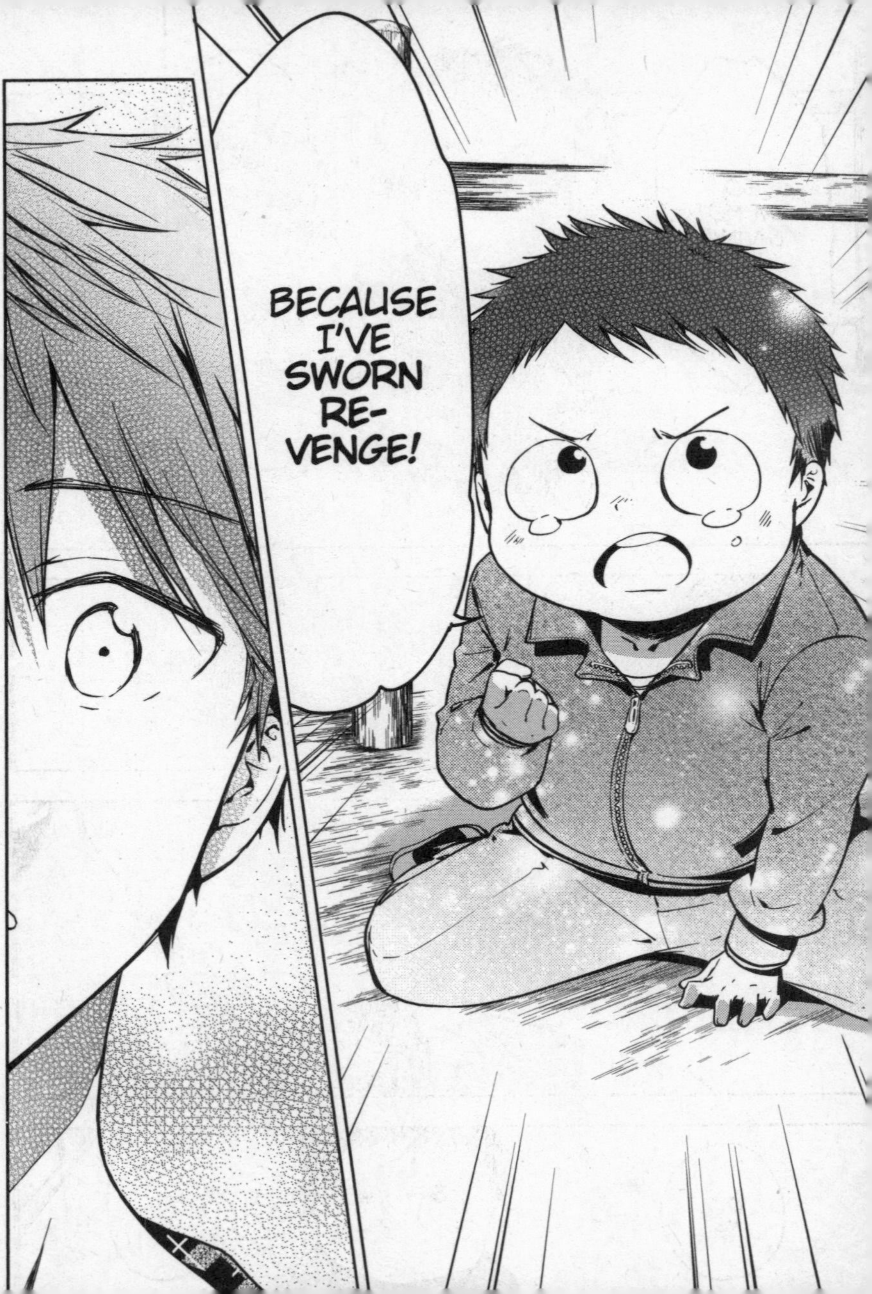
BECAUSE I'VE SWORN RE-VENGE!

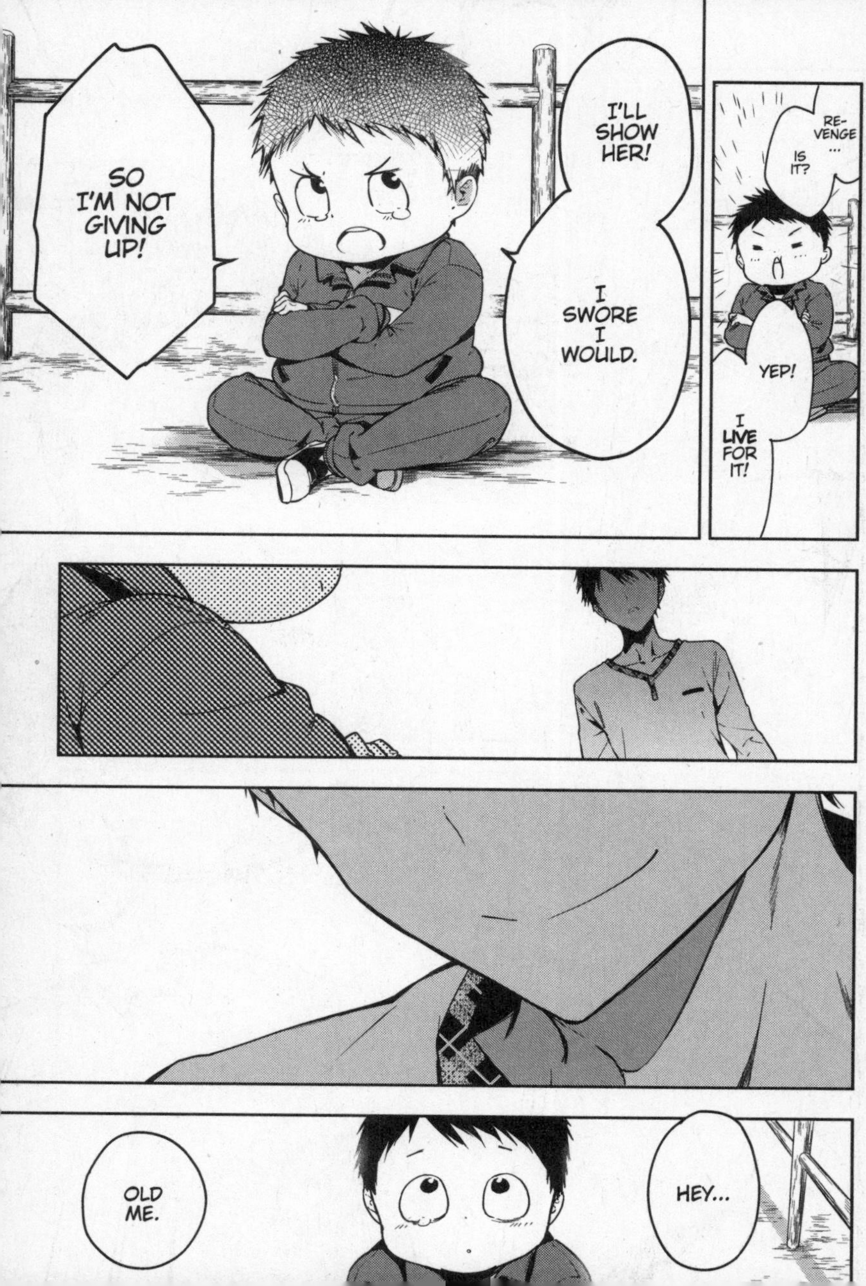
RE-VENGE... IS IT?
YEP! I LIVE FOR IT!
I'LL SHOW HER!
I SWORE I WOULD.
SO I'M NOT GIVING UP!
HEY...
OLD ME.

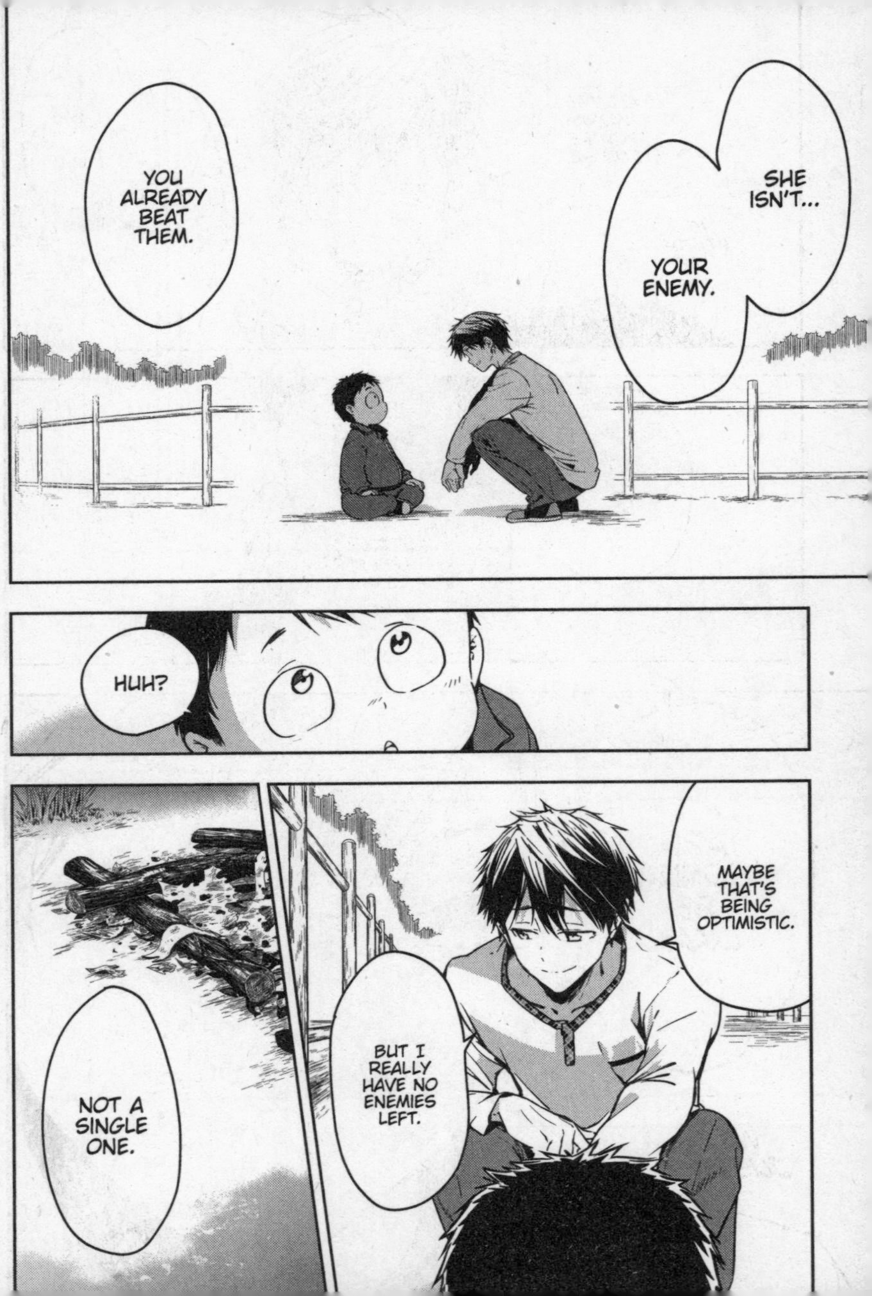
SHE ISN'T... YOUR ENEMY.
YOU ALREADY BEAT THEM.
HUH?
MAYBE THAT'S BEING OPTIMISTIC.
BUT I REALLY HAVE NO ENEMIES LEFT.
NOT A SINGLE ONE.

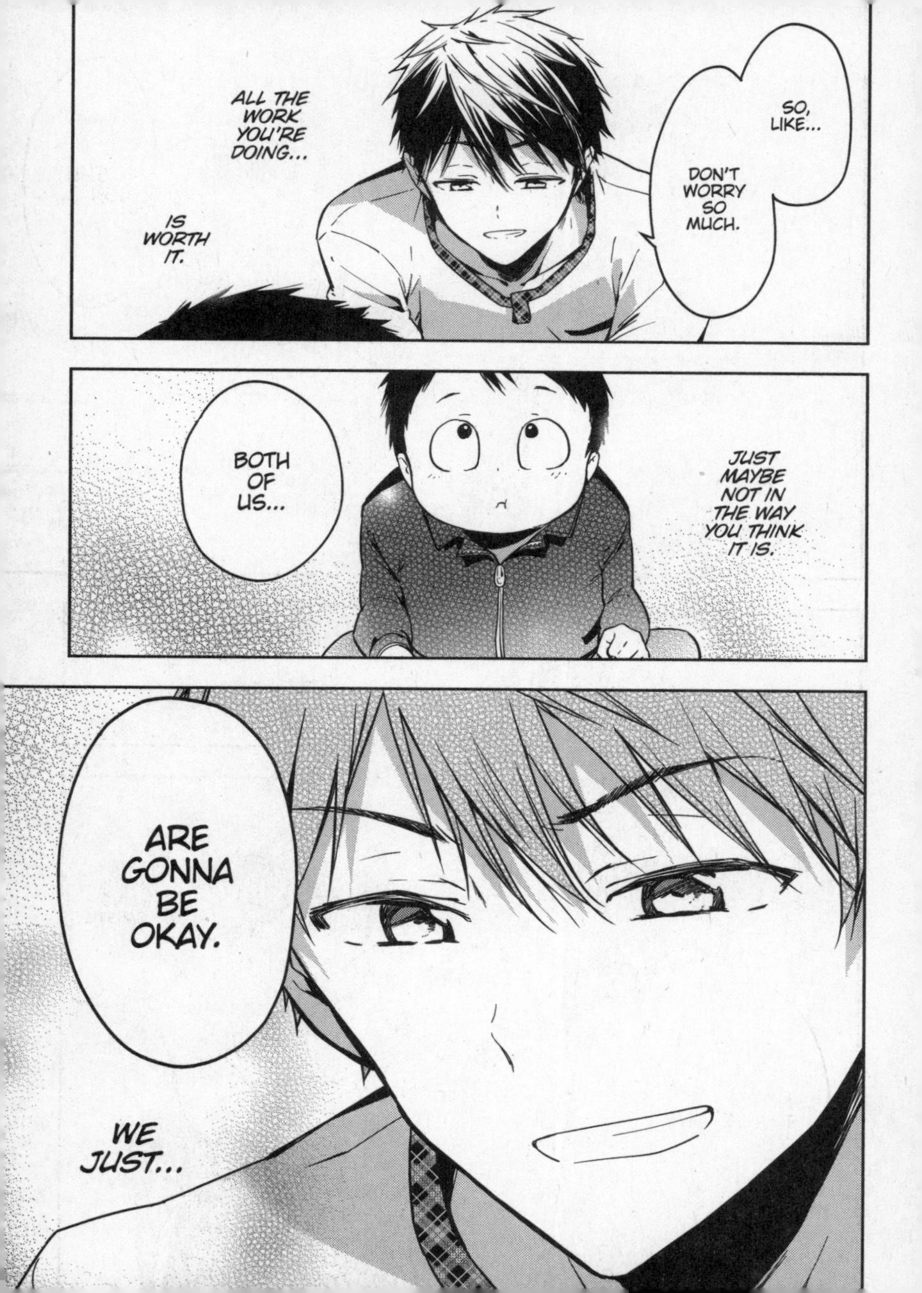
SO, LIKE...
DON'T WORRY SO MUCH.
ALL THE WORK YOU'RE DOING...
IS WORTH IT.
JUST MAYBE NOT IN THE WAY YOU THINK IT IS.
BOTH OF US...
WE JUST...
ARE GONNA BE OKAY.

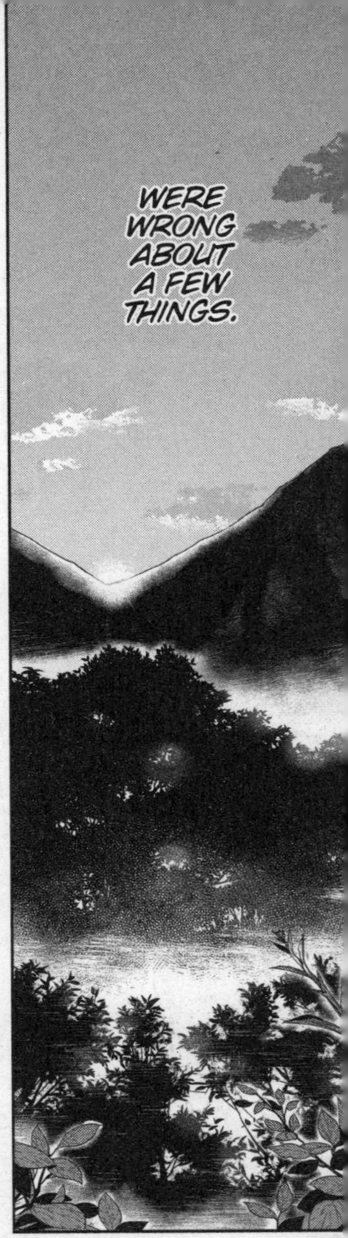
WERE WRONG ABOUT A FEW THINGS.

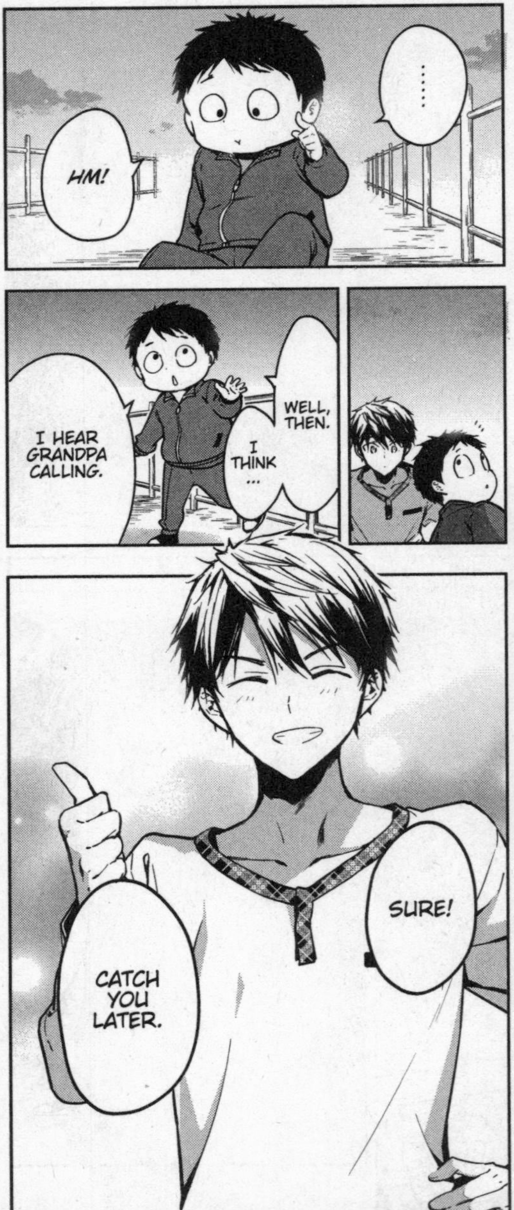
......
HM!
WELL, THEN.
I THINK ...
I HEAR GRANDPA CALLING.
SURE!
CATCH YOU LATER.

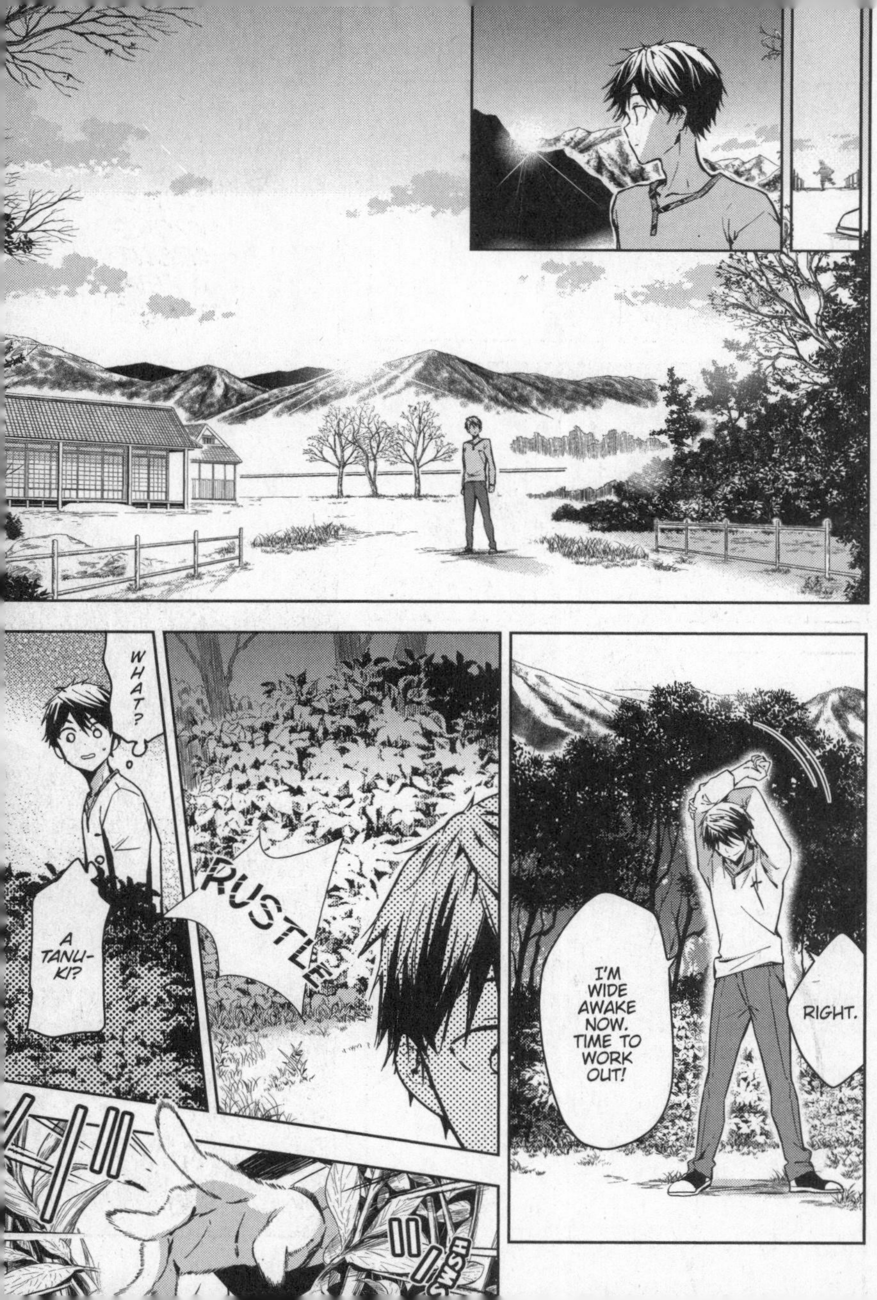
RIGHT.
I'M WIDE AWAKE NOW. TIME TO WORK OUT!
RUSTLE
WHAT?
A TANUKI?
SWSH

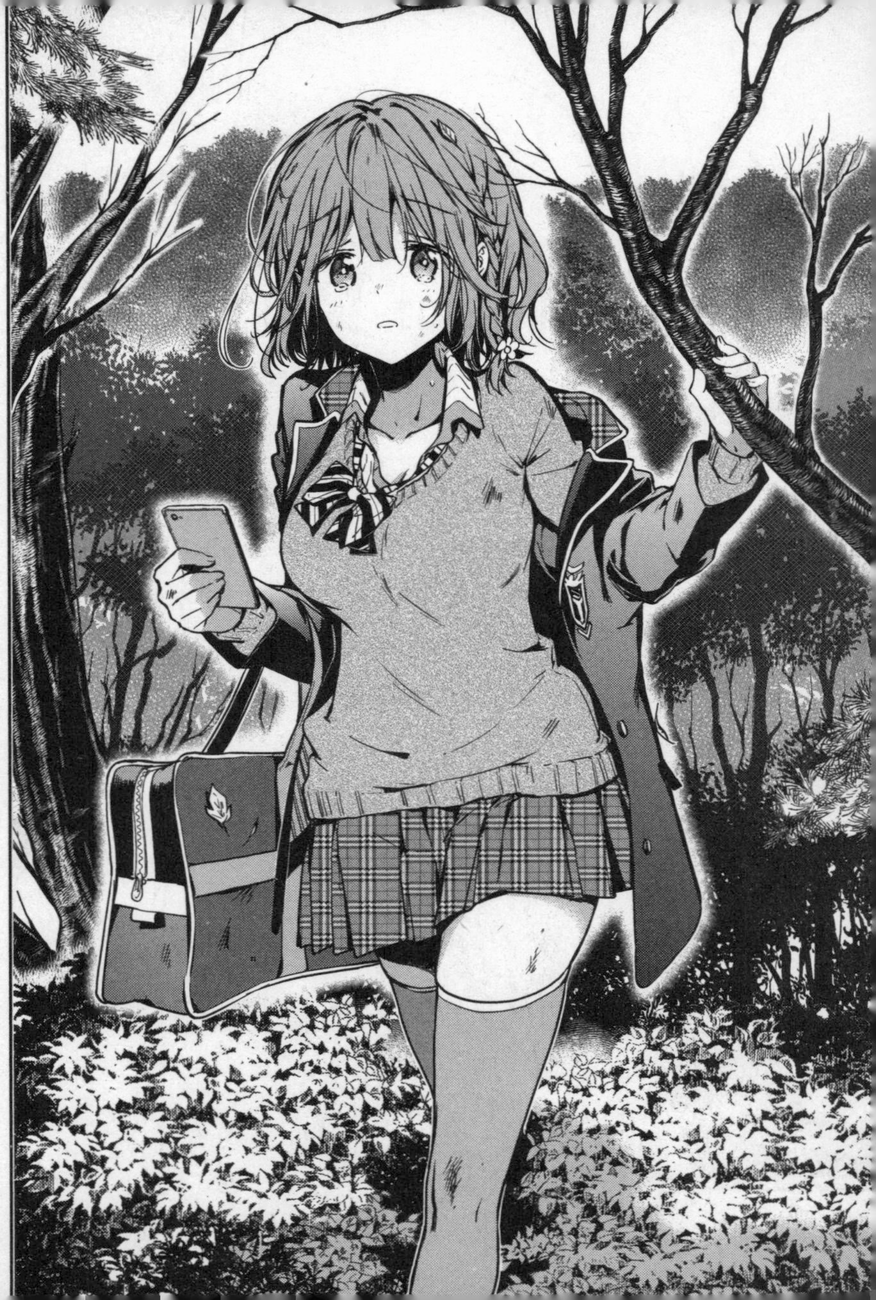

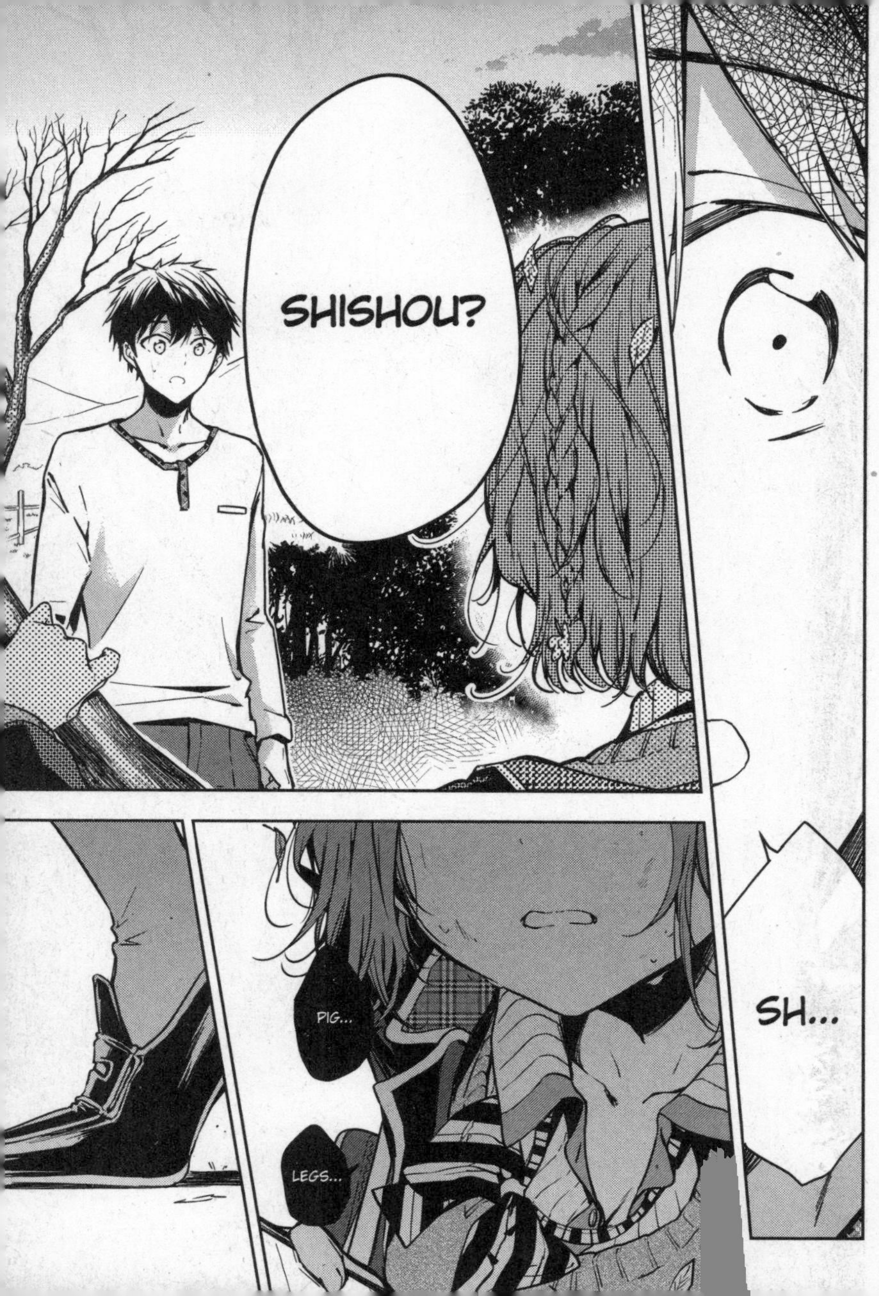
SHISHOU?
SH...
PIG...
LEGS...

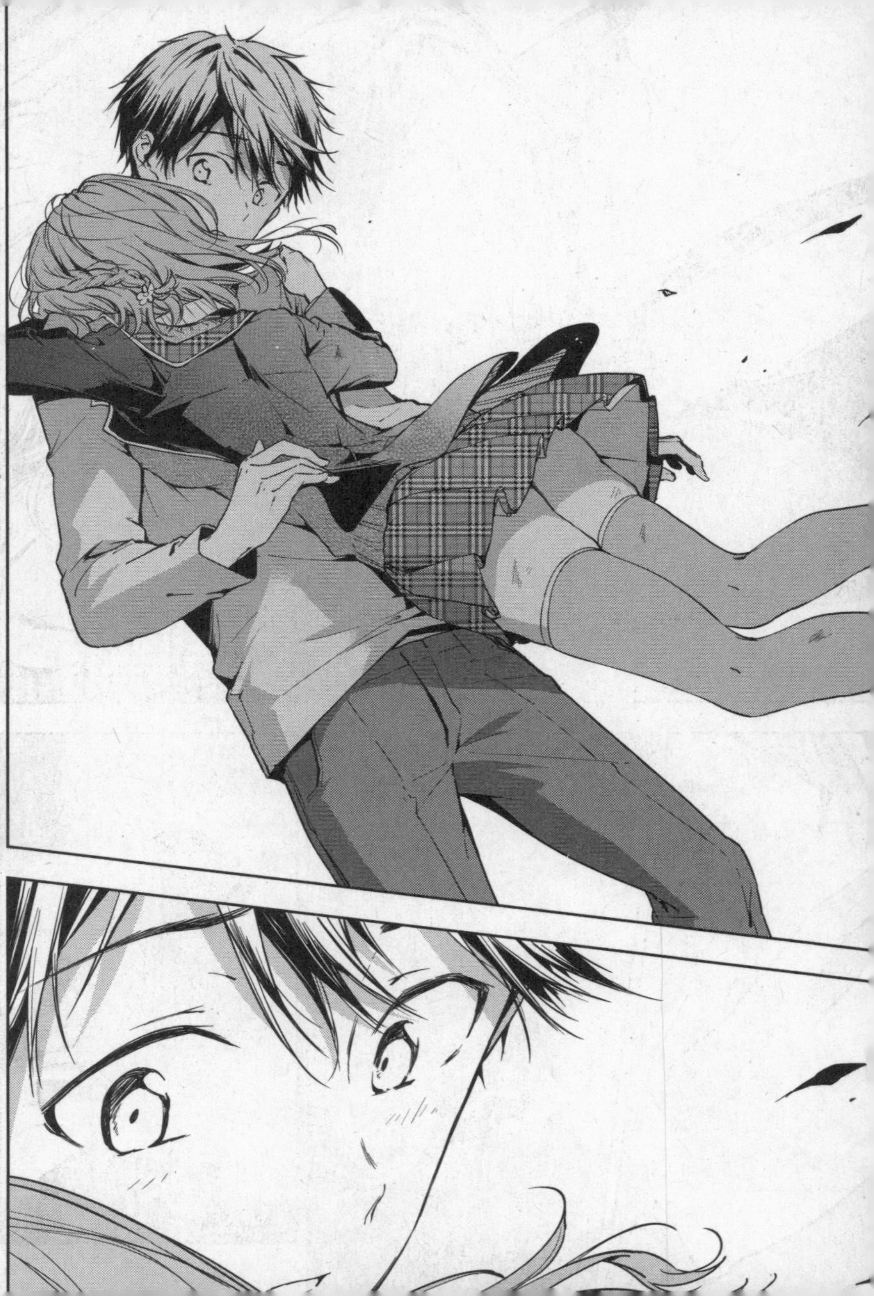

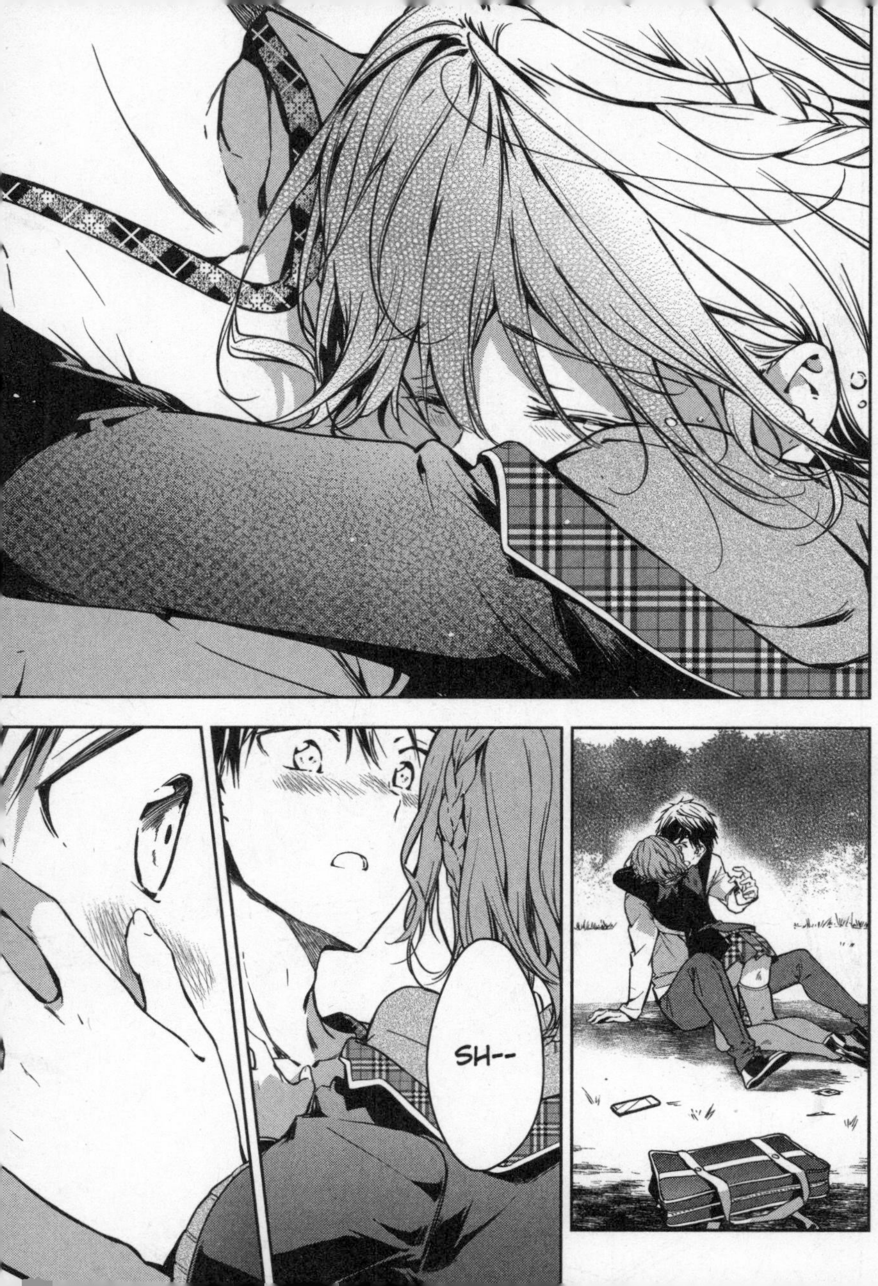
SH--

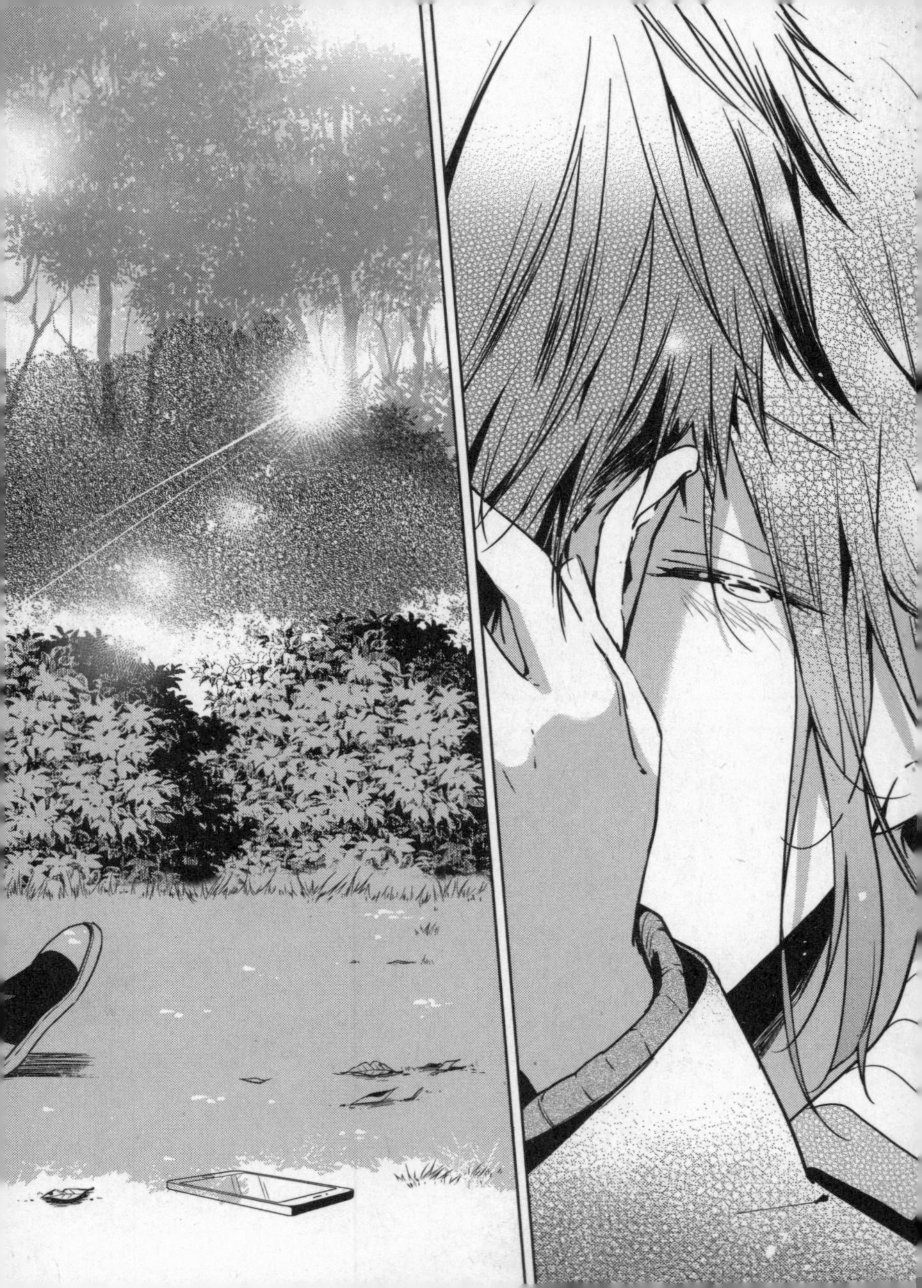

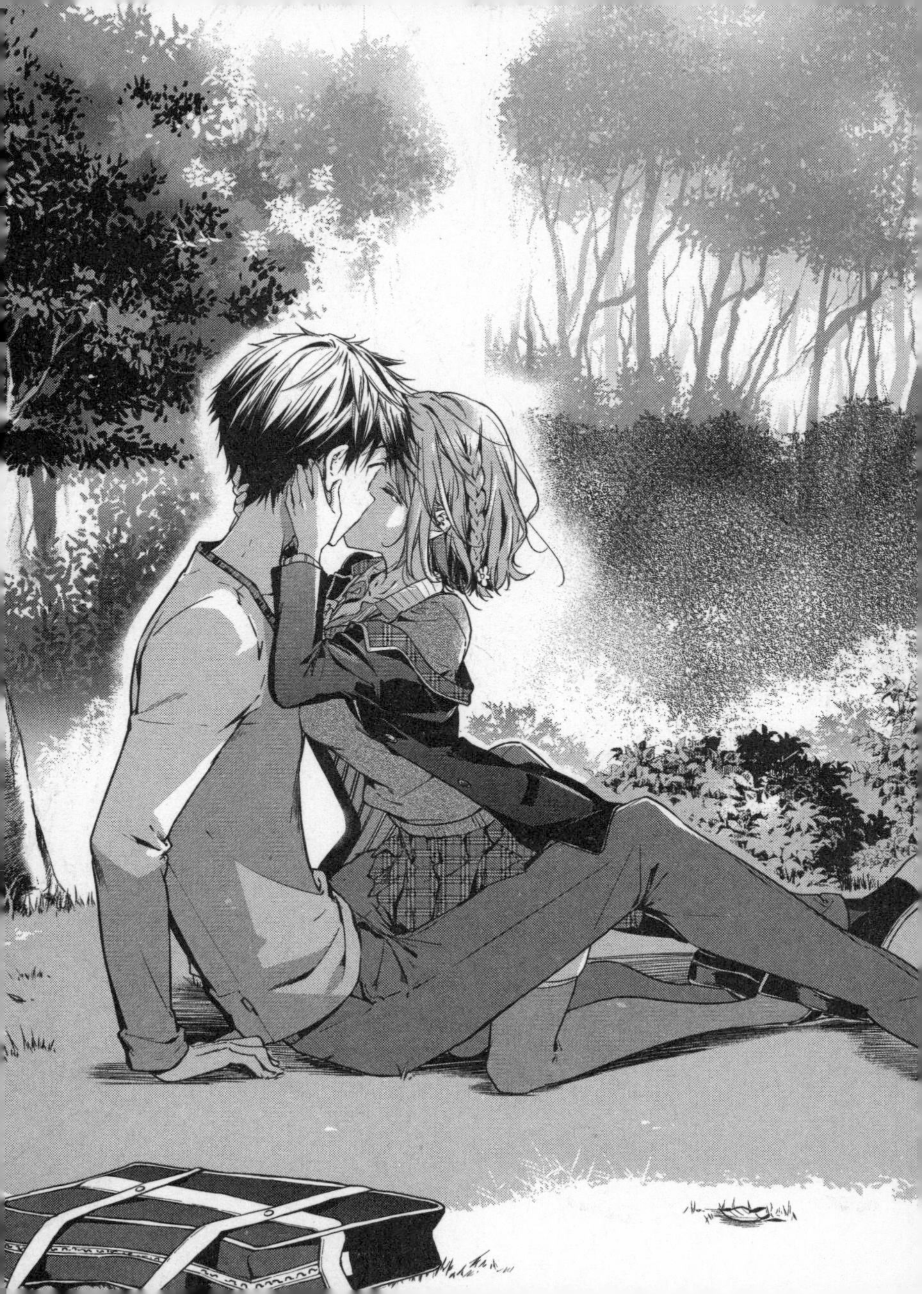

**10**

**Masamune-kun's**
**REVENGE**

Presented by Hazuki Takeoka & TIV

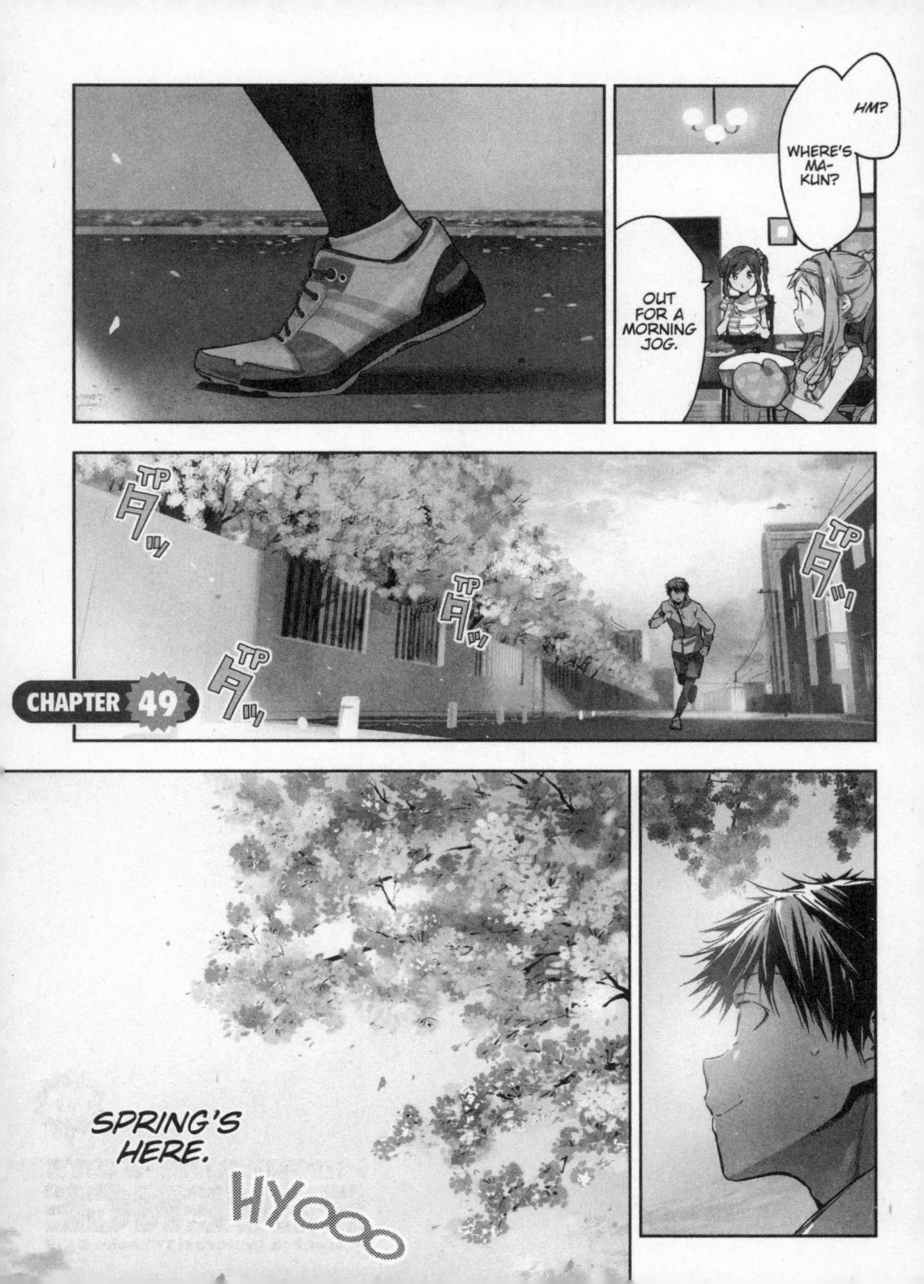
HM?
WHERE'S MA-KUN?
OUT FOR A MORNING JOG.
TP
TP
TP
TP
CHAPTER 49
SPRING'S HERE.
HYOOOO

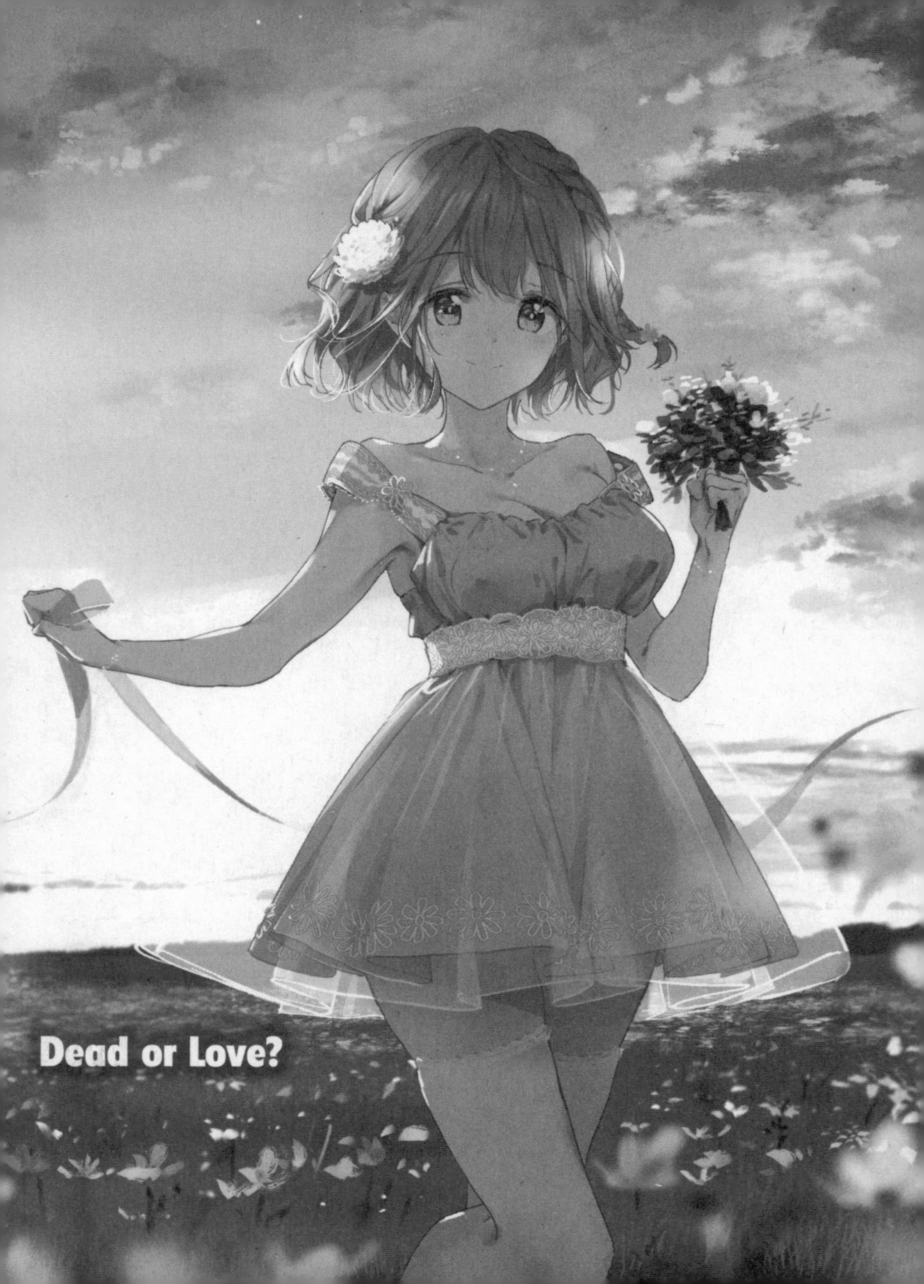
Dead or Love?

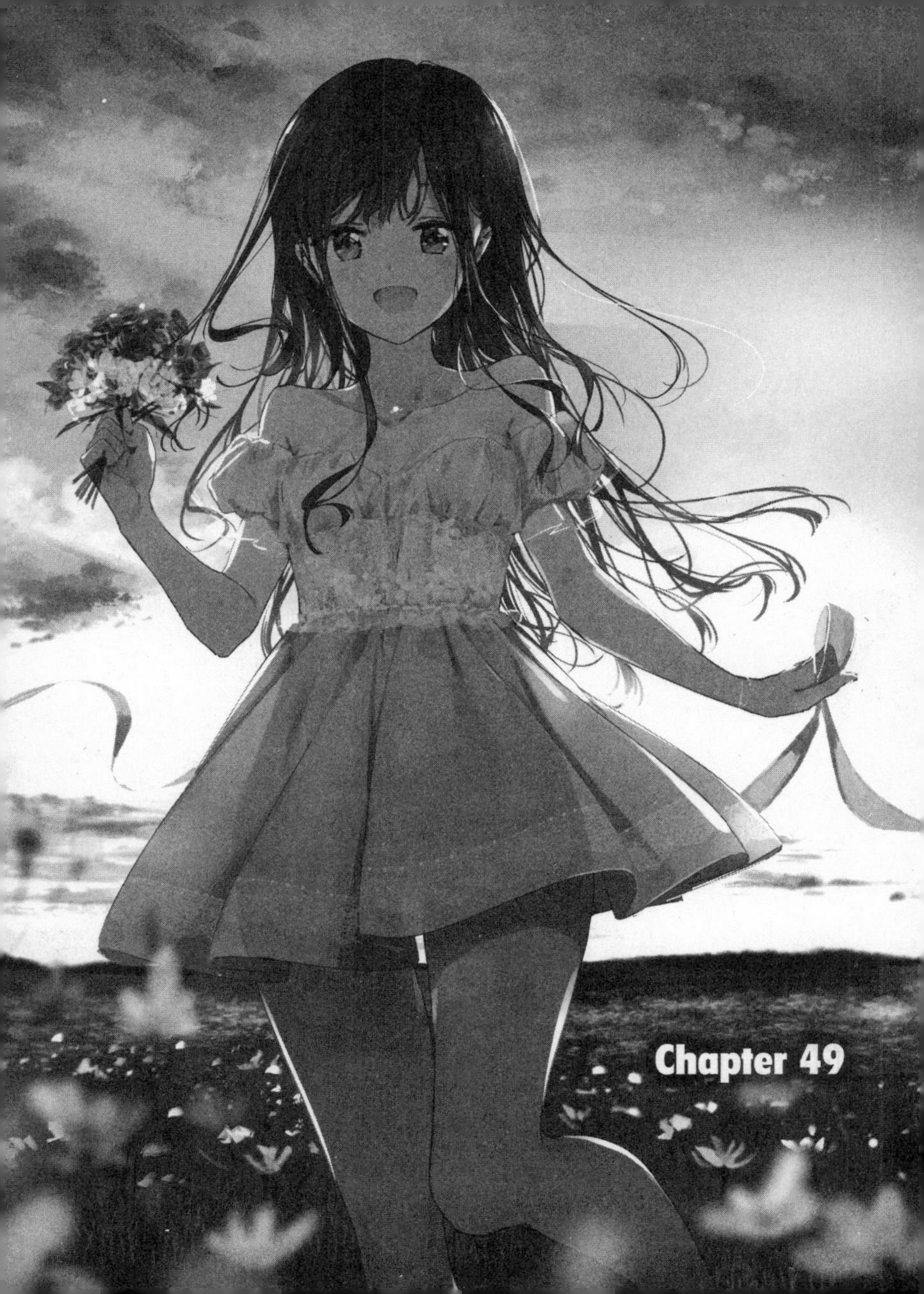
Chapter 49

**10**

**Masamune-kun's REVENGE**

Presented by Hazuki Takeoka & TIV

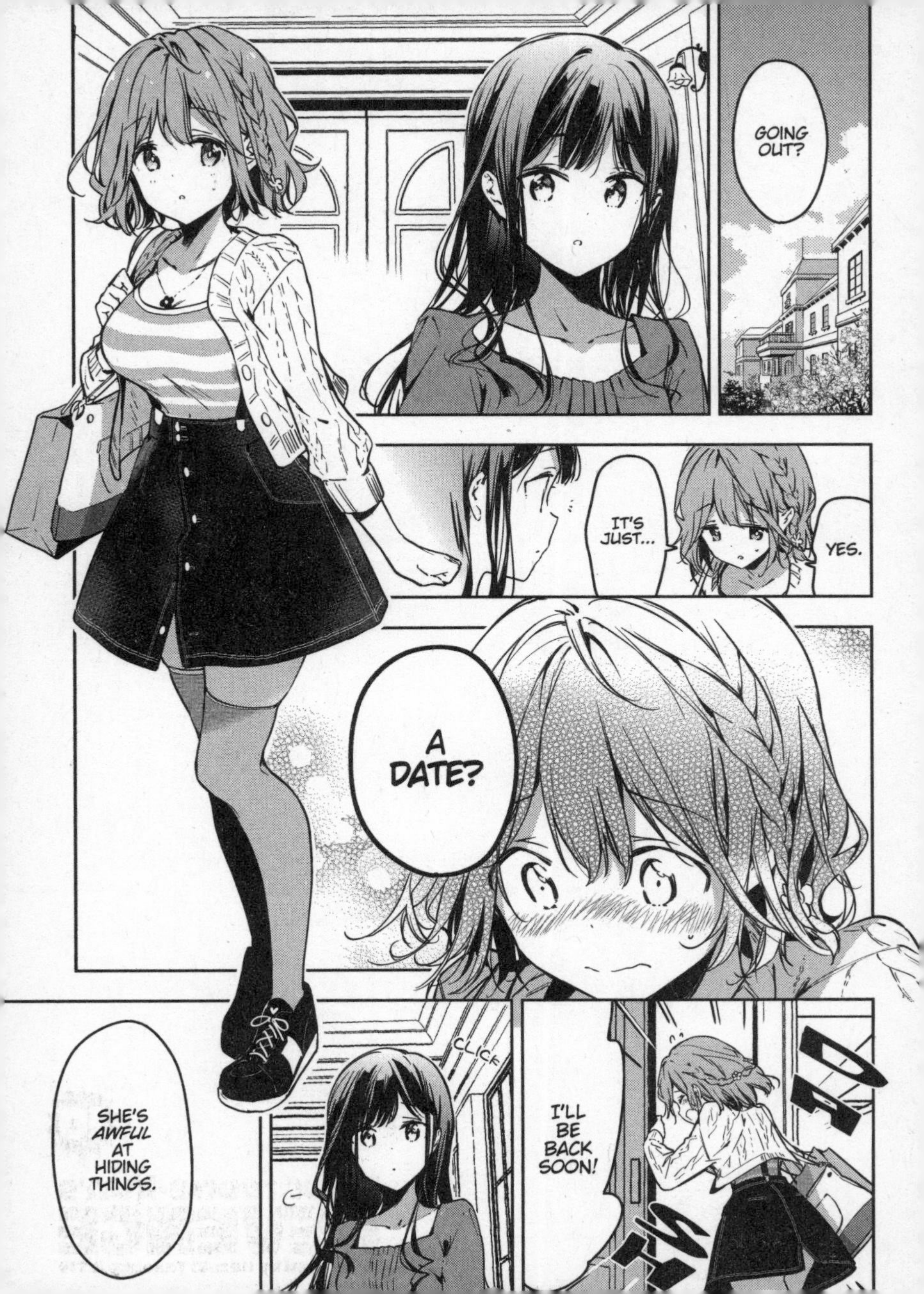
GOING OUT?
YES.
IT'S JUST...
A DATE?
I'LL BE BACK SOON!
CLICK
SHE'S AWFUL AT HIDING THINGS.

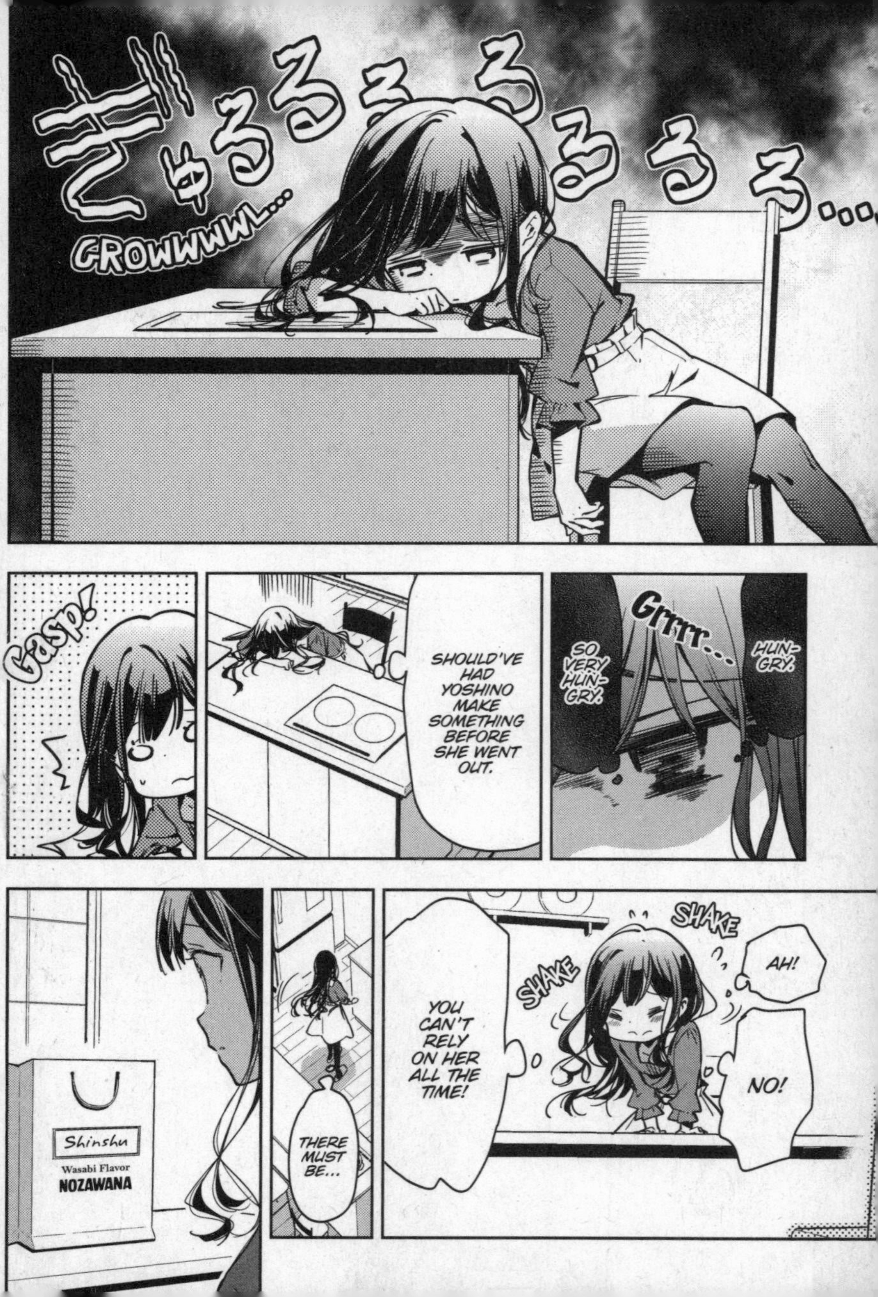
GROWWWWL...
Grrrrr...
HUN-GRY.
SO VERY HUN-GRY.
SHOULD'VE HAD YOSHINO MAKE SOMETHING BEFORE SHE WENT OUT.
Gasp!
AH!
SHAKE
SHAKE
NO!
YOU CAN'T RELY ON HER ALL THE TIME!
THERE MUST BE...
Shinshu
Wasabi Flavor
NOZAWANA

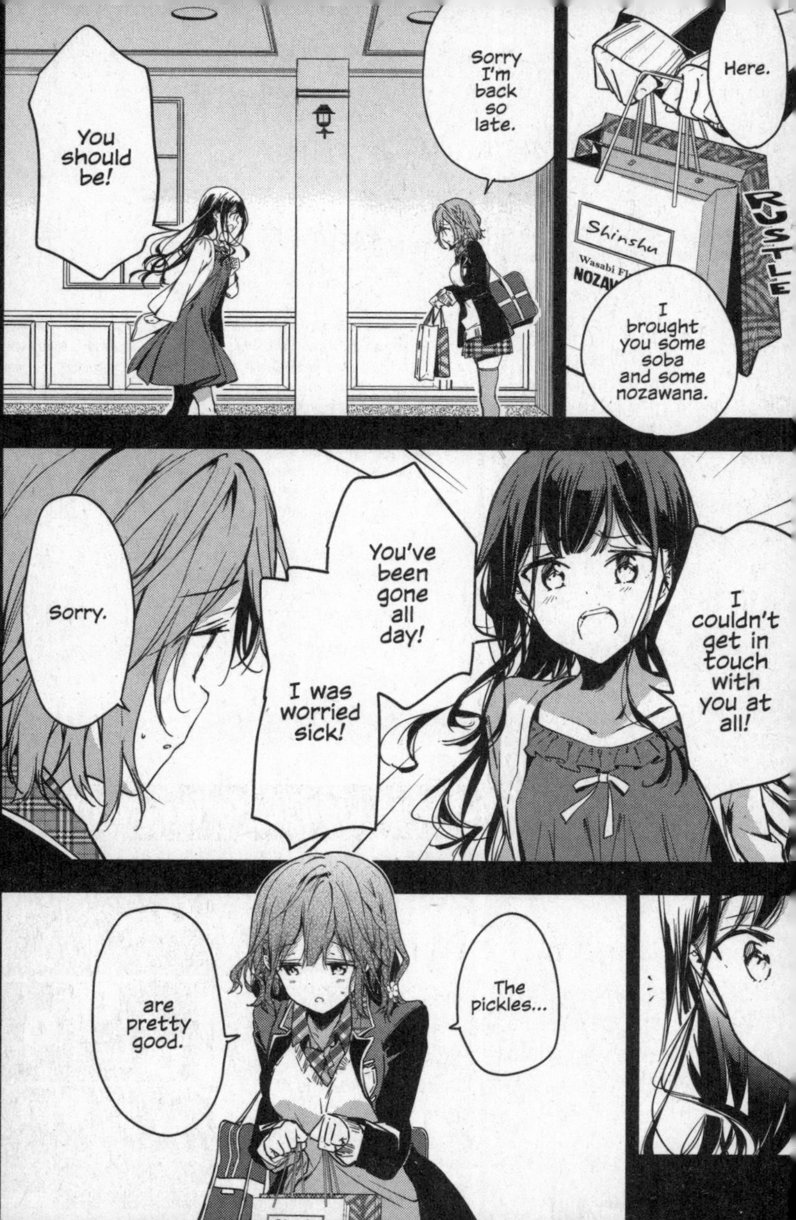
Here.
Shinshu
RUSTLE
I brought you some soba and some nozawana.
Sorry I'm back so late.
You should be!
I couldn't get in touch with you at all!
You've been gone all day!
I was worried sick!
Sorry.
The pickles...
are pretty good.

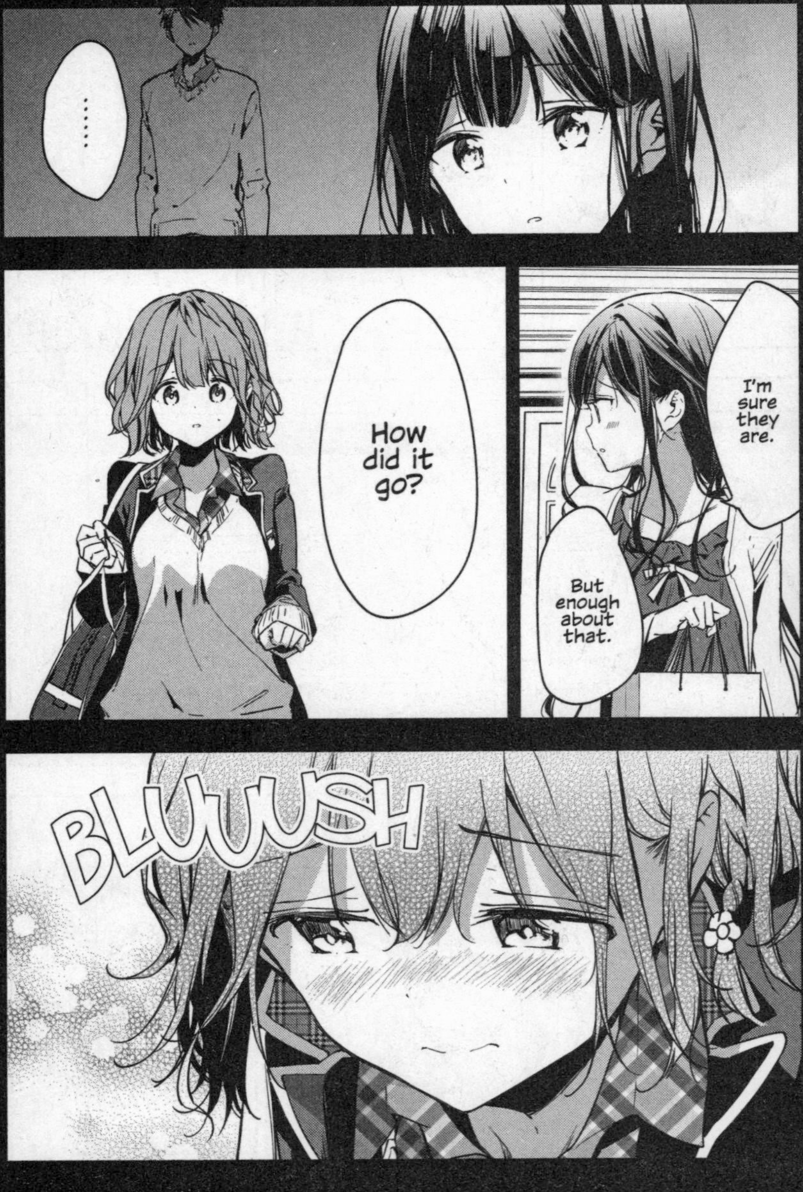
......
I'm sure they are.
But enough about that.
How did it go?
BLUUUSH

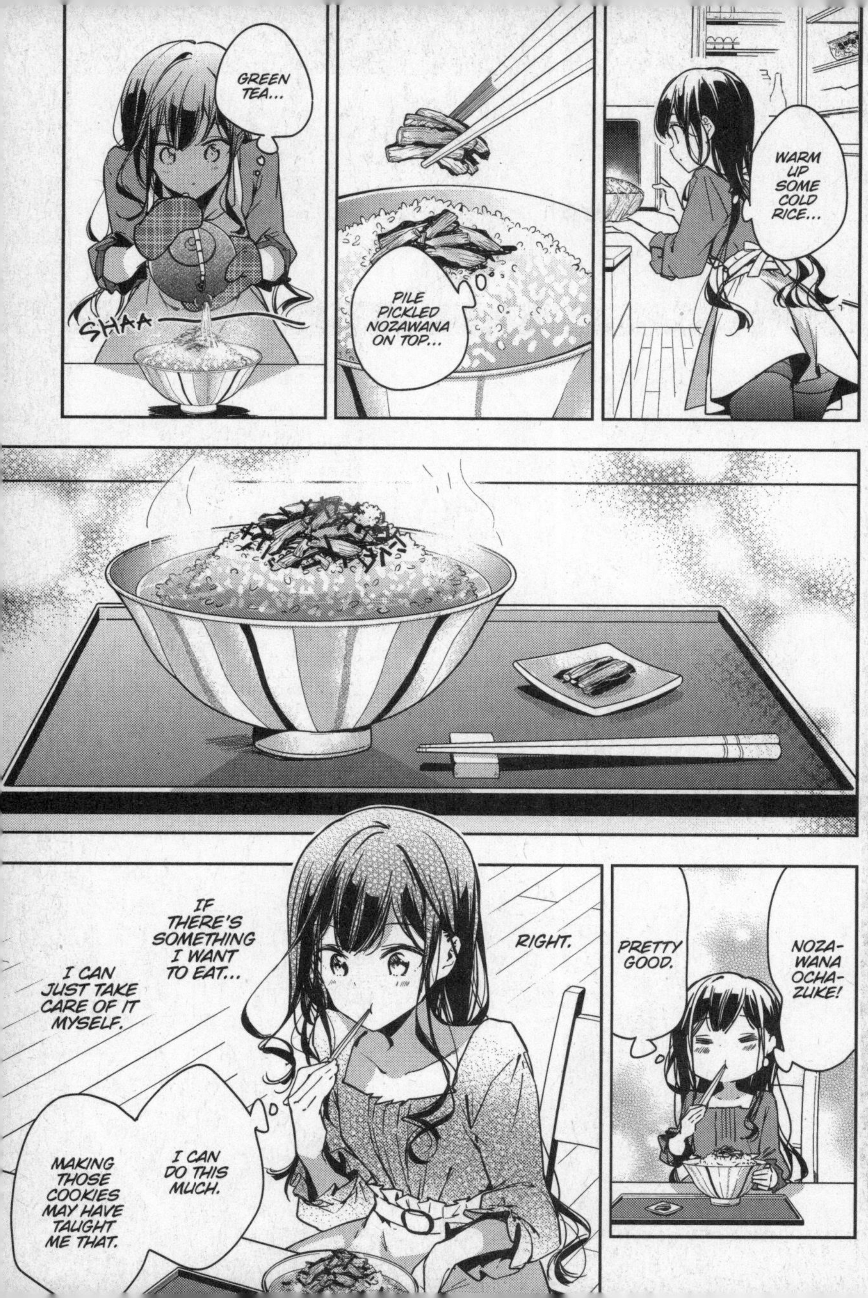
WARM UP SOME COLD RICE...
PILE PICKLED NOZAWANA ON TOP...
GREEN TEA...
SHAA
NOZA-WANA OCHA-ZUKE!
PRETTY GOOD.
RIGHT.
IF THERE'S SOMETHING I WANT TO EAT...
I CAN JUST TAKE CARE OF IT MYSELF.
I CAN DO THIS MUCH.
MAKING THOSE COOKIES MAY HAVE TAUGHT ME THAT.

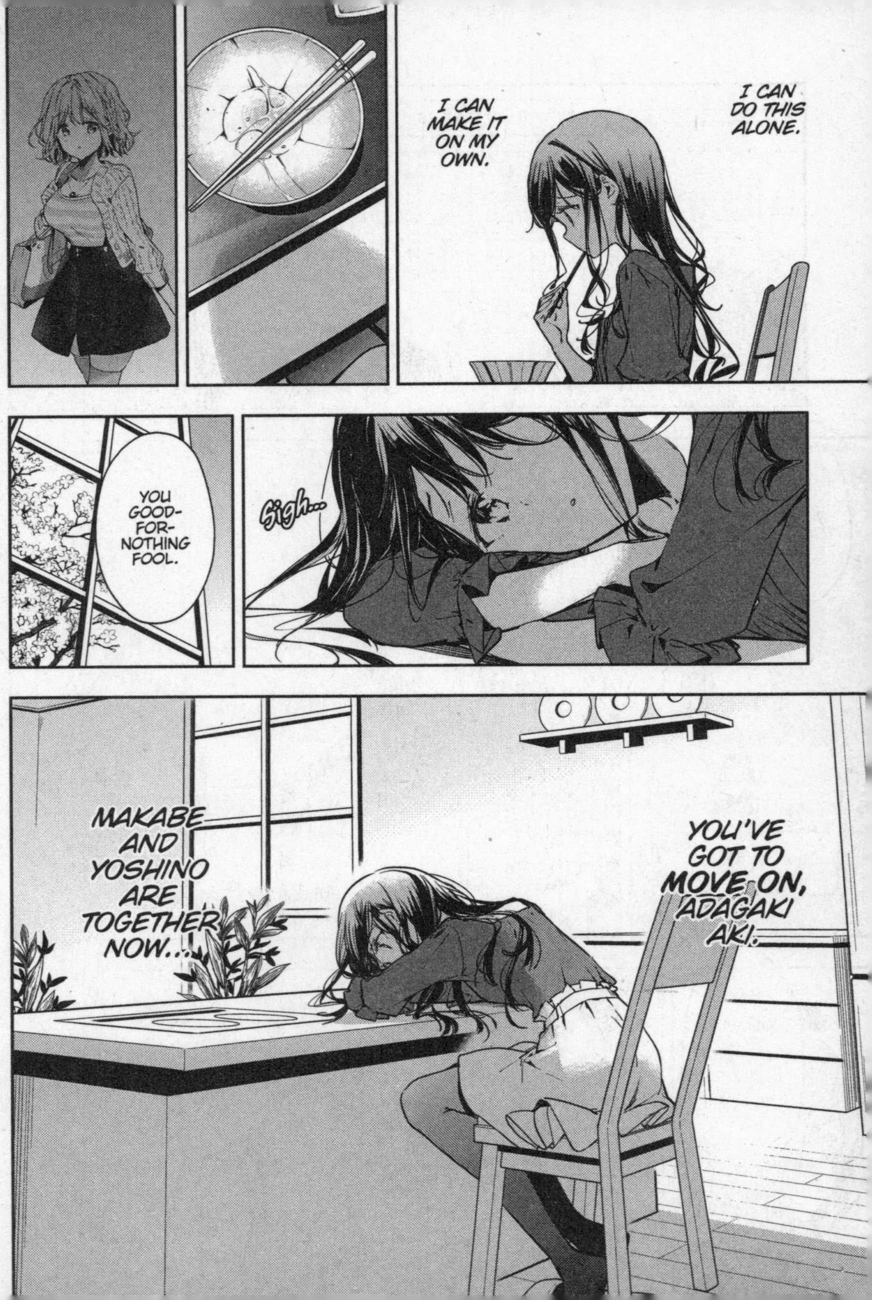
I CAN DO THIS ALONE.
I CAN MAKE IT ON MY OWN.
Sigh...
YOU GOOD-FOR-NOTHING FOOL.
YOU'VE GOT TO MOVE ON, ADAGAKI AKI.
MAKABE AND YOSHINO ARE TOGETHER NOW...

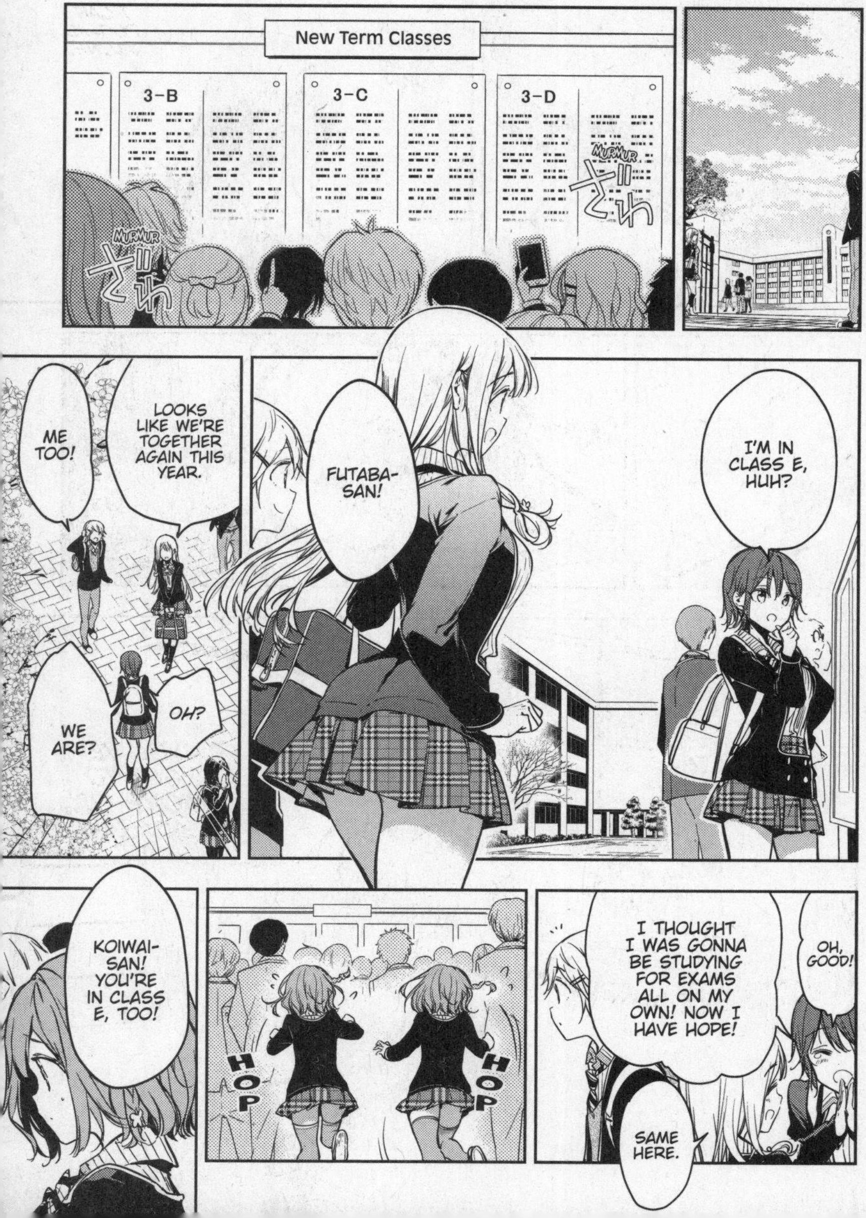
New Term Classes
3-B
3-C
3-D
MURMUR
MURMUR
I'M IN CLASS E, HUH?
FUTABA-SAN!
LOOKS LIKE WE'RE TOGETHER AGAIN THIS YEAR.
ME TOO!
OH?
WE ARE?
OH, GOOD!
I THOUGHT I WAS GONNA BE STUDYING FOR EXAMS ALL ON MY OWN! NOW I HAVE HOPE!
SAME HERE.
HOP
HOP
KOIWAI-SAN! YOU'RE IN CLASS E, TOO!

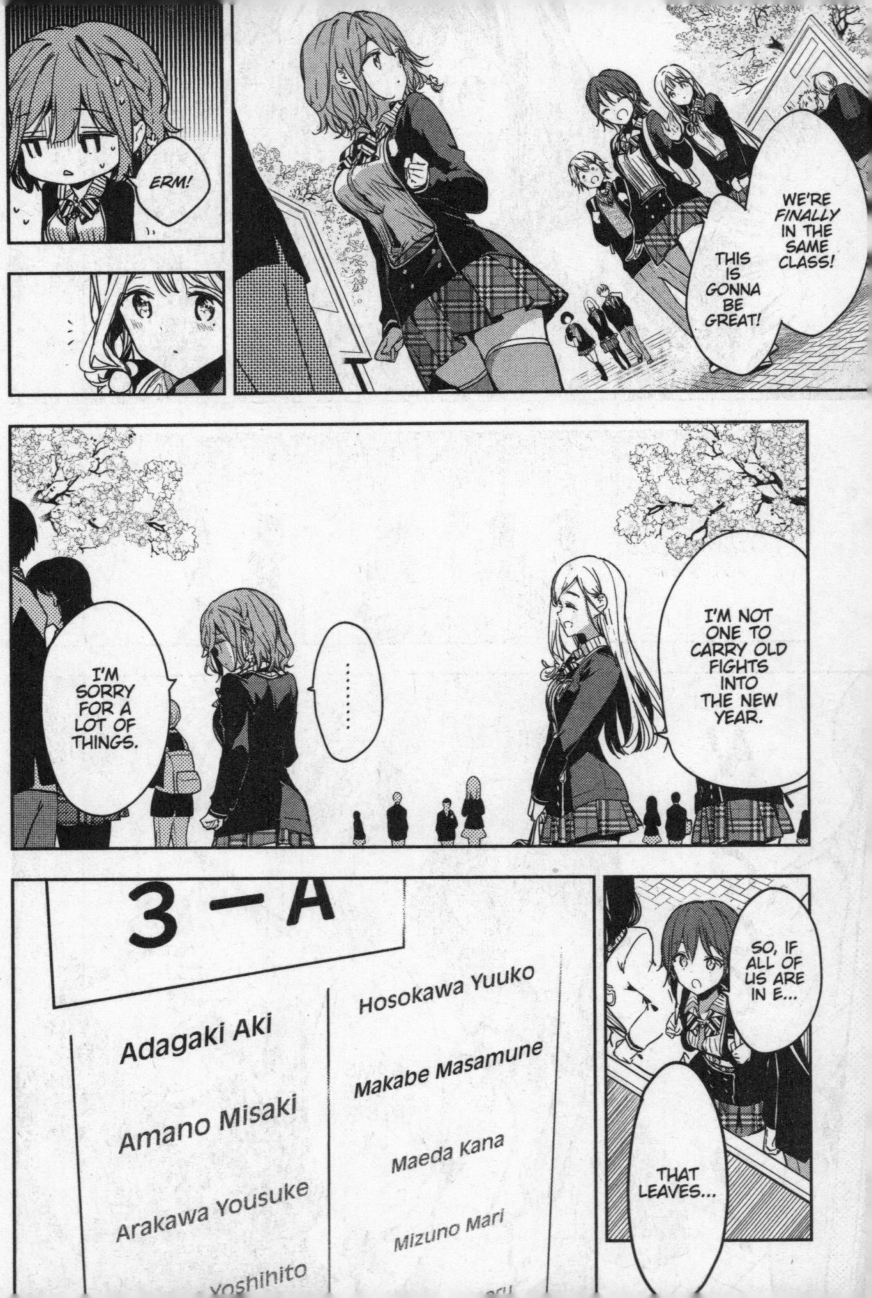
WE'RE FINALLY IN THE SAME CLASS!
THIS IS GONNA BE GREAT!
ERM!
I'M NOT ONE TO CARRY OLD FIGHTS INTO THE NEW YEAR.
......
I'M SORRY FOR A LOT OF THINGS.
SO, IF ALL OF US ARE IN E...
THAT LEAVES...
3 — A
Adagaki Aki
Amano Misaki
Arakawa Yousuke
Yoshihito
Hosokawa Yuuko
Makabe Masamune
Maeda Kana
Mizuno Mari

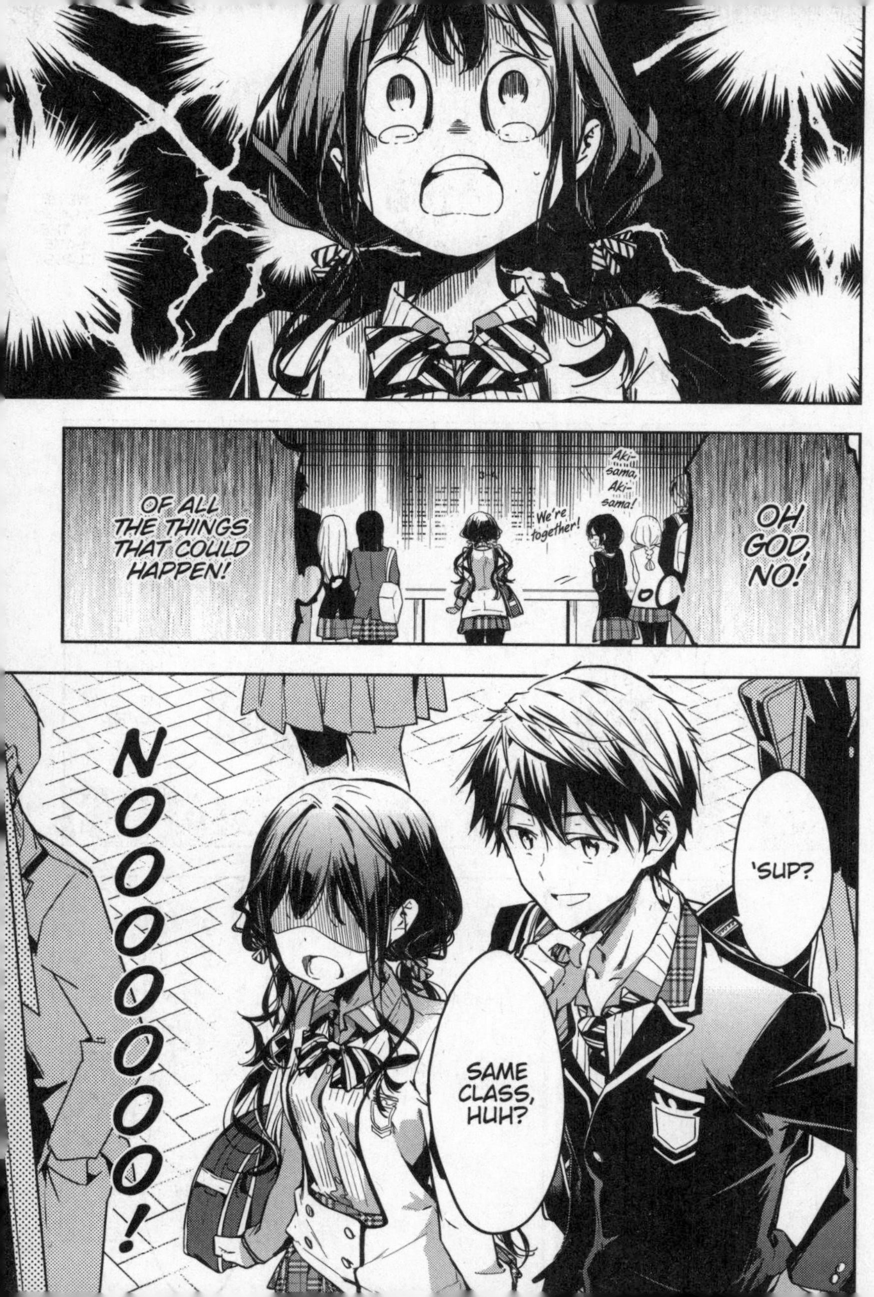
OH GOD, NO!
Aki-sama, Aki-sama!
We're together!
OF ALL THE THINGS THAT COULD HAPPEN!
'SUP?
SAME CLASS, HUH?
NOOOOOOOO!

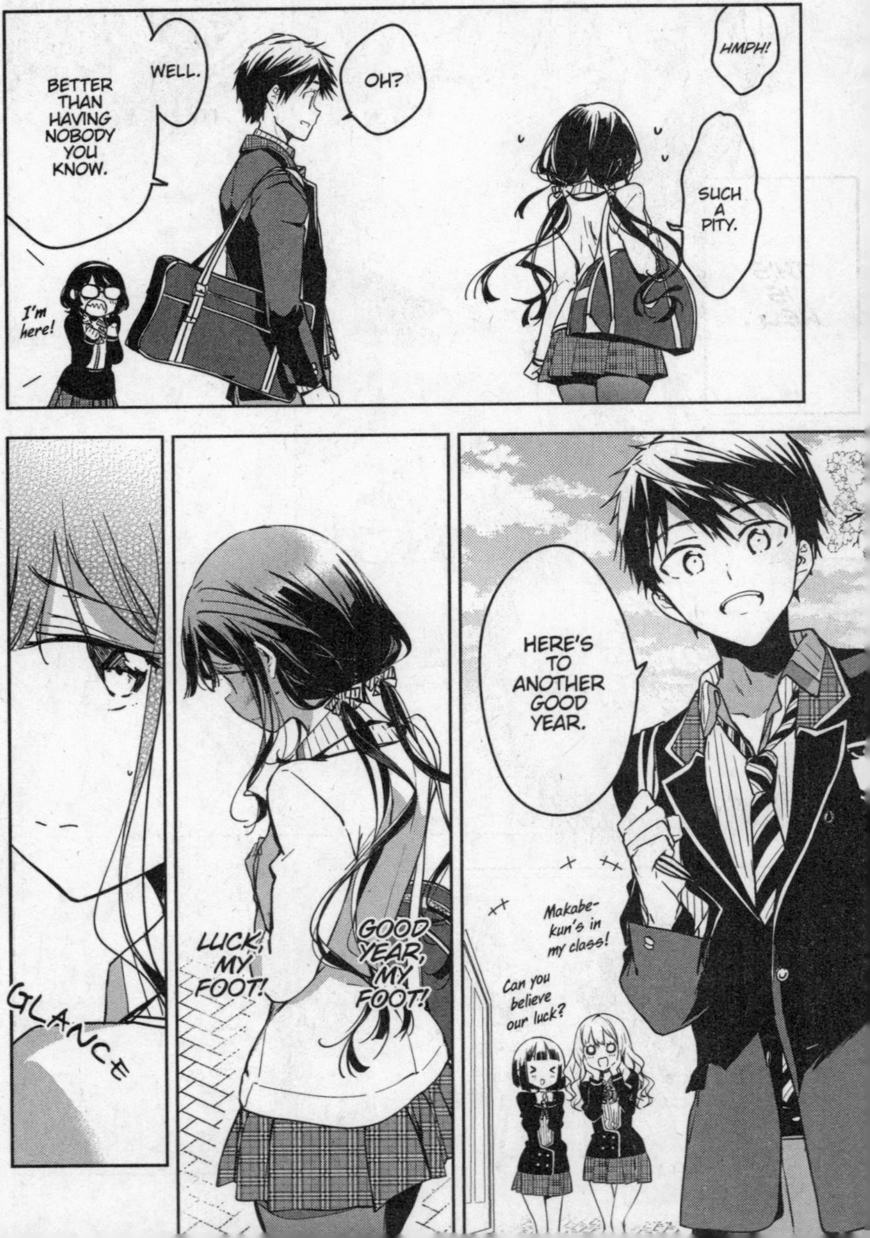
HMPH!
SUCH A PITY.
OH?
WELL.
BETTER THAN HAVING NOBODY YOU KNOW.
I'm here!
HERE'S TO ANOTHER GOOD YEAR.
Makabe-kun's in my class!
Can you believe our luck?
GOOD YEAR, MY FOOT!
LUCK, MY FOOT!
GLANCE

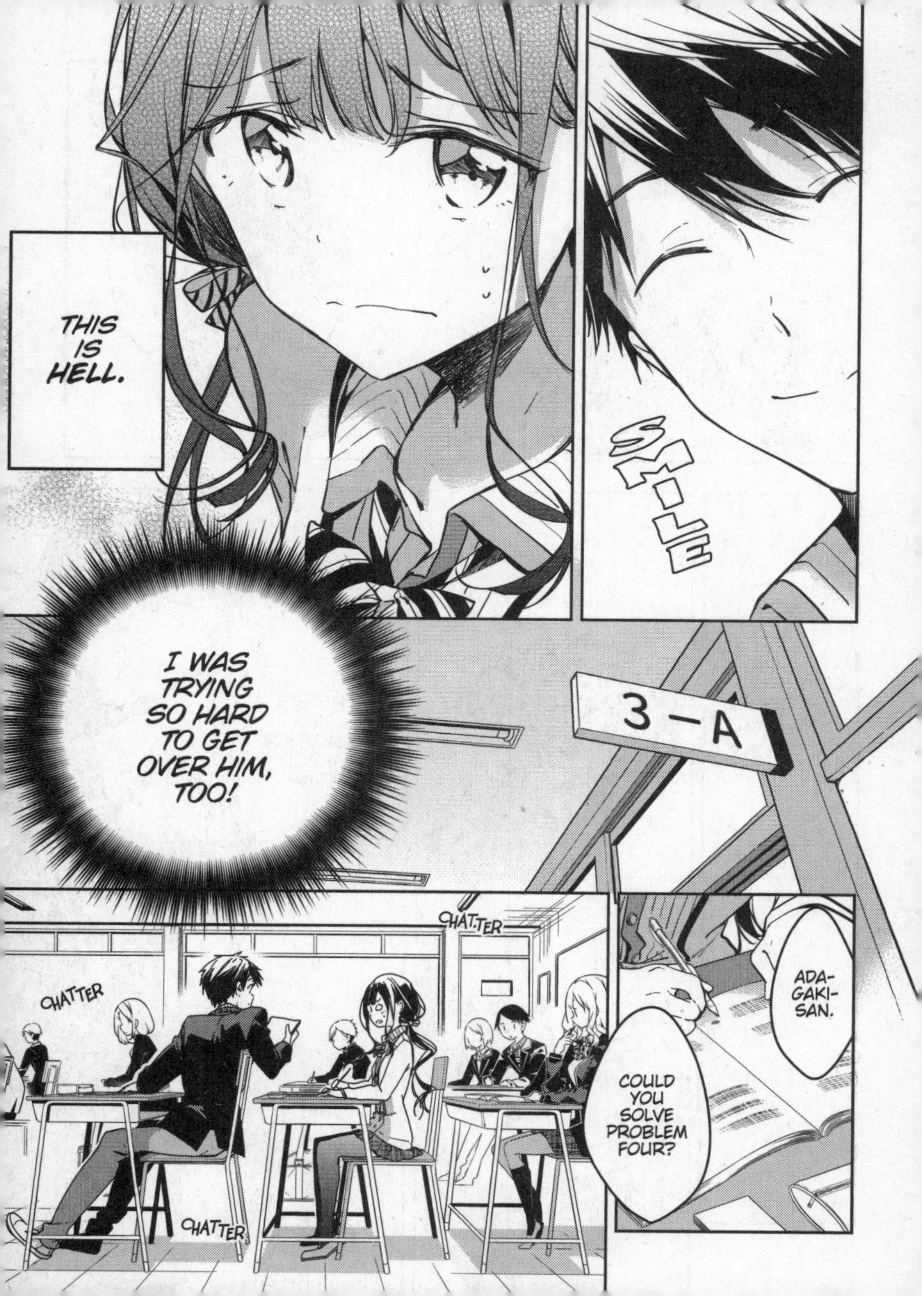
SMILE
THIS IS HELL.
I WAS TRYING SO HARD TO GET OVER HIM, TOO!
3-A
ADA-GAKI-SAN.
COULD YOU SOLVE PROBLEM FOUR?
CHAT-TER
CHATTER
CHATTER

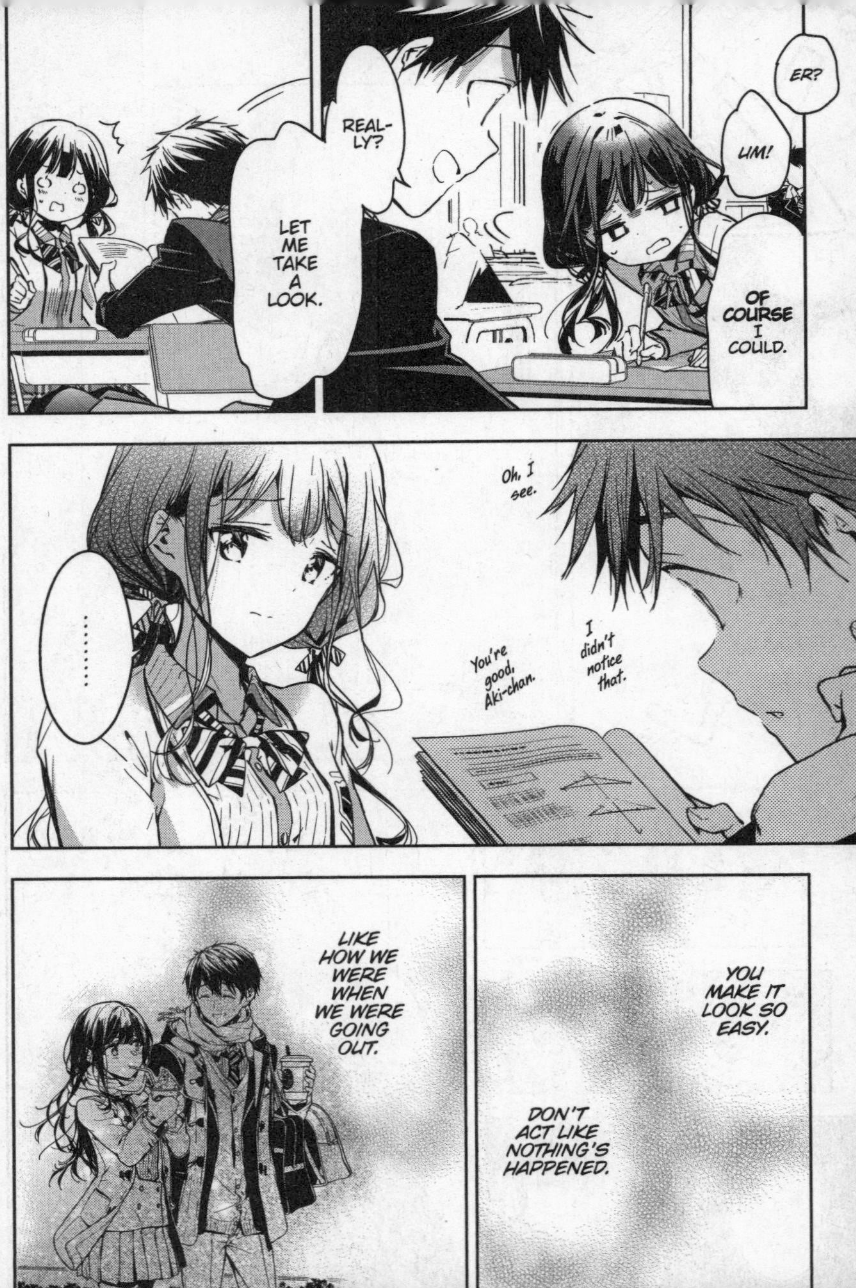
ER?
UM!
OF COURSE I COULD.
REAL-LY?
LET ME TAKE A LOOK.
Oh, I see.
I didn't notice that.
You're good, Aki-chan.
......
YOU MAKE IT LOOK SO EASY.
DON'T ACT LIKE NOTHING'S HAPPENED.
LIKE HOW WE WERE WHEN WE WERE GOING OUT.

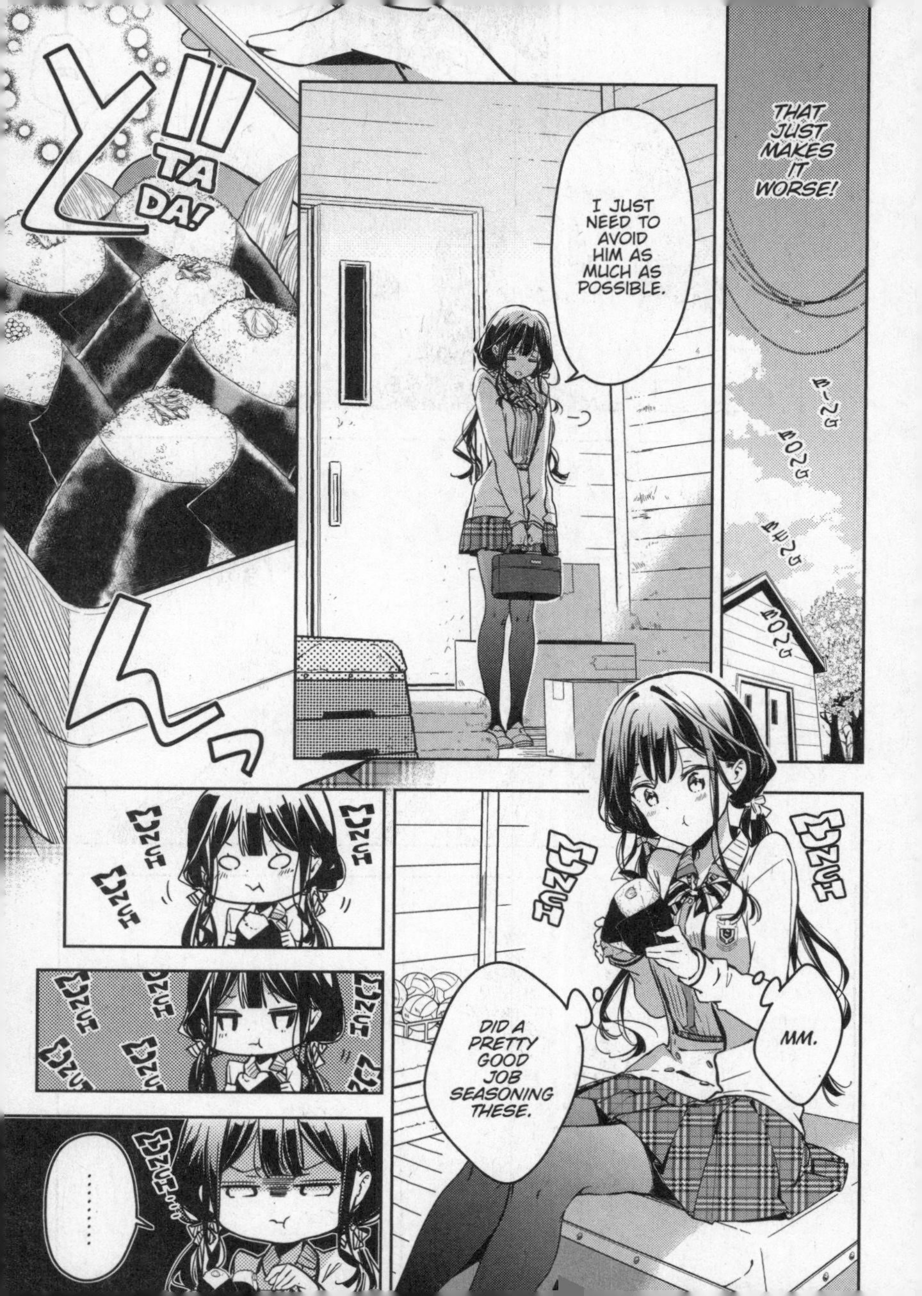
THAT JUST MAKES IT WORSE!
BING BONG BENG BONG
I JUST NEED TO AVOID HIM AS MUCH AS POSSIBLE.
TA DA!
MUNCH
MUNCH
MM.
DID A PRETTY GOOD JOB SEASONING THESE.
MUNCH MUNCH MUNCH
MUNCH MUNCH MUNCH MUNCH
MUNCH
......

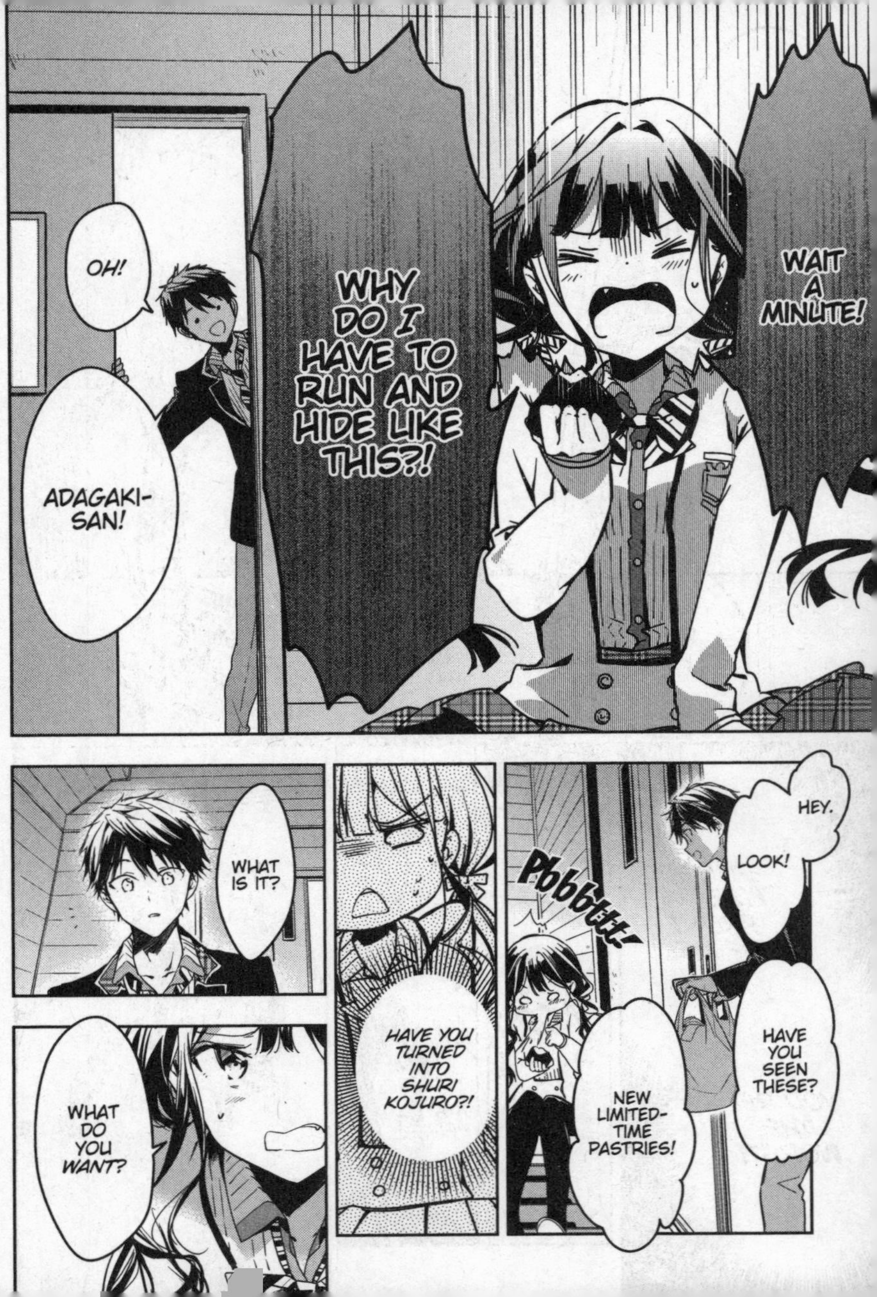
WAIT A MINUTE!
WHY DO I HAVE TO RUN AND HIDE LIKE THIS?!
OH!
ADAGAKI-SAN!
HEY.
LOOK!
Pbbbttt!
HAVE YOU SEEN THESE?
NEW LIMITED-TIME PASTRIES!
HAVE YOU TURNED INTO SHURI KOJURO?!
WHAT IS IT?
WHAT DO YOU WANT?

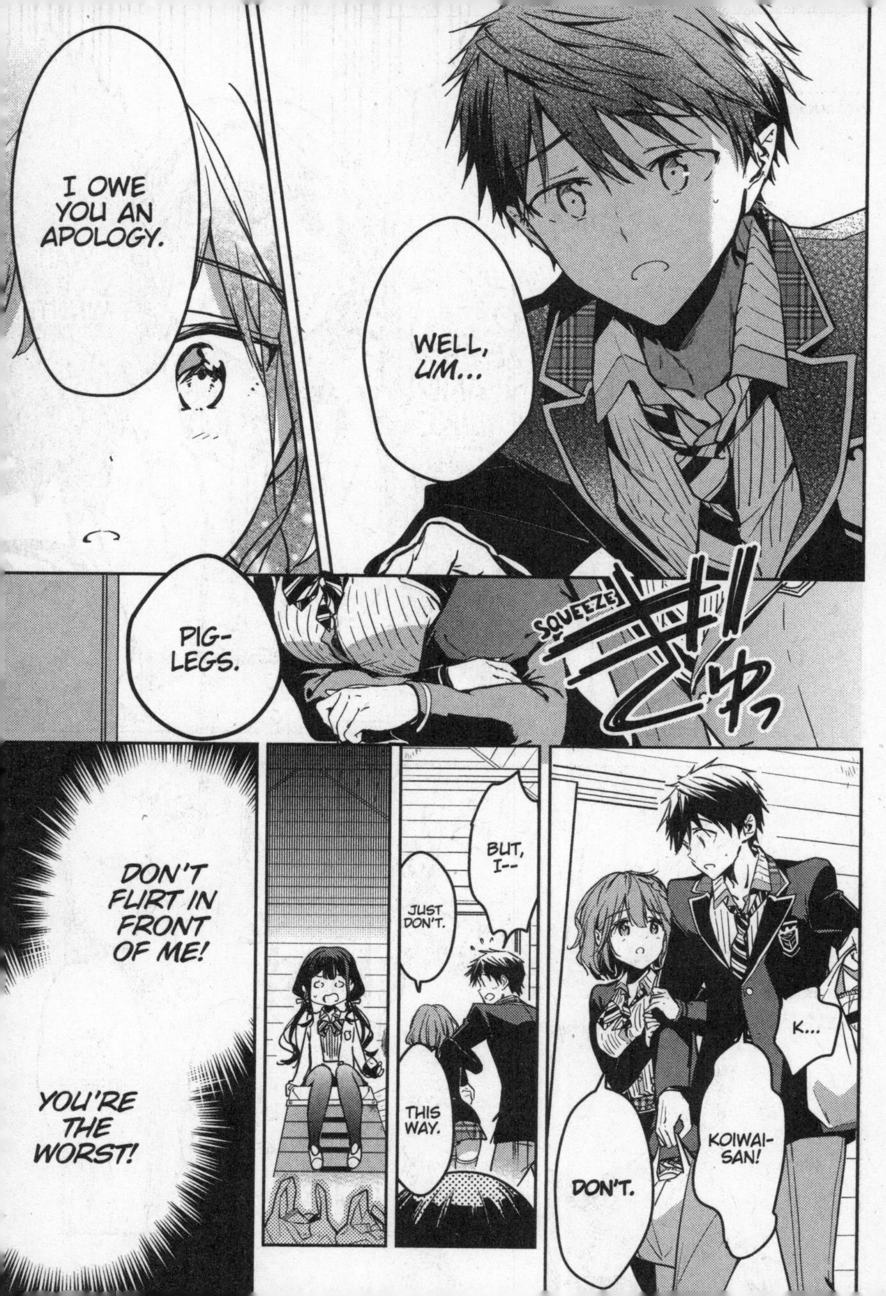
WELL, UM...
I OWE YOU AN APOLOGY.
SQUEEZE
PIG-LEGS.
K...
KOIWAI-SAN!
DON'T.
BUT, I--
JUST DON'T.
THIS WAY.
DON'T FLIRT IN FRONT OF ME!
YOU'RE THE WORST!

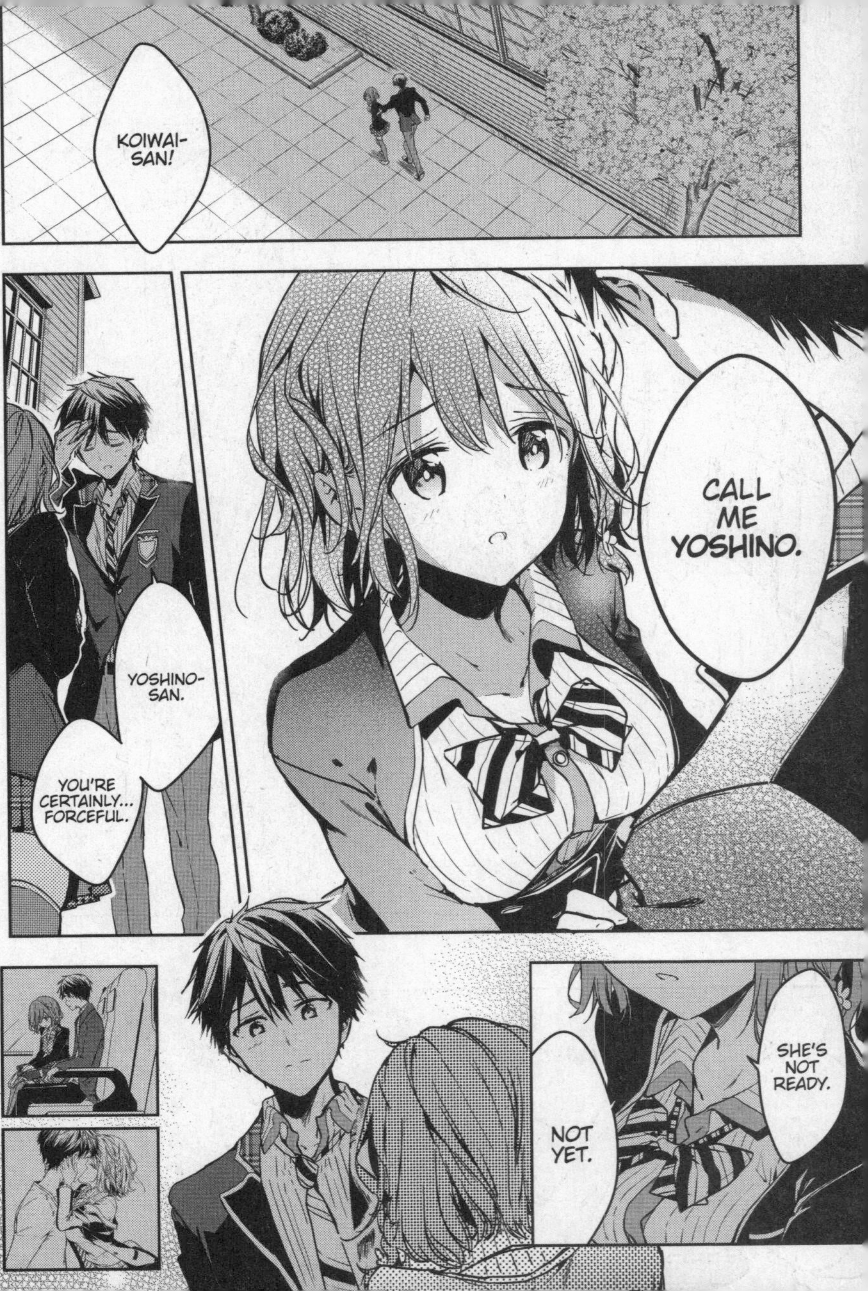
KOIWAI-SAN!
CALL ME YOSHINO.
YOSHINO-SAN.
YOU'RE CERTAINLY... FORCEFUL.
SHE'S NOT READY.
NOT YET.

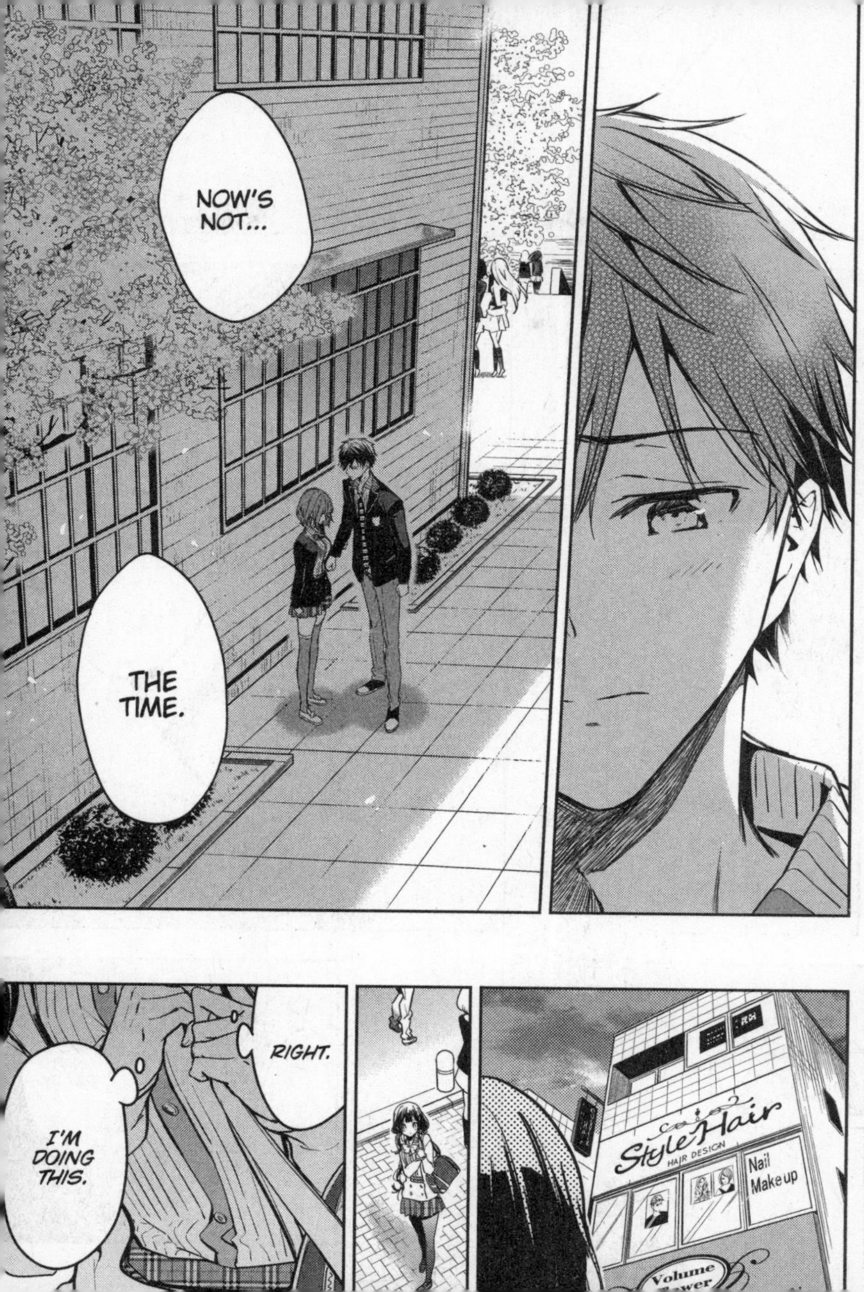
NOW'S NOT...
THE TIME.
Style Hair
HAIR DESIGN
Nail
Make up
Volume
RIGHT.
I'M DOING THIS.

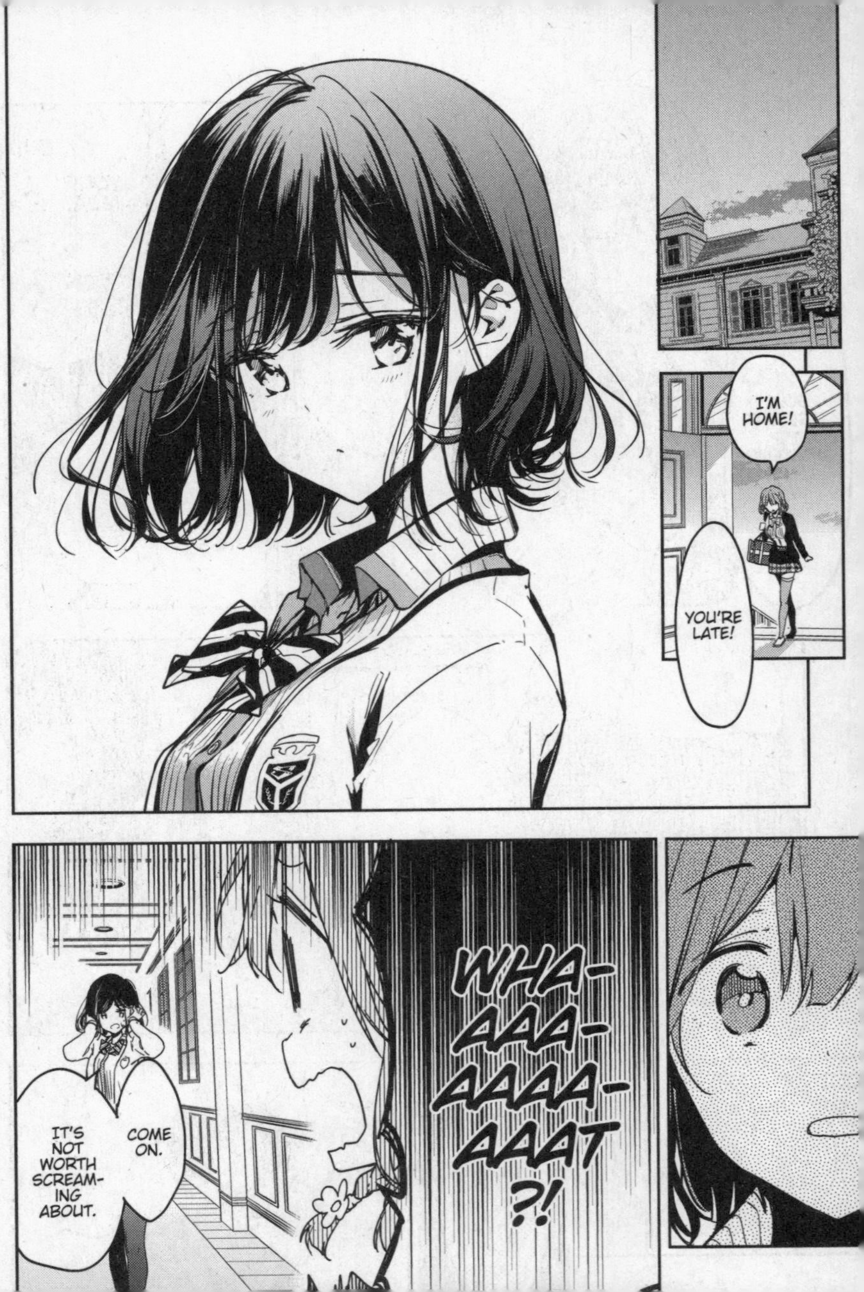
I'M HOME!
YOU'RE LATE!
WHA-AAA-AAAA-AAAT?!
COME ON.
IT'S NOT WORTH SCREAM-ING ABOUT.

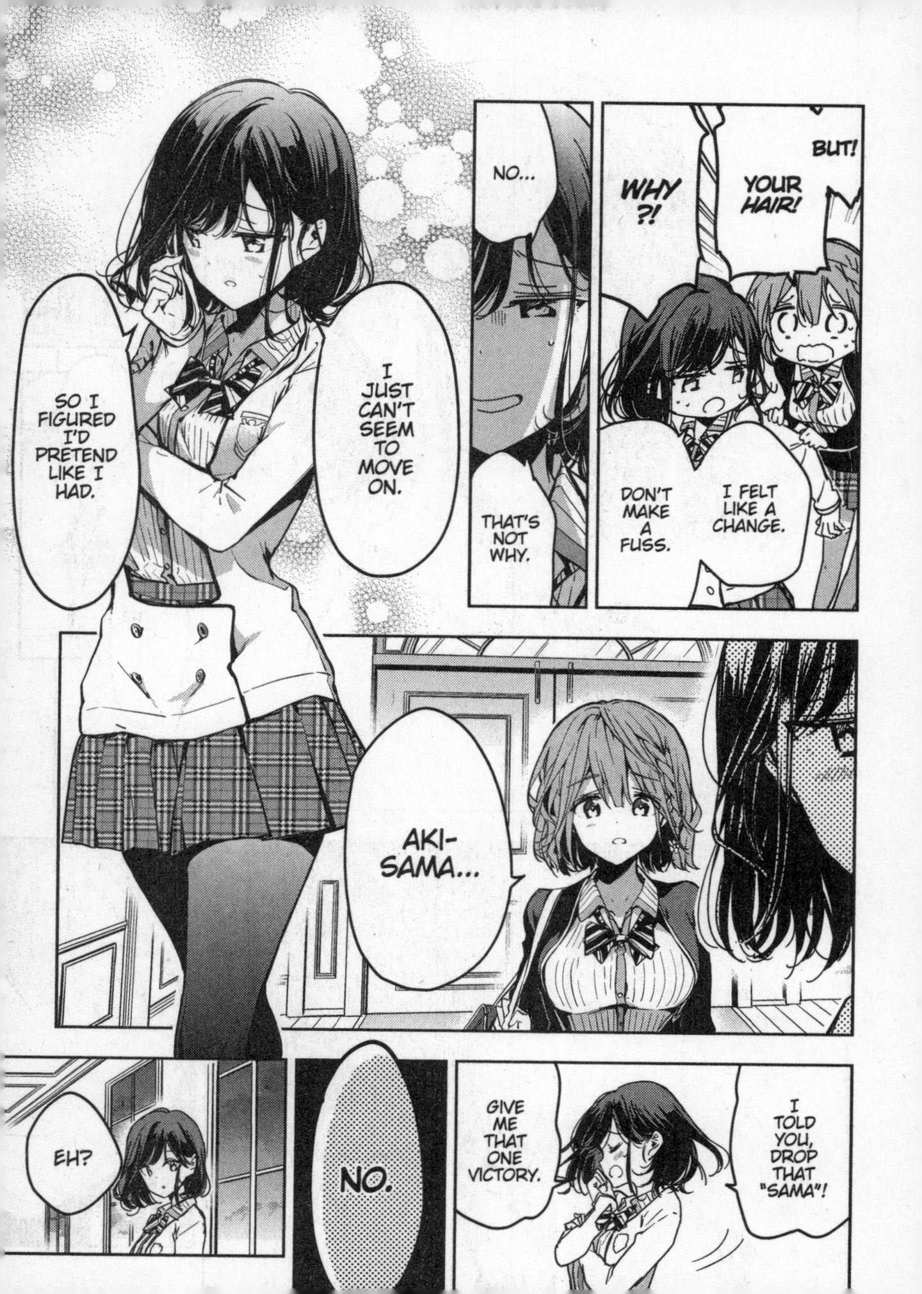
BUT!
YOUR HAIR!
WHY?!
I FELT LIKE A CHANGE.
DON'T MAKE A FUSS.
NO...
THAT'S NOT WHY.
I JUST CAN'T SEEM TO MOVE ON.
SO I FIGURED I'D PRETEND LIKE I HAD.
AKI-SAMA...
I TOLD YOU, DROP THAT "SAMA"!
GIVE ME THAT ONE VICTORY.
NO.
EH?

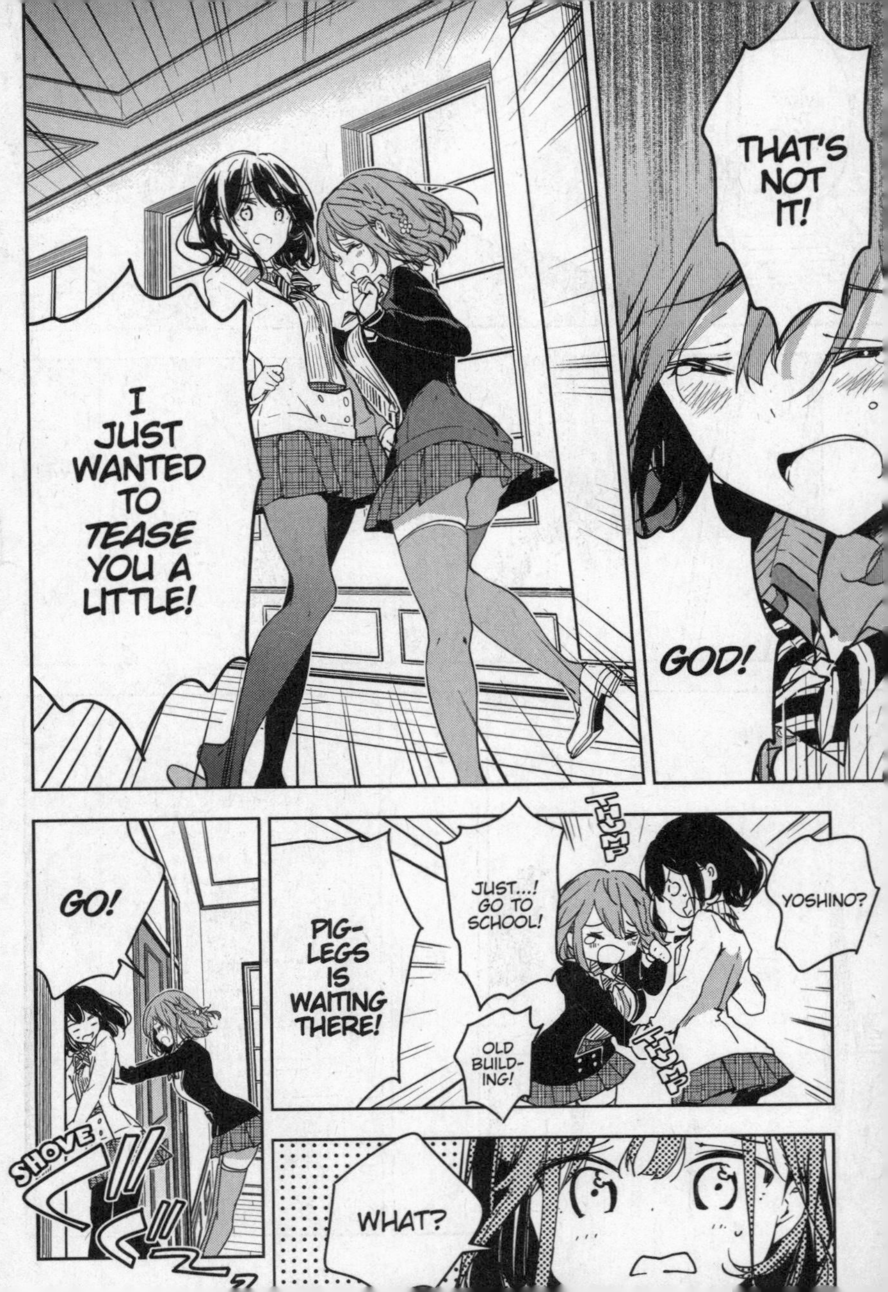
THAT'S NOT IT!
GOD!
I JUST WANTED TO TEASE YOU A LITTLE!
YOSHINO?
THUMP
JUST...! GO TO SCHOOL!
PIG-LEGS IS WAITING THERE!
OLD BUILDING!
THUMP
WHAT?
GO!
SHOVE

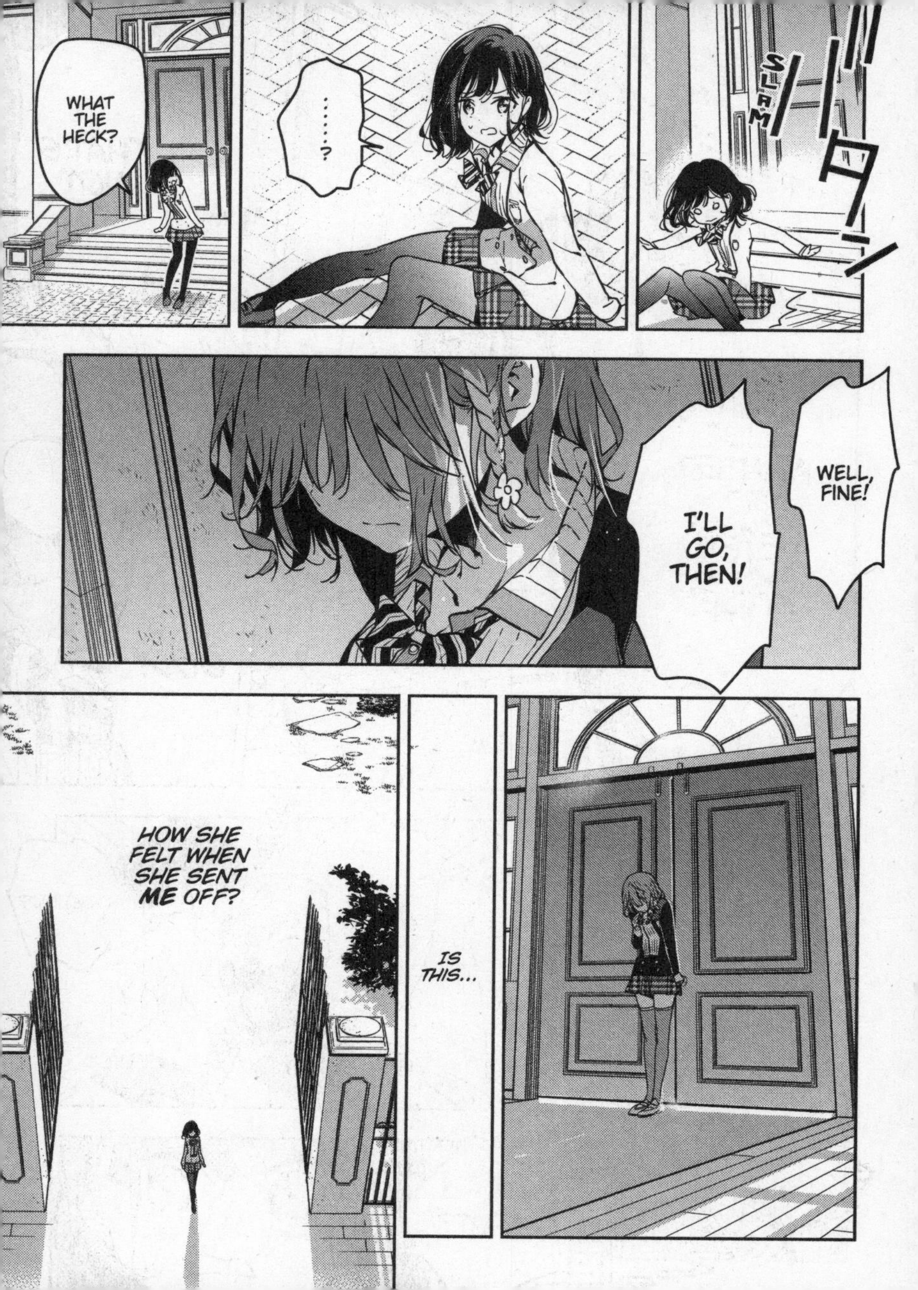
バタン
SLAM
......?
WHAT THE HECK?
WELL, FINE!
I'LL GO, THEN!
IS THIS...
HOW SHE FELT WHEN SHE SENT ME OFF?

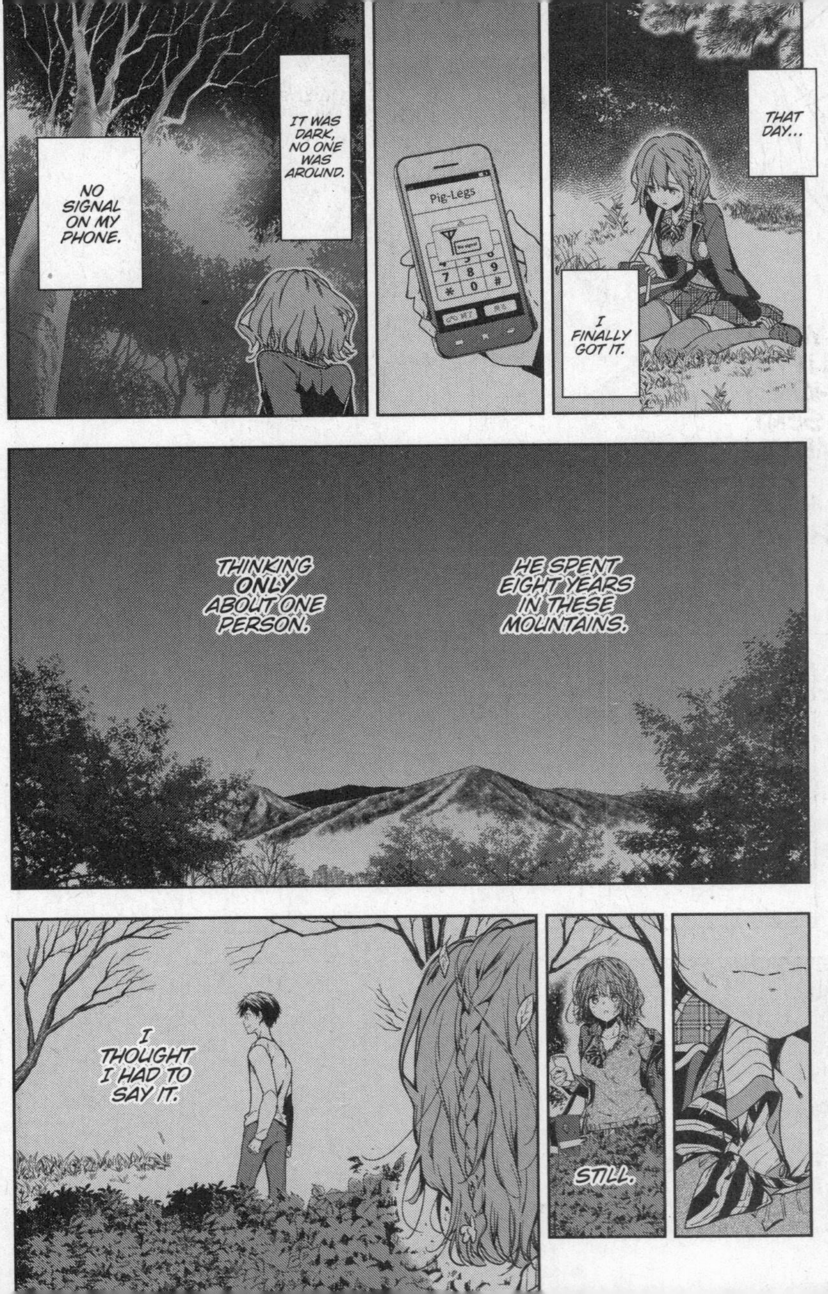
THAT DAY...
I FINALLY GOT IT.
Pig-Legs
IT WAS DARK, NO ONE WAS AROUND.
NO SIGNAL ON MY PHONE.
HE SPENT EIGHT YEARS IN THESE MOUNTAINS.
THINKING ONLY ABOUT ONE PERSON.
STILL.
I THOUGHT I HAD TO SAY IT.

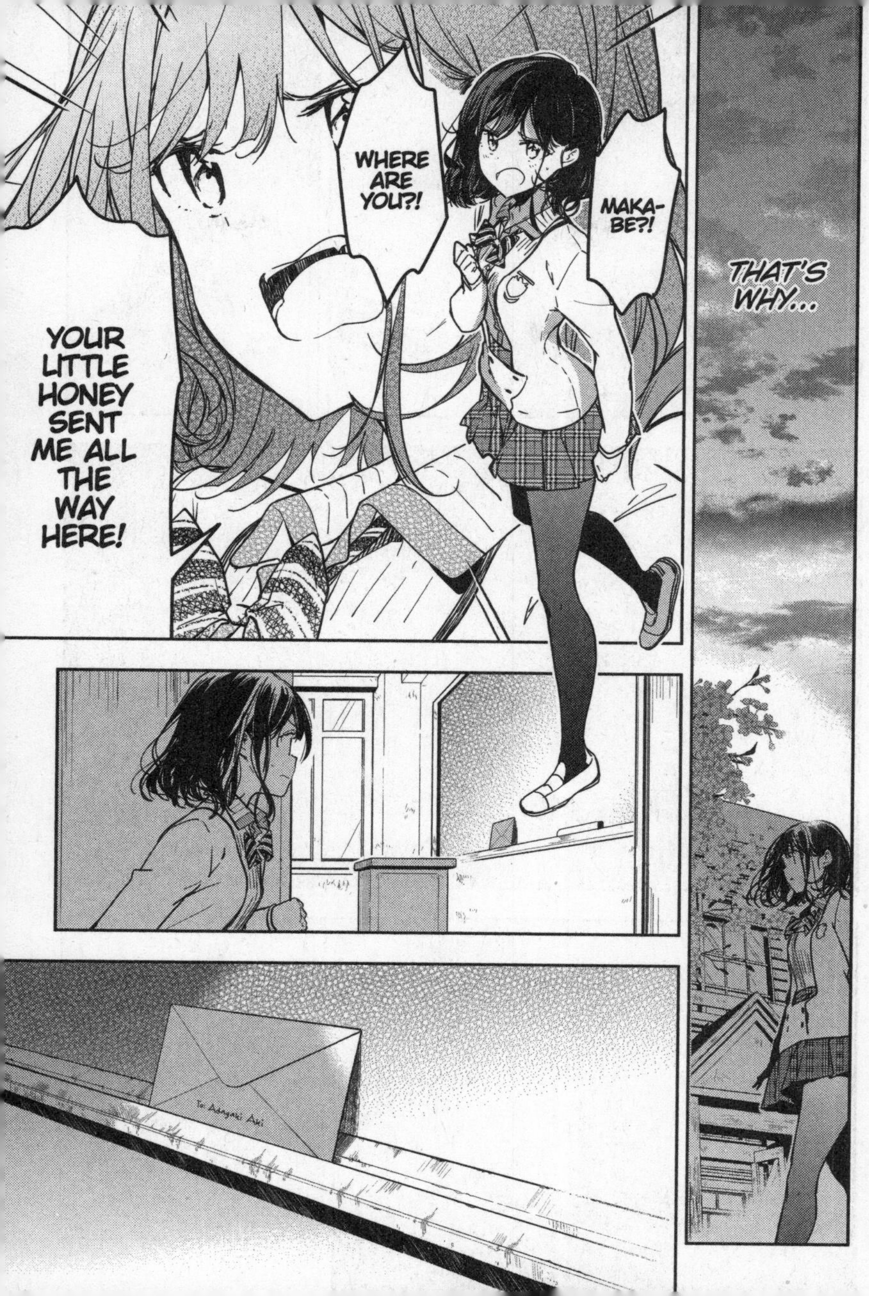
THAT'S WHY...
MAKA-BE?!
WHERE ARE YOU?!
YOUR LITTLE HONEY SENT ME ALL THE WAY HERE!
To: Adagaki Aki

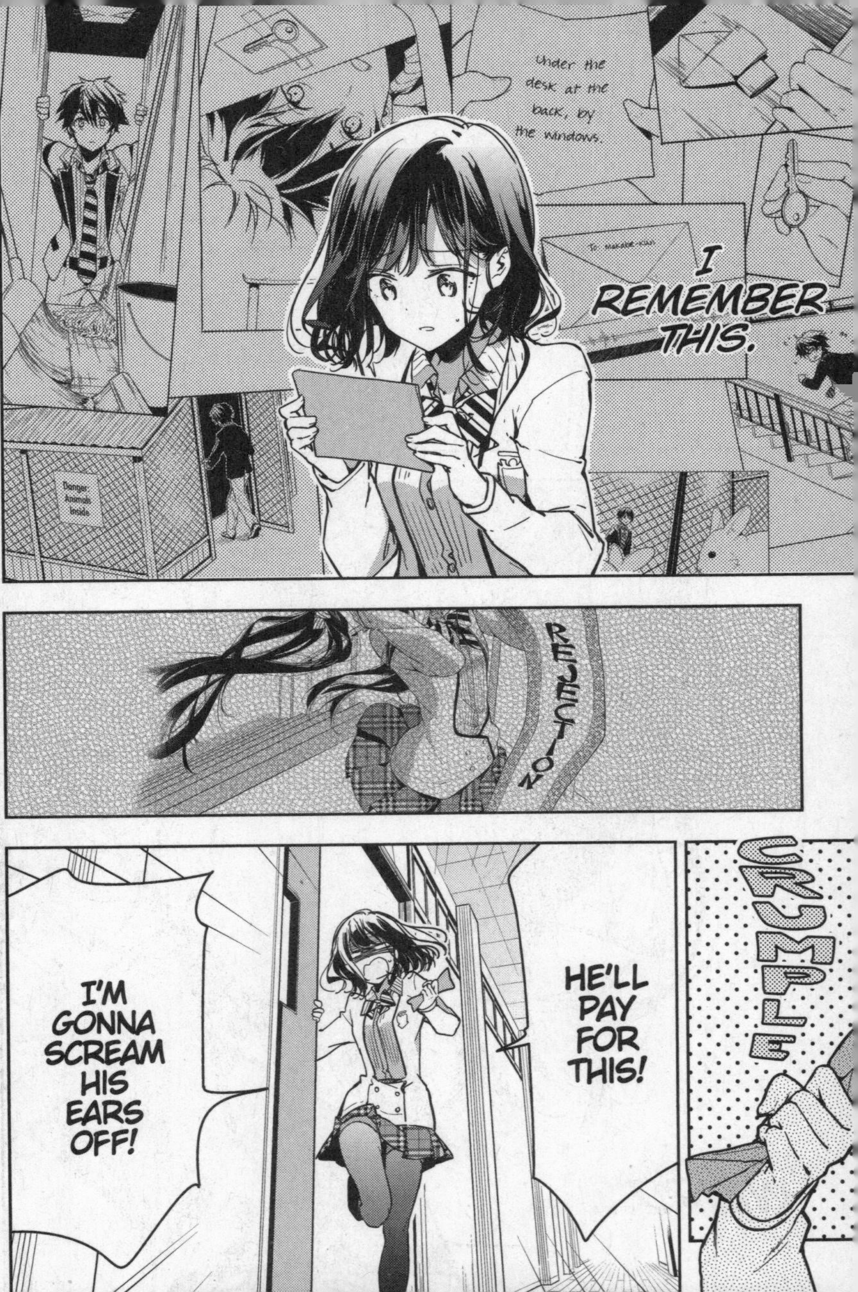
Under the desk at the back, by the windows.
I REMEMBER THIS.
Danger Animals Inside
REJECTION
CRUMPLE
HE'LL PAY FOR THIS!
I'M GONNA SCREAM HIS EARS OFF!

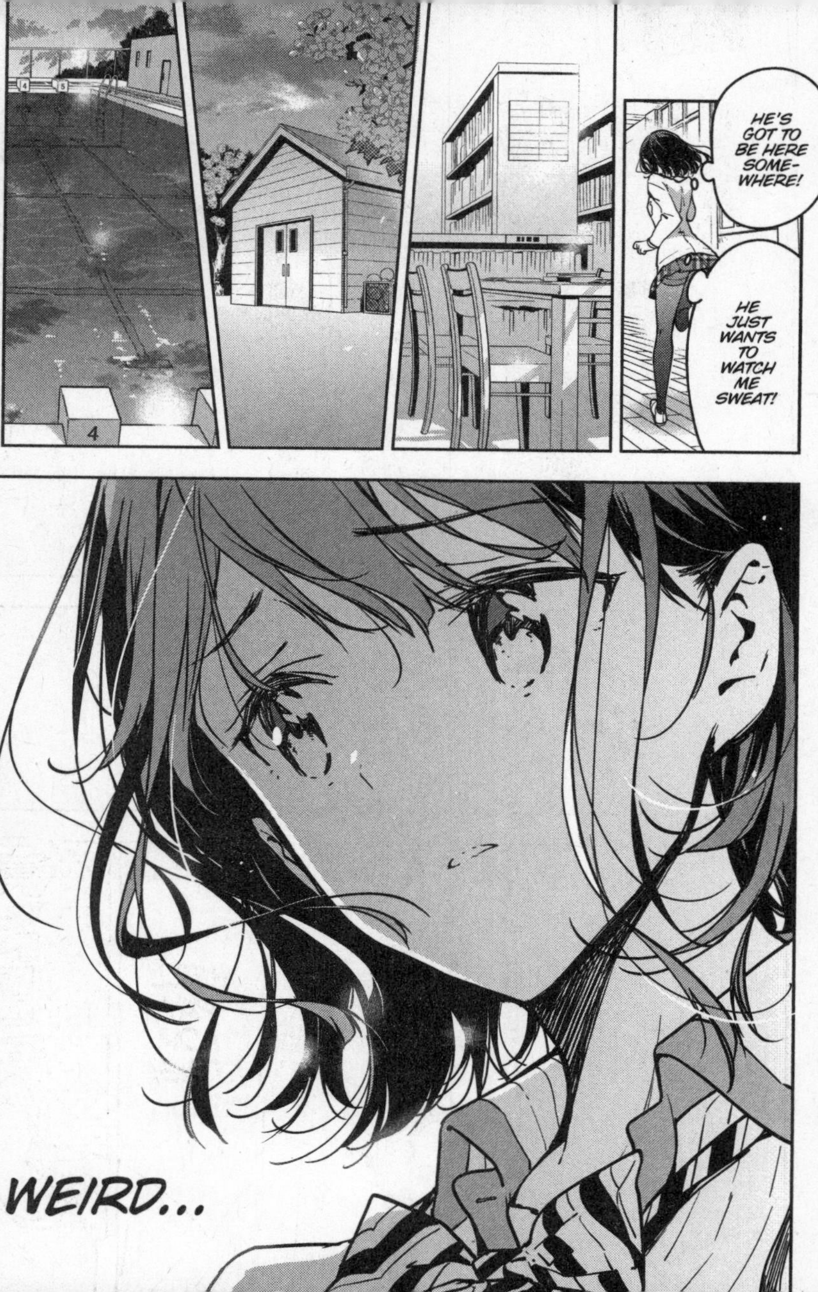
HE'S GOT TO BE HERE SOME-WHERE!
HE JUST WANTS TO WATCH ME SWEAT!
WEIRD...

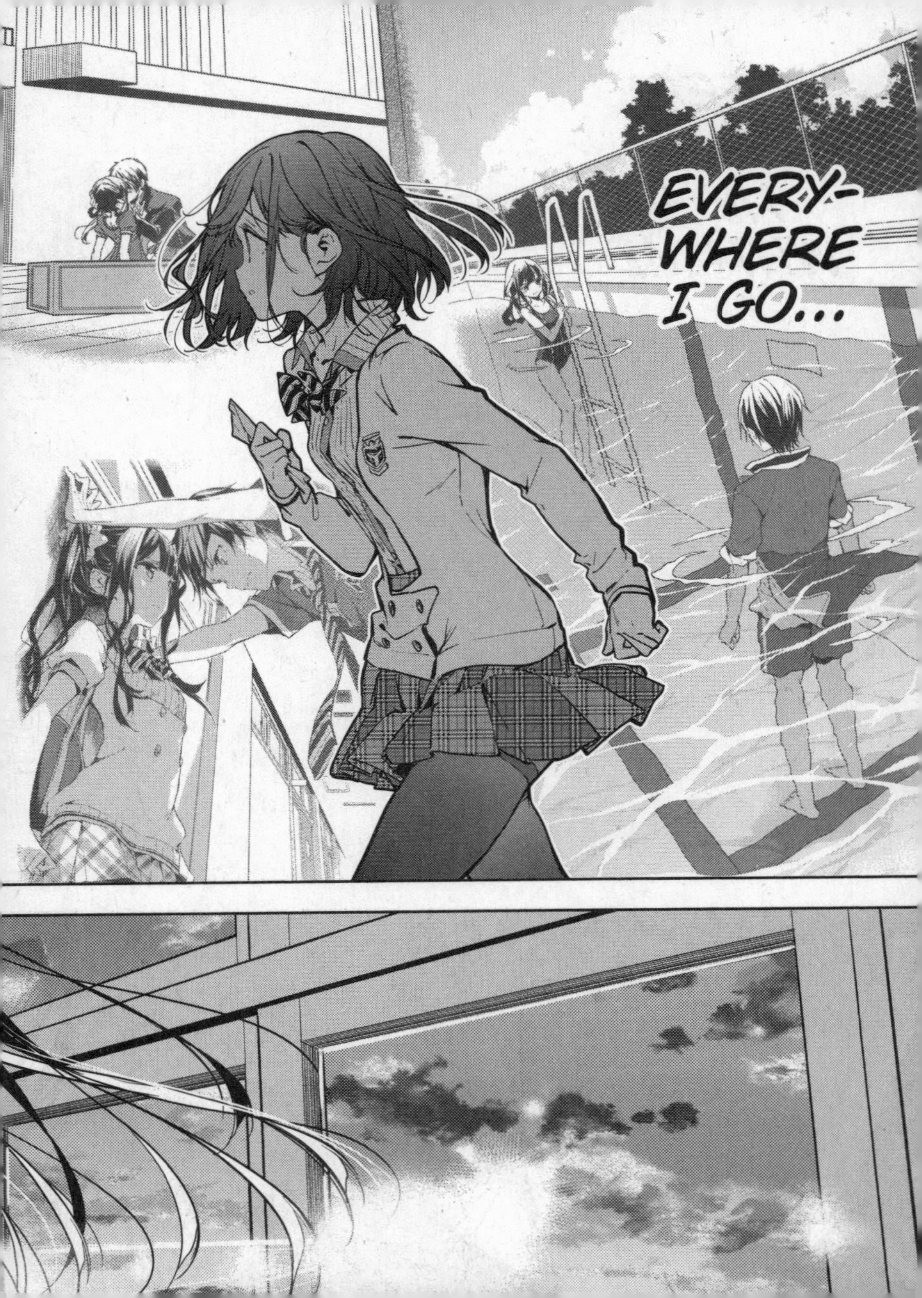
EVERY-WHERE I GO...

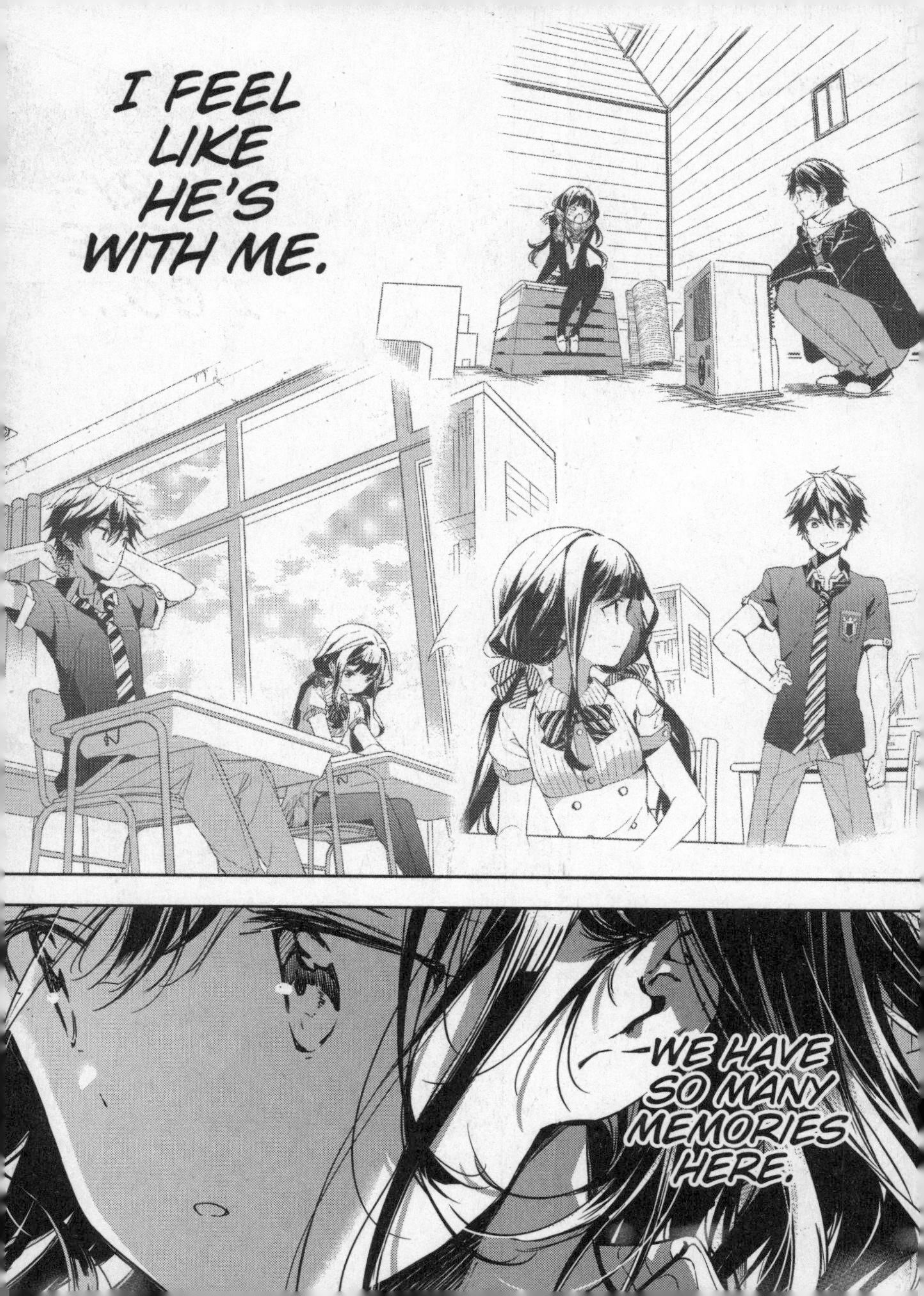
I FEEL LIKE HE'S WITH ME.
WE HAVE SO MANY MEMORIES HERE.

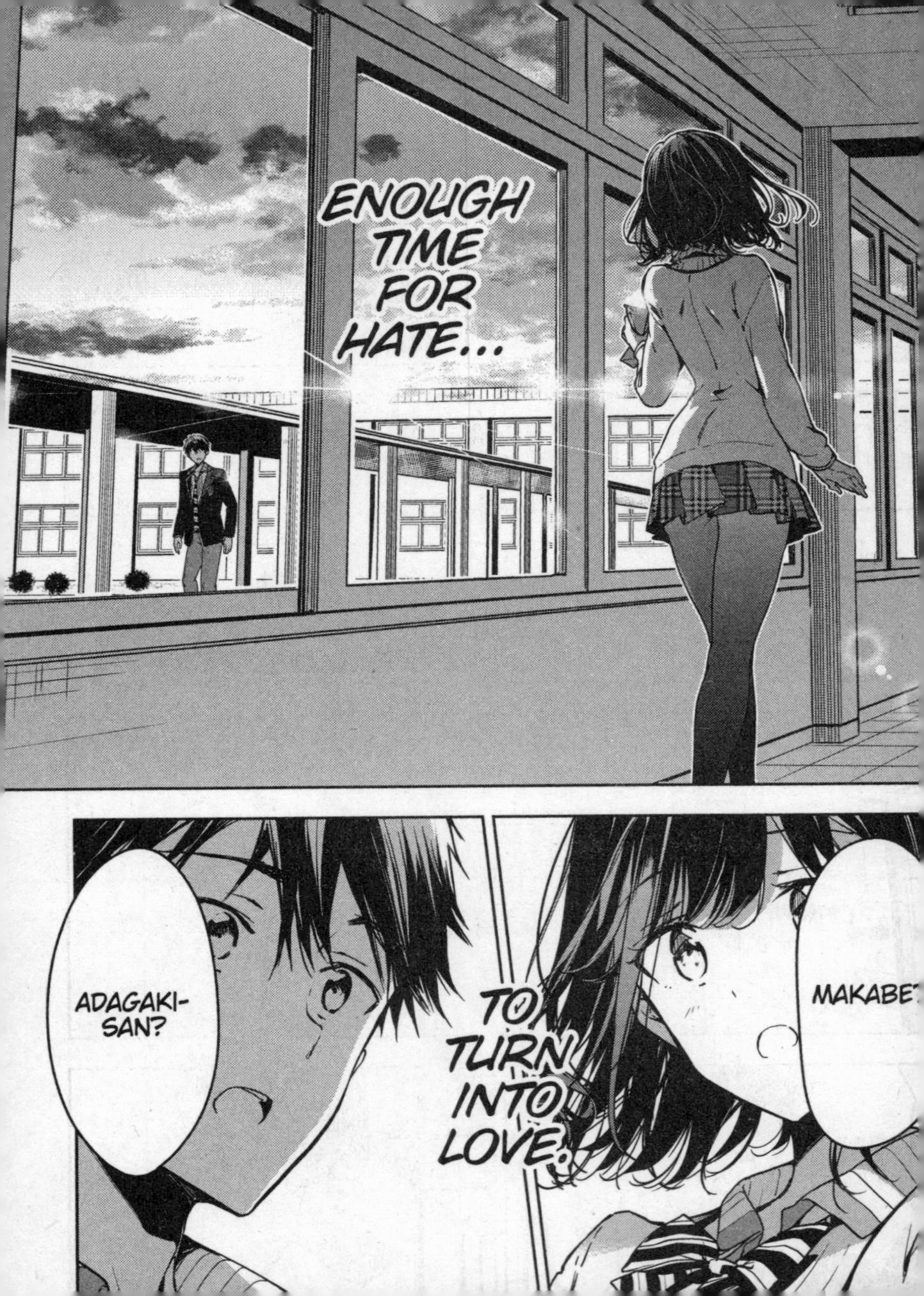
ENOUGH TIME FOR HATE...
MAKABE?
TO TURN INTO LOVE.
ADAGAKI-SAN?

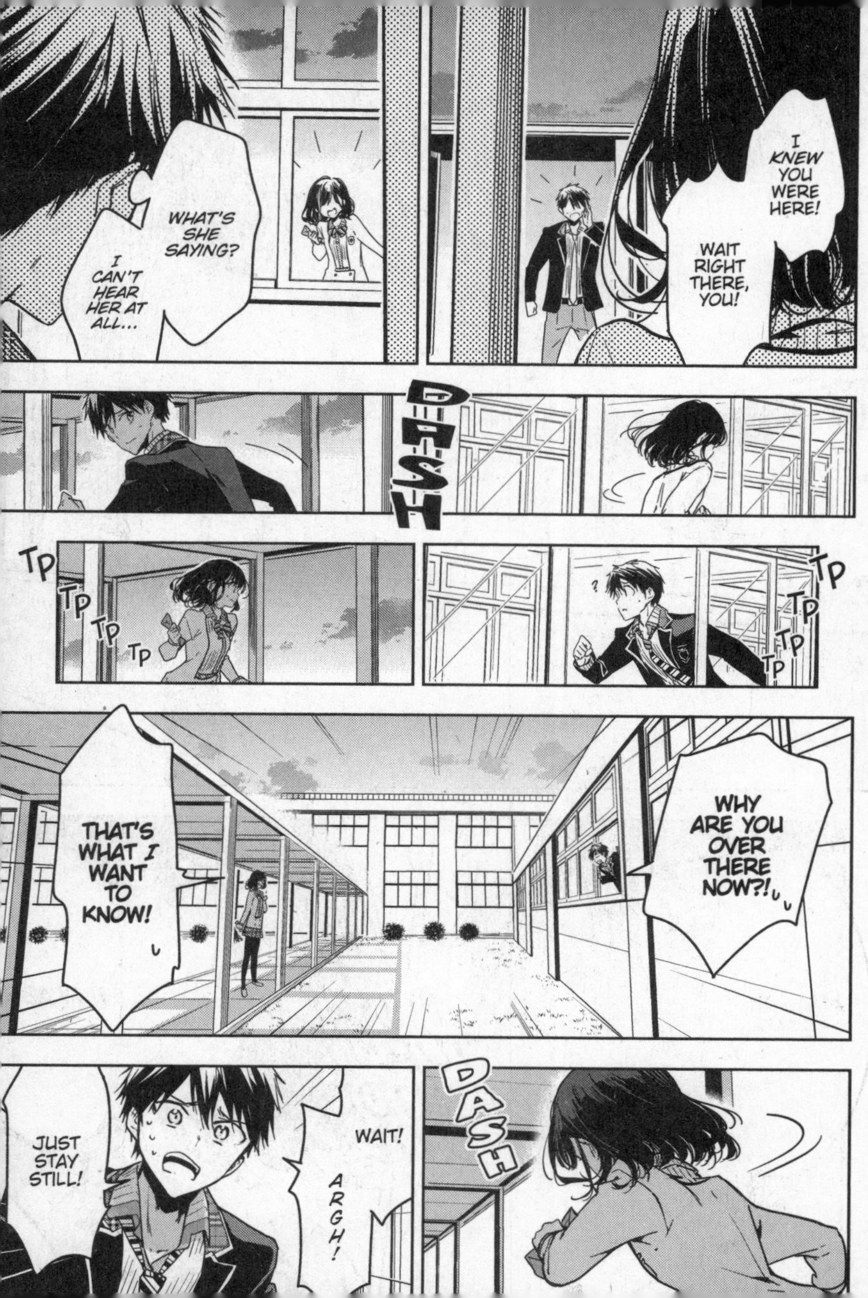
I KNEW YOU WERE HERE!
WAIT RIGHT THERE, YOU!
WHAT'S SHE SAYING?
I CAN'T HEAR HER AT ALL...
DASH
TP TP TP TP
TP TP TP TP TP
WHY ARE YOU OVER THERE NOW?!
THAT'S WHAT I WANT TO KNOW!
DASH
WAIT!
ARGH!
JUST STAY STILL!

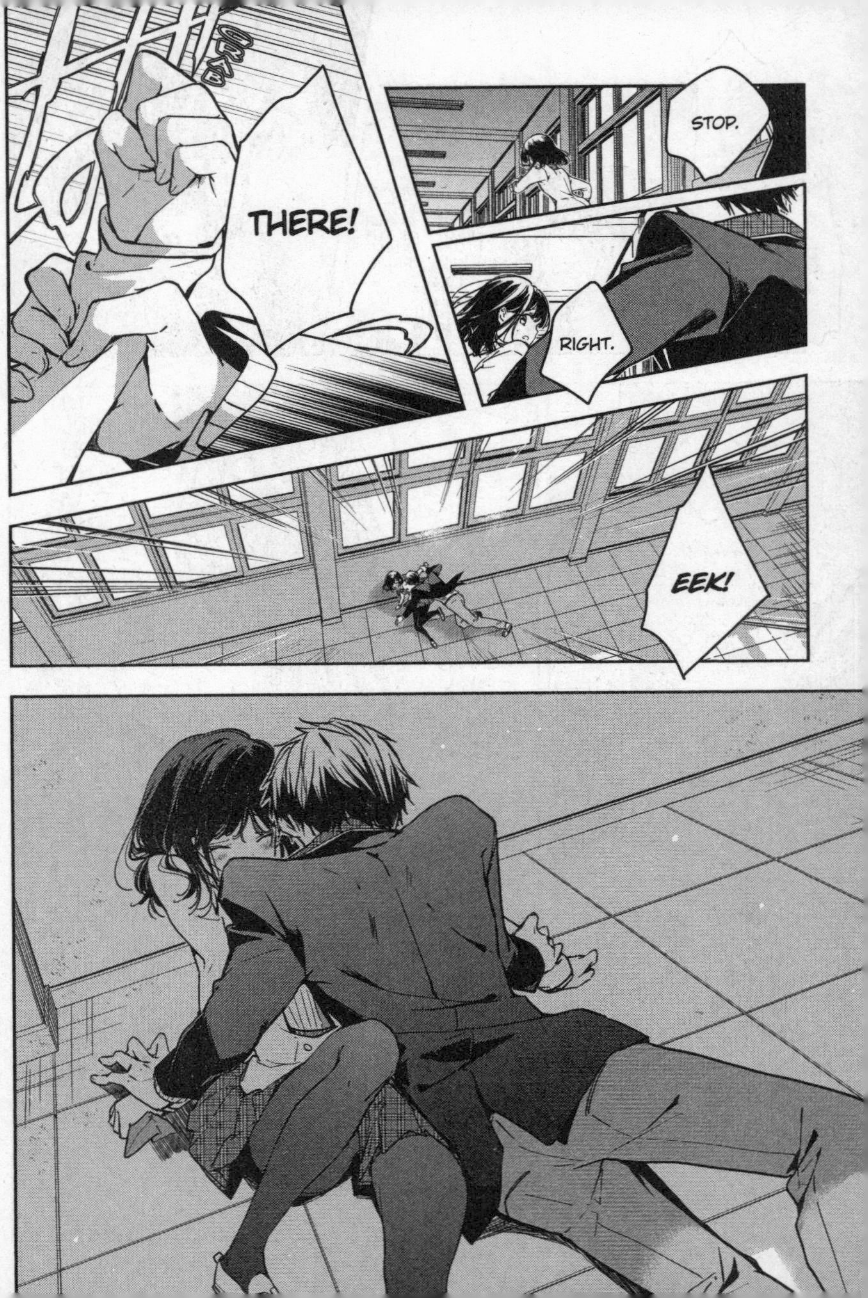
STOP.
RIGHT.
GRAB
THERE!
EEK!

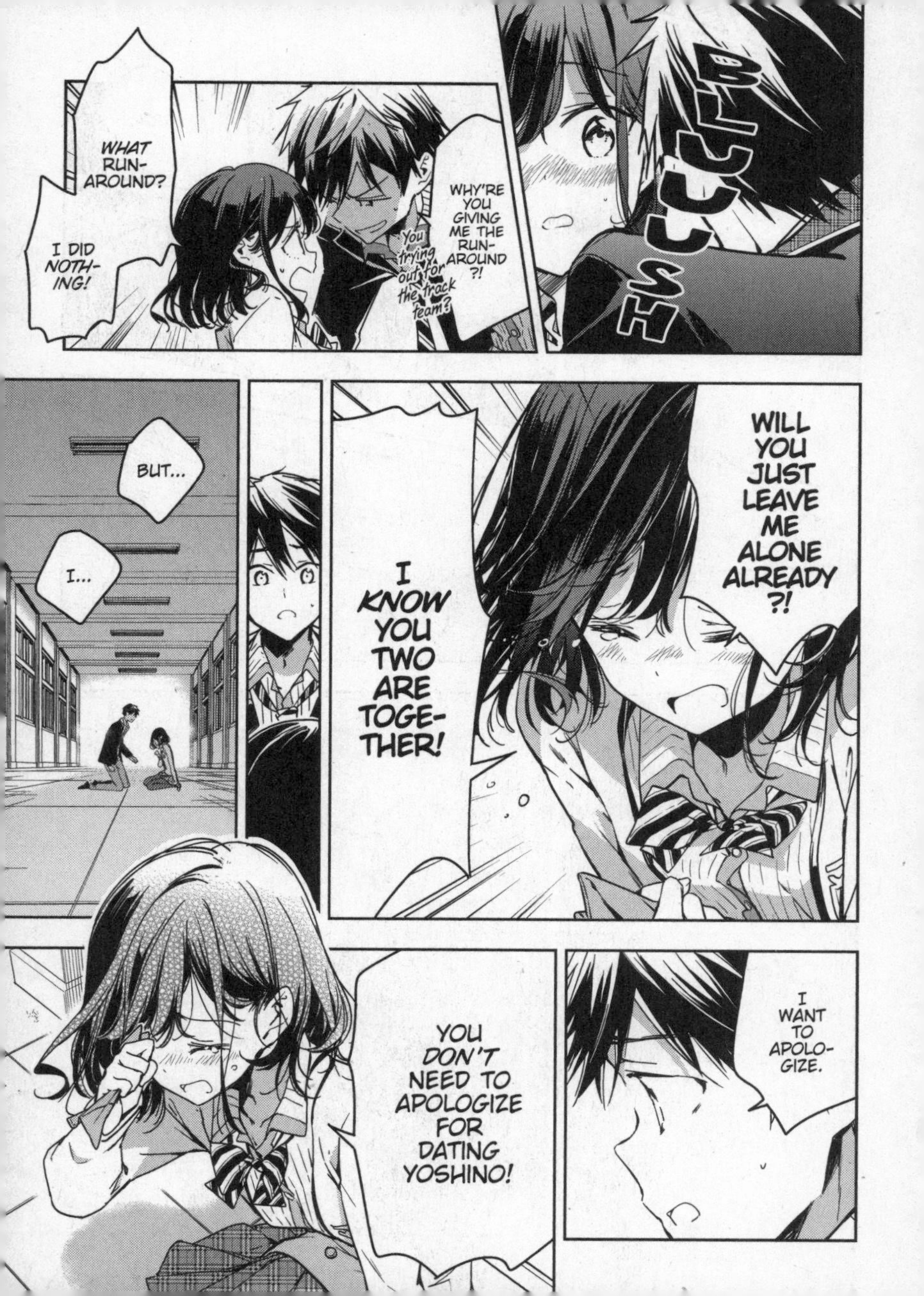
BLUUSH
WHY'RE YOU GIVING ME THE RUN-AROUND?!
You trying out for the track team?
WHAT RUN-AROUND?
I DID NOTHING!
WILL YOU JUST LEAVE ME ALONE ALREADY?!
I KNOW YOU TWO ARE TOGETHER!
BUT...
I...
I WANT TO APOLOGIZE.
YOU DON'T NEED TO APOLOGIZE FOR DATING YOSHINO!

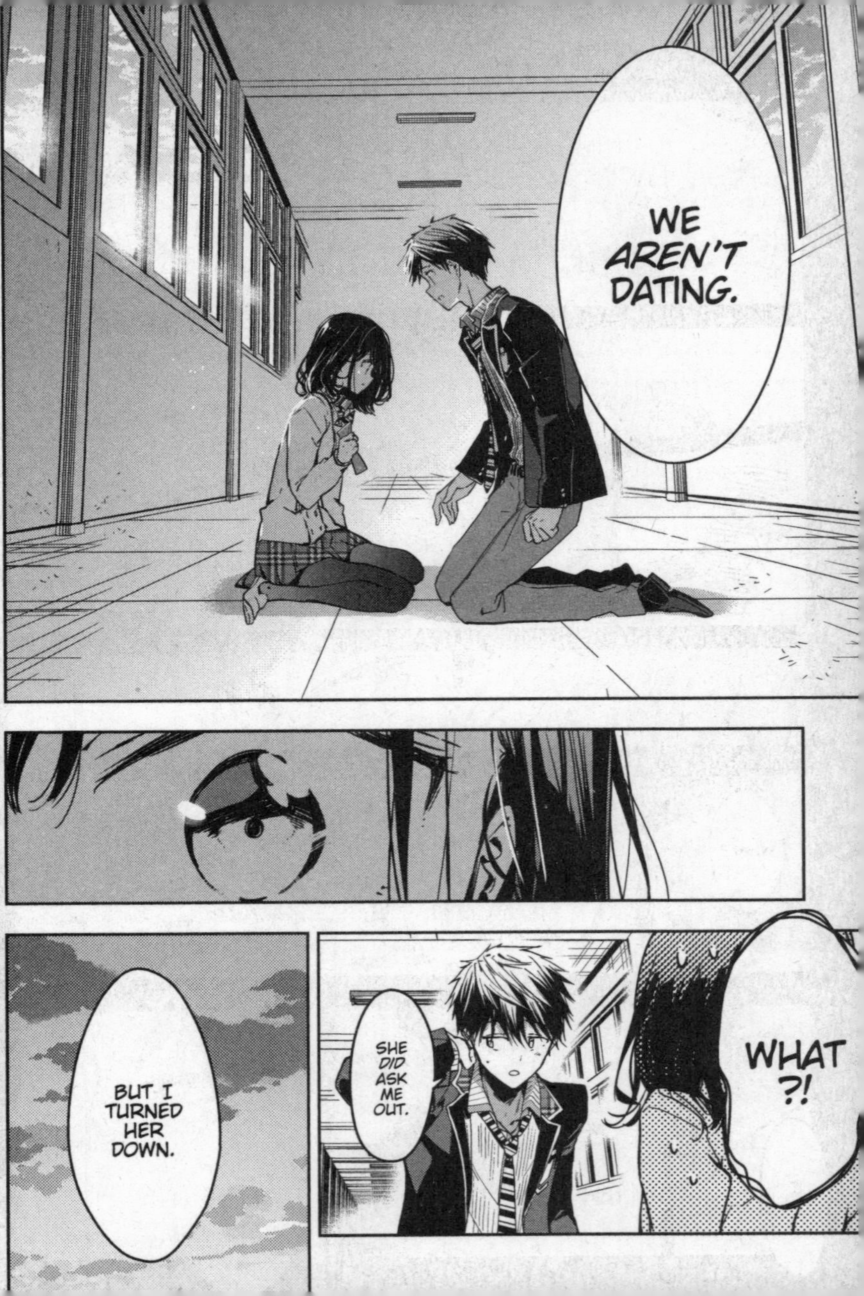
WE AREN'T DATING.
WHAT ?!
SHE DID ASK ME OUT.
BUT I TURNED HER DOWN.

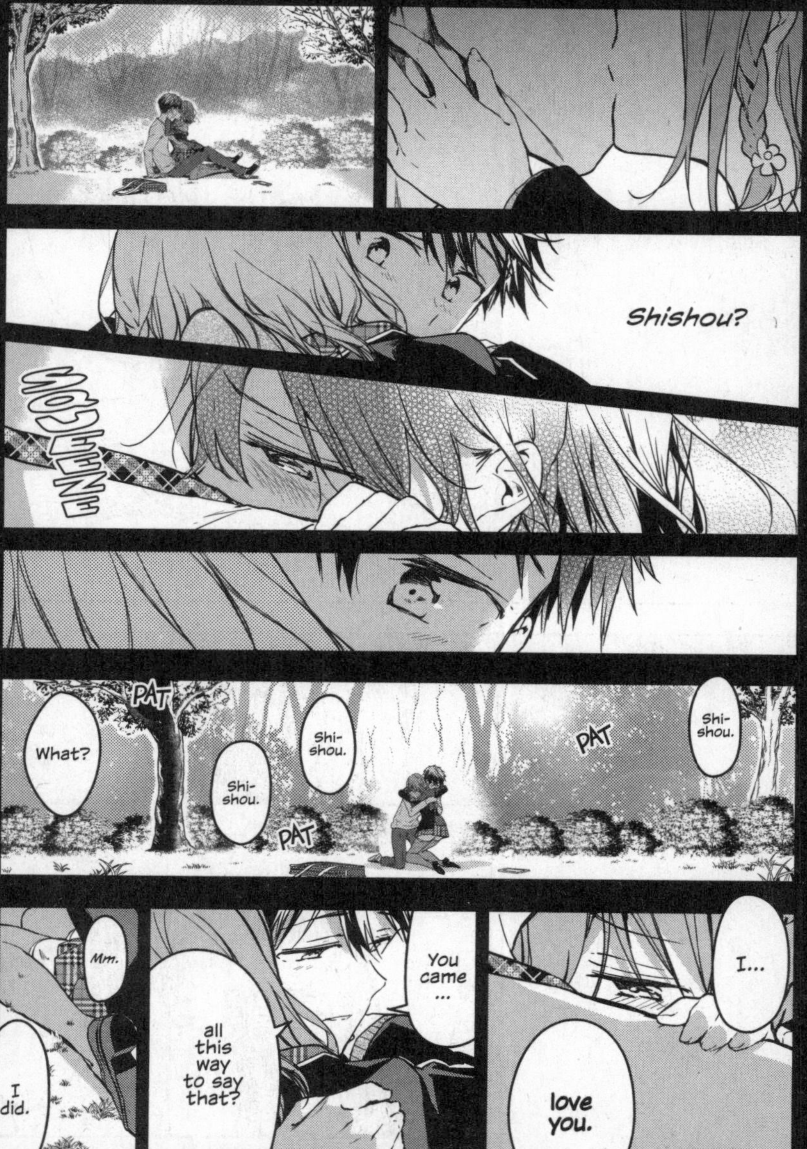
Shishou?
SQUEEZE
Shi-shou.
PAT
Shi-shou.
Shi-shou.
PAT
PAT
What?
I...
love you.
You came...
all this way to say that?
Mm.
I did.

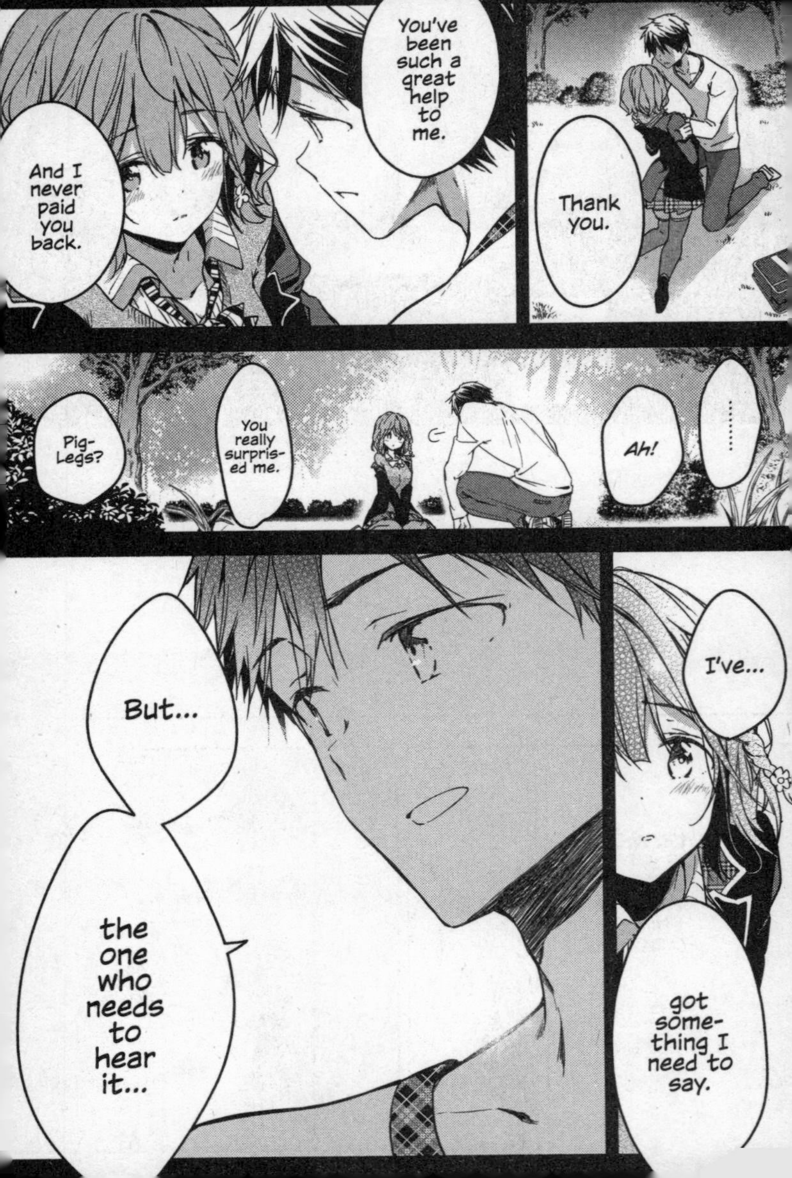
Thank you.
You've been such a great help to me.
And I never paid you back.
......
Ah!
You really surpris-ed me.
Pig-Legs?
I've...
got some-thing I need to say.
But...
the one who needs to hear it...

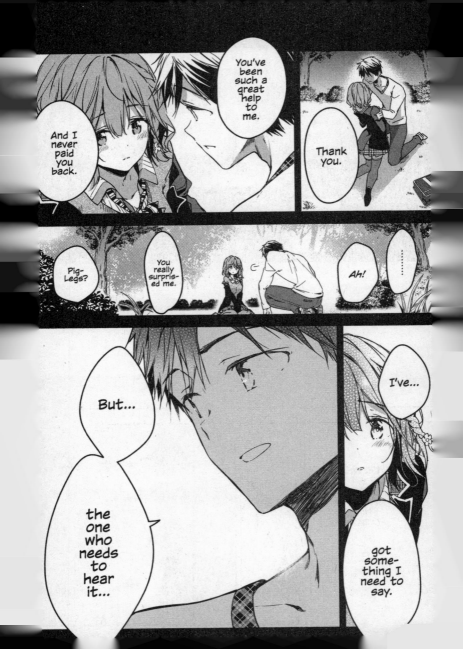

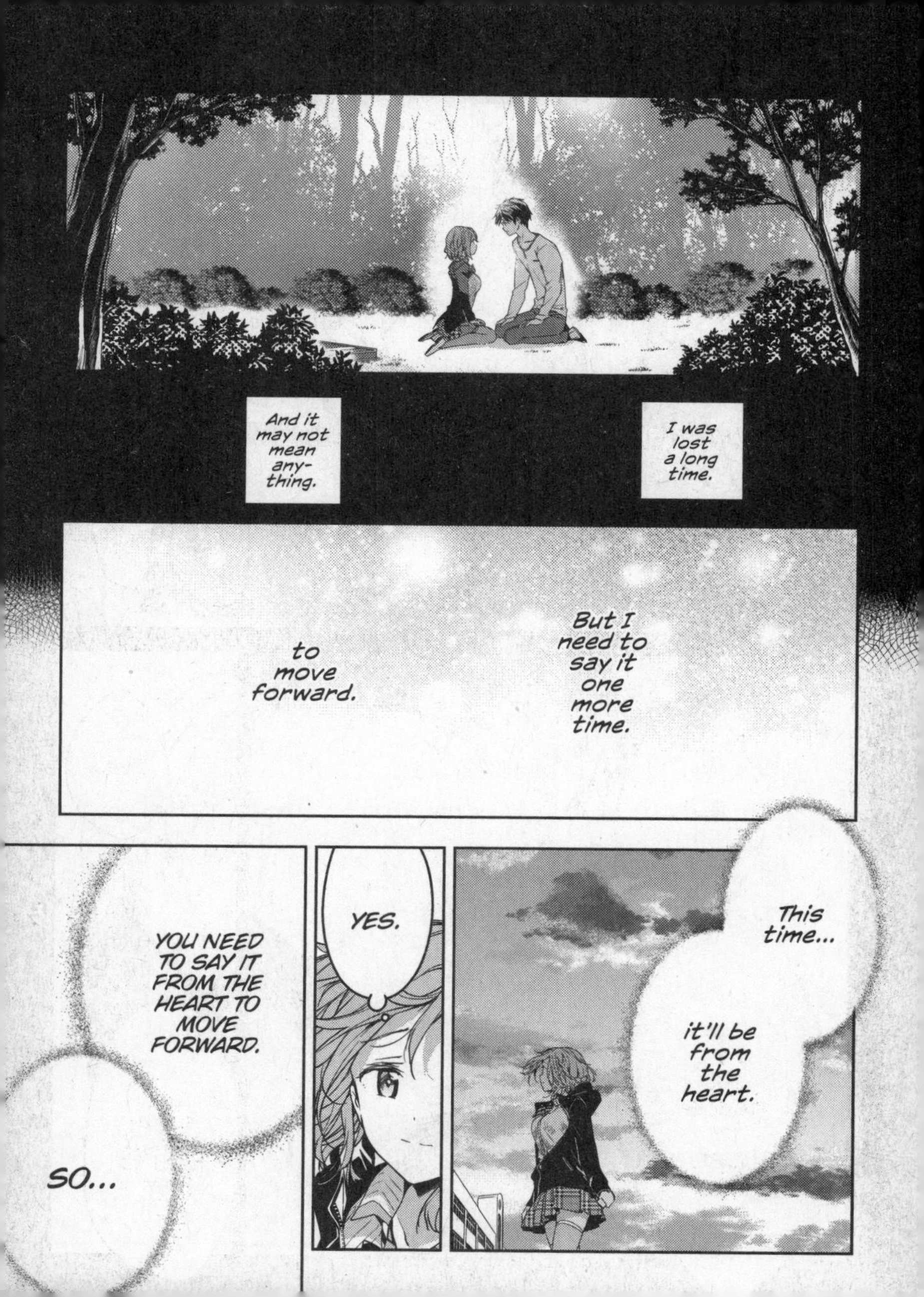
I was lost a long time.
And it may not mean anything.
But I need to say it one more time.
to move forward.
This time...
it'll be from the heart.
YES.
YOU NEED TO SAY IT FROM THE HEART TO MOVE FORWARD.
SO...

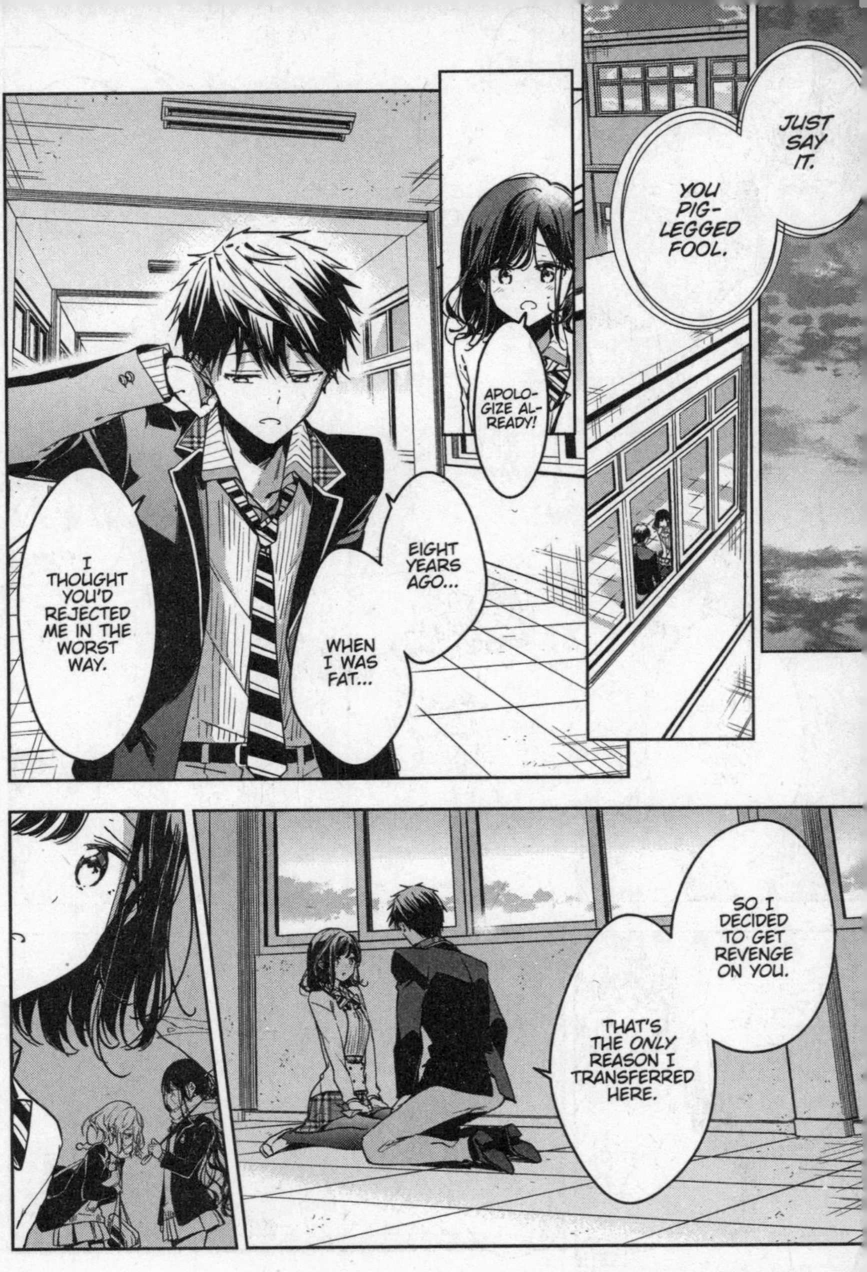
JUST SAY IT.
YOU PIG-LEGGED FOOL.
APOLOGIZE ALREADY!
EIGHT YEARS AGO...
WHEN I WAS FAT...
I THOUGHT YOU'D REJECTED ME IN THE WORST WAY.
SO I DECIDED TO GET REVENGE ON YOU.
THAT'S THE *ONLY* REASON I TRANSFERRED HERE.

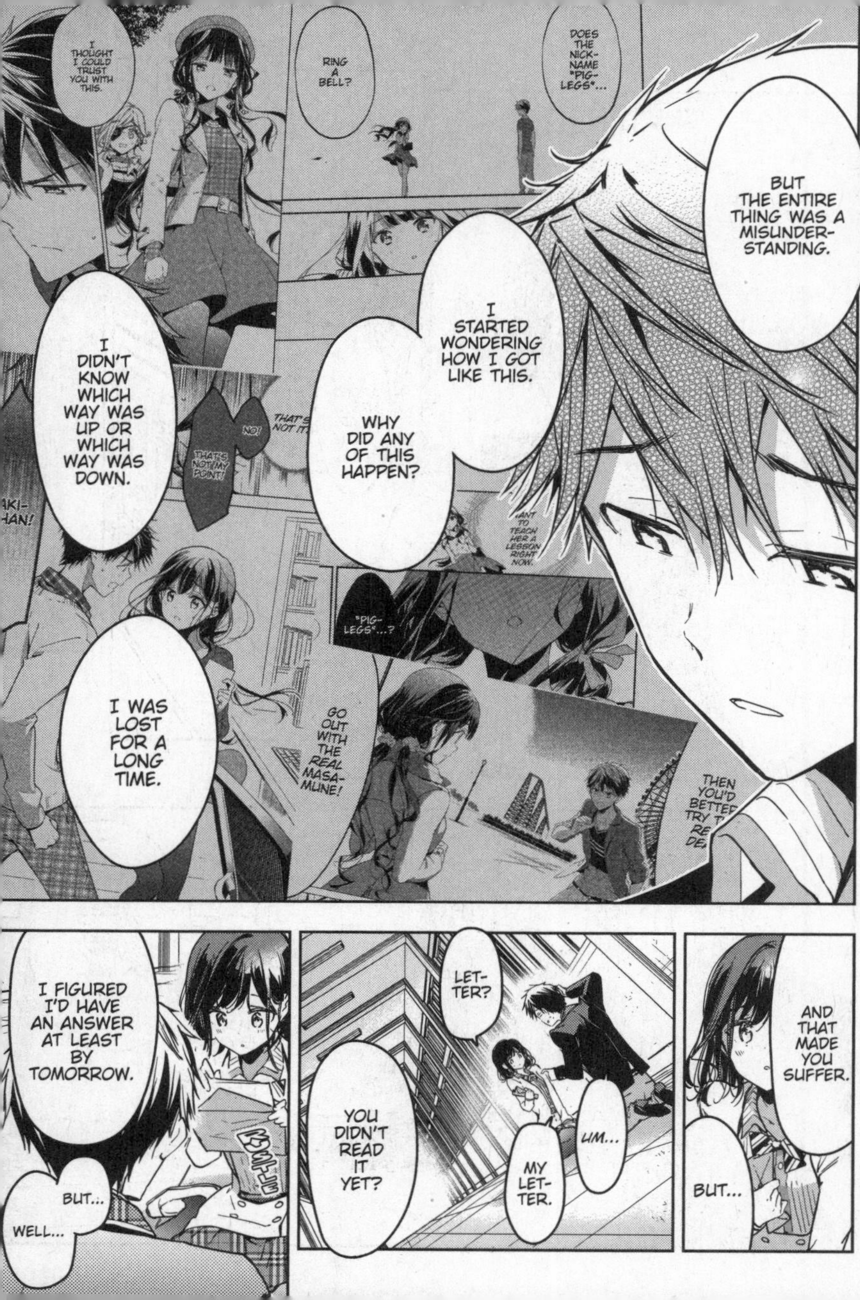
DOES THE NICK-NAME "PIG-LEGS"...
RING A BELL?
I THOUGHT I COULD TRUST YOU WITH THIS.
BUT THE ENTIRE THING WAS A MISUNDER-STANDING.
I STARTED WONDERING HOW I GOT LIKE THIS.
WHY DID ANY OF THIS HAPPEN?
THAT'S NOT IT!
NO!
THAT'S NOT MY POINT!
I DIDN'T KNOW WHICH WAY WAS UP OR WHICH WAY WAS DOWN.
"PIG-LEGS"...?
GO OUT WITH THE REAL MASA-MUNE!
I WAS LOST FOR A LONG TIME.
AND THAT MADE YOU SUFFER.
BUT...
UM...
MY LET-TER.
YOU DIDN'T READ IT YET?
LET-TER?
I FIGURED I'D HAVE AN ANSWER AT LEAST BY TOMORROW.
BUT...
WELL...

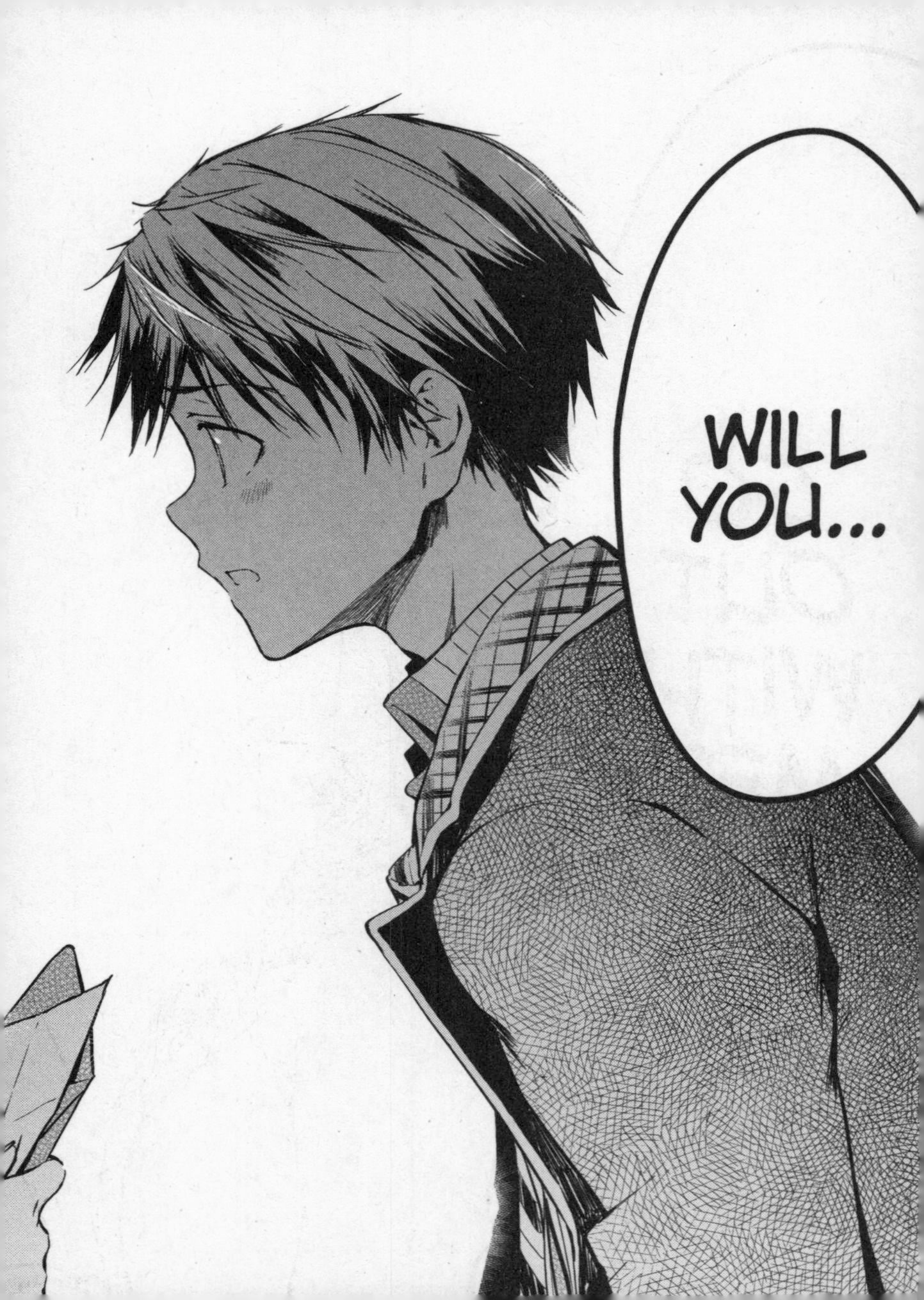
WILL YOU...

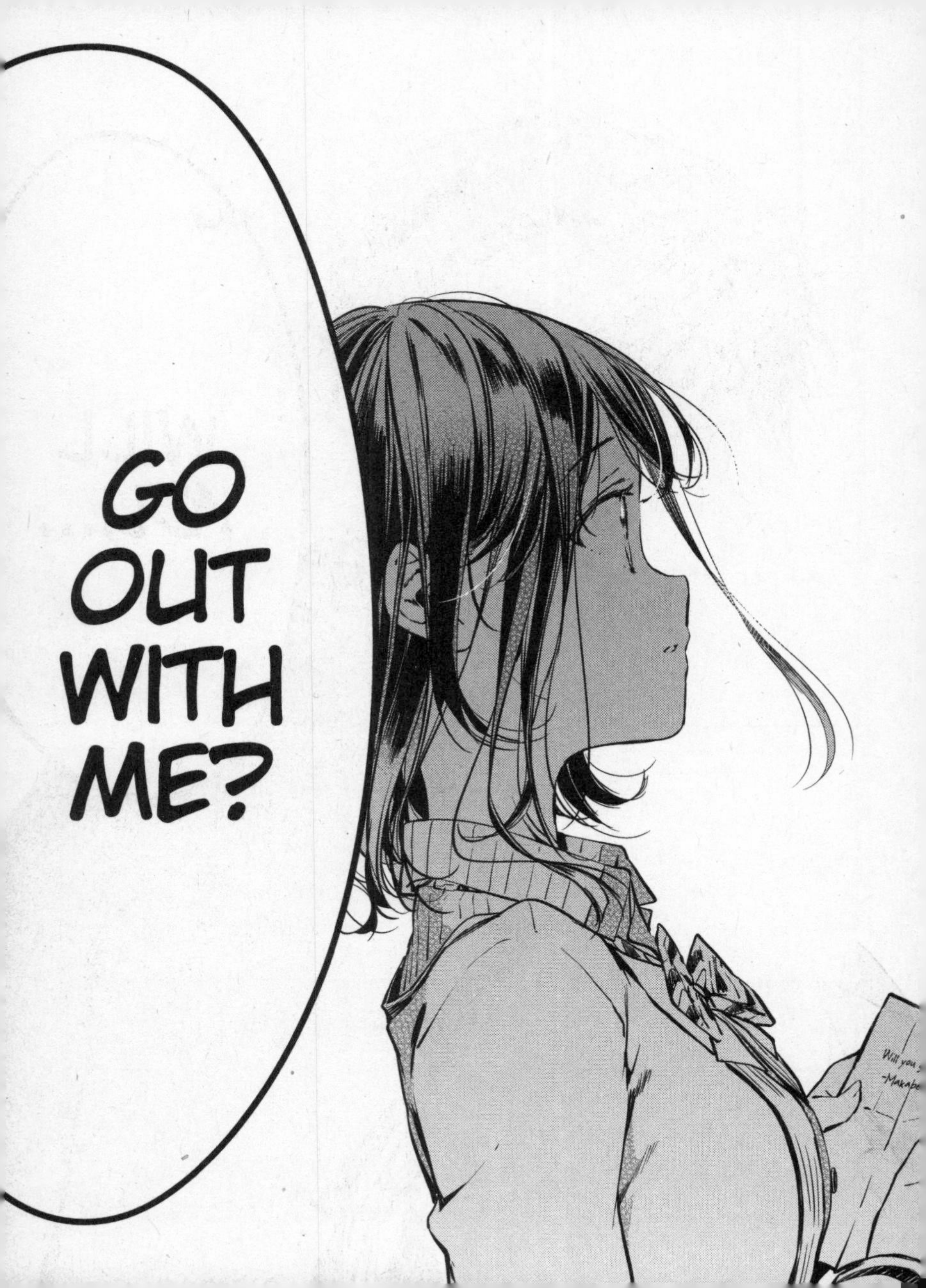
GO OUT WITH ME?

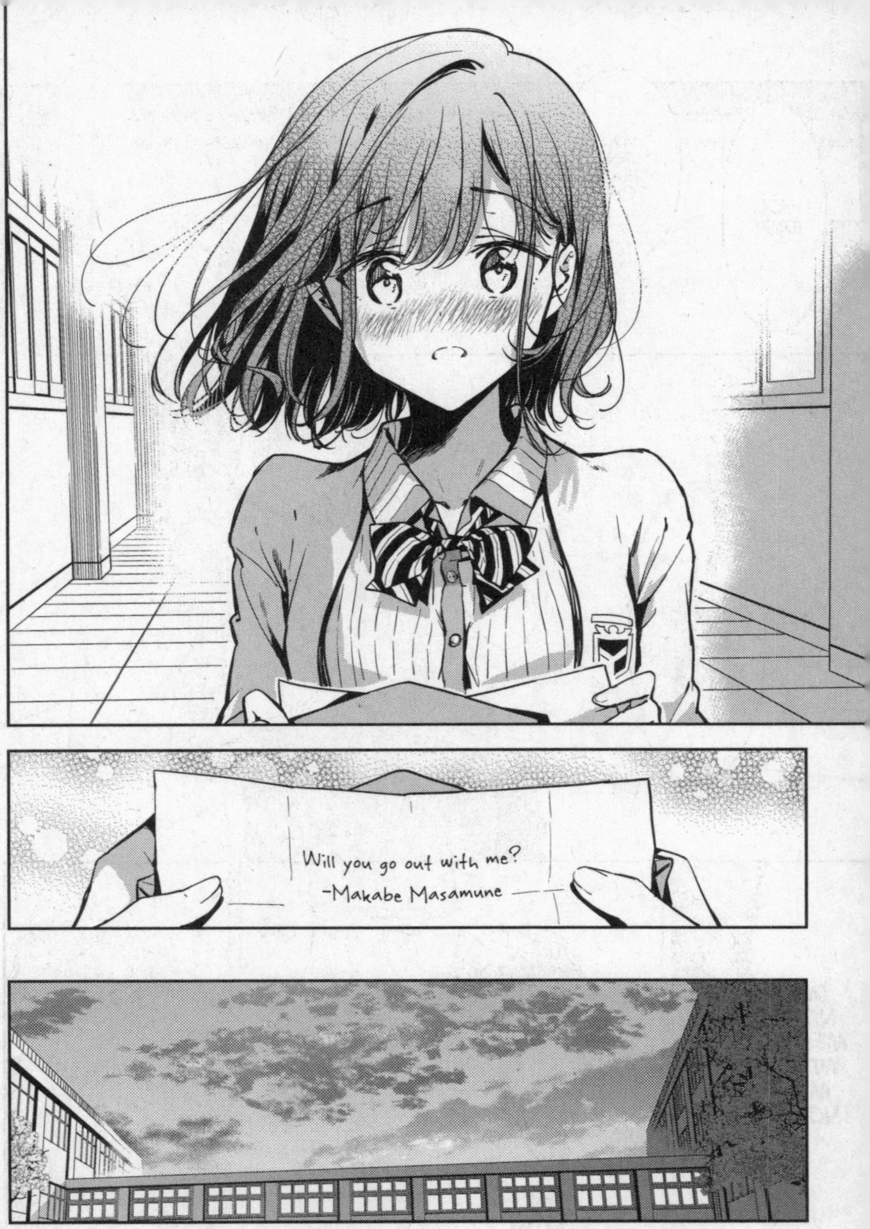
Will you go out with me?
-Makabe Masamune

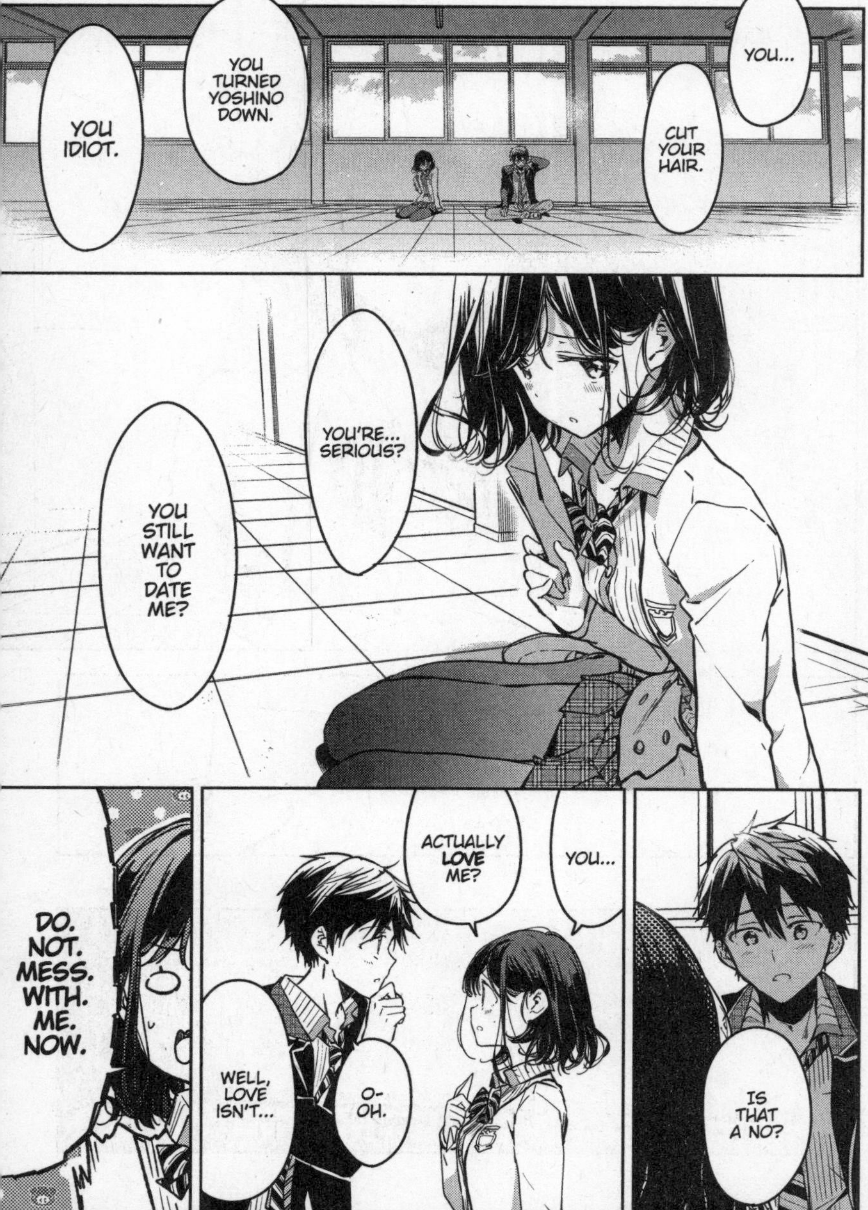
YOU...
CUT YOUR HAIR.
YOU TURNED YOSHINO DOWN.
YOU IDIOT.
YOU'RE... SERIOUS?
YOU STILL WANT TO DATE ME?
IS THAT A NO?
YOU...
ACTUALLY LOVE ME?
O-OH.
WELL, LOVE ISN'T...
DO. NOT. MESS. WITH. ME. NOW.

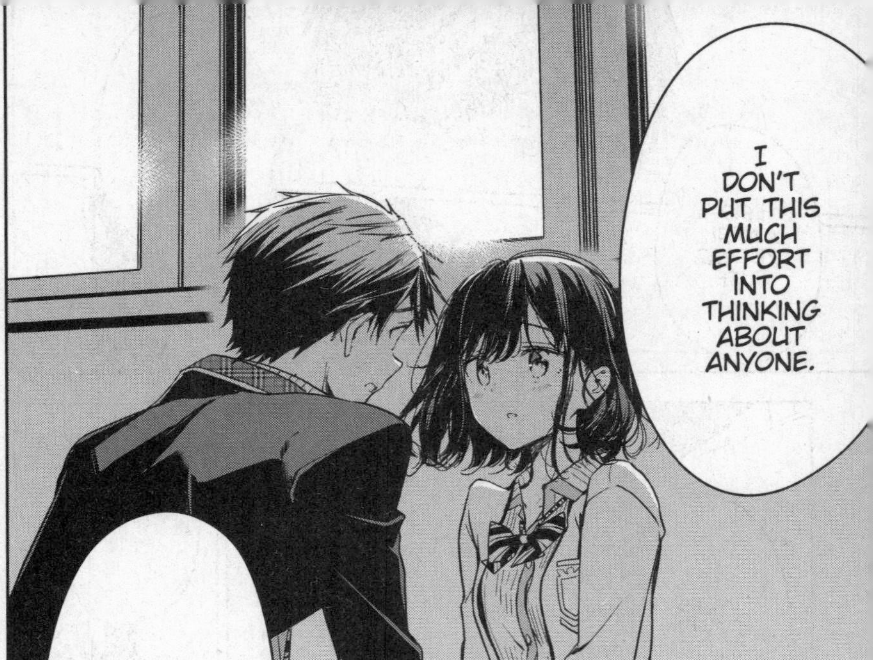
I DON'T PUT THIS MUCH EFFORT INTO THINKING ABOUT ANYONE.
JUST YOU.

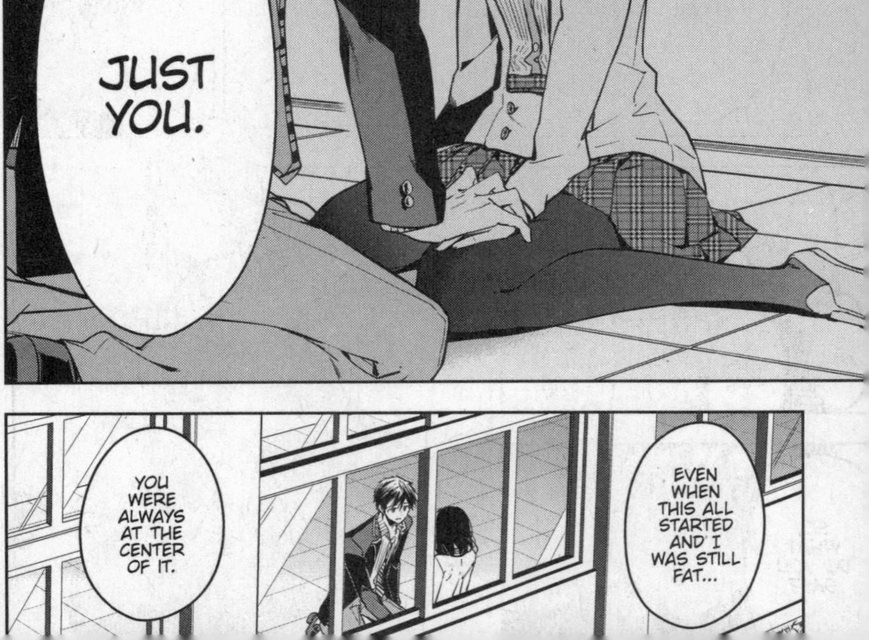
EVEN WHEN THIS ALL STARTED AND I WAS STILL FAT...
YOU WERE ALWAYS AT THE CENTER OF IT.

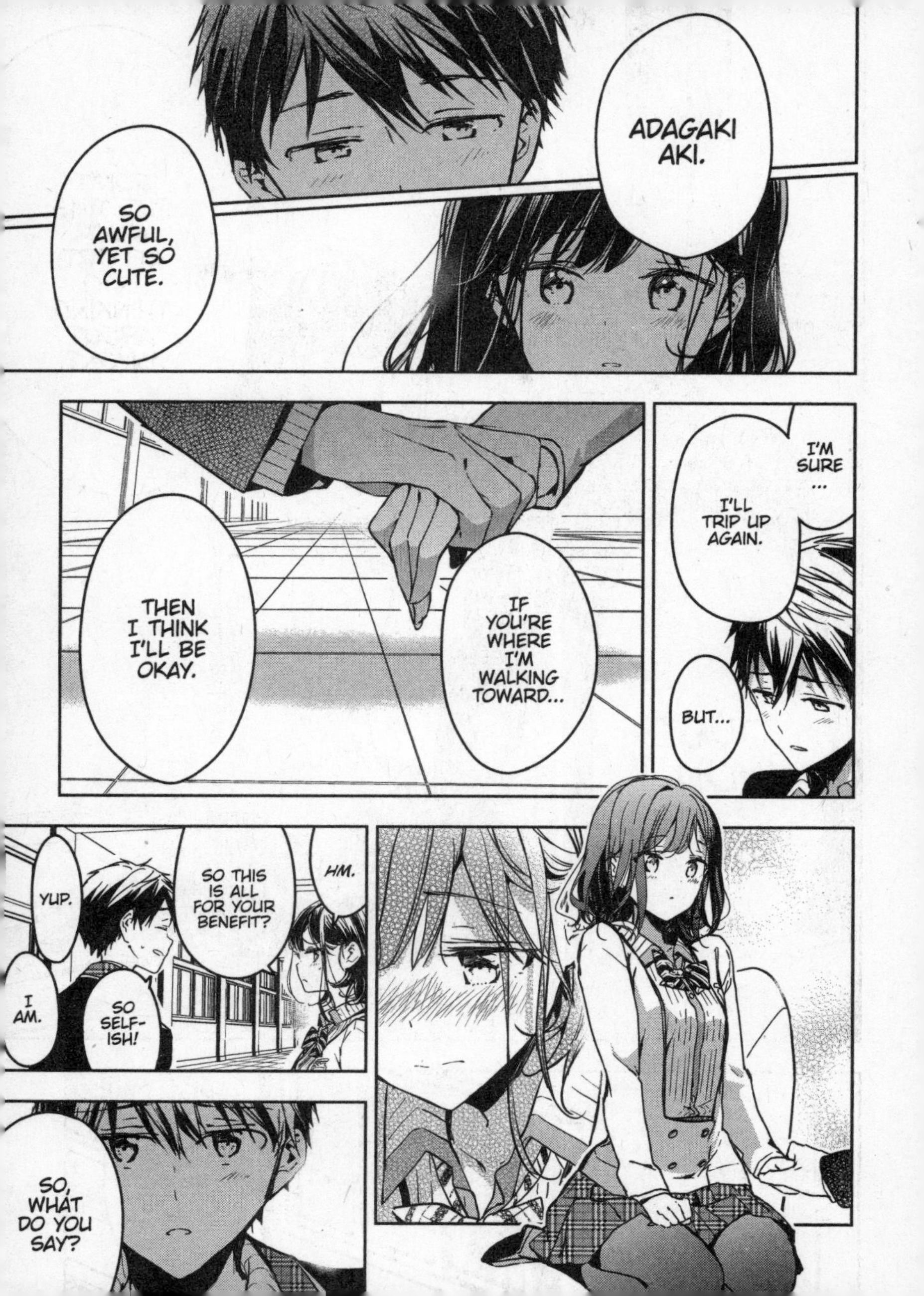
ADAGAKI AKI.
SO AWFUL, YET SO CUTE.
I'M SURE ... I'LL TRIP UP AGAIN.
BUT...
IF YOU'RE WHERE I'M WALKING TOWARD...
THEN I THINK I'LL BE OKAY.
HM.
SO THIS IS ALL FOR YOUR BENEFIT?
YUP.
SO SELF-ISH!
I AM.
SO, WHAT DO YOU SAY?

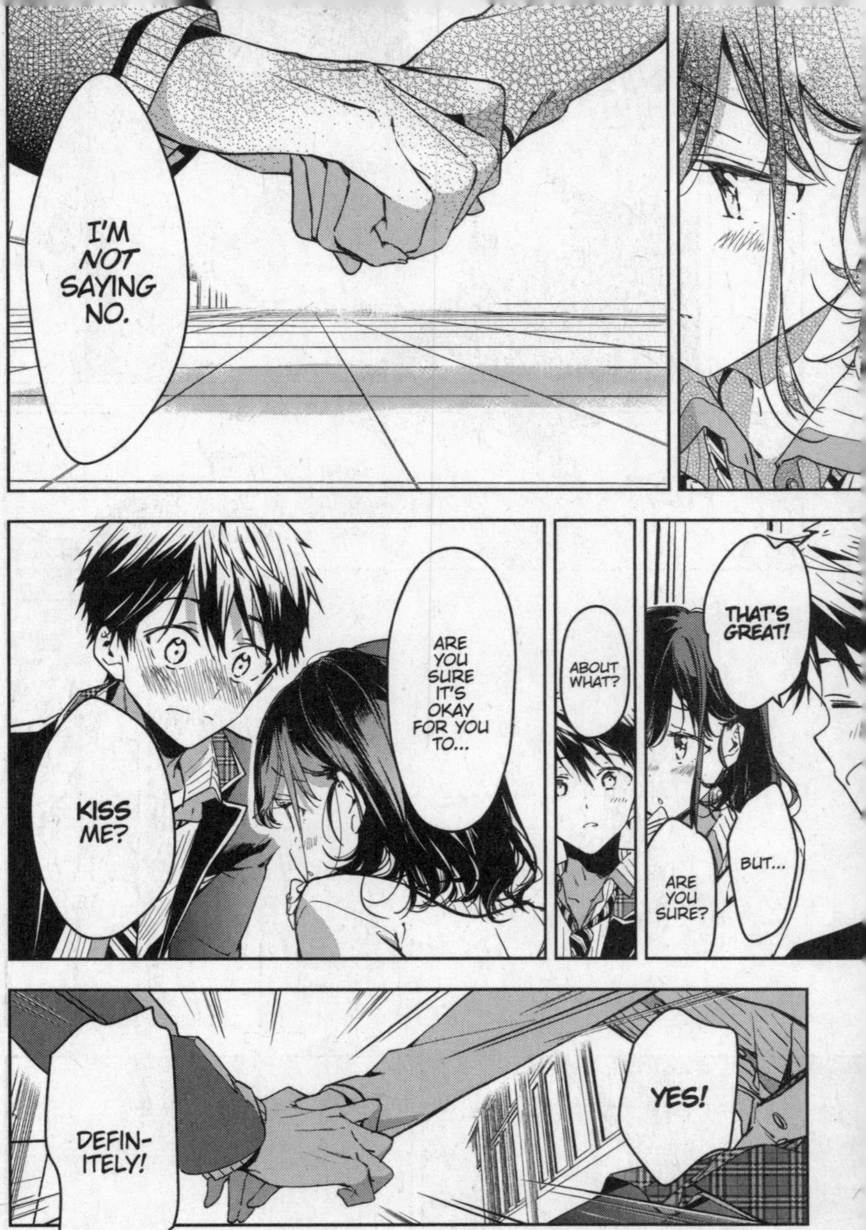
I'M NOT SAYING NO.
THAT'S GREAT!
BUT...
ARE YOU SURE?
ABOUT WHAT?
ARE YOU SURE IT'S OKAY FOR YOU TO...
KISS ME?
YES!
DEFIN-ITELY!

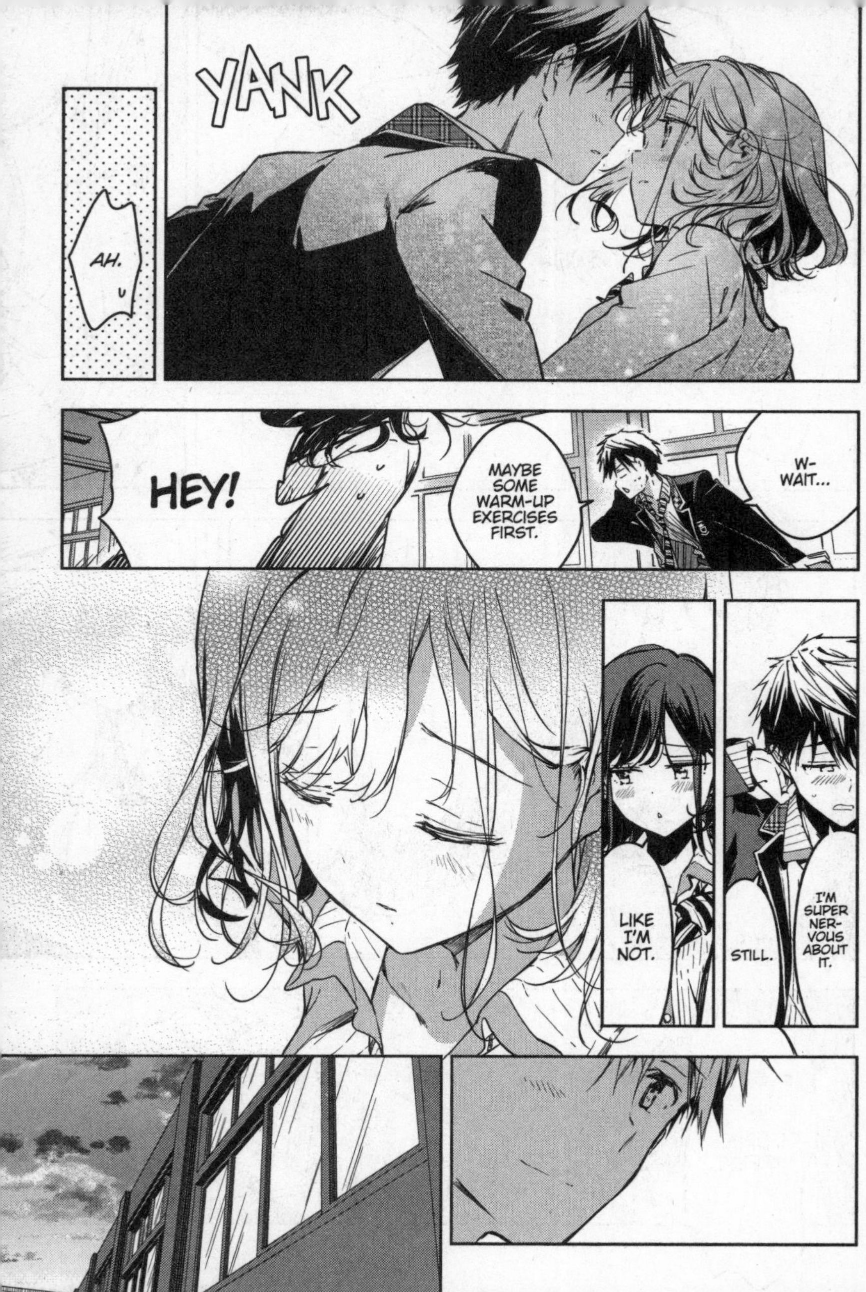
YANK
AH.
W-WAIT...
MAYBE SOME WARM-UP EXERCISES FIRST.
HEY!
I'M SUPER NERVOUS ABOUT IT.
STILL.
LIKE I'M NOT.

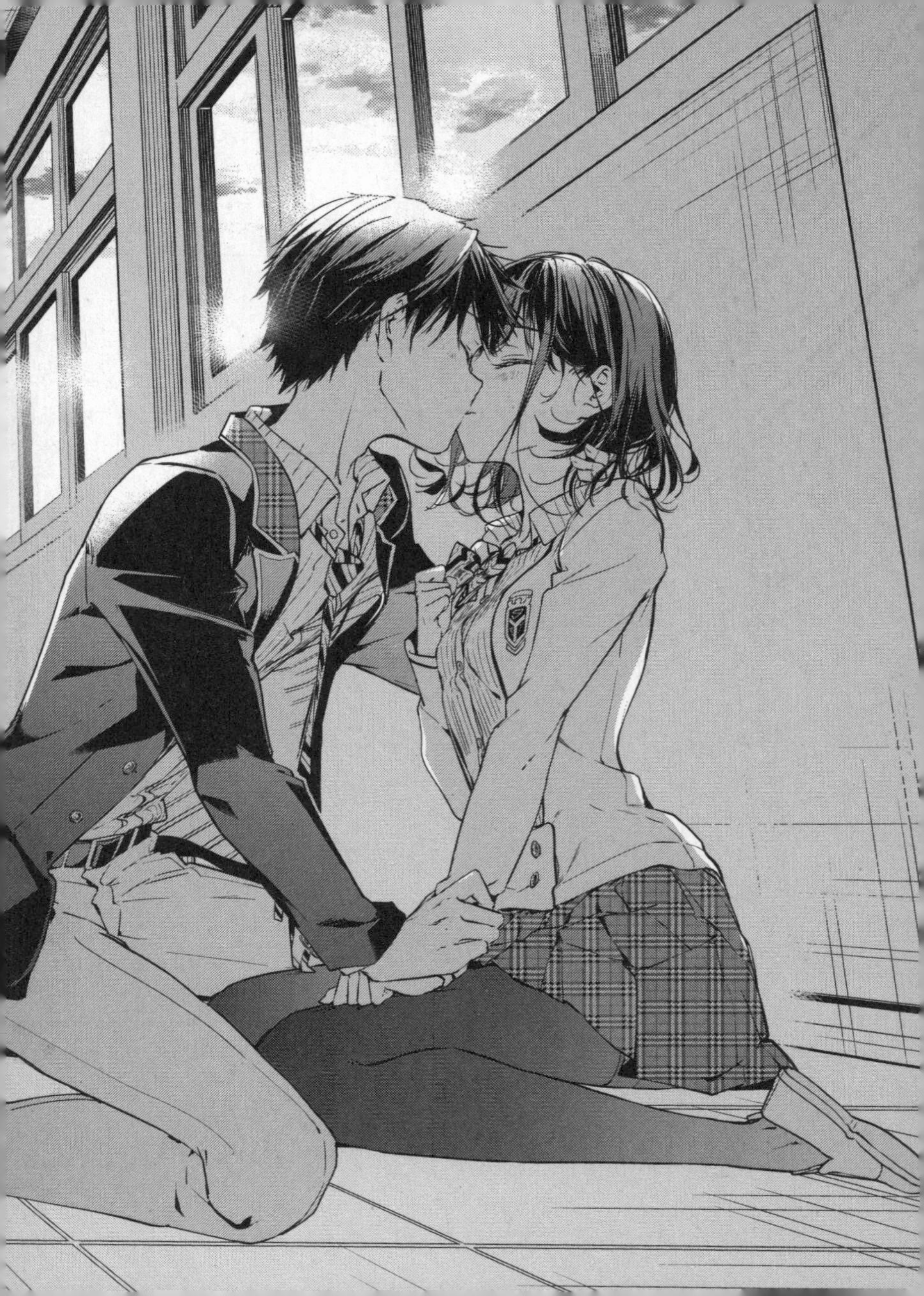

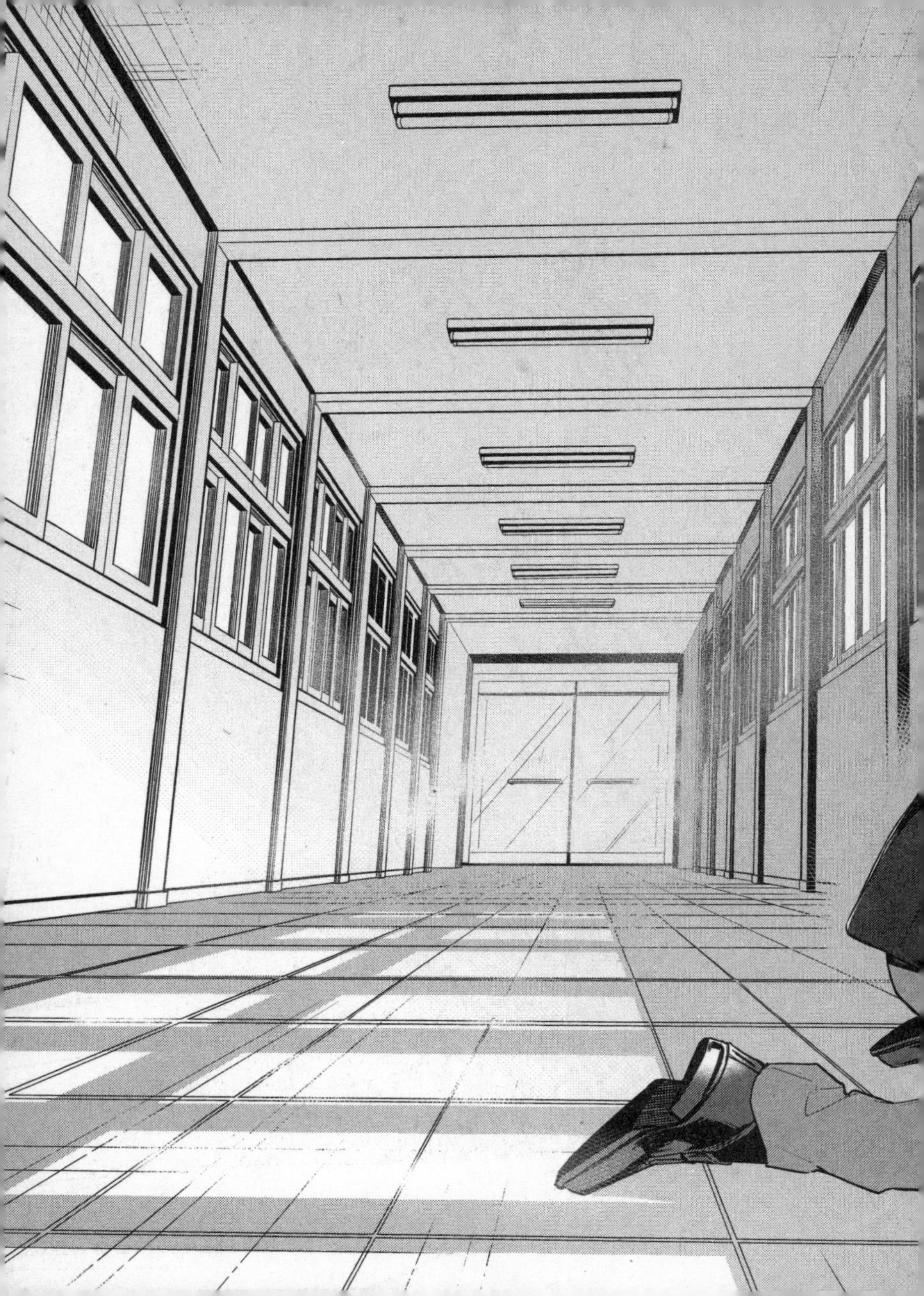

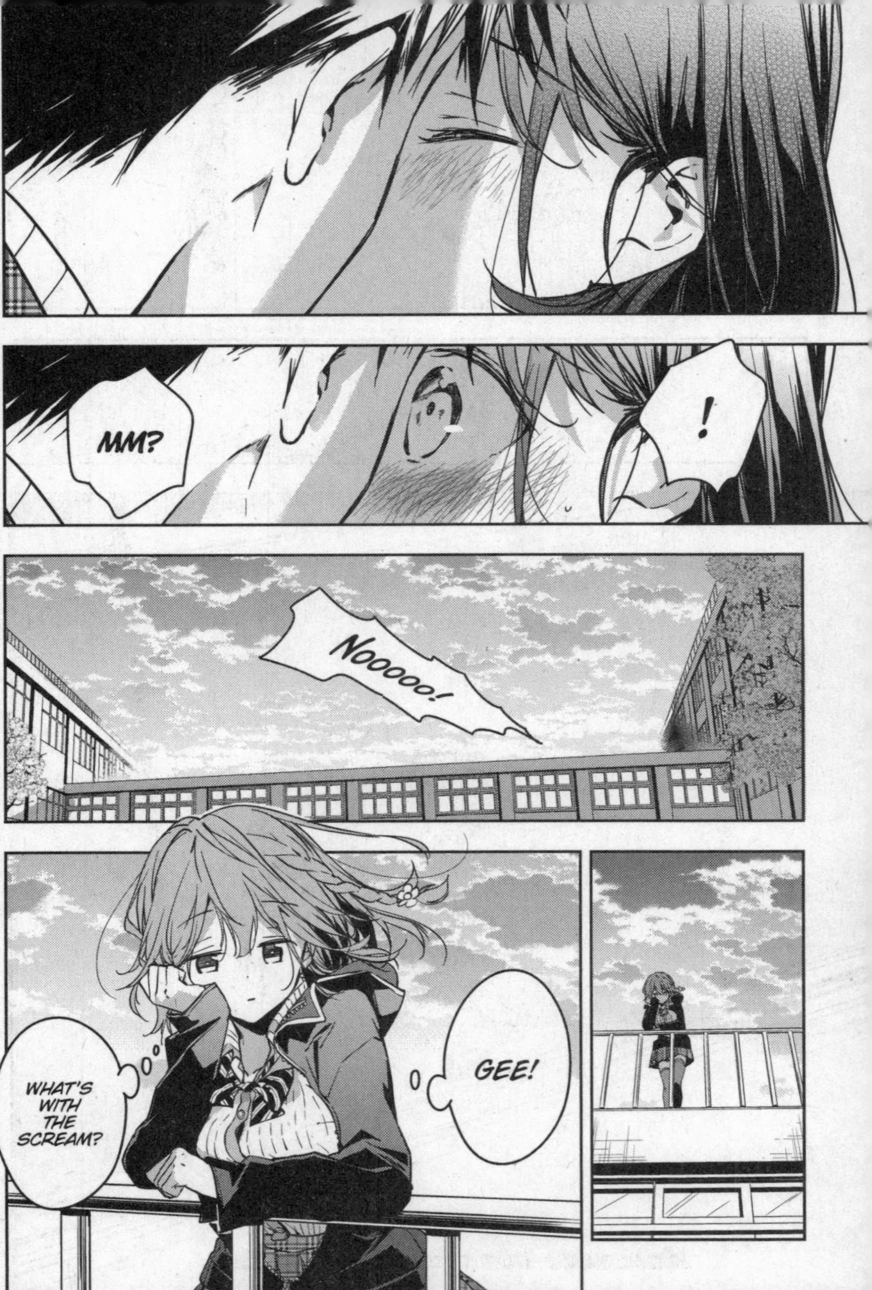
!
MM?
Noooooo!
GEE!
WHAT'S WITH THE SCREAM?

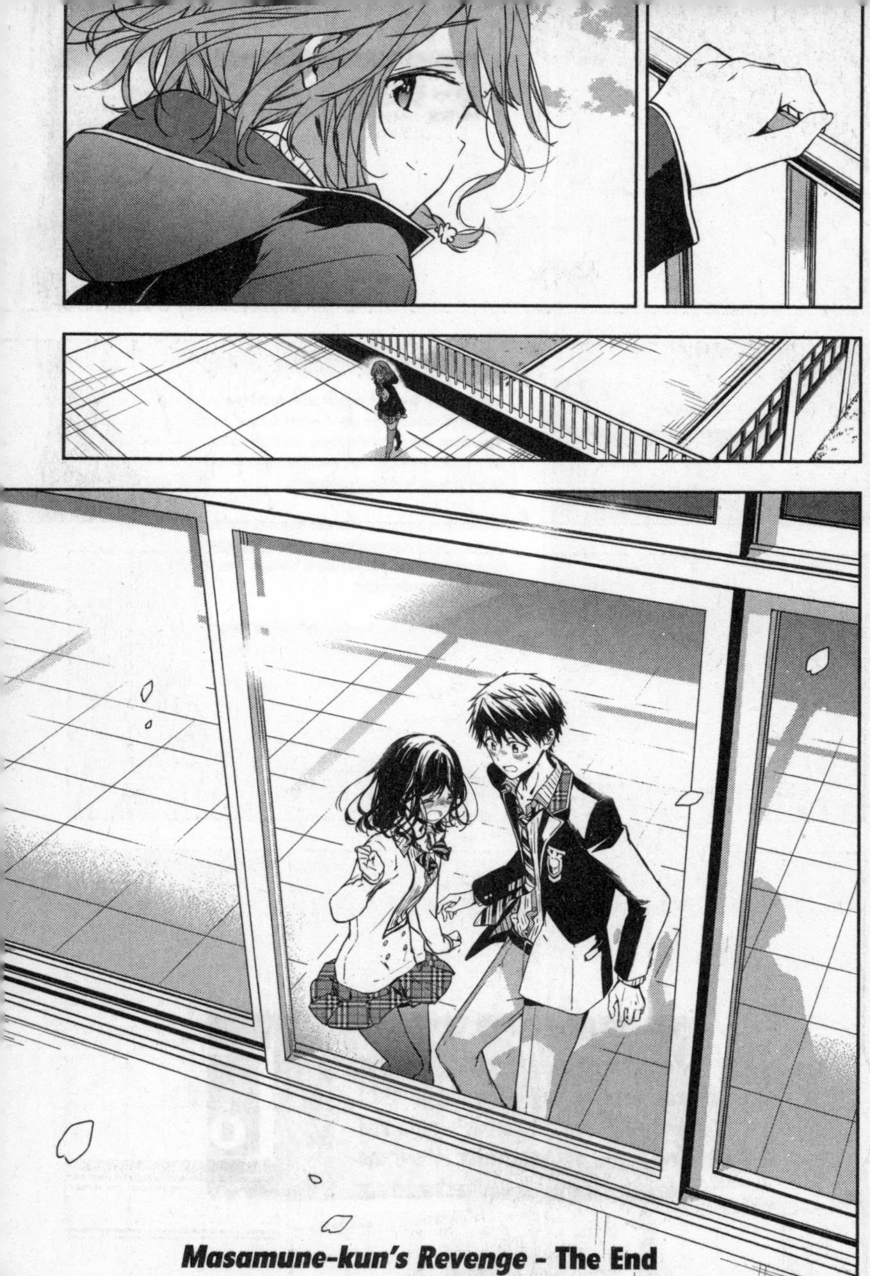

**Masamune-kun's Revenge - The End**

# SEVEN SEAS ENTERTAINMENT PRESENTS

## Masamune-kun's REVENGE 10

story by **HAZUKI TAKEOKA**  art by **TIV**

TRANSLATION
**Andrew Cunningham**

ADAPTATION
**Bambi Eloriaga-Amago**

MASAMUNE-KUN'S REVENGE VOL. 10
©HAZUKI TAKEOKA · TIV 2018
First published in Japan in 2018 by ICHIJINSHA Inc., Tokyo.
English translation rights arranged with ICHIJINSHA Inc., Tokyo.

**Lissa Pattillo**

MANAGING EDITOR
**Julie Davis**

EDITOR-IN-CHIEF
**Adam Arnold**

PUBLISHER
**Jason DeAngelis**

ISBN: 978-1-642750-80-5

Printed in Canada

First Printing: May 2019

10 9 8 7 6 5 4 3 2 1

## FOLLOW US ONLINE: *www.sevenseasentertainment.com*

# READING DIRECTIONS

This book reads
If this is your f
reading from th
take it from the
numbered diagr
first, but you'll get the hang of it! Have fun!!